The Future of Nature

Other Books from *Orion* Magazine

Finding Home: Writing on Nature and Culture from Orion *Magazine,*
    Edited by Peter Sauer
The Way to the Salt Marsh: A John Hay Reader, Edited and with an intro-
    duction by Christopher Merrill

From the Nature Literacy Series

Stories in the Land: A Place-Based Environmental Education Anthology,
    with an introduction by John Elder
Beyond Ecophobia: Reclaiming the Heart in Nature Education,
    by David Sobel
Into the Field: A Guide to Locally Focused Learning, by Claire Walker Leslie,
    John Tallmadge, and Tom Wessells, with an introduction by
    Ann Zwinger
Place Based Education: Connecting Classrooms & Communities,
    by David Sobel

The Future of Nature

Writing on a Human Ecology from Orion *Magazine*

SELECTED AND INTRODUCED BY

Barry Lopez

MILKWEED EDITIONS

Published 2007 by Milkweed Editions
Printed in Canada
Cover design by Christian Füenfhausen
Interior design by Wendy Holdman
The text of this book is set in Adobe Garamond Pro.
 18 19 20 21   10 9 8 7
First Edition

Special funding for this book was provided by
Furthermore: a program of the J. M. Kaplan Fund.

Milkweed Editions, a nonprofit publisher, gratefully acknowledges sustaining support from Emilie and Henry Buchwald; the Bush Foundation; the Patrick and Aimee Butler Family Foundation; CarVal Investors; the Timothy and Tara Clark Family Charitable Fund; the Dougherty Family Foundation; the Ecolab Foundation; the General Mills Foundation; the Claire Giannini Fund; John and Joanne Gordon; William and Jeanne Grandy; the Jerome Foundation; Dorothy Kaplan Light and Ernest Light; Constance B. Kunin; Marshall BankFirst Corp.; Sanders and Tasha Marvin; the May Department Stores Company Foundation; the McKnight Foundation; a grant from the Minnesota State Arts Board, through an appropriation by the Minnesota State Legislature, a grant from the National Endowment for the Arts, and private funders; an award from the National Endowment for the Arts, which believes that a great nation deserves great art; the Navarre Corporation; Debbie Reynolds; the St. Paul Travelers Foundation; Ellen and Sheldon Sturgis; the Target Foundation; the Gertrude Sexton Thompson Charitable Trust (George R. A. Johnson, Trustee); the James R. Thorpe Foundation; the Toro Foundation; Moira and John Turner; United Parcel Service; Joanne and Phil Von Blon; Kathleen and Bill Wanner; Serene and Christopher Warren; the W. M. Foundation; and the Xcel Energy Foundation.

Library of Congress Cataloging-in-Publication Data

The future of nature : writing on a human ecology from Orion magazine / edited and introduced by Barry Lopez. — 1st ed.
    p. cm.
  Includes bibliographical references.
  ISBN 978-1-57131-306-5 (pbk. : alk. paper)
  1. Human ecology. 2. Natural history. 3. Orion (New York, N.Y.)
I. Lopez, Barry Holstun, 1945– II. Orion (New York, N.Y.)
GF41.F88 2007
304.2—dc22

2007022207

The Future of Nature

Reverence

Monsters

Native

Acknowledgments

OUR UNDERSTANDING OF THE RELATIONSHIP BETWEEN PEOPLE AND the natural world is forever evolving. For twenty-five years, *Orion* has endeavored to capture the new thoughts, corrections, modifications, and breakthroughs that change the way we understand that relationship. *Orion* has also tried to document another phenomenon: for all of the terrible, greedy, and stupid mistakes humanity has made in its stewardship of the environment, there is no lack of love for the world and no lack of good ideas for living in a more sensible way.

The Future of Nature was shaped to give a sense of the fullness of the last fifteen years of *Orion*. (An earlier anthology, *Finding Home*, published by Beacon Press in 1992, covers the first ten years of *Orion*'s history.) In this book we tried not to collect the *Orion* essays that are necessarily the "best," but those that point toward a fuller understanding of the world and the possibility of a saner future. Its six sections map out the territories that the magazine's writers have returned to again and again. **Action** is devoted to the principle that real change happens from the bottom up, and within us. **Refugees** is dedicated to the human lives that are trampled in our abuse of the environment, and sometimes by the movement to protect the environment. **Boundaries** addresses the slippery question of what is natural, and what is not. **Reverence** underscores the notion that a worldview based in respect for nature is essential to any effort to protect nature. **Monsters** makes plain the insanity and short-sightedness of our treatment of the world. And **Native** reflects the belief of so many *Orion* writers that in order to heal the places we live in we must become a part of them.

Any rendition of an *Orion* anthology covering the last fifteen years was bound to omit writers whose ideas have been critical. The absence of the work of David Abram, Rick Bass, John Calderazzo, Mike Connelly, Jan DeBlieu, Brian Doyle, Jordan Fisher-Smith, David Ehrenfeld, John Elder, Chellis Glendinning, John Hay, Freeman House, Diana Kappel-Smith, Jeffrey Lockwood, Judith Larner Lowry, Ellen Meloy, Christopher Merrill, Kathleen Dean Moore, Richard Nelson, David Orr, John Price, Janisse Ray, Pattiann Rogers, Gary Snyder, John Tallmadge, Mitchell Thomashow, Terry

Tempest Williams, Ann Zwinger, and many others, makes clear that this collection is far from complete.

All of the articles included were edited by one of six editors: Aina Niemela Barten, Harlan Clifford, Emily Hiestand, Jennifer Sahn, Laird Townsend, and myself. Other members of the *Orion* editorial staff have been critical to the success of the magazine, among them Amanda Gardner Elkin, Tara Rae Gunter, Jason Houston, Laurie Lane-Zucker, Kim Leeder, Jennifer Marlow, Christina Rahr Lane, and Peter Sauer. Hannah Fries was essential to the process of assembling this anthology and played a major role in its creation.

Orion's efforts of the last twenty-five years would have not been possible without the support of four people in particular. M.G.H. Gilliam has been *Orion's* publisher through its history; Marion's singular vision has made *Orion* what it is today. Olivia Ladd Gilliam, who died in 1993, was the magazine's picture editor for its first ten years and created the spirit of community that those of us who work at *Orion* still feel. George K. Russell served as the magazine's Editor-in-Chief for its first twenty years and taught those of us who work here to remain focused on the themes that make it distinctive. Aina Barten almost single-handedly edited the magazine for its first ten years and still plays a vital role in its editorial process.

We are indebted to the individuals who have served on the board of The Orion Society and to the many individuals and institutions that have given the financial assistance to make *Orion* possible. We are especially grateful for the colleagueship and generous support of The Myrin Institute.

Daniel Slager, Hilary Reeves, Patrick Thomas, Ben Barnhart, Emily Cook, and the rest of the staff at Milkweed Editions have been true partners in every step of creating this book. Milkweed is a nonprofit publisher dedicated to the writing, ideas, and authors that are often left behind in a publishing world that is increasingly guided by profit alone. Every person who enjoys and depends on thoughtful writing should be grateful for nonprofit publishers like this one.

And we are grateful to our longtime friend Barry Lopez, who conceived of this book, urged us to move forward with it, and became its guiding spirit.

—*H. Emerson Blake*
Editor-in-Chief, Orion

Introduction

I HEARD AN UNFAMILIAR VOICE THIS MORNING, THE CALL OF A BIRD I could not identify. Birds calling are the conversations of neighbors. Not to know this voice urges me to leave my desk for a window where a pair of binoculars rests on the sill. The air is pale, the light flat. With the resolving power of the glasses I see snow slanting to the clearing below the house, particles fine as dust. A layer of fog wafts over the jade surface of the river, like an unfurled shroud, tattered and wind-buoyed.

I become so intent on the essence of the air I forget the unfamiliar call, until a flock of warbler-size birds bursts from the trees, a commotion tumbling through the lower branches of a red cedar, too far away to tell who they might be and then they're gone.

I've studied birds here for thirty-seven years. I've been on this wooded slope in the rural mountains of western Oregon long enough to know, now, how vast is my innocence. Long enough to know how much will stay hidden, even from the most diligent observer. I speak with my human neighbors about the particulars, because no one will ever know it all, and all of us together will never be able to explain the why of any of it. This isn't to wave away science or underestimate the sophisticated observation of Tsanchifin Kalapuya, earlier residents of this valley. It's to acknowledge—here, at least—the daily message: we don't know. Our plans for the future might go awry.

It is painful and old news that human life is in trouble. Fresh water, in ever-shortening supply for people around the world, is bottled in France to sell in America for more than the price of gasoline. A farrago of toxins, unsuspected and nameless, falls like mist over the dining table. Hormones designed to wrest market share for the manufacturer daily mock the integrity of the gamete. Corporations, not content as individuals merely to vote through their lobbyists, now have them write bills for an obeisant Congress. Free market missionaries, long fractious over the democratic obligation to respect the commonweal's health and to heed lawful restraints, can now ignore the disintegration of human communities in any market (country) doing business with the World Trade Organization.

The great challenge of our time is an ethical and metaphysical one, not a call to new technologies. Do we have the courage to face the carnage that industrialization has wrought, to face, everywhere, the social blight of hypercapitalistic aggression? And, having come to grips with injustice and terracide, can we find the mind to act? Can we imagine a way out?

The outline of an answer is in the small flock of birds bursting and weaving through the pendant branches of the cedar just now, backlit by fog on the water. The event itself is not a Rosetta stone of some kind, a solution to the hieroglyphics of our predicament. The physical allure of the event, how it pulls the eye—the convergence of light, animation, and color, the fleetness of the moment, the mysterious identity of the actors—can be successfully plumbed; but more of this apparition lies outside the senses, beyond the province of the intellect. It is within the ambit of wisdom. The few seconds of the birds' passing continue to resonate within the imagination, which observes the separate, individual movement of each bird even as it regards the weave of the community through the forest. The imagination extends the event in time, filling in the before and after that is opaque to the senses. Where did they come from? Where are they going? It perceives the illuminated riverscape beneath an overcast sky together with the pale air as an orchestration of light, congruent with the trajectory of the birds. The imagination beholds the movement of the birds, the movement of the river, and the movement of the overcast sky as perfectly scaled within each other.

A community of birds, moving relentlessly through subdued light, in harmony with all else, does not need a destination to be beautiful. They do not need an explanation to have meaning. They do not have to serve a purpose. Merely by moving through, they instigate wonder. They stir possibility. A wave of anonymous energy, the fate of which bears directly on our own.

In 1982, when the news of human fate was less scary than it is now, *Orion* set out to explore a separation few others were attending to, the scrim that western culture had lowered between nature and culture. Instead of staring grief-stricken at the natural world, on the one hand, or upbraiding the overdeveloped nations for their isolation and greed, the magazine chose the matrix between, the region where beleaguered nature encountered human society in both its innocence and ignorance. Like the sides of a clay pot, this thin wall maintains, in what was once continuous space, an inside together with an outside. A separation. For twenty-five years *Orion* has asked what is gained and what is lost in the division between nature and culture, and how the losses, which trouble us very deeply now, can be mitigated. What is required of us? The magazine has published declarations, offered policy statements and testimony, and championed political action, especially by grassroots groups; but *Orion*'s real strength has been the evolution of a philosophy of being, a way to incorporate, within a profound appreciation of the numinous dimension of nature, a sense of social and economic justice. The force behind much of what has appeared in *Orion*, then, has been the quest for just relations—between cultures and between cultures and nature.

What troubles us as a nation—the rise of a unilateral presidency, the pathology of consumption, the conniving of government with business, the presuming of religious groups, the poisoning and ravishment of the earth, the institutionalization of greed in corporate life and of lying in public life—can be understood as failures of virtue, specifically of the cardinal virtues. They are called cardinal virtues because they are found at the core of every religion. In fact they transcend religion. Among this handful are courage, justice, and reverence. The reason many in government feel no shame for the misery they inflict on humanity, for example, is because they have no reverence. The ability to feel awe before what is unfathomable and beyond human control has atrophied in them. Others are incapable of considering what might be just, because they are too wedded to sectarian beliefs in what is right. And some no longer know courage, because that place within them is now filled with strategies for securing advantage.

The largest positive social movement in the history of the world is afoot as I write these lines, a movement already apparent on the World Wide Web, but one that has not yet emerged in mainstream media. (Its best chronicler to date may be Paul Hawken, writing in *Blessed Unrest*, a portion of which appeared in a recent issue of *Orion*.) It's the movement toward civil society.

In brief, by acting locally on issues of social and economic justice, civil society seeks to re-establish, broadly speaking, environmental and social integrity. Civil society effectively marginalizes the agendas of both government and business. Instead it seeks to establish civil alliances in order to address local and global problems. Through the establishment of such alliances, civil society comes to resemble "of, by, and for the people" writ large. According to Hawken, more than a million such human groups worldwide are now in regular contact with each other. Civil society has no staff, no address, no nation, no religion, no stake in commerce or policy making. Its concerns are the achievement and the enhancement of justice, the encouragement of reverence, and the rise of courageously outspoken communities.

Writing, too, is a social as well as an artistic act. The writer, to varying degrees, is aware of the reader as part of the continuum of human fate. In the work collected here, the reader is not addressed as a pupil needing instruction but is treated instead as a companion. At one level the goal of both writer and reader is the same in these pieces—to become more informed and to understand better the shape of one's own resistance. The writers in *The Future of Nature* differ in their approaches, hail from many parts of the country, and are in no full philosophical agreement. Like the birds, though, they represent a visible, coherent trajectory through a confusing wood. They illuminate and provoke. Like the sudden appearance of the birds, what they write draws us up out of ourselves and into a larger reality.

In a glance out the window I see the birds, moving quickly through the cedar, are a civil society.

—Barry Lopez

The Future of Nature

Action

PETER SAUER

Reinhabiting Environmentalism

Picking up where Leopold and Carson left off

WHY IS THE ENVIRONMENT ALWAYS SO LOW ON THE POLITICAL agenda? It makes the list, but always near the bottom, way below where environmentalists, impatiently, longingly, wish it would be. Why has "environmental movement" become a generous generic term for a cacophony of bickering ideologies? What happened to its unity and idealism, and when did it fall into disarray?

By my reckoning it began the year Rachel Carson died, in 1964. That was the year the movement began to lose its grip on the principles declared by Carson and Aldo Leopold. That was also the year after which half of all Americans alive today were born. The majority of today's electorate has forgotten or never heard what the movement once stood for.

Sandra Steingraber was five years old in 1964. The story of her relationship to nature is a parable for the practice of Leopold's and Carson's politics in these times. In her childhood, Steingraber learned to love wild nature and aspired to be an ecologist and poet. Her bladder cancer was diagnosed during the summer of her sophomore year in college. During her outpatient years, she attempted to restore her dreams. She inventoried grasses in Illinois, and counted tree rings in Minnesota and ghost crabs in Costa Rica, but her life would be haunted by cancer—her own, her family's, neighbors', and a dear friend's. Eventually, at first against her will, she recognized that being a survivor had permanently changed her relation to nature. She turned her biologist's skills to understanding the ecology of her life growing up in a toxic land. In her 1997 book, *Living Downstream: A Scientist's Personal Investigation of Cancer and the Environment,* she describes the history and evidence of the relationships between synthetic chemicals and rising cancer rates, and—with exquisite poet's skills—explains their mechanisms.

Before the book was published, people who saw it (including me) expected *Living Downstream* to stir a great controversy, rocket to the top of the charts, and become another *Silent Spring.* The publisher banked on controversy and reviews to sell the book.

But no chemical company complained about it, and no major media reviewed it. Without the publicity they had anticipated, neither Steingraber nor her publicists imagined how well the book would sell or the response it would provoke.

Every venue on her low-budget book tour—church halls, college classrooms, independent bookstores—was filled to capacity with people who had read or heard about the book by word of mouth from relatives or friends, or from newsletters, or the Internet. She describes the book tour in the foreword to the second, paperback edition. She was greeted by

> wheat farmers in Montana, breast cancer activists in Montreal, and mothers of children with cancer in New Jersey . . . Massachusetts retirees fighting toxic dumping near their lakeside homes, Texans fighting contamination of their drinking water with pesticides, New England physicians . . . aquatic biologists . . .

They brought maps and printouts of cancer clusters in their neighborhoods, of cancer in the wildlife in their rivers; they brought poetry and funeral programs; one mother gave Steingraber the coat worn by her sister, who had died of cancer.

Like Rachel Carson before her, Steingraber's life was changed by the experience of having written her book. She discovered that she, her story, and her science had become part of thousands of conversations going on all over the country, and that she was a member of a new and powerful constituency. As cancers have increased at a rate of one percent each year for thirty-five years, the number of survivors and mourners has grown geometrically. Tens of thousands of family members, friends, and neighbors are impatient to right the wrongs indicted on the dead, eager to understand the relationship between the sorrow in their lives and the values, practices, policies, and laws of the society they have dedicated themselves to change, and hungry for stories that will unite them. Steingraber's book, like Carson's and Leopold's a generation earlier, was giving people a lingua franca with which to communicate with one another, and identify their common goal—to treat a healthy environment as a human right.

That same message appears in two recent documents, one from the fields of ethics, science, and law, the other from economists and agriculturists. The documents—the Wingspread Statement on the Precautionary Principle and the Vancouver Statement on the Globalization and Industrialization of Agriculture—are themselves syntheses of scattered conversations around the world that have been building and expanding their circles for several decades. These exchanges began spontaneously, in isolation, triggered by local concerns—toxins in their air, water, soil, and food; declining fisheries; rising sea level; the effects of globalization on their land, economies, and cultures; or cancers in their children. Slowly at first, one by one, door to door, through informal, then formal networks, people discovered they were all talking about the same thing: humanity and the environment are one.

This idea is not new. *Living Downstream,* the Vancouver Statement, and the Precautionary Principle pick up where Carson and Leopold left off. To connect the environment and human rights is an old refrain come round again. Reorchestrated for the times, it plays against the dissonance of a toxic and unjust world, and yet its message is the most hopeful I have heard in thirty-five years. It is also fragile and vulnerable, and I don't want to see it lost again.

I was eleven years old when Aldo Leopold died in 1948, the year the United Nations adopted the Universal Declaration of Human Rights. The nature I learned in childhood, the nature that inspired me to want to be a naturalist and artist, was taught to me by adults who were passionate about nature and about human rights, and who held a deep faith that there is a connection between these two. I learned about Leopold's Land Ethic from them.

"The Land Ethic," Leopold's most famous essay (from *A Sand County Almanac,* published posthumously in 1949), addressed the reciprocity between humanity (that's all of us and all our institutions—cultural, social, political, and economic—and our values, aspirations, our science and art) and the land (that's all of nature; "air, water, soils, plants and animals; collectively: the land"). Leopold wrote,

> There are two organisms whose processes of self-renewal have been subjected to human interference and control. One is man himself (medicine and public health), and the other is land (agriculture and conservation).

The genius of Leopold's ethic was its political ecology, which recognized that culture joins the fate of nature with the fate of humankind; that, for example, what humankind does in the realms of medicine and public health is in relationship to agriculture and conservation. He was urging the conservation community to engage in a great evolutionary conversation about responsibilities and obligations in a world in which the human and the biotic community could be one.

I remember the deep conviction with which my adult friends told me that, at last, Leopold had got it right—that if we heeded what he wrote, conservation would be an instrument for forging the peace and justice that the world was talking about then and deliberating at the new UN. Having learned my environmentalism in those brief salad days, before Russia got the bomb and the Cold War, Korea, and McCarthyism put America on a war footing again, I look back at the first Earth Day as the end, not the beginning, of a great movement.

For me, Earth Day ushered in a bio-biased environmentalism, one that separated human from natural ecology. From that time, Washington-based environmental organizations steered environmentalism toward the business of saving a nature that dwelt in a place that was separate from the world that most Americans live in. They lobbied Congress and the public on behalf of endangered (nonhuman) species, and for the establishment of new preserves and parks, and gained a tenfold expansion of the National Wilderness Preservation System. In the process, "wildness" was transformed into something so rare and precious that it had little to do with sustaining an ordinary human life. Nature was redefined as a collection of organisms to be saved like paintings in a well-endowed museum.

A founder of the Wilderness Society, Leopold writes at length in "The Land Ethic" in support of preserving wildlands. But he urges conservation not to choose park-making as its strategy—not to conserve nature by transferring parcels of private land into the public domain. Direct your energies, he says, to changing the values, aspirations, and beliefs of the private landowner. And the only way to do that is to work to change the fundamental values, beliefs, and aspirations of society as a whole. He chided conservation because it had never tried this strategy:

> The proof that conservation has not yet touched these foundations of conduct lies in the fact that philosophy and religion have not yet heard of it. In our attempt to make conservation easy, we have made it trivial.

The "landowner" he was describing was the farmer, who owned and worked forty-seven percent of America's land, and though there are a lot fewer farmers today, the amount of U.S. land in agriculture is still about the same. Conservation took a different route, collecting biota in bits and pieces. After fifty years of land-collecting, conservation's trophy is an archipelago of preserved real estate that represents not more than five or seven percent of a continent that has become universally toxic to wildlife and humans. No wonder so many people who are worried about the toxicity of their neighborhoods do not count themselves as environmentalists. It has been almost forty years since a human neighborhood has been defined as a natural environment.

In the years since Rachel Carson died, the use of chemical pesticides has more than doubled (to four pounds per person per year of chemicals for which toxic dosages most often begin at one-hundred-millionth of a pound). One hundred percent of the air in the Lower Forty-eight is now contaminated with eight cancer-causing industrial chemicals at levels that exceed safety standards. We are living with the epidemic of cancer and other debilitating diseases Carson warned of, and with the silence that she most feared—the silence of complacency, of muffled dissent, the silence born of the failure to connect what we do to nature with what we are doing to each other and ourselves.

Rachel Carson testified before the National Women's Press Club and a Senate subcommittee in 1962 that she had seen industry respond to her book with "a heavy dose of tranquilizing information, designed to lull the public into the sleep from which *Silent Spring* so rudely awakened it." She warned that the "chemical barrage" being "hurled against the fabric of life" constituted a violation of human rights. "These are matters of the most serious importance to society, I commend their study to you. . . ." As she spoke there were 11,500 American troops in Vietnam. Two years later, 60,000 Americans were "on the ground" there, and Rachel Carson was dead, and for the next eight years, the country studied and debated almost nothing but the war.

The Vietnam War debate transformed the nation's politics and its culture. Special interest politics became the political paralysis that stymies the Left today when the war divided civil rights, environment, and peace into separate camps. Soon, every political interest group sought to advance its cause by distancing itself from the controversies raised by every other interest group. When conservation separated its issues from those of civil rights, the campaign for environmental justice was launched. The environmentalism I grew up with ended when the environmental and social justice movements became adversaries.

That disconnect echoes across race and class. Hear it when a white nature writer expresses frustration and dismay that so few African-Americans speak out on nature's behalf and pursue instead the issues of civil and human rights, and the advocate for social justice replies that human rights must come first. Hear it in the protests of rural (poor-by-urban-standards) folk, from Maine to Oregon, against what they know as an invasion of urban environmentalists. Hear it in the voices of the residents of an Adirondack town who would rather have a prison in the nearby wild woods than wolves.

Hear it, also, when environmentalists in other countries express dismay that the U.S. citizenry will rally to save endangered species while ignoring issues involving the environment and human health. What you hear is Leopold's political ecology being pulled apart.

Separating human rights from nature's guaranteed that the environmental movement would not work for everyone. But the disconnect was beyond the movement's power to prevent. It was a political manifestation of a cultural schism that had been developing since before the end of World War II.

At the war's end, in the U.S. and around the world, the yearnings for peace and justice found expression in widespread public demand and support for the UN's Universal Declaration of Human Rights. The optimism inspired Leopold to write "The Land Ethic." In the U.S., however, aspirations for a just society had to compete with a desire to build a prosperous postwar economy with the muscle to prevail in the arms race. The conflict is the force that divided the movements for the environment and human rights. The clearest example of how it worked is the history of the nation's policies regarding toxic chemicals, and something called the precautionary principle.

The precautionary principle asserts that *if* harm is threatened, *if* there is uncertainty about the seriousness of that harm, then precautionary actions must be taken. An axiom as old as "First, do no harm," it gained new significance after World War II, when nations seeking a peace that would prevail began to apply it to environmental planning, policy, and law. By the 1970s the policy had been incorporated into Swedish environmental laws, and in Germany, as the *Vorsorgeprinzip* (the foresight, or taking care, principle), it formed the basis for a campaign to halt the contamination of rivers and the North Sea. At the same time, in the U.S., a public galvanized by *Silent Spring* had forced strong precautionary provisions into environmental legislation (the National Environmental Policy; Occupational Safety and Health; and Clean Air, Water, and Pesticide Control Acts). Examples are the bans, "without full scientific certainty" of their harm, on lead in gasoline, PCBs, and DDT.

In advocating precaution against potential, uncertain threats to the environment and to public health, the precautionary approach implicitly assumes the inevitable connection between the two. To win the legislation of the 1970s, its supporters had to contend with an approach that denied this connection: risk assessment.

Risk assessment came home from World War II along with the fantastic array of chemicals the nation had learned to mass-produce to win the war.

No sooner had these chemicals been redeployed for large-scale domestic use at home, than government regulators began to realize that these products were undeniably unsafe. Rather than ban these products and hinder the nation's conversion to a peacetime economy, regulators developed a strategy to manage and control their damage. By the early 1950s, the government had established licensing standards for "acceptable risks" at levels at which a product would kill not more than one in a million (or, in some cases, one in a hundred thousand) people.

Risk assessment works well for industry because it only assesses one substance at a time. By 1993, the policy had licensed 860 active ingredients for uses in 21,000 products, each one individually approved, with no assessments of how it might react with the other 859 on the list. In the last decade, the industry's product list has expanded further to include genetically engineered crops—companion plants for its pesticides and herbicides. Nurtured by risk assessment, postwar chemical companies have become major partners in the international agrochemical/biotechnology industry. Its worldwide sales topped $27.5 billion in 1998, and investors and governments around the world rely on the industry to lay the groundwork for a global economy.

By the end of the 1980s, deregulation and a series of Supreme Court decisions had weakened or eliminated many precautionary provisions from earlier environmental legislation, and risk assessment was the predominant policy for regulating environmental toxins. Meanwhile, scientists and lawyers who monitor the environment were discovering that decades of accumulated pollutants from many different sources, interacting in ways that were neither foreseen nor understood, were resulting in systemic problems—CO_2 in the atmosphere; endocrine disruptions in humans. The complexity of these processes obscures cause and effect, making the harm that any one toxin may do virtually untraceable, and making the laws based on establishing harm useless. By early in this decade, the limitations of risk assessment were becoming clear and the need for precautionary action obvious, but the principle had all but disappeared from public discourse.

At the end of her book tour in January 1998, Sandra Steingraber attended a conference on the precautionary principle at Frank Lloyd Wright's Wingspread in Racine, Wisconsin. The conference was called to revive the concept of the principle in the U.S., and to link its supporters here with the worldwide campaign against the excesses of industrialization.

Convened by the Science and Environmental Health Network, the conference brought together forty-two people; from the faculties of universities and law schools in Massachusetts, Illinois, Maryland, California, Virginia, and New Hampshire; from groups such as the Silicon Valley Toxins Coalition, Physicians for Social Responsibility, United Steelworkers of America, and the Indigenous Environmental Network. An international contingent came from organizations in Canada, Britain, Germany, and Sweden, concerned with global environmental issues.

The organizers of the Wingspread conference wished to develop strategies for making the precautionary principle operational in U.S. law. They write,

> the precautionary principle has four components: (1) preventative action should be taken in advance of scientific proof of causality; (2) the proponent of an activity, rather than the public, should bear the burden of proof of safety; (3) a reasonable range of alternatives, including a no action alternative (for new activities) should be considered when there may be evidence of harm caused by an activity; and (4) for decision making to be precautionary it must be open, informed and democratic and must include potentially affected parties.

Five months after the Wingspread conference, in June 1998, the International Forum on Food and Agriculture (IFA) held its inaugural strategy meeting in Vancouver, British Columbia. The fifty-four participants from five continents (twelve countries) included farmers and campesinos, academics, researchers, NGO leaders, and owners of food processing and distribution firms. Together they produced a statement that joins the precautionary principle with the struggle for human and cultural rights.

I keep a copy of the Vancouver Statement on my desk as a reminder that implicit in the marriage between the rights of humanity and the natural order of the planet's ecosystems, is the responsibility to correct abuses that threaten both. When Aldo Leopold wrote "The Land Ethic," he said he meant it as a first draft, a talking paper for a seminar in a thinking community. The whole first section of the essay was about ethics and farmers and farmland. If fifty years later, a group of farmers and agriculturists said, let us sit down and write another draft, to continue the seminar today, that draft would be the Vancouver Statement. It is perhaps the clearest statement of the last fifty years of what the environmental movement ought to be fighting for.

In this land where (quoting Steingraber) "if bottled and sold, the breast milk of many U.S. mothers is so contaminated with pesticide residues and industrial chemicals that it would be illegal for sale as a food commodity," the environmental movement will never be able to achieve Leopold's ideal, to "expand the boundaries of community to include the soil, air, water, plants, and animals; collectively: the land" unless it does more than affirm the beauty and sanctity of wild nature. There is a relationship between the toxicity of the continent we live on, the prison system we maintain, and the price of a bushel of corn (less than Corn Flakes) or the price of gas (less than bottled water). What's haywire in America, this increasingly farmless "supermarket to the world," is not merely our relationship to the land, but to each other and to the rest of the world.

For some this will not be an easy message to hear. And it will come from people who don't count themselves as environmentalists, who in fact would take offense if that label were applied to them. They will demand a shift in financial and professional resources from protecting wild nature in uninhabited enclaves to protecting public health in the environments where people live. They will want "index species" once again to refer to the miner's caged canary. Their politics will be passionate, more intolerant of delay or compromise. Theirs are issues of life and death and cannot wait seven generations.

Leopold urged his colleagues in the conservation community to work for an ethic that embraced human rights, for a society in which justice for all its members at last would establish a harmonious community with the land. Carson warned that the only way to stop the epidemic she was predicting was to declare the pollution of the environment a violation of human rights. History stole the opportunity to have the conversations they proposed. Now, those conversations have resumed. Leopold's classic statement, "A thing is right when it tends to preserve the integrity, stability, and beauty of the biotic community," is being reformulated for our time. What the parable of *Living Downstream* tells us, what the supporters of the precautionary principle are saying and the Vancouver Statement clarifies is that "we are the biotic community, our bodies are the biosphere, and human rights must apply to the ties that bind us—blood, bone, and tissue—and our communities to the land."

(1999)

Consent of the Governed

*The corporate usurpation of democracy and the valiant struggle
to win it back*

D ESCRIBING THE UNITED STATES OF THE 1830S IN HIS NOW-FAMOUS
work, *Democracy in America,* the young French aristocrat Alexis de
Tocqueville depicted a country passionate about self-governance. In the fifty
years since sovereignty had passed from the crown to the people, citizens of
the new republic had seized upon every opportunity "to take a hand in the
government of society and to talk about it. . . . If an American should be
reduced to occupying himself with his own affairs," wrote de Tocqueville,
"half his existence would be snatched from him; he would feel it as a vast
void in his life."

At the center of this vibrant society was the town or county government.
"Without local institutions," de Tocqueville believed, "a nation has not got
the spirit of liberty," and might easily fall victim to "despotic tendencies."

In the era's burgeoning textile and nascent railroad industries, and in its
rising commercial class, de Tocqueville had already detected a threat to the
"equality of conditions" he so admired in America. "The friends of democracy should keep their eyes anxiously fixed," he warned, on an "industrial
aristocracy. . . . For if ever again permanent inequality of conditions and
aristocracy make their way into the world it will have been by that door
that they entered." Under those conditions, he thought, life might very well
be worse than it had been under the old regimes of Europe. The old land-
based aristocracy of Europe at least felt obliged "to come to the help of its
servants and relieve their distress. But the industrial aristocracy . . . when it
has impoverished and brutalized the men it uses, abandons them in a time
of crisis."

As de Tocqueville predicted, the industrial aristocrats have prevailed
in America. They have garnered enormous power over the past 150 years
through the inexorable development of the modern corporation. Having
achieved extensive control over so many facets of our lives—from food and

clothing production to information, transportation, and other necessities—corporate institutions have become more powerful than the sovereign people who originally granted them existence.

As late as 1840, state legislators closely supervised the operation of corporations, allowing them to be created only for very specific public benefits, such as the building of a highway or a canal. Corporations were subject to a variety of limitations: a finite period of existence, limits to the amount of property they could own, and prohibitions against one corporation owning another. After a period of time deemed sufficient for investors to recoup a fair profit, the assets of a business would often revert to public ownership. In some states, it was even a felony for a corporation to donate to a political campaign.

But in the headlong rush into the Industrial Age, legislators and the courts stripped away almost all of those limitations. By the 1860s, most states had granted owners limited liability, waiving virtually all personal accountability for an institution's cumulative actions. In 1886, without comment, the United States Supreme Court ruled for corporate owners in *Santa Clara County v. Southern Pacific Railroad,* allowing corporations to be considered "persons," thereby opening the door to free speech and other civil rights under the Bill of Rights. By the early 1890s, states had largely eliminated restrictions on corporations owning each other, and by 1904, 318 corporations owned forty percent of all manufacturing assets. Corporate owners were replacing de Tocqueville's "equality of conditions" with what one writer of the time, W. J. Ghent, called "the new feudalism . . . characterized by a class dependence rather than by a personal dependence."

Throughout the twentieth century, federal courts have granted U.S. corporations additional rights that once applied only to human beings—including those of "due process" and "equal protection." Corporations, in turn, have used those rights to thwart democratic efforts to check their growth and influence.

Today, municipalities across the country are feeling the growing impact of corporate power. But in the conservative farming communities of western Pennsylvania, the commercial feudalism de Tocqueville warned against has evoked a response that echoes the defiant spirit of the Declaration of Independence. When agribusiness corporations obstructed local efforts to ban noxious farming practices, two townships in Clarion County did something that no municipal government had ever dared: They decreed that a corporation's rights do not apply within their jurisdictions.

The author of the ordinances, Thomas Linzey, an Alabama-born lawyer who attended law school in nearby Harrisburg, did not start out trying to convince the citizens of the heavily Republican county to attack the legal framework of corporate power. But over the past five years, Linzey has seen township supervisors begin to take a stand against expanding corporate influence—and not just in Clarion County. Throughout rural Pennsylvania, supervisors have held at bay some of the most well-connected agribusiness executives in the state, along with their lawyers, lobbyists, and representatives in the Pennsylvania legislature.

Linzey anticipated none of this when he cofounded the Community Environmental Legal Defense Fund (CELDF), a grassroots legal support group, in 1995. Initially, CELDF worked with activists according to a conventional formula. "We were launched to provide free legal services to community groups, specifically grassroots community environmental organizations," Linzey says. "That involved us in permit appeals and other typical regulatory stuff." But all that soon changed.

In 1997, the state of Pennsylvania began enforcing a weak waste-disposal law, passed at the urging of agribusiness lobbyists several years earlier, which explicitly barred townships from passing any more stringent law. It had the effect of repealing the waste-disposal regulations of more than one hundred townships, regulations that had prevented corporations from establishing factory farms in their communities. The supervisors, who had seen massive hog farms despoil the ecosystems and destroy the social and economic fabric of communities in nearby states, were desperate to find a way to protect their townships. Within a year, CELDF "started getting calls from municipal governments in Pennsylvania, as many as sixty to seventy a week," Linzey says. "Of 1,400 rural governments in the state we were interacting with perhaps ten percent of them. We still are."

But hog farms weren't the only threat introduced by the state's industry-backed regulation. The law also served to preempt local control over the spreading of municipal sewage sludge on rural farmland. In Pittsburgh and other large cities, powerful municipal treatment agencies, seeking to avoid costly payments to landfills, began contracting with corporate sewage haulers. Haulers, in turn, relied on rural farmers willing to use the sludge as fertilizer—a practice deemed "safe" by corporate-friendly government environmental agencies.

Pennsylvania required the sewage sludge leaving treatment plants, which contains numerous dangerous microorganisms, to be tested only at three-month intervals, and only for *E. coli* and heavy metals. Most individual batches arriving at farms were not tested at all. It was clear, from the local

vantage, that the state Department of Environmental Protection had failed
to protect the townships, turning many rural communities into toxic dumping grounds—with fatal results. In 1995, two local youths, Tony Behun and
Danny Pennock, died after being exposed to the material—Behun while
riding an all-terrain vehicle, Pennock while hunting.

"People are up in arms all over the place," said Russell Pennock, Danny's
father, a millwright from Centre County. "They're considering this a normal
agricultural operation. I'll tell you something right now: If anyone would
have seen the way my son suffered and died, they would not even get near
this stuff." After a U.S. Environmental Protection Agency scientist linked
the two deaths to a pathogen in the sludge, county supervisors tried to pass
ordinances to stop the practice, but found that the state had preempted
such local control with its less restrictive law.

The state's apparent complicity with the corporations outraged local
elected officials. People began to understand, Linzey recalls, "that the state
was being used by corporations to strip away democratic authority from
local governments."

Many small farmers in rural Pennsylvania were already feeling the devastating effects of increasing corporate control over the market. They often
had no choice but to sign contracts with large agribusiness corporations—
resulting in a modern form of peonage. By the corporate formula, a farmer
must agree to raise hogs exclusively for the corporation, and to build specialized factory-farm barns, which typically cost $250,000 or more. Yet the
corporation can cancel the contract at any time. The farmer doesn't even
own the animals—except the dead ones, which pile up in mortality bins
as infectious diseases ravage the crowded pens. The agribusiness company
takes the lion's share of the profits while externalizing the costs and liabili-
ties; the farmer is financially and legally responsible for all environmental
harms, including groundwater contamination from manure lagoons.

Even if farmers could find a way to market their hogs on their own, loan
officers often deny applications from farmers unless they are locked into a
corporate livestock contract. "The once-proud occupation of 'independent
family farmer' has become a black mark on loan papers," Linzey writes on
the CELDF Web site.

A bespectacled thirty-four-year-old, Linzey speaks with a tinge of
Southern drawl. Under the tutelage of historian Richard Grossman of the
Program on Corporations, Law, and Democracy, he has become an eloquent speaker on organizing tactics, constitutional theory, and the history
of corporations in this country. But he is also an excellent listener. He heard

the indignation as incredulous supervisors came to understand their lack of authority in the regulatory arena. The rights and privileges that corporations were able to assert seemed incomprehensible to them. "There's disbelief," he says. "Then the clients attack you, and then you have to explain it to them, giving prior examples of how this works."

Township supervisors were quick to see that the problem was not simply factory farms or sludge, "but the corporations that were pushing them," Linzey says. Enormously wealthy corporations were able to secure rulings that channeled citizen energies into futile battles. The supervisors started to realize, according to Linzey, "that the only thing environmental law regulates is environmentalists."

By 1999, with CELDF's help, five townships in two counties had adopted a straightforward ordinance that challenged state law by prohibiting corporations from farming or owning farmland. Five more townships in three more counties followed suit. Also in 1999, Rush Township of Centre County became the first in the nation to pass an ordinance to control sludge spreading. Haulers who wanted to apply sewage sludge to farmland would have to test every load at their own expense—and for a wider array of toxic substances than required by the weaker state law. Three dozen townships in seven counties have unanimously passed similar sludge ordinances to date. Citing a township's mandate to protect its citizens, Licking Township Supervisor Mik Robertson declares, "If the state isn't going to do the job, we'll do it for them."

So far, the spate of unanimous votes at the municipal level has halted both new hog farms and the spreading of additional sludge in these townships.

In de Tocqueville's time, local communities like those in rural Pennsylvania had enormous strength and autonomy. The large corporation was nonexistent, and the federal government had little say over local affairs. Americans by and large reserved patriotic feelings for their state. People, at least those of European descent, played a more active role in local governance than they do today. Their only direct experience with the federal government was through the post office. As de Tocqueville pointed out, "real political life" was not concentrated in what was called "the Union," itself a telling term; before the Civil War the "United States" was a plural noun, as in, "The United States *are* a large country."

Since the consolidation of the Union and throughout the twentieth century, the autonomy of state and local governments has continued to wane as corporations have grown larger and gained more extensive rights under the

U.S. Constitution. In two decisions in the mid-1970s, the Supreme Court affirmed a corporation's right to make contributions to political campaigns, considering money to be a form of "free speech." And over the past few decades, corporations have won increasingly generous interpretations of the Interstate Commerce Clause of the Constitution. Originally intended to prevent individual states from obstructing the flow of goods and people across their borders, the clause has been used by corporations to challenge almost any state law that might affect activity across state lines. In 2002, for example, the federal courts ruled that a Virginia law prohibiting the dumping of trash from other states violated a waste hauler's rights. In early 2003, Smithfield Foods, one of the nation's largest factory-farm conglomerates, sued on similar grounds to overturn Iowa's citizen initiative banning meatpacking companies from owning livestock, a practice the citizens believed undercut family farms.

Elsewhere, corporate rights have posed increasingly absurd threats to sovereignty. In 1994, for example, Vermont passed a law requiring the labeling of milk from cows that had received a bioengineered bovine growth hormone; in 1996 the federal courts overthrew that law, saying that the mandated disclosure violated a corporation's First Amendment right "not to speak." Four years later, a Pennsylvania township tried to use zoning laws to control the placement of a cell-phone tower; the telecommunications company sued the township and won, citing a nineteenth-century civil rights law designed to protect newly freed slaves.

Until recently, these incidents might have been seen simply as aberrations or "corporate abuse." But an increasing number of Americans have begun to consider a whole range of single-issue cases as examples of "corporate rule." The role that government has played, in their view, is merely that of a referee who enforces the rules defined by corporations for their own benefit rather than the public's.

It was this perception that motivated the townships to take their revolutionary stand. But their successes in halting factory farming and sludge applications within their borders didn't prohibit corporations from attempting to press their case in the courtroom.

In 2000, the transnational hauler Synagro-WWT, Inc. sued Rush Township, claiming its antisludge ordinance illegally preempted the weaker state law and violated the company's constitutional right of due process. It also sued each supervisor personally for one million dollars. In response, Linzey recalls, one township supervisor asked, "What the hell are the constitutional rights of corporations?" A year later, PennAg Industries Association, a statewide agribusiness trade group, funded its own suit against the factory farm ordinance in Fulton County's Belfast Township on similar constitutional grounds. Rulings on both suits are expected in mid-2004.

It was only after those suits had been filed that the two Clarion County townships, Licking and Porter, took the historic step of passing ordinances to decree that within their townships, "Corporations shall not be considered to be 'persons' protected by the Constitution of the United States," a measure that effectively declared their independence from corporate rule. For Mik Robertson, the issue is simple: "Those rights are meant for individuals." He and his two fellow supervisors later revised their ordinance to also deny corporations the right to invoke the Constitution's Interstate Commerce Clause; Porter Township is considering a similar amendment. Several other townships are preparing their own versions of the corporate rights ordinance, according to Linzey.

Now, when a corporation claims that an antisludge ordinance violates its rights, the townships can simply say those rights don't apply here. The corporation would then be forced to defend corporate personhood in a legal battle. That hasn't happened yet, but Linzey and his allies have energized a statewide coalition that has vowed to fight the issue all the way to the Supreme Court, raising awareness along the way about a basic question of sovereignty: By what authority can a conglomeration of capital and property, whose existence is granted by the public, deny the right of a sovereign people to govern itself democratically? Linzey predicts that such a suit could happen within a decade, and that it could ignite populist sentiment across the country—even around the world.

Growing support for these issues was put to the test in 2002, when agribusiness interests, displeased by the spread of ordinances prohibiting factory farming, began prodding the Pennsylvania state legislature to pass an even more severe bill than the 1997 directive. This time there was no disguising it as waste-disposal regulation. The 2002 bill had one explicitly stated purpose: To strip away a township's right to control agriculture—including sludge applications—within its borders. When it stalled in a senate committee, the Pennsylvania legislators renumbered the bill and rammed it through before their constituents noticed. By the time CELDF found out about the bill, it was up for a vote in the house.

"We ignited opposition almost overnight," Linzey recalls. "We were working with 100-plus townships already. All we had to do was notify them."

Within two weeks, the coalition included four hundred local townships, five countywide associations of township officials, the Sierra Club, two small-farmers groups, the citizens' rights group Common Cause—even the United Mine Workers (whose members had been sickened by sewage sludge applied on mine reclamation sites), which invited in the formidable AFL-CIO.

"It was like Sam Adams in 1766, when the Townsend Acts were passed," says Linzey. "He had already built the mob, the rabble, and just had to alert the people that this was happening as an act of oppression."

Because the issue had been defined as protection of a community's right to self-determination, the bill became unpopular and was tabled indefinitely. On Thanksgiving Eve 2002, it met its end when a mandated voting period elapsed. For the moment, the coalition had won.

The deliberations in Clarion County and elsewhere in Pennsylvania resonate far beyond state lines. In recent years, judges, mayors, and a host of local and state legislators nationwide, whose authority as democratically elected representatives is similarly threatened by the increasing legal power of corporations, have begun to take action:

- In Minnesota, State Representative Bill Hilty has introduced a state constitutional amendment eliminating corporate personhood.
- The Arizona Green Party is campaigning for the passage of a similar amendment in their state.
- In the northern California town of Gualala, legislators passed nonbinding resolutions in opposition to corporate personhood.
- Iowa, Kansas, Minnesota, Missouri, Nebraska, Oklahoma, North Dakota, South Dakota, and Wisconsin have all passed laws outlawing corporate ownership of farms.

But in the age of globalization, questions of sovereignty can no longer be addressed strictly within U.S. borders. Clarion County's townships may pass an ordinance saying that a sludge hauler's constitutional rights don't apply. "But if there is foreign participation, say if they are partially German-owned or Canadian," says Victor Menotti of the International Forum on Globalization, "you run up against another set of corporate rights under [international] trade agreements."

It was this other set of rights, the understanding of global "corporate rule," that brought many of the forty thousand demonstrators to the streets of Seattle in December 1999 to shut down the meeting of the World Trade Organization (WTO). It is also what incited subsequent demonstrations at the meeting of the World Bank in Prague in 2000, the meeting of the G-8 (the eight most economically powerful countries) in Genoa in 2001, the Free Trade Area of the Americas meeting in Québec in 2001, and most recently, the WTO meeting in Cancún. Through it all, protesters have held fast to one principle: the right of a people to govern themselves, through their representatives, without obstruction by corporations.

A growing number of public officials in the U.S. face challenges to their sovereignty similar to those confronted by their counterparts in the Pennsylvania townships. One is Velma Veloria, chair of the Washington State legislature's Joint Committee on Trade Policy. For fifty-three-year-old Veloria, the 1999 Seattle demonstration against the WTO was a defining event. Veloria realized that behind the tumult in the streets, "there was a whole movement that was asking for accountability and transparency." She imagined what might happen if a tanker that was not double-hulled spilled oil in Puget Sound. She and her colleagues could pass a law requiring double hulls in Seattle harbor, but under the emerging rules of the WTO, such a law could meet the same fate as a Clarion County antisludge ordinance: It could be attacked as interfering with the rights of corporations, as a barrier to trade. "It opened a whole new field for me about the sovereignty of the state," Veloria says.

California State Senator Liz Figueroa, chair of the Senate Select Committee on International Trade Policy and State Legislature, has faced similar quandaries. In 2000, Figueroa authored a bill that made it illegal for the state to do business with companies that employed slave or forced labor. Figueroa explained to the city councils and constituents in her district that foreign trade imports produced by slave labor could undercut the local economy. But as pragmatic and ethically incontestable as the bill sounds, it could potentially be challenged under the WTO's rules.

"Our job is monumental," she says, referring to her efforts to explain how trade agreements can usurp democracy. "We have to make sure our own legislative offices even know of the conflict . . . we have to explain the reality of the situation."

Figueroa and Veloria are not alone. International trade agreements such as the North American Free Trade Agreement (NAFTA), the WTO's General Agreement on Trade and Tariffs (GATT), and the pending Free Trade Area of the Americas (FTAA) threaten the jurisdiction of any elected or appointed representative of a sovereign people at any level of government. A National League of Cities resolution declared that the trade agreements could "undermine the scope of local governmental authority under the Constitution." Last year, the Conference of Chief Justices, consisting of the top judges from each state, wrote a letter to the U.S. Senate stating that the proposed FTAA "does not protect adequately the traditional values of constitutional federalism" and "threatens the integrity of the courts of this country." In California, Minnesota, Oregon, Washington, Massachusetts, and New Hampshire, state legislatures have expressed concern over trade agreements, as has the National Council of State Legislators. Their statements, however more discreet, nonetheless echo the chants from the streets of Seattle: "This isn't about trade, this isn't about business; this is about democracy."

Despite their enormous ramifications, most international trade agreements remain a mystery to the average American. At the core, they are simple.

GATT and NAFTA cover the trade of physical goods between countries. They can be used to override any country's protection of the environment, for example, or of workers' rights, by defining relevant laws and regulations as illegal "barriers to trade." They provide for a "dispute resolution" process, but the process routinely determines such laws to be in violation of the agreements.

In the case of GATT, a WTO member country can sue another member country—on behalf of one of its corporations—on the grounds that a country's law has violated GATT trade rules. The case is heard by a secret tribunal appointed by the WTO. State and local officials are denied legal representation. If the tribunal finds that a law or regulation of a country—or state or township—is a "barrier to trade," the offending country must either rescind that law or pay the accusing country whatever amount the WTO decides the company had to forgo because of the barrier, a sum that can amount to billions of dollars. In short, democratic lawmakers and regulators at any level can be penalized for interfering with international profit-making.

Through this process, WTO tribunals have overturned such U.S. laws as EPA standards for clean-burning gasoline and regulations banning fish caught by methods that endanger dolphins and sea turtles. The WTO has also effectively undermined the use of the precautionary principle, by which practices can be banned until proven safe—in one recent instance superseding European laws forbidding the use of growth hormones in beef cattle. A WTO tribunal dismissed laboratory evidence that such hormones may cause cancer because it lacked "scientific certainty." On similar grounds, the U.S., on behalf of Monsanto and other American agribusiness giants, recently initiated an action under GATT challenging the European Union's ban on genetically modified food.

Under NAFTA, which covers Canada, Mexico, and the U.S., a corporation can sue a government directly. The case would also be heard by a secret tribunal, such as when Vancouver-based Methanex sued the U.S. over

California's ban on a cancer-causing gas additive, MTBE. The company, which manufactures the additive's key ingredient, claimed that the ban failed to consider its financial interests. Since July 2001, three men—one former U.S. official and two corporate lawyers—have held closed hearings on the thirteenth floor of World Bank headquarters in Washington, D.C., to decide whether, in this instance, a democratically elected governor's executive order to protect the public should cost the U.S. $970 million in fines. The FTAA, recently fast-tracked for negotiations to put it into effect by 2005, would extend NAFTA's provisions to all of Latin America.

GATS, the General Agreement on Trade in Services, a recent trade agreement under the WTO, takes the usurpation of democracy one step further. While GATT deals with the exchange of goods across international borders, GATS establishes certain privileges for transnational companies operating within a country. It covers "services," meaning almost anything from telecommunications to construction to mining to supplying drinking water. It even includes functions that traditionally have been carried out or closely controlled by government, like postal services and social services such as welfare—even libraries. Activists point out that the primary focus of GATS is to limit government involvement, "whether in the form of a law, regulation, rule, procedure, decision, administrative action or any other form," to quote the treaty itself. Public Citizen's Lori Wallach has called GATS a "massive attack on the most basic functions of local and state government."

Under GATS, any activity the federal government agrees to declare a "service" would be thrown open to privatization. The supply and treatment of water is a timely example, since the European Union is currently pressing the United States to make water among the first of the services it places under GATS. If clean drinking water is so declared, no government body in the U.S. could insist that it remain publicly managed. If any government wanted to create a publicly owned water district, foreign corporate "competitors" would have the right to underbid the government for control of the service. Just as important, a transnational company could challenge any rules—including environmental and health regulations—that would hamper its ability to profit from a business that is related to a service under GATS.

On March 28, 2003, twenty-nine California state legislators signed a letter of concern to U.S. Trade Representative Robert Zoellick about the provisions contained in GATS. The letter states that GATS could usurp any government regulation, including nurse-to-patient staffing levels, laws against racial discrimination, worker health and safety laws, regulatory limits to oil drilling, and standards for everything from waste incineration to trace toxins in drinking water. As a result, the letter states, GATS would "jeopardize the public welfare and pose grave consequences for democratic governance throughout the world."

Veloria and Figueroa both believe that if state legislators are to challenge this "power grab," in Veloria's words, they will have to organize among themselves. "One state cannot do it alone. We need to do it on a national scale." Otherwise U.S. citizens may find themselves under the thumb of NAFTA and WTO trade tribunals, "unelected bodies that have no accountability to the people." At that point, Veloria asks, "Why have state legislators, why have elected officials?"

In his work with the rural Pennsylvania supervisors, Thomas Linzey's approach to domestic corporate rights may well illuminate how individuals, states, and nations can deal with international trade treaties.

"Clarion County is one of many emerging examples of local communities reasserting their own authority to define how they want land managed and what sort of protections they want for their community," says antiglobalization organizer Victor Menotti. "It's when things like this come to light that people question what the hell we've gotten ourselves into. These local communities stand up, and others say, 'if they can do that, we can do that.'"

On many issues of local governance, Linzey believes, a state or local legislature "could declare null and void the federal government's signature on GATT." To him it would be the "ultimate act of insurrection: saying governments have no constitutional authority to give away sovereign and democratic rights to international trade tribunals that operate in secrecy."

For now, Velma Veloria is still working through traditional channels. In an attempt to remove the antidemocratic provisions of the trade treaties, her committee will take up the issue with the state's delegation to Congress. But she is well aware that her colleagues, and the people of Washington State, may find that traditional route closed to them, as the Pennsylvania townships did in 1997.

If that happens, the practice of democracy at the local level would require legislators to defy the trade agreements. "At some point we might get to where the people working with Linzey are," she says. "We may end up saying we don't recognize parts of the international trade agreements that impact us. But that depends on the grassroots, on people demanding it."

There, too, the Pennsylvania coalition may offer some inspiration. "When the agribusiness folks filed suit over our anticorporate farming laws," Linzey recalls, "page one of the lawsuit said 'we the corporations are people and this ordinance violates our personhood rights.' When we photocopied that, people immediately understood how they're ruled by these constitutional rights and privileges. It sparks a conversation."

The Pennsylvania township supervisors are backed by a determined grass-roots movement, with a constituency "ready to go to the mat for their binding law to establish a sustainable vision that doesn't include corporate rights and privileges," says Linzey. "The product is not the ordinance," he adds. "The product is the people."

The Pennsylvania ordinances express the will of a sovereign people who are exercising their right to create institutions that support their vision of how they wish to live. And, as one would expect in a democratic society, the people of Pennsylvania wish to be the ones who define the rules under which those institutions may operate, be they governments or corporations.

History repeats itself. In the course of asserting their sovereign rights, the citizens of rural Pennsylvania have undergone a profound change in personal identity and political consciousness not unlike that of their forebears in the years leading up to the signing of the Declaration of Independence. As historian Lawrence Henry Gipson noted, "The period from 1760 to 1775 is really the history of the transformation of the attitude of the great body of colonials from acquiescence in the traditional order of things to a demand for a new order." People who for generations had considered themselves loyal Englishmen suddenly declared themselves to be citizens of a new nation, one based on the sovereignty of its citizens.

Veloria believes we are at a similar juncture today. "I have faith that the American people will stand up for themselves and for democracy—that they can only be pushed so far."

(2003)

Beyond Hope

Removing a major stumbling block to acting on behalf of the Earth

THE MOST COMMON WORDS I HEAR SPOKEN BY ANY ENVIRONMEN-
talists anywhere are, *We're fucked.* Most of these environmentalists
are fighting desperately, using whatever tools they have—or rather whatever legal tools they have, which means whatever tools those in power
grant them the right to use, which means whatever tools will be ultimately
ineffective—to try to protect some piece of ground, to try to stop the manufacture or release of poisons, to try to stop civilized humans from torment-
ing some group of plants or animals. Sometimes they're reduced to trying
to protect just one tree.

Here's how John Osborn, an extraordinary activist and friend, sums up
his reasons for doing the work: "As things become increasingly chaotic, I
want to make sure some doors remain open. If grizzly bears are still alive in
twenty, thirty, and forty years, they may still be alive in fifty. If they're gone
in twenty, they'll be gone forever."

But no matter what environmentalists do, our best efforts are insufficient. We're losing badly, on every front. Those in power are hell-bent on
destroying the planet, and most people don't care.

Frankly, I don't have much hope. But I think that's a good thing. Hope
is what keeps us chained to the system, the conglomerate of people and
ideas and ideals that is causing the destruction of the Earth.

To start, there is the false hope that suddenly somehow the system may
inexplicably change. Or technology will save us. Or the Great Mother.
Or beings from Alpha Centauri. Or Jesus Christ. Or Santa Claus. All of
these false hopes lead to inaction, or at least to ineffectiveness. One reason
my mother stayed with my abusive father was that there were no battered
women's shelters in the '50s and '60s, but another was her false hope that
he would change. False hopes bind us to unlivable situations, and blind us
to real possibilities.

Does anyone really believe that Weyerhaeuser is going to stop deforest-
ing because we ask nicely? Does anyone really believe that Monsanto will

stop Monsantoing because we ask nicely? If only we get a Democrat in the White House, things will be okay. If only we pass this or that piece of legislation, things will be okay. If only we *defeat* this or that piece of legislation, things will be okay. Nonsense. Things will not be okay. They are already not okay, and they're getting worse. Rapidly.

But it isn't only false hopes that keep those who go along enchained. It is hope itself. Hope, we are told, is our beacon in the dark. It is our light at the end of a long, dark tunnel. It is the beam of light that makes its way into our prison cells. It is our reason for persevering, our protection against despair (which must be avoided at all costs). How can we continue if we do not have hope?

We've all been taught that hope in some future condition—like hope in some future heaven—is and must be our refuge in current sorrow. I'm sure you remember the story of Pandora. She was given a tightly sealed box and was told never to open it. But, being curious, she did, and out flew plagues, sorrow, and mischief, probably not in that order. Too late she clamped down the lid. Only one thing remained in the box: hope. Hope, the story goes, was the only good the casket held among many evils, and it remains to this day mankind's sole comfort in misfortune. No mention here of action being a comfort in misfortune, or of actually *doing something* to alleviate or eliminate one's misfortune.

The more I understand hope, the more I realize that all along it deserved to be in the box with the plagues, sorrow, and mischief; that it serves the needs of those in power as surely as belief in a distant heaven; that hope is really nothing more than a secular way of keeping us in line.

Hope is, in fact, a curse, a bane. I say this not only because of the lovely Buddhist saying "Hope and fear chase each other's tails," not only because hope leads us away from the present, away from who and where we are right now and toward some imaginary future state. I say this because of *what hope* is.

More or less all of us yammer on more or less endlessly about hope. You wouldn't believe—or maybe you would—how many magazine editors have asked me to write about the apocalypse, then enjoined me to leave readers with a sense of hope. But what, precisely, is hope? At a talk I gave last spring, someone asked me to define it. I turned the question back on the audience, and here's the definition we all came up with: hope is a longing for a future condition over which you have no agency; it means you are essentially powerless.

I'm not, for example, going to say I hope I eat something tomorrow. I just will. I don't hope I take another breath right now, nor that I finish writing this sentence. I just do them. On the other hand, I do hope that the next time I get on a plane, it doesn't crash. To hope for some result means you have given up any agency concerning it. Many people say they hope the dominant culture stops destroying the world. By saying that, they've assumed that the destruction will continue, at least in the short term, and they've stepped away from their own ability to participate in stopping it.

I do not hope coho salmon survive. I will do whatever it takes to make sure the dominant culture doesn't drive them extinct. If coho want to leave us because they don't like how they're being treated—and who could blame them?—I will say goodbye, and I will miss them, but if they do not want to leave, I will not allow civilization to kill them off.

When we realize the degree of agency we actually do have, we no longer have to "hope" at all. We simply do the work. We make sure salmon survive. We make sure prairie dogs survive. We make sure grizzlies survive. We do whatever it takes.

When we stop hoping for external assistance, when we stop hoping that the awful situation we're in will somehow resolve itself, when we stop hoping the situation will somehow not get worse, then we are finally free—truly free—to honestly start working to resolve it. I would say that when hope dies, action begins.

People sometimes ask me, "If things are so bad, why don't you just kill yourself?" The answer is that life is really, really good. I am a complex enough being that I can hold in my heart the understanding that we are really, really fucked, and at the same time that life is really, really good. I am full of rage, sorrow, joy, love, hate, despair, happiness, satisfaction, dissatisfaction, and a thousand other feelings. *We are really fucked. Life is still really good.*

Many people are afraid to feel despair. They fear that if they allow themselves to perceive how desperate our situation really is, they must then be perpetually miserable. They forget that it is possible to feel many things at once. They also forget that despair is an entirely appropriate response to a desperate situation. Many people probably also fear that if they allow themselves to perceive how desperate things are, they may be forced to do something about it.

Another question people sometimes ask me is, "If things are so bad, why don't you just party?" Well, the first answer is that I don't really like to party. The second is that I'm already having a great deal of fun. I love my life. I love life. This is true for most activists I know. We are doing what we love, fighting for what (and whom) we love.

I have no patience for those who use our desperate situation as an excuse for inaction. I've learned that if you deprive most of these people of that particular excuse they just find another, then another, then another.

The use of this excuse to justify inaction—the use of any excuse to justify inaction—reveals nothing more nor less than an incapacity to love.

At one of my recent talks someone stood up during the Q and A and announced that the only reason people ever become activists is to feel better about themselves. Effectiveness really doesn't matter, he said, and it's egotistical to think it does.

I told him I disagreed.

Doesn't activism make you feel good? he asked.

Of course, I said, but that's not why I do it. If I only want to feel good, I can just masturbate. But I want to accomplish something in the real world.

Why?

Because I'm in love. With salmon, with trees outside my window, with baby lampreys living in sandy stream bottoms, with slender salamanders crawling through the duff. And if you love, you act to defend your beloved. Of course results matter to you, but they don't determine whether or not you make the effort. You don't simply hope your beloved survives and thrives. You do what it takes. If my love doesn't cause me to protect those I love, it's not love.

A wonderful thing happens when you give up on hope, which is that you realize you never needed it in the first place. You realize that giving up on hope didn't kill you. It didn't even make you less effective. In fact it made you more effective, because you ceased relying on someone or something else to solve your problems—you ceased *hoping* your problems would somehow get solved through the magical assistance of God, the Great Mother, the Sierra Club, valiant tree-sitters, brave salmon, or even the Earth itself—and you just began doing whatever it takes to solve those problems yourself.

When you give up on hope, something even better happens than it not killing you, which is that in some sense it does kill you. You die. And there's a wonderful thing about being dead, which is that they—those in power—cannot really touch you anymore. Not through promises, not through threats, not through violence itself. Once you're dead in this way, you can still sing, you can still dance, you can still make love, you can still fight like hell—you can still live because you are still alive, more alive in fact than ever before. You come to realize that when hope died, the you who died with the hope was not you, but was the you who depended on those who exploit you, the you who believed that those who exploit you will somehow stop on their own, the you who believed in the mythologies propagated by those who exploit you in order to facilitate that exploitation. The socially constructed you died. The civilized you died. The manufactured, fabricated, stamped, molded you died. The victim died.

And who is left when that you dies? You are left. Animal you. Naked you. Vulnerable (and invulnerable) you. Mortal you. Survivor you. The you who thinks not what the culture taught you to think but what you think. The you who feels not what the culture taught you to feel but what you feel. The you who is not who the culture taught you to be but who you are. The you who can say *yes,* the you who can say *no.* The you who is a part of the land where you live. The you who will fight (or not) to defend your family. The you who will fight (or not) to defend those you love. The you who will fight (or not) to defend the land upon which your life and the lives of those you love depends. The you whose morality is not based on what you have been taught by the culture that is killing the planet, killing you, but on your own animal feelings of love and connection to your family, your friends, your land base—not to your family as self-identified civilized beings but as animals who require a land base, animals who are being killed by chemicals, animals who have been formed and deformed to fit the needs of the culture.

When you give up on hope—when you are dead in this way, and by so being are really alive—you make yourself no longer vulnerable to the co-option of rationality and fear that Nazis inflicted on Jews and others, that abusers like my father inflict on their victims, that the dominant culture inflicts on all of us. Or is it rather the case that these exploiters frame physical, social, and emotional circumstances such that victims perceive themselves as having no choice but to inflict this cooption on themselves?

But when you give up on hope, this exploiter/victim relationship is broken. You become like the Jews who participated in the Warsaw Ghetto Uprising.

When you give up on hope, you turn away from fear.

And when you quit relying on hope, and instead begin to protect the people, things, and places you love, you become very dangerous indeed to those in power.

In case you're wondering, that's a very good thing.

(2006)

The Union Makes Them Strong

A blue-green alliance on climate change adopts a new agenda: jobs

THE ARRIVALS PREDICTABLY DIVIDE THEMSELVES INTO TWO CAMPS, and even the dinner choices—vegetarian pasta or prime rib—reinforce stereotypes of people who, when they aren't coming to blows over logging, mining, or environmental laws, are doing their best to ignore one another—as they seem to be doing tonight. Like wallflowers, the environmentalists cluster at a table near the door: Most are college students; one is a college professor. Many of the younger environmentalists seem nervous, ill at ease, as they talk quietly among themselves. A timid twenty-something with a complicated haircut turns to his tablemates and says, "I'm afraid of the steelworkers."

On the far side of the room, wearing union jackets and caps, the steelworkers trade war stories in defiant tones. One worker describes a 2003 meeting in which Terry Bonds, the United Steelworkers of America (USWA) District 12 director, railed at mining company officials for breaking their contract with the union. "'Wherever you're going to go,'" the unionist quotes Bonds as saying, "'you're going to look up, and we're going to be in your face.'" A smirking blond chimes in with a story about management that ends, "They'd love to get rid of me, but they can't." Such bravado seems foreign to the green side of the room.

But later, during official introductions, dessert forks go down when USWA representative Wayne Holland describes his "passionate dislike" for President George W. Bush. "This is the worst president we've ever seen for workers' rights and issues," he says. "And he's been a disaster, no doubt, for environmental issues." When Sierra Club member Mark Clemmons says he's proud to be a "squeaky little rust atom on the hinge of history," everyone breaks into laughter.

On this weekend in Salt Lake City in March 2004, steelworkers from nearby Kennecott Utah Copper have come together with members of the Utah chapter of the Sierra Club under the guidance of the Public Health Institute, a New York-based nonprofit that helps people build coalitions.

The task at hand: train thirty-year veterans of the labor movement and devoted young conservationists to tally their similarities, pool their resources, and explore whether the jobs-versus-environment debate has distracted them from common aims, or even a common identity.

The 2004 training was but one piece of a broader labor movement, spearheaded in recent years largely by the USWA, to wean the United States off fossil fuels. The goal is to reverse climate change and to start planning for the inevitable: the disappearance of the nation's dominant energy source, probably within a few generations given current rates of use. To leaders of the steelworkers union—which represents 1.2 million members in metalworking, welding, tire making, shipbuilding, transportation, communication, and health care—a shift away from fossil fuels may also be a matter of short-term economic survival. The U.S. economy, including the energy industry, is hemorrhaging jobs overseas and across borders; in the last three years alone, nearly three million jobs have left U.S. soil. And of those jobs remaining, fewer are industrial and fewer are unionized, prompting labor leaders to take some untraditional stances.

"If we hope to maintain a strong industrial economy, we need to reject the notion of a clean environment versus industrial jobs," Leo Gerard, USWA international president, said in October. "We need to get real and get those quality jobs back. And we can't do that without the clean energy industry." By retrofitting buildings to make them energy efficient, Gerard says, by manufacturing energy-efficient appliances, and by building wind turbines, labor could reclaim lost jobs—and protect the environment.

Gerard's vision isn't just a pipe dream: In October, an alliance of six labor unions and environmental groups released a report showing that if the United States pursued a clean energy economy, it would generate 1.4 million new jobs over the next twenty years. Granted, that's not enough to keep pace with current job losses overall, but it's more than enough to offset the ongoing losses in fossil fuel-related industries. And if labor gets in on the ground floor, those could be 1.4 million union jobs.

Steelworker Andy Triplett had no interest in the environment before this March weekend. Tall, with a thin mustache and a goatee, Triplett looks much younger than forty-five, and it seems impossible that he's worked at Kennecott Utah Copper for twenty-six years. He has a high school education and works as a millwright. He fixes machinery—everything from pumps and furnaces to gearboxes and cranes—and manufactures new parts as necessary. Though he's quiet and exceedingly polite, Triplett, Local 392's unit chair at Kennecott's copper refinery, burns with the political fire of labor's activist past. The prospect of spending the weekend with a bunch of Sierra Club members was a tough sell for him: "I was thinking, 'Why would I want to go into a deal where people are so closed-minded about mines?'"

With a Sierra Club partner, Triplett is assigned to teach a session about the term "environment." The two are given a primer defining the term as "the place where people live, work, study, play, and worship." By the time he stands in front of the class, Triplett seems to have undergone an epiphany— his face is lit up, his body language invigorated. The definition, he explains in animated tones, means that the "environment" is not a distant place that only wealthy backpackers can reach; it's part of everyday experience. "We could get the fear out of the debate by educating people about this defini-tion," he says to the class. Later he would say of the experience, "My eyes were opened so wide. I saw how much more we have in common."

Throughout the weekend, union members continue to pair up with environmentalists to teach the group an assigned topic related to global change. After each pair presents its lesson, the teams debate it in more depth at their tables. A miner might hear about sustainable logging from a Sierra Club member, who might in turn hear what it's like to worry about outsourced industrial jobs. By the second day, when the topic turns to con-serving resources and cutting carbon emissions, the ideas around the tables have become confident and far-reaching: Construction workers should use local products to cut down on transportation pollution; electricity should be generated locally to decrease energy loss over transmission lines, thus cutting energy demand; industrial workers should educate their employers about their ability to cut pollution—and then demand that employers ac-tually do so. Other strategies include helping communities fight local pol-luters and educating consumers to boycott offenders.

But the invisible backdrop to all of the discussion is the topic of job security. Perhaps because it's designed mainly to break down cultural bar-riers, not forge strategy, the Public Health Institute training deliberately omits any formal session on the grim statistics of industrial employment. Nobody mentions that from 1980 to 1999, according to the U.S. Bureau of Labor Statistics, employment in U.S. coal mining and oil refining fell 66 percent and 40 percent respectively, amid an overall decline in industrial jobs. Nobody mentions that oil and gas industry jobs are expected to de-cline by 28 percent through 2012 as automation increases, domestic supplies dwindle, and companies shift exploration and production overseas. Nobody mentions how far the United States lags behind Europe, where employment in wind energy alone tripled from 1998 to 2003 and is expected to triple again, to two hundred thousand jobs, by 2020.

Still, there is a palpable sense that jobs are disappearing, that blue and green alike are going to have to deal with something after fossil fuels, and that global warming is undoubtedly an issue that unions must tackle with all the force they have historically mustered. Tom Maki, a steelworkers representative living in Rock Springs, Wyoming, a hub of the nation's current coal bed methane boom, is particularly insistent: "If we don't do it, who will?"

He could have put it another way: If we don't do it, what will we do? In 2003, union membership levels were at their lowest ever. Only 12.9 percent of all workers belonged to a union, compared with 20.1 percent just twenty years earlier. Those numbers are even more dismal outside the public sector. Only 8.2 percent of the private labor force was organized in 2003. "Our side is weak because progressive political forces spend more time being divided than coming up with a plan," says Les Leopold, executive director of the Public Health Institute. "Our theory is that unless labor becomes green, it will die."

The labor movement was once the heart of the liberal movement in the United States. Trade unionists were the ones, after all, who successfully fought for a five-day workweek, unemployment insurance, the minimum wage, child labor laws, health and safety regulations, and workers' compensation. Beginning in the late nineteenth century, labor pioneered sit-down strikes, boycotts, and work stoppages, which influenced all subsequent progressive movements in the United States. Suffragists, civil rights leaders, feminists, consumer advocates, and environmentalists have all used tools perfected by labor whether they realized it or not.

Once upon a time, labor was a force to be reckoned with by corporations, the federal government, and corrupt union leaders themselves. The head of the United Mine Workers of America, John L. Lewis, not only negotiated directly with President Franklin Roosevelt, but also defied him and President Harry S. Truman with three coal strikes during World War II. When Roosevelt seized the mines, workers struck again against their federal operators. In 1969, when corrupt union leaders collaborated with mine operators to block new worker safety laws and provisions for black-lung compensation, forty thousand coal miners organized a wildcat strike in defiance of the United Mine Workers leadership.

Despite the radical decrease in union membership in the last twenty years, labor remains the largest progressive bloc in the country, representing about a fifth of the voters in the 2000 election, according to a University of

Pennsylvania survey. As with any social movement, the strength of unions lies with its rank-and-file members—the ones willing to trudge out into the snow, to bring new and sometimes controversial information to union hall meetings, the ones willing to trust their leaders enough to set aside stereotypes and hang out with a bunch of Sierra Club members for a weekend.

This would not be the first time labor has advocated a shift away from fossil fuels and contributed thoughtful planning to achieve it. In the 1960s Tony Mazzocchi, a legendary organizer with the Oil, Chemical and Atomic Workers Union, began a campaign for a federal plan to ease the transition to clean energy—a plan he called "'a Superfund for workers,'" says Joe Anderson, director of the nonprofit Labor Institute West, an arm of the Public Health Institute. "He used to say 'we want these workers to be treated as well as we treat dirt.'"

Recently revived by steelworkers and others under the moniker "Just Transitions," Mazzocchi's plan is loosely modeled on the G.I. Bill of 1944, which provided returning World War II veterans with a living wage and college tuition. Just Transitions, funded by a tax on polluting corporations, would offer assistance to communities disrupted by mine or refinery shutdowns, train workers to work in the clean energy industry, and continue providing them health insurance and benefits while they find new jobs.

Mazzocchi, a coalition builder par excellence, provided the intellectual inspiration for today's blue-green movement. In the late '50s, he helped found the Committee for a Sane Nuclear Policy, and in the early '70s he co-chaired the first Earth Day and worked with Ralph Nader to pressure Congress to pass the Occupational Safety and Health Act. In 1996 he formed the Labor Party. By moving beyond the "bread and butter" issues—Do you have a job? How much money do you make? What are the benefits like?—Mazzocchi left a trail for today's union leaders to follow.

Steelworker David Foster, elected in 1997 as the director of USWA District 11, appears to have inherited Mazzocchi's role. His job involves working with members from Iowa to Alaska. He represents everyone from steel-mill workers and coal miners to bus drivers and nurses. A former bricklayer, Foster is the consummate working guy who moved up the ranks and gained respect from his fellow workers as an effective organizer.

But he has also become an increasingly familiar face on the environmental circuit. In 1999, Foster scaled a 180-foot-tall redwood to meet with forest activist and tree-sitter Julia Butterfly Hill. His efforts not only symbolized the lengths to which he would go to reach environmentalists, but also lent credibility to a movement easily dismissed by industrial workers. He is part of a new generation of unionists that sees the dichotomy between environmental stewardship and jobs as false. "Environmentalists are our prime allies in how to regain control over the economy," he says firmly. "The wave of job loss in the last four years—2.5 million industrial jobs—has nothing to do with environmental regulations and everything to do with a global economy that is bent on maximizing profits. Labor is fighting the erosion of workers' rights, and the environmental movement is fighting the erosion of environmental protection." Given the growing extremism in the corporate world, Foster says, the opportunities to work together "are limitless."

Foster's point is easily illustrated by the birth of the Salt Lake City conference, which grew out of a nearby conflict that epitomized corporate excesses.

Union jobs are scarce in Utah, but USWA Local 392 represents more than one thousand miners, refinery and smelter workers, maintenance workers, and truck drivers at Kennecott Utah Copper. Each day at Kennecott, workers pull a quarter-million tons of rock out of an open-pit copper mine west of Salt Lake City that was once a mountain. Drivers on Interstate 80, which skirts the eastern shore of the Great Salt Lake, can see the smelter's twelve-hundred-foot smokestack. If you're an environmentalist here, you've probably fumed about the crater that's now almost three miles wide and three-quarters of a mile deep, or about the smokestack emissions. And if you're a mine worker, chances are you've assumed environmentalists were out to kill your job.

But those stereotypes hid a common cause that became apparent in the spring of 2003. Rio Tinto, the Melbourne-based corporation that owns Kennecott and has mining operations on six continents, was trying to quietly settle a groundwater pollution case with state and local officials. When the company and the state tried to fast-track Rio Tinto's plan to dump its mine sludge into the Great Salt Lake, local Sierra Club member Ivan Weber hit the roof and looked for allies. He found them in steelworkers, who packed the next public hearing on the dumping permit, making up more than half the crowd. Faced with increased public pressure, the company withdrew its proposal and has since had to revise its groundwater cleanup plans.

Steelworkers, it turned out, had been primed to help environmentalists by Rio Tinto itself. In June of 2003, after twenty months of talks, Rio Tinto and the Kennecott Coordinated Bargaining Committee agreed upon a union contract. Two days later, Rio Tinto laid off 120 workers. Although many of those workers have since retired or returned to work, the case is still under arbitration and union members are still seething over the company's actions.

"That torqued my jaw," says Terry Bonds, USWA District 12 director and head of the bargaining committee. A former roughneck in the Gulf Coast oil fields, and not one to back down from a good fight, Bonds speaks with a Texas drawl that can convey bitter rage and sweet humor in the span of a sentence. "We were in a labor dispute; we were going to take them on in whatever avenue we could find," he says. "We learned that when green-collar workers and blue-collar workers get together, we're stronger." The honey comes back into his voice as he adds that groundwater problems ultimately affect the lives of an entire community. "We're tree huggers, too," he says, smiling. "We just don't fall in love with the tree."

At the time of the groundwater victory, the steelworkers union had been holding weekend trainings on global warming throughout the country. Six months later, the union hired the Public Health Institute to bring Kennecott's mine workers and environmentalists together in Salt Lake City.

"I think the Kennecott story is one that will be replicated around the country," says Tanya Tolchin with the Sierra Club's Partnerships Program. "Now more than ever, people are looking to form new alliances and find more common ground."

Other blue-green alliances have been coalescing in fits and starts for more than a decade. About ten years ago, Andy Stern and Jane Perkins created the Blue-Green Working Group around their kitchen table. Stern, president of the Service Employees International Union (SEIU), and Perkins, former head of Friends of the Earth, invited friends from both movements to start talking about green solutions, particularly for global warming, that keep workers in mind.

"It represents a maturity or an epiphany for the environmental community," says Kevin Knobloch, president of the Union of Concerned Scientists and a member of the working group, "that we've come to recognize how important it is to support policies that preserve and create jobs."

The working group originally included members of SEIU, the steelworkers, and the latest incarnation of Mazzocchi's oil and atomic workers union; it also included representatives of the former Union of Needletrades, Textiles and Industrial Employees, which in 2004 merged with the Hotel Employees and Restaurant Employees International Union to become UNITE HERE!

Members of the United Auto Workers, United Mine Workers of America, and the International Brotherhood of Boilermakers attended early meetings, says Dan Becker, director of the Sierra Club's global warming program and the "green" co-chair of the Blue-Green Working Group. "Sometimes [the alliances] worked; other times they were blown up by people who didn't want blue-green actions."

Eventually, a nucleus formed and the group met regularly. In one of the group's first public announcements in 2002, members of the Sierra Club and the Natural Resources Defense Council stood with their union counterparts at a press conference that challenged President Bush's climate change plan, which the coalition said would increase carbon emissions over the next ten years. After that salvo, however, the group's recommendations gathered dust and the members drifted apart.

But in early fall of 2004, the Oakland-based nonprofit Redefining Progress approached the Blue-Green Working Group with a report outlining how the United States would benefit economically from a clean energy policy. Redefining Progress, which provides economic analyses to promote sustainable development, recommended an industrial policy that would cut U.S. carbon emissions in half in twenty years and create 1.4 million jobs. The plan included a fifty-state breakdown on the job growth. In October 2004, the Working Group, of which Mazzocchi's spiritual heir, David Foster, is the "blue" co-chair, held press conferences in ten states, touting the plan. The group also took out advertisements in eight regional newspapers, taunting President Bush for his refusal to recognize that jobs and the clean energy industry go hand in hand.

The Redefining Progress report, based on the U.S. Department of Energy's own data, said that some of the new jobs would come directly from building new renewable energy sources and energy efficiencies. Other jobs would result indirectly, the report says, since the average household would save $1,275 per year—that's $76 billion nationwide—on energy costs. That money could then stimulate jobs unrelated to energy production.

Daniel Kammen, founding director of the Renewable and Appropriate Energy Laboratory, recently analyzed thirteen independent studies concerning clean energy and employment in Europe and the United States. A physicist, engineer, and economist at the University of California at Berkeley, Kammen found that every technology in the renewables industry generates more jobs per average megawatt of power than does the coal and natural gas industry. How many jobs, exactly, depends on the assumptions made about the particular mix of solar, wind, and biomass. Wind, for example, creates far more jobs than fossil fuels initially do (from milling steel for the wind turbines, then installing them) and employs modestly more people than fossil fuels after the initial surge. But that advantage eventually decreases because wind farms are rather reliable. Both photovoltaic and biomass systems employ dramatically fewer workers at first, but gain strong advantages over fuel processing for coal and gas plants in the long term, mostly in operations and maintenance jobs.

In any case, mainly because of increasing automation, the once job-rich fossil fuel-related industries now have a relatively poor record of creating employment. According to the U.S. Bureau of Labor Statistics, fuel production over the last ten years has increased at the same time that jobs in mining and in the oil and gas industry have declined.

"Conventional energy isn't labor intensive; it's capital intensive," explains Howard Geller, an energy expert who heads the Boulder, Colorado-based Southwest Energy Efficiency Project. Geller cites coal as an example. Across the nation, he points out, the coal industry accounts for about sixty thousand jobs—half the workforce of twenty years ago, despite a 37 percent increase in coal production over the same period. Through 2012, coal-mining jobs are expected to decline by another 15 percent, even factoring in increased production.

Part of the reason, says Geller, is that domestic coal production is shifting from the Appalachian region to places like Wyoming, where the norm is mechanized strip mining that employs enormous haul trucks, not vast labor forces. According to the Wyoming Mining Association, the state produced 264 million tons of coal in 1995 and employed about 4,400 people; in 2003, the state produced a record 376 million tons with only 4,700 employees. That's a 42 percent increase in production and only a 9.5 percent increase in jobs.

Leaders in Europe have already caught on to the benefits, including increased employment, of shifting to renewable energy. Many countries in the European Union have established subsidies to guarantee renewable-electricity providers a profitable price per kilowatt-hour of electricity, which stimulates investment and will eventually lower the cost of such electricity. The European Union has also directed that 12.5 percent of its energy must come from renewable sources by 2010; has set a greenhouse gas reduction goal of 15 percent by the same deadline; and has signed on to the Kyoto Protocol. To meet those latter two commitments, the portion of the European energy pie served up by renewables could exceed 12.5 percent.

"Ten years ago Germany had no wind [energy]," says Kammen, "Now they have three times the wind [energy] the United States has. And in some parts of the country, they get a quarter of their energy from wind. It doesn't have to be that hard a thing to do." In Denmark, which makes half the world's turbines, the wind industry employs twenty thousand people.

According to the European Wind Energy Association, European companies currently control 85 percent of the world market for wind turbine manufacturing. U.S. companies account for only 9 percent. It may be no coincidence that, in 1999 alone, the last year for which figures are available, the federal government gave the oil, natural gas, coal, and nuclear industries $2.8 billion in subsidies, according to the U.S. Department of Energy. By comparison, the subsidies for solar and wind energy totaled only $134 million.

Since the early '80s, economists have known that the money going to fossil fuels and nuclear power plants would create more jobs if it were channeled into renewable energy, says Richard Grossman, who worked on blue-green alliances over energy and jobs almost thirty years ago and who now works with the nonprofit Program on Corporations, Law and Democracy. "We're no closer than we were twenty-five years ago. It's about money and the law and the will and who's making the decisions."

To catch up with Europe, the federal government would need to boost its research and development budget for energy. Since 1980, Kammen says, federal research and development budgets for energy have dipped from about $7 billion in 1980 to less than $3 billion in 1995. Congress also would need to set a generous goal of generating 20 percent of U.S. energy consumption from renewable sources, which Kammen says could yield three times the number of jobs produced by fossil fuels. Although eighteen states currently have individual goals ranging from 10 percent to 20 percent renewable, there is no talk of implementing a national standard.

For Triplett, the millwright and refinery unit chair at Kennecott Utah Copper, these are serious times. Aside from Bush's assault on labor and the general decline of unions, Triplett is faced with a likely outsourcing of his own job to a nonunion company in the United States. A grandfather at age forty-five, he knows he's too old to start a new career, too young to retire. But he finds hope in new alliances forged with environmentalists, and in the Just Transitions plan that he and other workers might someday follow.

Now that the environment means something tangible to him, he's also bent on figuring out his role in its protection. "It is incumbent upon us as union workers and miners to live up to these [environmental] laws," he says now. "We have a personal responsibility to make sure companies are living up to what they're supposed to do." To Triplett, this is not just about protecting local hunting grounds or fishing holes. At the union hall in dusty downtown Magna, between Salt Lake City and the Great Salt Lake, he shows a video about global warming and passes out booklets titled "Global

Warming and Working People." He admits that the blue-green movement is only beginning to get traction, but says he wants to let steelworkers know "the Sierra Club is not this evil thing out to take your job."

Triplett came to the Public Health Institute training with his buddy Scott Mullins, his counterpart in Kennecott's smelter unit. Mullins, a stocky guy with blond hair and a formidable jaw that visibly tenses when he mentions Rio Tinto, has not embraced his newfound green cause as fervently as Triplett. Mullins has little immediate reason to fear for his job. As a materials handler who works in the blast-furnace environs of the copper smelter, he does skilled work in a dangerous job that won't likely be contracted out to nonunion private companies.

"Is my every waking minute consumed with the environment?" he asks. "No. I would not consider myself an environmentalist. But now I ask myself, 'What would I do on a certain issue to help fight that fight?' This is going to sound corny, but we only have one Earth, and we're responsible for what we do with it. We've got to do everything we can for our children, grandchildren, and the generations after that."

(2005)

Got Tape?

Keeping a grassroots group together when everyone feels out of place

I'M STANDING IN MY DRIVEWAY ON A SPIT-FREEZING COLD MORNING, waving my mittened hand to a friend who has declined to join me. "No one in this neighborhood's going to listen to you," she yells through the fog.

I shrug. "I'll be back by dark." And I step into the frothy jaws of the suburban winter. Within a few strides I'm standing by a mailbox I see every day but have tried to ignore. It's candy-apple purple with red flames swooshing back toward the house—the kind of design you see on hot rods. Parked on the lawn beside a stack of worn tires is a Chevy truck draped with bumper stickers: I AM THE NRA, RUSH IS RIGHT, and so on. My friend's voice rings in my ears. Just then, I see some movement to my left.

"You think he looks good here?" a woman asks.

The man to whom she is speaking ponders the life-sized Rudolph at the head of Santa's sleigh. He sets his baby Jesus down on top of Santa's gift bag to help secure Rudolph's ties.

"Excuse me," I call out toward Santa. "Do you know about the plans to build a SuperTarget and HyperMart?"

They look at me through the haze.

"On the land behind our houses . . . the old apple orchards and ponds?"

"Asshole!" the guy says.

About now I'm thinking of hot cocoa, fireplaces, and moving to another city.

The man walks toward me. "I met that asshole. He's tryin' a sell us a bag a bullshit."

"I . . . I have some letters, a petition against it."

He drops Rudolph cold. I hold out my pen, jittery with thanks. "If you could both sign, and maybe jot a note in your own words, make it more individual."

I hear the pen scratching, then he shoves the clipboard in my direction. "This is OUR town," he's written, underlining it about ten times.

His note hits the nail on the head. In order to Target our neighborhood, this developer must override the Comprehensive Land Use Plan—the single document created by city officials and residents in concert. It states that this land should never be used for retail. I'm out here going door to door because I believe the collective voice of the citizens should not be silenced by a nonresident whose annual income trumps ours by a few million.

"What're you gonna do with them papers?" the man asks.

"Deliver them to city council. Maybe organize a group."

"You name the place and time, we'll be there." He shakes my hand. I wave goodbye through the maze of lights and plastic figurines and run back home.

"It's great. You should come along," I beg my friend.

"They signed?"

"And volunteered!"

My excitement gets to her and she joins me.

Next house. A stout man wearing perma-seamed slacks, white shirt, necktie. If it weren't for his slippers, I'd think he was on his way to work. I smile. "Morning! You heard about the plans for the SuperTarget?"

"No."

"On the land where the ponds are." I position the clipboard so it will slide easily into his hand.

"I don't care," he says. And he shuts the door.

My friend goes home to her hot cocoa. When I return that evening, though, she flips through the letters, surprised. "You got all these signed?"

I nod. "And this is the list of volunteers."

Up to this time, my only attempt at civic duty had been to attend a few "COG" (Community Organized Government) meetings. At my first COG, five people attended, three of them city employees. My fellow attendee was mainly concerned about how he could keep kids from setting his fence posts on fire.

At the next COG it was just the city volunteer coordinator and me. She had a projector and we watched a movie about the problem of Canada geese in the area. I learned some nifty tips about how to keep them from defecating willy-nilly on my lawn.

Recalling these vibrant evenings, I feared my list of volunteers might be so many empty promises. Against my better judgment, I rented a conference room, capacity 300, in a hotel. My workouts that week consisted of running from door to door, delivering fliers that announced the gathering.

I arrived that night just before it was time to start. It was not a bad showing: about twenty-five people, sitting at great distances from one another. I introduced myself and began. People trickled in as I spoke. They trickled and trickled. Thirty minutes later there was standing room only.

I was nervous and excited. "We need a volunteer for community actions leader, someone who can set up eye-catching booths, stuff like that," I said.

A hand shot up. "Me and the missus could do that," said Silas, the fellow with the holiday lawn display.

The momentum continued. I ticked down the list of task forces needed—legal research, fundraising, media relations, city relations, planning liaison, etc.—and soon we had ten task-force leaders and a dozen or so people on each team. At the end of the meeting, we brainstormed and planned for our first organizational meeting.

For several days afterward, I tried to figure out why so many people had shown up that evening. There was no precedent for it. Our neck of the woods is known locally as "outletville." The indoor mall brims with ninety-nine-cent stores, wholesale clubs, and those new "security" stores that sell mace, brass knuckles, and a variety of small knives. People here are generally working toward moving out of the area, not coming together.

It's true I'm out of place here—probably the only person who voted Nader/LaDuke—but everyone else is out of place, too. There's scarcely a common thread between us, except this: we're buffered from endless strip malls and a twenty-four-plex theater by the 108-acre tract of land that is now at risk. Deer, herons, bald eagles, ibis, and fox live here. The property hooks up circuitously with miles of open country, a narrow paradise gasping beneath the wide Colorado sky, snaking all the way up to the Rocky Mountains. Aside from its beauty, this land offers the only occasion I've ever had to talk to my neighbors. People walk their dogs there. They fish in the ponds. Silas stables his horse at the old pony farm that will be condemned if this project is allowed to go through.

In any other situation, the leaders who came that night—a gay couple, a former Black Panther who is now a conservative Republican, two college kids, a Hmong couple, a right-wing Libertarian, a born-again Christian, and a handful of liberal-leaning Democrats—would never have gathered under one roof. If diversity's what it's all about, then our neighborhood is all that and a bag of chips. But without a shared sense of purpose, diversity spells conflict and isolation, not opportunity. I figure that tract of land is what brought us together. None of us is about to give that up.

The group agrees to meet after the holidays. In the interim we're all supposed to do a little research. My job is to sign us up for a city council meeting. That's easy. One phone call, it's done. I e-mail the group and ask them to prepare. My e-mail, however, crosses with an incoming note from the city clerk. "I'm sorry. We have to delete you from the agenda." Furthermore, she says, "No one from your group will be allowed, under any circumstances, to address your elected officials concerning this matter."

What?

This lights a fire under our melting pot. "It's unconstitutional," says Silas.

"Gag order," says John, the former Black Panther. But after several meetings with the city attorney, we feel powerless. The city is within the law. In Colorado, if there's a public land dispute between two "groups" (in this case, the developer's corporation and our grassroots group), the case becomes a trial and the city councilors become judges. If a judge hears "testimony" a priori, that testimony (i.e., the voice of our group) will be thrown out. Furthermore, if we wish to hold public meetings, we must, by law, invite the developer. Otherwise we'll have an "ex parte" meeting, which—you guessed it—turns us mute at the public hearing.

I take this as my first occasion to contact the press. "Sure, that's the law, but most city councils don't opt to employ it," says the reporter. Off the bat, our city is playing hardball.

Our first official meeting as an organization takes place at my house, and we learn some other sobering facts. "The average amount of retail in most cities is twenty-five square feet per person," says Donna. "You know what it is here? Fifty-three square feet per person. Lucky us. We have an extra two-car garage's worth of shopping opportunities for every man, woman, and child."

Silas's findings add more. He flips through paperwork, then reads aloud, "Better'n seventeen percent a' them stores stand empty. Look at this chart. We been on a steady decline in retail success since 1998."

"How can the city think we need more new stores?" asks Celia.

Sadly, we all know the answer. Cities east of the Mississippi have a much better chance at fending off excess commercial development than we do because, in general, eastern cities gain their greatest revenue from property taxes. In the West, it's retail taxes that hum the number. City officials are bound to respond more favorably to commercial developers who actually bring in revenue than to citizens who drop very little cash into city coffers.

We also learn that keeping a grassroots group together takes a lot of work. It's pretty easy to sign a piece of paper saying we all oppose the development. But it's another matter for people who have never had reason to talk to one another to sit together in one room and focus on a common goal. A typical meeting goes like this: Cherry has recently resigned from her job because her colleagues were "too abrupt" with her. One of them, she says, actually said to her, "Shut up!"

"I mean, I don't have to take that, do I?"

Everyone shakes their heads, no.

"I'm divorced. I have two kids."

"You did the right thing."

I place my hand on Cherry's hand and smile. "Okay. Do you think we should tape the fliers to the doors, or just tuck them?"

"Because, that woman, my co-worker, she had it out for me. I'm good at what I do. I'm a good worker. Aren't I?"

"Yes."

She pauses. I begin to speak.

"And I'm bringing up two boys. I'm divorced. Bringing them up alone."

Oh, no, I missed again. The others are tremendously patient. "Yes," the whole group says, in harmony.

"Because, you know, he doesn't give them tough love and I do, and they don't like it much, but it's better, don't you think it's better?"

"Oh, yes. Tough love," someone replies.

Cherry pauses again. I know I have to speak, speak now, say something, anything, except "Shut up!" which is oh-so-perched on my taste buds, but I swallow it and say, "Do you think we should use tape?"

Cherry looks lost. She takes a deep breath as if to talk again, and John jumps right in. "Tape, yes, good. Tape!"

One issue down. How many to go?

The meetings go on like this, month after month. While discovering our strengths, we learn everyone's foibles. We find that Celia is detail-oriented and—good for her—she can take notes and do research. But occasionally, she asks things like, "Where will we put the letters?"

"What's that?"

"The letters to city council. Should they go right or left of the fliers on the table?"

I'm quick to respond. "Either."

"Or maybe behind?"

"No," Donna says. "Not behind. They'll be harder to reach."

"They'll have to reach over the fliers?" I ask.

"Yes," says Donna.

Celia relaxes visibly.

Rita, on the other hand, comes to meeting after meeting and barely breathes a sentence. She's our accountant, does a great job, and keeps her conversations to the financial report. But soon, she finds her forum. Within a few weeks, we're all getting weekly e-mail updates on her health, her husband's health, the health of the dog, who is incontinent, but has medication to control the problem. Her notes trigger an electronic deluge of notes about divorce and tough love and dinner recipes.

I try to keep the group on track, but I feel awkward—even intimidated. I don't fit. I don't have a day job or a motorized vehicle, and I am by nature introverted. Each week I give a little pep talk: "We just have to hang in there, folks. We'll win this thing. We will." As I speak, I'm wondering what I've done with the letters I collected last week—did I deliver them, or are they waterlogged in the pocket of my raincoat—and the petitions? I can't recall, and, oh my, is there anyone out there who's good at keeping things organized?

From my lips to God's ears.

"Look, I don't mind being the big fat bitch of the group . . ." This was Marie's self-introduction at our third meeting. "If it gets the job done, so be it." Marie owns a successful ad agency and, ironically, was instrumental in developing one of the most controversial commercial sites along Colorado's Front Range. "Sound hypocritical?" she asked. "Well, that project was consistent with the Land Use Plan. I'm not against development. I'm against silencing citizens' voices."

A few weeks later, Norma joined. Norma had, of all things, a flip chart and the facilitation skills to use it. After a few weeks with Norma and chart, tough love and recipes were distant echoes.

The following meeting, Hogan arrived with a box of sample T-shirts and news that a local company had cut us a deal for a custom design. At the same time we learned that Wild Oats and REI had agreed to let us set up booths in their stores. Indeed, we were becoming a real community force—even without breathing a word to city council.

After a few press interviews a reporter said, off record, "You know, the developer hates you guys. I mean, he actually said *hate*." I smiled. Hate's a strong word, and it gave us strength. We celebrated every attack as a coup. The press we received incited others to contact us. Soon we had a venture capitalist and pro bono attorney working with us. Our constituency grew. Our recognition snowballed.

Still, it was no open-and-shut case. While the elected officials who would determine the "case" were not supposed to have ex parte conversations with the developer, there was no way to monitor that. When John's Motown band played at the local Rotary Club, for instance, he watched the developer and several city councilors twist and turn on the dance floor together. Meanwhile, we sat at our monthly meetings eating finger sandwiches and imagining how slick the developer's presentation would be at the hearing and how feeble ours might seem in comparison.

That's when the obvious became clear: if we were really going to make a difference, we had to quit fighting against something, and begin fighting for something. If you build it, they will come. And if it's a strip mall you build, well, they'll come to that. But if it's a place that incites pride and involvement in your community, they'll also come to that. We envisioned a nature and cultural center, maybe a historical orchard—something to encourage people to stay here, rather than using it as a stepping-stone to elsewhere.

Donna had organized a good bit of fundraising—local garage sales that contributed profits; a bird walk on the land for a small donation; some straightforward requests for contributions. Marie and I had created a paid-subscription newsletter. Through these efforts, we'd garnered some revenue. "So, let's hire an architect," I said.

Shortly after the newspaper reported our plans, we received a phone call from the landowner's attorney. He said the landowner had been following our work in the news and was interested in meeting with us.

The call threw us into fear. We'd been told by opponents that we were stepping on landowner's rights, that if his profits were diminished by our efforts, he could sue us. Our attorney assured us this was not possible and offered to accompany us to the meeting. "Too aggressive," Norma said. "We'll bring you in later if there's a need."

The day of the meeting arrives. Marie drives. We pull onto the dirt road and travel through walnut groves and cottonwoods, past grazing horses and stables. A man with gray hair down to his waist greets us at the fence, introduces himself as Oliver. He's smoking a filterless Camel. "Reason I brought you here today," he says, and just then a small plane flies overhead, propeller slapping the air. Oliver looks up. "Christ, I had my fill a' helicopters in 'Nam, right. Can't stand that sound, right."

He ducks into the house, and we follow. The place is empty. No furniture, curtains, lamps, rugs—nothing. Greasy pizza boxes are scattered like lily pads that we must step over on the way to Oliver's room: a cubicle with a sleeping bag and computer. Along the top of the monitor are a dozen or so stickers of endangered wildlife. Peregrine, otter, whale. Along the bottom are stickers of atomic bombs in various stages of detonation.

"So, anyway," Oliver continues, but then stops abruptly. Across the street from the property sits a miniature golf course. In it, there's a volcano that spews real fire when someone scores. As we speak, a kid lands a hole-in-one, the volcano roars, and Oliver takes cover. He doesn't dive to the ground or anything, but a stormy look brims in his eyes and he hunches over. "To put that thing there—it's an insult to the men who fought for this country. Sounds like mortar fire, right. Nights I wake up sweating, right."

Oliver hops from one subject to the next without shifting gears or turning on the blinker, from Vietnam to childhood in a puff of smoke. "Yeah, me and my best buddy Henry, we built that thing way back when."

"The volcano?"

I follow his line of sight, and my eyes light on a tree house nestled in a tangle of branches.

"Still there," he says.

He stares for a while, then exhales. "You know, homeless people could set up camp on this land, right." No blinker, new topic. "Got nothin' against 'em. Got homeless buddies, right. But if they come here and start cookin' Top Ramen on Coleman stoves, well, it's a fire hazard." He drops his cigarette onto the plywood floor and crushes it out with his boot. "Yeh, I'm the past of this land. You guys're the future." The volcano blows again. Oliver's eyes glaze.

On the drive home, I'm convinced that Oliver was siding with us.

"Oh, right," says Marie. "He's going to nix the retail deal and donate his land." I consider it. He's got the long hair, the Woodstock gaze. Marie and Norma laugh and laugh. They help me see that Oliver is just one more quirky character in our cast of players. I have a bit of a Woodstock gaze myself, I guess.

For the next few weeks, our group is a mess. We're nervous about whatever it was Oliver wanted from us, and there's a new topic on the table. The city has plans to house a sex offenders' rehab center nearby. Folks are up in arms.

"We need to move on. Let them build the damn Target."

"You want to quit now?"

"This sex offenders thing's more important."

"Look, nobody wants a sex offenders' rehab in their backyard, but they have to be built somewhere," says Billy, one half of the gay couple.

"Well, to those of us who have families . . ." says John.

"You suggesting I don't have a family?"

"Oh, don't hit me with your liberal bullshit. You guys are immoral."

"Immoral? You're the closed-minded bigot, but we're immoral?"

I would love to say that just then, the phone rang and the director of open space acquisitions said, "Hey, Oliver's donating a portion of land and we're hoping to buy the rest, with your help." But that would be implausible.

Except, it's what happened. Okay, she didn't call during that meeting, but the rest is true. Just when we'd sunk to name-calling, the city was ready to work with us on our terms.

A week later we trudge over to Celia's. There are apologies, but most people agree it's time to quit. We've won the biggest battle.

Then Rita, who rarely speaks, says, "I can't believe we've come this far just to turn our power over to the city." She says it softly, and for a moment, it stuns us all silent.

"Well," says Marie, eventually, "I'll put out another newsletter."

"I'll contact the architect," says Celia.

An energy slowly fills the room. I can't help but smile.

Before I stepped out of my house that cold morning three years ago, I might have told you "community" was some kind of Up With People fantasy—like-minded folks sharing a Norman Rockwell moment. Now I think community has little to do with like minds. It has to do with very differently minded people finding a way to get along because we all live in, are connected to, and share a sense of place.

When I hear the coyotes howl at night, all the people in this room hear the same thing. Maybe one of us is making dinner, the other one just rising to go to the graveyard shift. At the same time in our different lives, we stop; we listen. We feel the migrations of birds that pass through here, see the coming of summer on the wings of swallows, and ready ourselves for winter when the herons depart and the bald eagles return. In these moments, a sense of community crashes through our suburban walls.

If I tried to say what made our mongrel group a success, I couldn't pinpoint any one thing. It was as if we were working together to create one sculpture so big that, as we were working, we couldn't see it for what it was. One person chiseled here, another chiseled there until, one day, we stepped back and saw something beginning to take form: our own community. There was no unveiling, no ceremony. But each tap of the sculptor's mallet—the support of a business, the help of an attorney, some economic research—helped shape our little corner of the world into something we intended.

Working together like this, we won our fight against unnecessary development. Now we have to work toward forming the community center we want in its place. In the process, we'll learn even more about one another, and maybe dislike each other more, which means our fondness will also grow.

It's November, and as we leave our meeting, Silas starts soliciting help to set up his next Christmas display.

"That's some hideous shit, man," says John.

"You were the one who reported us for light pollution?"

"That's right."

"I always liked those wiseacres who showed up with myrrh at a baby shower," says Marie.

"Well that's just disrespectful," says Silas.

"So what time you want us to be there?" asks John.

Silas ponders. "About ten o'clock?"

Yeah, we'll be there.

(2003)

A License to Be Human

Being an activist is as much about the self as it is about problems in the larger world

THE STARTING POINT MIGHT SOUND FAMILIAR: A FAVORITE HILLSIDE bulldozed, an ancient grove of redwood trees felled, a loved one killed on the streets, a loved one dying of lung cancer, a country's resources squandered, its principles trampled. Anger and outrage are the typical response, compelling you to attend meetings, write letters, paste flyers, organize people, blockade entrances, perhaps even go to jail. It seems as if you have no choice. The war is on. But what if the war is not just on the outside, but also churns within you? What if you share more with the wrongdoers, and the larger society that sanctions the wrongdoing, than it's convenient to acknowledge?

In the last decade, a new generation of moral leaders has begun to envision a more reflective approach to saving the world. Loosely termed the "reverence" movement, this current of activism has had a wide range of devotees—from redwoods activist Julia Butterfly Hill to former gang member Aqueela Sherrills, who organized youth in South Central Los Angeles to secure a historic truce between the Bloods and the Crips. There is no joint Web site, no blueprint of tactics, no manifesto of what to do or how. But those at the heart of the movement agree on one thing: being an activist can't just be about being right or showing others how they're wrong.

Van Jones, the executive director of the Ella Baker Center for Human Rights, a nonprofit organization dedicated to reforming the nation's criminal justice system, says: "A reverence perspective is, at the end of the day, taking corrective steps to further enhance the beauty of others and the beauty of yourself." This simple reformulation demands of its practitioners as much personal honesty as any spiritual pursuit. But it can produce surprisingly effective results within individuals, their organizations, and in the larger world. *Orion* Features Editor Laird Townsend talked with Mr. Jones at his office in Oakland, California.

Laird Townsend: Where does the idea of a reverence perspective come from?

Van Jones: It's really Aqueela Sherrills's idea. Aqueela and his brother led the effort to establish a successful peace treaty between warring gangs in Los Angeles in 1992. And going through that really deepened him spiritually. Then his son was killed—shot to death by a young man in the neighborhood. Aqueela had to walk the path of forgiveness in the wake of that, and arrived at the idea that we need a reverence movement, so that people have more respect for life.

LT: To transcend the fighting?

VJ: To hold a reverential perspective even in the midst of confrontation. Sometimes it's good to be passive and polite; sometimes it's good to interrupt business as usual with protests, et cetera. I think it's a huge mistake in a society as unequal and unjust as ours to primarily put the onus on oppressed people to be saints. I think that's wildly unfair. But there's been an addiction to the politics of confrontation among a certain tier of activists. Speaking truth to power, confronting injustices is a good thing, but when people start to use confrontational tactics in their own coalitions, their own organizations, then you have a movement that is too injured internally to play a healing role externally.

I think we've all been in situations where people have been shorter with each other, sharper with each other, meaner to each other than we should have been. The results have been less unity, weaker organizations, more brittle ties, collapsed coalitions. If you ask people what their actual experience of being on the left is, lots of people say, "Oh, we're saving the world, blah, blah, blah." I say: "No, no, no, what's your experience—like, Thursday?" They say: "Oh, it was horrible."

It's like the difference between using diesel versus solar as your energy source. Anger is a messy fuel that eventually causes more problems than it can solve.

LT: So the reverence perspective also implies introspection?

VJ: Usually whatever the external thing is that we're fighting, there is an internal manifestation of it. For instance, I'm challenging the incarceration industry. But there are ways in my own life that I'm punitive and unforgiving. So I want society to be rehabilitative and give people second chances, but I'm not that way myself. I think that people who want to change society have a double duty. We have to be willing to confront the warmonger within and without, the punitive incarcerator within and without, the polluter within and without, the greedy capitalist developer within and without. We have to really look at how we are—combative, punitive, self-destructive, greedy; we're passionate about changing that in the external world, even as we enact it in our internal world and in our relationships with each other.

If you can figure out how it is that you're like your target, it doesn't necessarily give you any answers, but it's the right question to ask. "How am I like my target?" opens up a different world of possibilities in terms of how I am going to relate to my target.

LT: And we activists need to relate to our targets differently?

VJ: We have this whole David and Goliath syndrome. If you're an activist, that has a positive side: you want to confront unjust authority, fight against long odds, hold out the possibility of miraculous outcomes. And that's a good thing.

But there's a shadow side to David and Goliath, which is that there's got to be some big mean *other*. You've got to be the small underdog all the time and there's got to be some confrontation between absolute good (you) and absolute evil (the other). If you're an activist then you know what I'm talking about; you know what it's like when you try to lead a meeting and somebody's got to challenge you on every point. You know what it's like when you get everyone riled up to attack the mayor, and the mayor doesn't show up, and everybody attacks you. It's part of the toxic stuff that we're playing with.

Also, you have to have enough respect to realize that Goliath has probably figured out the slingshot thing by now. So to continue to do the same thing over and over again, which is what we've been doing since the '60s, keeps us from being creative. And it's probably going to yield worse results over time.

LT: Keeping it in the realm of metaphor, how do you approach Goliath differently?

VJ: There's a way of being in conflict like a barbarian, and a way of being in conflict like a ninja. I think that we need a lot more ninja energy and a lot less barbarian energy. When it's time to fight, you want to be as surgical and precise with your intervention as you possibly can be. You want to use just as much conflict as required, just as much force as required and no more. There's a call for a wiser kind of warrior. Less wild, belligerent. More grounded, more dignified.

The other thing is, it could be that you're just in the wrong book of the Bible altogether. It could be that it's not really about David and Goliath; it's really about Noah. The kinds of really serious challenges that are coming up will feel more like what happened down in New Orleans. It's easy to say there's an evil Goliath called George Bush who's letting bad things happen to good people. But even if George Bush were to leave the planet, we've still got major, major climate destabilization to deal with. And so it could be that we need to figure out new ways to win—to be open to the possibility that sometimes we can win Goliath over to helping us build the ark.

We have so many mixed metaphors, it's humorous, but I'll throw a few more at you. Among social justice activists we have this view that spaceship Earth is really slave ship Earth, and there's this incredible need to free people from exploitation. The slave revolt movie that most people have heard about is *Amistad*: righteous enslaved Africans stick up for themselves and take over the slave ship. It's really a metaphor for the last century's version of revolution; the people at the bottom rise up and take over slave ship Earth. But I say that if for whatever reason you look out and you notice the name of the ship is not *Amistad,* it's the *Titanic,* you suddenly have a very different set of leadership challenges. Now you've got to not only liberate the captives, you also have to save the ship. If you try to deal with that from a position of outrage and confrontation, you'll last about twenty-three seconds. A reverence perspective, where you're really, really committed to saving all the life on board as sustainably as you can and as effectively as you can, is really the only approach that will work.

LT: But you're talking about saving a society that doesn't necessarily want to be saved. . . .

VJ: Suicide is another way to look at it. Suicidal economy, suicidal foreign policy. It looks homicidal, and it is. But it's also deeply suicidal.

LT: What makes the economy appear homicidal and how is it suicidal?

VJ: It's obscured from U.S. eyes sometimes: "Look at all these nice cheap sneakers." We force people to work in production lines in horrible, brutal conditions, killing them when they resist—and wipe out whole ecosystems to make way for cash crops or mines. If you look at the way the economy works, it takes living things and turns them into dead things and calls them products. The faster it does that, the more economic growth you have. So if you zoom in on it, it's homicidal—it's destroying ecosystems and lives. You can't keep doing this indefinitely. At some point either you or your grandkids are going to have to deal with the consequences, and they're just starting to come due—from running the country on a credit card to the melting of polar ice caps.

LT: So where should environmentalists focus their energies?

VJ: There's already a big countercurrent. It looks like a bunch of static at first. But if you look deeply enough you see that there's a coherency—people taking different approaches, but for the same aspirations: so that we have healthy communities, and people's daily work can be adding to the health of their communities and ecosystems. As Dan Carol of the Apollo Alliance and others have said, we need a Green New Deal. You have problem-makers in the economy: the warmongers, polluters, clear-cutters, the incarcerators, despoilers—and we all participate in those economies of destruction. Then you have the problem-solvers, trying to create a politics of reconstruction: coaches, counselors, art instructors, solar engineers, organic farmers, permaculturists. The problem-solvers get pennies from the government compared to the dollars for the problem-makers. You want to move the government from the side of the problem-makers to the side of the problem-solvers.

LT: What would that look like?

VJ: You're working in a factory; the water comes out cleaner than it went in. You drive a car; only air and water come out, because the engine is designed not to pollute. You go into the store; it's owned locally and sells affordable products made locally by people who are paid well. Right now we go to a corporate franchise to buy products that are made by people who are poorly paid. The products are shipped all around the world at great expense—and 50 percent of that weight will be in the trashcan the minute you unwrap it. It's mostly packaging—not to mention the waste in petroleum or emissions to get it there. We have an extraordinarily wasteful society.

LT: Your work takes on what you call the incarceration industry, especially as it relates to juvenile detention. How is that related to conservation?

VJ: Putting a generation of kids in a prison is like clear-cutting a forest. We deeply believe we have a throwaway planet—throwaway species, resources, neighborhoods, nations, continents. Young people and adults in prison have been thrown away as well. Once they're outside the circle of people who deserve dignity and respect, then they can be preyed upon. The prisoners can be worked—in the South in the fields like enslaved people: Angola in Louisiana is a classic example. Or by big corporations here in California: Microsoft, for some of their packaging; Victoria's Secret and United Airlines, for telemarketing orders. It's complicated. Often prisoners feel better about having that opportunity than sitting in a cell or working for the state making license plates and furniture. But when you get out of prison, those companies are never going to hire you because you are a felon. The entire incarceration process is destructive of people and people's spirits.

It also destroys communities. When you take a young parent away from a family, leaving behind a two-year-old who takes years off the lives of grandparents, and then throw that person back into the community with no resources, you're not helping the family reintegrate the person. You're making the community worse. You're making it harder for families to re-cover from the mistakes anybody makes. Politically, it destroys those com-munities as well. In New York State they count you in the county you're incarcerated in. That allows a congressional district around a prison—usually white and rural—to claim a bigger population and access to more congressional clout, even though incarcerated people can't vote. Meanwhile, the community the prisoner came from will have less congressional clout. It's further disenfranchisement.

But it's all related. The polluters, the clear-cutters, the incarcerators, they're all enacting the same story: money is more important than life, and we have the technology or the guns to protect ourselves from any con-sequences of our heedlessness.

LT: And so this is where the reverence perspective comes in?

VJ: The reverence perspective promotes a restorative approach to the econ-omy and to politics. It's a rearticulation of our better wisdom, a rearticula-tion of things that have been a part of human consciousness for thousands and thousands of years—indeed, things that have allowed us to be around for those thousands and thousands of years. The ancient understanding of limits and consequences needs to find its way back into modern discourse. But a return to that wisdom requires the deepest possible changes—and those start at a personal level.

Activists have gotten trapped by "either/or," which says that since ulti-mately there are real limits to our freedom under the present system, we have to change the system first. "I'm going to change them, and then I'm going to change me," as opposed to saying, "Well, I've got to change both them and me, and probably the first step to changing them is changing me." You do need a structural analysis to understand the way capitalism works, but you can't do all your work from that perspective. The transformation that we seek in the world is very deep. In order for us to be in service to that, our transformation has to be very deep as well.

LT: The new generation of moral leaders, people who have become an effective force in their own right, people like yourself, Aqueela, Julia Butterfly, Latifa Simon of the Center for Young Women's Development, Jody Evans of Code Pink—what distinguishes your work, or your approach to the work?

VJ: I think we're all trying to be honest with ourselves, about ourselves, and our motives, however mixed. I think this newer crop of people is not trying to create an image of ourselves as flawless saints and, in fact, the opposite: we're deliberately trying to tell on ourselves as much as possible. We confess as much as we accuse. The confessional quality, the unmasking quality, gives other people license to be human. Other people can feel that it's okay that they have dirty laundry. That eliminates a lot of the posturing: people wanting to be more revolutionary than thou.

It's a real leadership challenge to inspire people to take collective action based on shared motivations and at the same time stay human doing it, to avoid becoming self-righteous, other-blaming banshees. One thing that I know from my own experience is that demonization and deification are the same process, two sides of the same coin, and if you set yourself up to be deified, then you can't be mad when the other half demonizes you. The idea that either you're this egomaniac who's only out there for yourself or you're this pure martyr with no personal ambitions or desires—both of those are false.

You have to be willing to state the truth, even mixed motives. Like myself: on the one hand I want to help everybody, and on the other hand I'm the child of a somewhat turbulent upbringing trying to prove myself to myself. So once you put that out there, the weird ego-driven parts have a lot less power. It doesn't go away, but it just doesn't have the same ability to sneak around under the table to determine outcomes. Put it at the table along with everything else and then you can feed your ego appropriately without it causing a lot of chaos.

LT: Can you tell me what personal experiences have led you to some of these insights?

VJ: Just screwing up my own life: womanizing, crashing organizations and coalitions over my ego, self-destructing with someone else's ego. All those disaster stories that you can tell from the perspective of "I was victimized."

But if you're looking at it through the lens of a video camera, it looks like your own conduct helped to create the outcome. I've been practicing progressive activism on the left for twenty years—I'll be thirty-seven this month. So that's most of my life. Most of my wisdom now doesn't come out of reaction to mean people at the bar or selfish people at the mall. Most of my life has been spent interacting with other people who are supposedly trying to change the world. And I've got just as many scars, and just as many enemies, and just as much conflict in my life as somebody who's worked in a corporation. And that can't be all everybody else's fault.

LT: I've heard you say, "Based on my confession I'm inviting you to a higher place than me." That encourages other people to transcend where you happen to be in that moment.

VJ: Yeah, that's one way to climb a mountain range. Get as far as you can go and then help someone else climb above where you are. This is a collective process. Those of us who are doing this work are standing on the shoulders of pretty impressive people. Ella Baker, an indispensable organizer in the movement associated with Dr. King, used to say: give light, and the people will find the way. But she also said strong people don't need strong leaders.

I think people have this image of somebody with a cape and a rod and a staff and all the answers. And my experience has been that whenever I've been in that mindset—more often than I'd like to admit—that's usually the beginning of some awful farce. And then when I'm not doing that at all, when I'm just trying to be present to myself and understand what's going on, all of a sudden people start wanting me to take on more responsibilities. And then I'll hear that I'm a good leader from somebody, and that wasn't what I was trying to do. I was just trying to help or be of service or be present or make an observation—just trying to assist.

LT: So that's the best way to be effective?

VJ: If I can do something myself and make a big difference, I'll do it. Often people will not make a change that they can make, even if it's small, waiting for some other person—if only the mayor would do this, or Bush would do that, or if only somebody in the red states would understand this then everything would be fine. Those kinds of conversations I don't find to be constructive. You know, for a while Nelson Mandela could only make a difference inside a cell. But look at the difference he made in the world by focusing there for more than two decades.

That's the difference between the real giants of the last century and a lot of what we see now. You lose one campaign and you want to give up and move to Canada. That's not the way. It has to be a protracted struggle. And part of that struggle is looking at the shadow side, the broken part of ourselves as activists in these movements. We have to stop seeing that as a distraction from the real work and start seeing it as part of the real work. If you don't have those kinds of conversations that really look for error in yourself and in your cause, then your cause over the long term begins to lose power and lose persuasiveness.

I'm not saying we should only look within. If all you're doing is navel-gazing then you're not carrying out the mission either. I'm saying we have to both confess and accuse, we have to be able to look within and without, fight for changes both in society and within ourselves.

(2006)

Refugees

MARK DOWIE

Conservation Refugees

When protecting nature means kicking people out

A LOW FOG ENVELOPS THE STEEP AND REMOTE VALLEYS OF SOUTH-western Uganda most mornings, as birds found only in this small corner of the continent rise in chorus and the great apes drink from clear streams. Days in the dense montane forest are quiet and steamy. Nights are an exaltation of insects and primate howling. For thousands of years the Batwa people thrived in this soundscape, in such close harmony with the forest that early-twentieth-century wildlife biologists who studied the flora and fauna of the region barely noticed their existence. They were, as one naturalist noted, "part of the fauna."

In the 1930s, Ugandan leaders were persuaded by international conservationists that this area was threatened by loggers, miners, and other extractive interests.

In response, three forest reserves were created—the Mgahinga, the Echuya, and the Bwindi—all of which overlapped with the Batwa's ancestral territory. For sixty years these reserves simply existed on paper, which kept them off-limits to extractors. And the Batwa stayed on, living as they had for generations, in reciprocity with the diverse biota that first drew conservationists to the region.

However, when the reserves were formally designated as national parks in 1991 and a bureaucracy was created and funded by the World Bank's Global Environment Facility to manage them, a rumor was in circulation that the Batwa were hunting and eating silverback gorillas, which by that time were widely recognized as a threatened species and also, increasingly, as a featured attraction for ecotourists from Europe and America. Gorillas were being disturbed and even poached, the Batwa admitted, but by Bahutu, Batutsi, Bantu, and other tribes who invaded the forest from outside villages. The Batwa, who felt a strong kinship with the great apes, adamantly denied killing them. Nonetheless, under pressure from traditional Western conservationists, who had come to believe that wilderness and human community were incompatible, the Batwa were forcibly expelled from their homeland.

These forests are so dense that the Batwa lost perspective when they first came out. Some even stepped in front of moving vehicles. Now they are living in shabby squatter camps on the perimeter of the parks, without running water or sanitation.

Tomas Mtwandi, who was born in the Mgahinga and evicted with his family when he was fourteen, is adapting slowly and reluctantly to modern life. He is employed as an indentured laborer for a local Bantu farmer and is raising a family in a one-room shack near the Bwindi park border. He is regarded as rich by his neighbors because his roof doesn't leak and he has a makeshift metal door on his mud-wall home. As a "registered resource user," Mtwandi is permitted to harvest honey from the Bwindi and pay an occasional visit to the graves of his ancestors in the Mgahinga, but he does so at the risk of being mistaken for a poacher and shot on sight by paid wardens from neighboring tribes. His forest knowledge is waning, and his family's nutrition is poor. In the forest they had meat, roots, fruit, and a balanced diet. Today they have a little money but no meat. In one more generation their forest-based culture—songs, rituals, traditions, and stories—will be gone.

It's no secret that millions of native peoples around the world have been pushed off their land to make room for big oil, big metal, big timber, and big agriculture. But few people realize that the same thing has happened for a much nobler cause: land and wildlife conservation. Today the list of culture-wrecking institutions put forth by tribal leaders on almost every continent includes not only Shell, Texaco, Freeport, and Bechtel, but also more surprising names like Conservation International (CI), The Nature Conservancy (TNC), the World Wildlife Fund (WWF), and the Wildlife Conservation Society (WCS). Even the more culturally sensitive World Conservation Union (IUCN) might get a mention.

In early 2004 a United Nations meeting was convened in New York for the ninth year in a row to push for passage of a resolution protecting the territorial and human rights of indigenous peoples. The UN draft declaration states: "Indigenous peoples shall not be forcibly removed from their lands or territories. No relocation shall take place without the free and informed consent of the indigenous peoples concerned and after agreement on just and fair compensation and, where possible, with the option to return." During the meeting an indigenous delegate who did not identify herself rose to state that while extractive industries were still a serious threat to their welfare and cultural integrity, their new and biggest enemy was "conservation."

Later that spring, at a Vancouver, British Columbia, meeting of the International Forum on Indigenous Mapping, all two hundred delegates signed a declaration stating that the "activities of conservation organizations now represent the single biggest threat to the integrity of indigenous lands." These are rhetorical jabs, of course, but they have shaken the international conservation community, as have a subsequent spate of critical articles and studies, two of them conducted by the Ford Foundation, calling big conservation to task for its historical mistreatment of indigenous peoples.

"We are enemies of conservation," declared Maasai leader Martin Saning'o, standing before a session of the November 2004 World Conservation Congress sponsored by IUCN in Bangkok, Thailand. The nomadic Maasai, who have over the past thirty years lost most of their grazing range to conservation projects throughout eastern Africa, hadn't always felt that way. In fact, Saning'o reminded his audience, "we were the original conservationists." The room was hushed as he quietly explained how pastoral and nomadic cattlemen have traditionally protected their range: "Our ways of farming pollinated diverse seed species and maintained corridors between ecosystems." Then he tried to fathom the strange version of land conservation that has impoverished his people, more than one hundred thousand of whom have been displaced from southern Kenya and the Serengeti Plains of Tanzania. Like the Batwa, the Maasai have not been fairly compensated. Their culture is dissolving and they live in poverty.

"We don't want to be like you," Saning'o told a room of shocked white faces. "We want you to be like us. We are here to change your minds. You cannot accomplish conservation without us."

Although he might not have realized it, Saning'o was speaking for a growing worldwide movement of indigenous peoples who think of themselves as conservation refugees. Not to be confused with ecological refugees—people forced to abandon their homelands as a result of unbearable heat, drought, desertification, flooding, disease, or other consequences of climate chaos—conservation refugees are removed from their lands involuntarily, either forcibly or through a variety of less coercive measures. The gentler, more benign methods are sometimes called "soft eviction" or "voluntary resettlement," though the latter is contestable. Soft or hard, the main complaint heard in the makeshift villages bordering parks and at meetings like the World Conservation Congress in Bangkok is that relocation often occurs with the tacit approval or benign neglect of one of the five big international nongovernmental conservation organizations, or as they have been nicknamed by indigenous leaders, the BINGOs.

The rationale for "internal displacements," as these evictions are officially called, usually involves a perceived threat to the biological diversity of a large geographical area, variously designated by one or more BINGOs as an "ecological hot spot," an "ecoregion," a "vulnerable ecosystem," a "biological corridor," or a "living landscape." The huge parks and reserves that are created often involve a debt-for-nature swap (some of the host country's national debt paid off or retired in exchange for the protection of a parcel of sensitive land) or similar financial incentive provided by the World Bank's Global Environment Facility and one or more of its "executing agencies" (bilateral and multilateral banks). This trade may be paired with an offer made by the funding organization to pay for the management of the park or reserve. Broad rules for human use and habitation of the protected area are set and enforced by the host nation, often following the advice and counsel of a BINGO, which might even be given management powers over the area. Indigenous peoples are often left out of the process entirely.

Curious about this brand of conservation that puts the rights of nature before the rights of people, I set out last autumn to meet the issue face to face. I visited with tribal members on three continents who were grappling with the consequences of Western conservation and found an alarming similarity among the stories I heard.

Khon Noi, matriarch of a remote mountain village, huddles next to an open-pit stove in the loose, brightly colored clothes that identify her as Karen, the most populous of six tribes found in the lush, mountainous reaches of far northern Thailand. Her village of sixty-five families has been in the same wide valley for over two hundred years. She chews betel, spitting its bright red juice into the fire, and speaks softly through black teeth. She tells me I can use her name, as long as I don't identify her village.

"The government has no idea who I am," she says. "The only person in the village they know by name is the 'headman' they appointed to represent us in government negotiations. They were here last week, in military uniforms, to tell us we could no longer practice rotational agriculture in this valley. If they knew that someone here was saying bad things about them they would come back again and move us out."

In a recent outburst of environmental enthusiasm stimulated by generous financial offerings from the Global Environment Facility, the Thai government has been creating national parks as fast as the Royal Forest Department can map them. Ten years ago there was barely a park to be found in Thailand, and because those few that existed were unmarked "paper parks," few Thais even knew they were there. Now there are 114 land parks and 24 marine parks on the map. Almost twenty-five thousand square kilometers, most of which are occupied by hill and fishing tribes, are now managed by the forest department as protected areas.

"Men in uniform just appeared one day, out of nowhere, showing their guns," Kohn Noi recalls, "and telling us that we were now living in

a national park. That was the first we knew of it. Our own guns were confiscated . . . no more hunting, no more trapping, no more snaring, and no
more 'slash and burn.' That's what they call our agriculture. We call it crop
rotation and we've been doing it in this valley for over two hundred years.
Soon we will be forced to sell rice to pay for greens and legumes we are
no longer allowed to grow here. Hunting we can live without, as we raise
chickens, pigs, and buffalo. But rotational farming is our way of life."

A week before our conversation, a short flight south of Noi's village, six
thousand conservationists were attending the World Conservation Congress
in Bangkok. Lining the hallways of a massive convention center were the
display booths of big conservation, adorned with larger-than-life photos of
indigenous peoples in splendid tribal attire. At huge plenary sessions praise
was heaped on Thailand's beloved Queen Sirikit and her environment minister, who came accompanied by a sizable delegation from the Royal Forest
Department.

But if delegates had taken the time to attend smaller panels and workshops, some held outside the convention center in a parking lot, they would
have heard Khon Noi's story repeated a dozen times or more by indigenous
leaders who came to Bangkok from every continent, at great expense, to
lobby conservation biologists and government bureaucrats for fairer treatment. And they would have heard a young Karen father of two boys ask
why his country, whose cabinet had ordered its environmental bureaucracy
to evict his people from their traditional homeland, was chosen by IUCN
to host the largest conservation convention in history.

The response of big conservation, in Bangkok and elsewhere, has been
to deny that they are party to the evictions while generating reams of pro-
motional material about their affection for and close relationships with indigenous peoples. "We recognize that indigenous people have perhaps the
deepest understanding of the Earth's living resources," says Conservation
International chairman and CEO Peter Seligmann, adding that, "we firmly
believe that indigenous people must have ownership, control and title of
their lands." Such messages are carefully projected toward major funders of
conservation, which in response to the aforementioned Ford Foundation
reports and other press have become increasingly sensitive to indigenous
peoples and their struggles for cultural survival.

Financial support for international conservation has in recent years expanded well beyond the individuals and family foundations that seeded
the movement to include very large foundations like Ford, MacArthur,
and Gordon and Betty Moore, as well as the World Bank, its Global
Environment Facility, foreign governments, USAID, a host of bilateral
and multilateral banks, and transnational corporations. During the 1990s

USAID alone pumped almost $300 million into the international conservation movement, which it had come to regard as a vital adjunct to economic prosperity. The five largest conservation organizations, CI, TNC, and WWF among them, absorbed over 70 percent of that expenditure. Indigenous communities received none of it. The Moore Foundation made a singular ten-year commitment of nearly $280 million, the largest environmental grant in history, to just one organization—Conservation International. And all of the BINGOs have become increasingly corporate in recent years, both in orientation and affiliation. The Nature Conservancy now boasts almost two thousand corporate sponsors, while Conservation International has received about $9 million from its two hundred fifty corporate "partners."

With that kind of financial and political leverage, as well as chapters in almost every country of the world, millions of loyal members, and nine-figure budgets, CI, WWF, and TNC have undertaken a hugely expanded global push to increase the number of so-called protected areas (PAs)—parks, reserves, wildlife sanctuaries, and corridors created to preserve biological diversity. In 1962, there were some 1,000 official PAs worldwide. Today there are 108,000, with more being added every day. The total area of land now under conservation protection worldwide has doubled since 1990, when the World Parks Commission set a goal of protecting 10 percent of the planet's surface. That goal has been exceeded, as over 12 percent of all land, a total area of 11.75 million square miles, is now protected. That's an area greater than the entire landmass of Africa.

At first glance, so much protected land seems undeniably positive, an enormous achievement of very good people doing the right thing for our planet. But the record is less impressive when the impact upon native people is considered. For example, during the 1990s the African nation of Chad increased the amount of national land under protection from 0.1 to 9.1 percent. All of that land had been previously inhabited by what are now an estimated six hundred thousand conservation refugees. No other country besides India, which officially admits to 1.6 million, is even counting this growing new class of refugees. World estimates offered by the UN, IUCN, and a few anthropologists range from 5 million to tens of millions. Charles Geisler, a sociologist at Cornell University who has studied displacements in Africa, is certain the number on that continent alone exceeds 14 million.

The true worldwide figure, if it were ever known, would depend upon the semantics of words like "eviction," "displacement," and "refugee," over which parties on all sides of the issue argue endlessly. The larger point is that conservation refugees exist on every continent but Antarctica, and by most accounts live far more difficult lives than they once did, banished from lands they thrived on for hundreds, even thousands of years.

The practice of removing people from protected areas began in the United States in 1864 with the military expulsion of Miwok and Ahwahnee Indians from their four-thousand-year-old settlements in Yosemite Valley. During the California Gold Rush the valley and its native communities had been "discovered" by white settlers. One of them, a miner and wilderness romantic named Lafayette Burnell, swooned over the lush beauty of the valley as he watched James Savage, commander of the Mariposa Battalion, burn Indian villages and acorn caches to the ground—a first step to starving and freezing the Miwok into submission.

Burnell approved of the torching. Fancying himself a passionate conservationist, he was determined to "sweep the territory of any scattered bands that might infest it." And swept it was, a process that lasted until 1969 when the last Miwok village was evacuated from the national park. Similar treatment was experienced by the Shoshone, Lakota, Bannock, Crow, Nez Perce, Flathead, and Blackfeet, all of whom at one time or another occupied and hunted in what is now Yellowstone National Park. And many parks have followed, followed by many evictions.

John Muir, a forefather of the American conservation movement, argued that "wilderness" should be cleared of all inhabitants and set aside to satisfy the urbane human's need for recreation and spiritual renewal. It was a sentiment that became national policy with the passage of the 1964 Wilderness Act, which defined wilderness as a place "where man himself is a visitor who does not remain." One should not be surprised to find hardy residues of these sentiments among traditional conservation groups. The preference for "virgin" wilderness has lingered on in a movement that has tended to value all nature but human nature, and refused to recognize the positive wildness in human beings.

Expulsions continue around the world to this day, albeit under less violent circumstances than the atrocious Miwok massacres. The Indian government, which evicted one hundred thousand *adivasis* (rural peoples) in Assam between April and July of 2002, estimates that another 2 or 3 million more will be displaced over the next decade. The policy is largely in response to a 1993 lawsuit brought by WWF, which demanded that the government increase PAs by 8 percent, mostly in order to protect tiger habitat. A more immediate threat involves the impending removal of several Mayan communities from the Montes Azules region of Chiapas, Mexico, a process, begun in the mid-1970s with the intent to preserve virgin tropical forest, which could still quite easily spark a civil war. Conservation International is deeply immersed in that controversy, as are a host of extractive industries.

Tensions are also high in the Enoosupukia region of Kenya, where two thousand members of the ancient Ogiek community were recently ordered to leave the Mau Forest, where they have thrived as hunter-gatherers for centuries. ANY PERSON FOUND INSIDE THE TRUST LAND AREA SHALL BE EVICTED/ARRESTED, reads a warning posted by the government. Once the Ogiek villages were cleared, all structures were burned to the ground. And while the stated intent of the Kenyan government is environmental, the Ogiek note that their land has been deeded over to powerful members of former president Daniel arap Moi's Kalenjin tribe, and that vast regions of the forest are being clear-cut. An Ogiek defender, Kenya Deputy Minister of Environment Wangari Maathai, recently told *Newsweek* magazine that "the Ogiek are a class of their own." A lifelong environmental activist and Nobel laureate, Maathai remembers what the Mau Forest was like when the Ogiek lived there: no roads, no logging, plenty of biodiversity. The World Wildlife Fund, which is active in the area, has been careful not to promote the Ogiek eviction, but has also done nothing to stop it.

Meanwhile, over the past decade each of the BINGOs and most of the international agencies they work with have issued formal and heartfelt declarations in support of indigenous peoples and their territorial rights. The Nature Conservancy's "Commitment to People" statement declares, "We respect the needs of local communities by developing ways to conserve biological diversity while at the same time enabling humans to live productively and sustainably on the landscape." After endorsing the UN's draft declaration on the rights of indigenous peoples, WWF adopted its own statement of principles upholding the rights of indigenous peoples to own, manage, and control their lands and territories—a radical notion for many governments. In 1999 the World Commission on Protected Areas formally recognized indigenous peoples' rights to "sustainable, traditional use" of their lands and territories.

The following year the IUCN adopted a bold set of principles for establishing protected areas, which states unequivocally, "The establishment of new protected areas on indigenous and other traditional peoples' . . . domains should be based on the legal recognition of collective rights of communities living within them to the lands, territories, waters, coastal seas and other resources they traditionally own or otherwise occupy or use."

Tribal people, who tend to think and plan in generations, rather than weeks, months, and years, are still waiting to be paid the consideration promised in these thoughtful pronouncements. Of course the UN draft declaration is the prize because it must be ratified by so many nations. The declaration has failed to pass mainly because powerful leaders such as Tony Blair and George Bush threaten to veto it, arguing that there is not and should never be such a thing as collective human rights.

Sadly, the human rights and global conservation communities remain at serious odds over the question of displacement, each side blaming the other for the particular crisis they perceive. Conservation biologists argue that by allowing native populations to grow, hunt, and gather in protected areas, anthropologists, cultural preservationists, and other supporters of indigenous rights become complicit in the decline of biological diversity. Some, like the Wildlife Conservation Society's outspoken president, Steven Sanderson, believe that the entire global conservation agenda has been "hijacked" by advocates for indigenous peoples, placing wildlife and bio-diversity in peril. "Forest peoples and their representatives may speak for the forest," Sanderson has said, "They may speak for their version of the forest; but they do not speak for the forest we want to conserve." WCS, originally the New York Zoological Society, is a BINGO lesser in size and stature than the likes of TNC and CI, but more insistent than its colleagues that indigenous territorial rights, while a valid social issue, should be of no concern to wildlife conservationists.

Human rights groups, such as Cultural Survival, First Peoples Worldwide, EarthRights International, Survival International, and the Forest Peoples Programme argue the opposite, accusing some of the BINGOs and governments like Uganda's of destroying indigenous cultures, the diversity of which they deem essential to the preservation of biological diversity.

One attempt to bridge this unfortunate divide is the "market-based solution." BINGOs endorse ecotourism, bioprospecting, extractive reserves, and industrial partnerships that involve such activities as building nature resorts, leading pharmaceutical scientists to medicinal plants, gathering nuts for Ben and Jerry's ice cream, or harvesting plant oils for the Body Shop as the best way to protect both land and community with a single program. Global conservation Web sites and annual reports feature stunning photographs of native people leading nature tours and harvesting fair-trade coffee, Brazil nuts, and medicinal plants. But no native names or faces can be found on the boards of the BINGOs that promote these arrangements.

Market-based solutions, which may have been implemented with the best of social and ecological intentions, share a lamentable outcome, barely discernible behind a smoke screen of slick promotion. In almost every case indigenous people are moved into the money economy without the means to participate in it fully. They become permanently indentured as park rangers (never wardens), porters, waiters, harvesters, or, if they manage to learn a European language, ecotour guides. Under this model, "conservation" edges ever closer to "development," while native communities are assimilated into the lowest ranks of national cultures.

Given this history, it should be no surprise that tribal peoples regard conservationists as just another colonizer—an extension of the deadening forces of economic and cultural hegemony. Whole societies like the Batwa, the Maasai, the Ashinika of Peru, the Gwi and Gana Bushmen of Botswana, the Karen and Hmong of Southeast Asia, and the Huarani of Ecuador are being transformed from independent and self-sustaining into deeply dependent and poor communities.

When I traveled throughout Mesoamerica and the Andean-Amazon watershed last fall visiting staff members of CI, TNC, WCS, and WWF I was looking for signs that an awakening was on the horizon. The field staff I met were acutely aware that the spirit of exclusion survives in the headquarters of their organizations, alongside a subtle but real prejudice against "unscientific" native wisdom. Dan Campbell, TNC's director in Belize, conceded, "We have an organization that sometimes tries to employ models that don't fit the culture of nations where we work." And Joy Grant, in the same office, said that as a consequence of a protracted disagreement with the indigenous peoples of Belize, local people "are now the key to everything we do."

"We are arrogant," was the confession of a CI executive working in South America, who asked me not to identify her. I was heartened by her admission until she went on to suggest that this was merely a minor character flaw. In fact, arrogance was cited by almost all of the nearly one hundred indigenous leaders I met with as a major impediment to constructive communication with big conservation.

Luis Suarez, the new director of CI in Ecuador, seems to be aware of that. "Yes," he said, "CI has made some serious blunders with indigenous organizations within the past four years, not only in Ecuador but also in Peru." And he admitted to me that his organization was at that very moment making new enemies in Guyana, where CI had worked with the Wai Wai peoples on the establishment of a protected area, but had simultaneously ignored another tribe, the Wapishana, whose six communities will be encompassed by the park.

If field observations and field workers' sentiments trickle up to the headquarters of CI and the other BINGOs, there could be a happy ending to this story. There are already positive working models of socially sensitive conservation on every continent, particularly in Australia, Bolivia, Nepal, and Canada, where national laws that protect native land rights leave foreign conservationists no choice but to join hands with indigenous communities and work out creative ways to protect wildlife habitat and sustain biodiversity while allowing indigenous citizens to thrive in their traditional settlements.

However, in most such cases it is the native people who initiate the creation of a reserve, which is more likely to be called an "indigenous protected area" (IPA) or a "community conservation area" (CCA). IPAs are an invention of Australian aboriginals, many of whom have regained ownership and territorial autonomy under new treaties with the national government, and CCAs are appearing around the world, from Lao fishing villages along the Mekong River to the Mataven Forest in Colombia, where six indigenous tribes live in 152 villages bordering a four-million-acre ecologically intact reserve. The tribes manage a national park within the reserve and collectively own considerable acreage along its border. Before the Mataven conservation area was created, the indigenous communities mapped the boundaries of the land to be protected, proposed their own operating rules and restrictions, and sought independent funding to pay for management of the reserve, which is today regarded worldwide as a model of indigenous conservation.

The Kayapo, a nation of Amazonian Indians with whom the Brazilian government and CI have formed a co-operative conservation project, is another such example. Kayapo leaders, renowned for their militancy, openly refused to be treated like just another stakeholder in a two-way deal between a national government and a conservation NGO, as is so often the case with co-operative management plans. Throughout negotiations they insisted upon being an equal player at the table, with equal rights and land sovereignty. As a consequence, the Xingu National Park, the continent's first Indian-owned park, was created to protect the lifeways of the Kayapo and other indigenous Amazonians who are determined to remain within the park's boundaries.

In many locations, once a CCA is established and territorial rights are assured, the founding community invites a BINGO to send its ecologists and wildlife biologists to share in the task of protecting biodiversity by combining Western scientific methodology with indigenous ecological knowledge. And on occasion they will ask for help negotiating with reluctant governments. For example, the Guarani Izoceños people in Bolivia invited the

Wildlife Conservation Society to mediate a comanagement agreement with their government, which today allows the tribe to manage and own part of the new Kaa-Iya del Gran Chaco National Park.

Too much hope should probably not be placed in a handful of successful comanagement models or a few field staffs' epiphanies. The unrestrained corporate lust for energy, hardwood, medicines, and strategic metals is still a considerable threat to indigenous communities, arguably a larger threat than conservation. However, the lines between the two are being blurred. Particularly problematic is the fact that international conservation organizations remain comfortable working in close quarters with some of the most aggressive global resource prospectors, such as Boise Cascade, Chevron-Texaco, Mitsubishi, Conoco-Phillips, International Paper, Rio Tinto Mining, Shell, and Weyerhaeuser, all of whom are members of a CI-created entity called the Center for Environmental Leadership in Business. Of course if the BINGOs were to renounce their corporate partners, they would forfeit millions of dollars in revenue and access to global power without which they sincerely believe they could not be effective.

And there are some respected and influential conservation biologists who still strongly support top-down, centralized "fortress" conservation. Duke University's John Terborgh, for example, author of the classic *Requiem for Nature,* believes that comanagement projects and CCAs are a huge mistake. "My feeling is that a park should be a park, and it shouldn't have any resident people in it," he says. He bases his argument on three decades of research in Peru's Manu National Park, where native Machiguenga Indians fish and hunt animals with traditional weapons. Terborgh is concerned that they will acquire motorboats, guns, and chainsaws used by their fellow tribesmen outside the park, and that biodiversity will suffer. Then there's paleontologist Richard Leakey, who at the 2003 World Parks Congress in South Africa set off a firestorm of protest by denying the very existence of indigenous peoples in Kenya, his homeland, and arguing that "the global interest in biodiversity might sometimes trump the rights of local people."

Not all of Leakey's colleagues agree with him. Many conservationists are beginning to realize that most of the areas they have sought to protect are rich in biodiversity precisely because the people who were living there had come to understand the value and mechanisms of biological diversity. Some will even admit that wrecking the lives of 10 million or more poor, powerless people has been an enormous mistake—not only a moral, social, philosophical, and economic mistake, but an ecological one as well. Others have learned from bitter experience that national parks and protected areas surrounded by angry, hungry people who describe themselves as "enemies of conservation" are generally doomed to fail. As Cristina Eghenter of WWF observed after working with communities surrounding the Kayan Mentarang National Park in Borneo, "It is becoming increasingly evident that conservation objectives can rarely be obtained or sustained by imposing policies that produce negative impacts on indigenous peoples."

More and more conservationists seem to be wondering how, after setting aside a "protected" land mass the size of Africa, global biodiversity continues to decline. Might there be something terribly wrong with this plan—particularly after the Convention on Biological Diversity has documented the astounding fact that in Africa, where so many parks and reserves have been created and where indigenous evictions run highest, 90 percent of biodiversity lies outside of protected areas? If we want to preserve biodiversity in the far reaches of the globe, places that are in many cases still occupied by indigenous people living in ways that are ecologically sustainable, history is showing us that the dumbest thing we can do is kick them out.

(2005)

Jeremiad for Belarus

Countryside contaminated by Chernobyl reminds an Iowan of home

I'VE LOST COUNT OF THE TIMES I'VE DRIVEN LUSH, ROLLING IOWA hills to go to see how the local nuclear power plant responds to terrorist threats or Homeland Security's latest "orange alert." The front entrance has been altered since my first investigation. Now, instead of two lanes of vehicles passing easily through open gates, portable concrete medians channel traffic into a single lane. At a small wooden building in front of the open gates, a middle-aged man checks the identification of plant workers. I wonder if he ever notices me, slowly turning the car around and circling the plant on a county road edged in cornfields. I turn onto gravel, wind past small acreages of retired farmers in their new houses. I turn again, onto a lonely service road. Over and over since September 2001, I've been astonished to find this back entrance to the Duane Arnold Energy Center unguarded. The chain link gates blocking the road are usually padlocked. But all they do is span the road; on either side there's nothing but a farmer's barbed-wire fence.

Today though, construction crews are reworking the road's surface and the gates stand wide open. I drive my rusting Taurus onto the property, twist among the working vehicles, pull over, park, and watch the men work. I stay there for an hour, and no one approaches and asks, "What're you doing sitting alone in that car within firing distance of a nuclear reactor?"

Like most Americans, I hadn't thought much about Chernobyl since the spring of 1986. For a few weeks back then, speculative coverage of the disaster at a Ukrainian nuclear plant filled the evening news. Like everyone, I watched it, horrified. But slowly the name "Chernobyl" became just another echo of the horrible nuclear events in recent memory—Hiroshima, Nagasaki, Bikini Atoll, and the irradiating of the Marshall Islands—an anniversary sound bite, the subject of an occasional documentary.

Then in the fall of 2000, the Frankfurt International School, where I was teaching, asked if I'd join a delegation to Cherikov. A small town in southeastern Belarus, Cherikov was the terminus of one of the school's humanitarian service projects.

"Belarus?" I asked. "What's Belarus?"

"The country most contaminated by Chernobyl," answered a German colleague.

"I thought that was Ukraine," I said.

She sighed, "Most Americans seem to."

Nothing she could tell me, and nothing I'd read, had warned me that Belarus would look and smell just like home, like Iowa, like the upper Midwest. On a five-hour drive from Minsk to Cherikov, we passed mile after mile of undulating autumn prairie grasses covered with burst pods and dark dried flowers. Green coniferous forests trimmed with white-barked birch trees broke the prairie vistas; I could smell Thanksgiving on the wind. Only the robin's-egg-blue cemetery fences reminded me that I wasn't home.

I had expected ashen land, naked trees, barren fields. I remembered Edward Teller's response to the news about Chernobyl: "The chances of a real calamity at a nuclear power station are infinitesimally small," he said on the "ABC Evening News" in late April 1986. "But should it happen, the consequences are impossible to imagine." Certainly I didn't imagine that the most radioactive landscape on Earth would make me homesick. As our van rolled across the moraine-ribbed hills of rural Belarus it finally sank in: radioactivity isn't visible, tactile, odoriferous.

Twenty-three percent of Belarus was contaminated with Chernobyl's fallout, 32,592 square miles—that's two-thirds of Iowa, more land than six eastern states combined. But it isn't a solid swath of land, nor neat concentric circles emanating from Ukraine. On maps the contamination looks like rusty puddles and large tannin-stained lakes. Color variations denote concentration levels of the radioactive isotope mapped most clearly, cesium-137.

The average level of contamination on the polluted territories, thirty-seven curies (Ci) per square kilometer, is notated scientifically as $37Ci/km2$. The International Atomic Energy Agency (IAEA) set the "safe for residency limit" at a maximum of $5Ci/km2$. Eighty-eight percent of contaminated Belarus is 111 to 370 times more contaminated than that. Two million people still live on that land.

"We did not know what you would like," Irene (pronounced Ear-ay-na) Kulbakina apologizes on my first night in Cherikov. "It is too simple."

On the table is spread the largesse of the most humble people with whom I've ever shared food, a beautiful meal prepared in a kitchen with neither refrigerator nor sink. Small plates of open-faced sandwiches cover the table: pale pink tomatoes on a cream spread, apple slices beneath melted sheets of cheese, tiny smoked fish supine on white bread. Ceramic bowls cradle colorful vegetables in brine, canned corn in something creamy, and three different preparations of mushrooms.

It is a small moment of truth. I've been told vaguely to "try to avoid" eating dairy products, fish, local produce, or "forest gifts." I've read that when the radiological community began to study the effects of Chernobyl's pollution on Belarus, one of the most disturbing discoveries was that grains and legumes absorb cesium-137 and accumulate it much more quickly and in much greater quantities than was predicted. But I'm the guest of a schoolteacher and her truck driver husband, full-time workers earning less than $80 a month between them, and paying $2.50 a liter for uncontaminated drinking water for their six-year-old daughter, Olya. When they proudly spread that meal before me, I receive a whole paper napkin while Irene and her husband, Sasha, split one.

"It looks lovely," I say, accepting a glass of garnet-colored wine they handle like gold. Irene translates for her Belarusan husband. The big, pale-skinned man smiles shyly.

"My husband has made it," Irene explains. "His education was to be a chef. But there is no place to practice it now, and it would not pay enough. He enjoys it though, and he has spent the week preparing. Yesterday, all afternoon, he picked the mushrooms from the woods. Eat, please, eat."

According to the Belarusan Ministry of Emergencies' report, "Belarus and Chernobyl: The Second Decade," 2,500 square miles of Belarus have plutonium levels three times higher than the IAEA considers safe for human habitation. No one argues with the fact that a particle of plutonium absorbed by the lung will eventually cause cancer. But, I reason, studying the colorful food Sasha has prepared, I'm not likely to breath plutonium from this meal. Tomorrow maybe, as we walk down the packed-dirt roads of a village on the edge of an evacuated zone, but not here, tonight.

Cesium-137 and strontium-90, on the other hand, are quite likely to be stewing in the rich brown mushrooms Sasha has collected from the woods. The Kulbakinas and their friends live, work, and garden in a village where the level of cesium-137 is thirty-seven times above the IAEA's maximum safe-limit. I help myself to small servings of several of the dishes, and my host's face falls. "Can we get you something else?" Irene asks.

"No, no," I say, "let me go slowly so I can taste everything. Tell me what I'm eating."

Measuring external exposure to radiation is a fairly straightforward exercise, if one has the equipment with which to do it. Computing internal exposure is much more complicated. The IAEA, which still insists that only thirty-two people have died as a direct result of Chernobyl, doesn't measure internal contamination levels in their judgments of safety, nor in their counting of Chernobyl-influenced deaths. Yet scientists do not dispute that once ingested, long-lived radionuclides, and many of the chemical progeny produced as they decay, remain in the body, irradiating tissues they've nestled into. (Nor does the irradiation stop when the host dies.)

Some radionuclides find their way from soil to plant to herbivore and carnivore. They accumulate in particular organs. Thousands of Belarusan autopsies already show that cesium settles in heart and optical muscles, speeding their degeneration. Strontium-90 likes teeth and snuggles into bone marrow, irradiating the stem cells responsible for our blood and immune systems.

Given Cherikov's initial contamination levels, the IAEA's 5Ci/km2 "safe for residency limit," and the time it takes each radioactive isotope to decay, I figure it'll be 2136 before it will be safe to be outdoors here—if it's the cesium you're worried about. If it's the strontium-90 that scares you, it'll be 2154 before eating, drinking, and breathing are not akin to buying a Shirley Jacksonesque lottery ticket.

I eat Sasha's mushrooms. The deep brown forest gifts taste only of the autumn forest floor.

In the most contaminated of Belarus's territories, what the Ministry of Emergencies calls the "Zones of Alienation," the only legal activities are scientific research or jobs linked to radiation control, like soaking down dry prairies so that fires don't rerelease plutonium into the air. Ten minutes from Cherikov, a thousand-square-mile "alienation zone" is posted with large white billboards warning the trespasser in Russian that she'll be fined ten months' salary if caught inside. The zone isn't fenced. The armed guards at an intersection leading into it merely nod and let our rickety van of humanitarian sightseers pass.

For miles it looks like a normal coniferous forest opening onto green pastures that flow into ancient orchards. But there are freshly cut tree stumps, wet and golden in the weak sunlight. On the edge of the timber a crane loads tree trunks onto a flatbed lumber truck.

"Milling wood doesn't prevent it from emitting radioactivity, does it?" I ask our van driver and translator, Mikhail Koslovski, a representative of

With Hope for the Future, one of the many projects that have stepped into the post-Soviet funding vacuum to aid victims of Chernobyl.

"No," he answers, meeting my eyes in the rearview mirror.

"Then what are they doing?"

"Belarus is poor, Hope," he says. "It goes to Minsk to be made into furniture."

I want to make sure I've understood him. "People in Minsk make furniture out of radioactive trees and then sell it to unsuspecting buyers?"

"Da," he says quietly.

We move from the forest to an enormous open prairie, so flat, the uninterrupted grasses so tall, that I can't see the road anywhere on the horizon. The van slows and makes a right-angle turn. At first I'm puzzled, and then I realize that the road's precise geometry is all that speaks of a settlement. After the accident that "could never happen here," Belarusan conscripts dug holes and buried the village that once stood in this spot. They did the same with over a hundred other settlements. To prevent surface contamination from leaching into groundwater, they backed cement trucks up to village wells and filled them to the brim with concrete.

Still, under a clump of trees in the distance, houses hunker behind wooden fences. When we get closer, I see a man, his chapped hands ungloved, his feet wrapped in pig hide tied below his knees, standing beside an ancient wooden wagon to which he has harnessed a lean Holstein milk cow.

"*Samosely?*" I ask Mikhail, using the term for the old people who have returned without permission to their confiscated homes.

"*Refusniks,*" he replies. "The old women said, 'We survived starvation and Hitler and starvation and Stalin, and now you tell us something invisible will kill us? We will die here.'"

Watching the huddle of houses recede, I connect the sweet odor of the village with smoke from a chimney. "Is it peat they're burning?" I ask, imagining the plutonium coming out of that chimney. "Peat dug here in the alienation zone?"

"Da," he says again.

More miles of undulating prairie, and then swamps with trees burned from the top down. "The Swedes said 3,000 curies here," Mikhail explains. "It is not safe for more than five minutes." We're 150 miles from Chernobyl. I don't want to know 3,000 curies of what; I want him to keep driving.

Ten miles later, he slows down. On our right is an empty, long-weathered village. "This village is relocated," Mikhail says, irony overriding the Russian accent in his German. "The village is relocated there." He points to a set of five-story apartment buildings on our left, nearly new, and abandoned, curtains blowing through broken windows. "When Lukashenko [president of Belarus since 1994] had to show that he was doing something, this he did. Television cameras showed people moving into their new homes. They did not turn around to show that the people came only across the field."

"It took years," he explains, backing the van around, "to know what the contamination levels were, and more to know what is uninhabitable. Now the people are relocated again, and dying."

In the main street of the deserted village several ragged men have gathered. They huddle together near a porch, watching us, their shoulders curled in fear. "Mikhail?" I ask, pointing. He studies them a moment.

"Chechens," he sighs as we drive away. "Better to die of radiation than a bullet in the head."

Watching the refugees watching us, I ponder the impossibility of resettling two million people. I begin to understand what Ivan Kenik, Belarus's Minister for Extraordinary Situations and Protection of the Population from the Consequences of the Chernobyl Catastrophe, was trying to convey. In March 1995 in the magazine *Sovetskaya Belorussiya,* he warned that the cost of his country's Chernobyl mitigation would amount to thirty-two times his country's annual budget through 2015. No one from any government or international organization contested his claim.

But there were Chernobyl-related arguments going on in the nuclear and radiological communities, as Western authorities refused to believe reports of illnesses appearing in Belarus much earlier than anyone had predicted. Among the first radionuclide assaults after a nuclear explosion is iodine-131, which our thyroids mistake for stable iodine and readily absorb. During the week after what Belarusans have come to call simply "the catastrophe," all ten million citizens were exposed to untold amounts of it.

Western predictions of Chernobyl's consequences were based on Hiroshima-Nagasaki data, and on the then-current belief that iodine-131 had a low carcinogenic potential. But within a year after the accident, Belarusan scientists reported increases in a childhood thyroid cancer that has a one-in-a-million spontaneous incidence. "The appearance of several tens of cases in the region around Chernobyl from a population of under half a million children . . . should have left little room for doubt that something was seriously amiss," said Keith Baverstock, a leading radiation scientist with the World Health Organization's European Center for Environment and Health, in 1998.

"Many people predicted a small increase in thyroid cancer, with a ten-year latency period, and they were reluctant to accept reports of a large increase four to five years after the explosion," admitted Sir Dillwyn Williams, a Cambridge thyroid cancer expert, in 2001.

Yet while scientists and nuclear regulatory bodies argued about the reliability of Belarusan data, the incidence of thyroid cancer in Belarus continued to rise. The most recent statistic is 2,000 cases in a population of 400,000 children—5,000 times its spontaneous occurrence in "clean" countries. That's only one of the reasons that Vasily Nesterenko, head of the independent Institute of Radiation Safety in Minsk, wrote in 2000 that "Belarus is facing alone a disaster it's not responsible for. . . . Only massive international aid and strong logistical support by the government will ensure the survival of my people."

On a cold November day two years later, on a sidewalk in Cherikov, I watch a crying woman plead with Svetlana Vladimirovna, the director of the local kindergarten. The woman wants the nonexistent orphanage opened, NOW. Fourteen parentless children have been waiting for months. She's just discovered five more, siblings, the oldest age twelve, in a barn on the edge of town, feeding themselves on stolen eggs and radioactive apples. "Their parents?" I ask.

Lovely Svetlana looks at me sadly. "Dead," she says, "dying."

"Why?" I ask.

She shrugs. "Chernobyl. Vodka. Chernobyl."

She, the teachers, and a woman in a white lab coat lead us on a tour of the kindergarten. In every room they point to donations from the Frankfurt International School and Den Kindern von Tschernobyl, a Bad Homburg, Germany-based group of chemical factory workers who have become Cherikov's major benefactors. "*Danke, danke, spasiba, danke,*" the teachers chorus as they point to crayons and construction paper, toys and books, cribs and linens.

Then the woman in clinical garb takes us into a three-room suite filled with medical equipment and vitamins delivered by Den Kindern's latest six-truck convoy. The first room is surrounded on three sides by tables low enough for three-year-olds. Every three feet all around the room tiny chairs are pulled up before ventilators and nebulizers. Photographs and diagrams on the walls that show children how to place the plastic tubes in their mouths help me picture what it looks like when they are all sitting here, a roomful of toddlers using machines to ease their breathing.

"Allergies," the school's doctor explains. "The children now have all kinds of allergies. Each year more. Most have asthma. Acute asthma, so, the ventilators."

"We could use more," Svetlana says shyly. Twelve is not enough to serve her thirty-seven charges, far fewer children than she once cared for. And with the help of German humanitarians, she'll soon be turning her school into an orphanage. "These children," she explains, "are certain to have illness."

While no one knows which health issues are consequences of radioactive exposure and which are not, it's obvious that living conditions in Belarus exacerbate all forms of illness. First and foremost is lack of food. The people in the contaminated zones are hungry. What little food is available in shops—where I've never seen fresh fruit and the only fresh vegetables are cabbage and potatoes—is beyond their economic reach. They garden in contaminated community plots, spend their late summers putting up radioactive vegetables, and hope they have canned and dried enough nourishment to last until spring.

In the spring of 2002, Irene wrote, "The situation at the state factory, Sasha's job, is very difficult. They produce not only mineral water but tinned food as well. But the state has no money to buy vegetables or fruit, and they have no money to pay for electricity and gas, and so every month they work half of the month, or have whole month holiday—no pay. You know, in March there were some days when we had not even a piece of bread, no potato, rice or anything. The children cried and we had not anything to eat." Irene's breast milk had not come in after the birth of their second daughter, Lena, and the night after receiving this letter I dreamed of them, the whole family, sitting down to a meal made only of the infant formula my friends and I had been shipping to Cherikov all winter.

Nutritional deficiencies are legion in Belarus, and of course they compound the deleterious effects of constant exposure to radiation. So does being continually chilled through a six-month winter because the state can't provide enough fuel to heat apartment-complex boilers. So does lacking the means to fight germs. The average salary in the contaminated zones is forty dollars a month. The last time I was there a bar of soap was nearly two dollars, toothpaste and a toothbrush four dollars. Neither laundry nor dish soap was available in Cherikov at all. Yes, boiling water kills germs, but it concentrates the accumulation of radionuclides.

These are the sorts of complications, variables difficult to account for in medical research, that make it easy for skeptics to question any seriously scary reports based on studies of Belarusan health post-Chernobyl. But post-Chernobyl demographics make plain trends that are harder to dismiss.

According to the 2000 report on Minsk's United Nations Development Program (UNDP), life expectancy in Belarus in the 1960s was almost level with that in Western Europe. By 1999, thirteen years after Chernobyl, it had fallen 12 to 14 years for men and 7 to 9 years for women. A baby boy born in rural Belarus today can expect to live 59 years.

But they may be very hard years. Nearly half of Belarus's teenagers have serious health problems. Forty-five to 47 percent of those graduating from high school have physical disorders like gastro-intestinal anomalies, weakened hearts, and cataracts; 40 percent of them have chronic "blood disorders" and malfunctioning thyroids. The number of handicapped adolescents trebled in the last decade.

These people are coming into their reproductive years already ill. They make the grim forecast for a country trying to survive an ecological catastrophe even grimmer. Despite a rise in the number of young Belarusan women twenty-six and under—the sector of the population that gives birth to more than 70 percent of humanity's children—the last decade has seen no national increase in births. For the first time in history, the decline in births occurred in both rural and urban populations. Between the censuses of 1989 and 1999, the number of children under age five in Belarus dropped a breathtaking 42 percent, while in the U.S. it rose 5 percent.

And, not only are birth rates decreasing, but every year since 1993 Belarus has experienced more deaths than births. In 1994, 10,000 more Belarusans died than were born. That figure has increased in each successive year. By 1999 (the last year for which there are figures), the difference had reached 25,000, and no leveling-off is predicted. Statisticians at Belarus's Institute of Economics maintain that if present trends continue, in fifty years the population of Belarus will be between 4 and 4.5 million, less than half what it is today. Over the next hundred years, they predict, the total population of Belarus will fall to one-tenth of today's 10 million people.

What a bleak time that next hundred years will be if the international community doesn't organize and help Belarus. Before Chernobyl, Belarus was the only one of the fifteen Soviet Republics with a birth defects registry, noted Richard Stone in a 2001 article in *Science*. The Minsk Institute for Hereditary Diseases has been keeping track of birth anomalies since 1979, and so they have one of the few reliable databases from which to draw comparisons between the lightly contaminated (1Ci/km2), moderately contaminated (2-15Ci/km2), and heavily contaminated (more than 15Ci/km2) regions. In all three, birth defects skyrocketed after 1986. In both the lightly and moderately contaminated areas they rose 50 percent, in heavily contaminated areas 83 percent.

On my first trip, in November 2000, I spent three days touring schools in Cherikov and the even more contaminated areas of the Mogilev district. Then we traveled to children's hospitals in Minsk. What I saw there still shows up in nightmares: children with eyes in the sides of their heads, and children with no eyes at all, children with fingers that look like toes, and children whose genitals are so poorly formed one can't determine their sex. Those nightmares are audible with infant wails like the cries of wounded wild animals.

In one of the rural schools, the principal told us we'd come at a good time because the children had just returned from weeks of potato harvesting. Part of the contaminated crop comes to the school. The children participate not only in the harvest but also in the canning of fruits and vegetables for their school meals. For many, it is the only certain meal of the day. Seventy percent of the students' parents are alcoholics, many of whom begrudge the school its share of potatoes, which they otherwise distill into vodka.

The consequences of want and alcohol are visible everywhere. Hunger and fetal alcohol syndrome (FAS) growl in the corners of every primary classroom. Belarus's children are often so small I mistake them for being three and four years younger than they are. Many have the scalloped ears and widely spaced eyes of FAS, children whose brains cannot function mathematically, who cannot follow more than two steps in any oral sequence.

The rampant alcoholism embarrasses Belarusans like Irene and Sasha, struggling to be good, strong, sober parents. And in many circles, from the United Nations Scientific Committee on the Effects of Atomic Radiation (UNSCEAR), to the IAEA, to scholars of post-Soviet communism, experts cite alcoholism as a reason to discredit the dire reports of illness in the contaminated territories. In turn, they explain away the alcoholism and the fragility of mental health among those living on permanently contaminated land with the insidious term "radiophobic." A fear of radiation and radiation-related illnesses, it is said over and over, makes them ill. They are, more than anything else, sick in the head.

Who wouldn't be, I wonder each time I read this argument. Hungry, sick, forgotten, with no relief in sight. Their children are suffering and they can't produce more, and even when they can, what chance will those children have? The very ground is contaminated. The half-life of plutonium is twenty-four thousand years, and it will be five times that long before some of Belarus is "free" of plutonium contamination.

Anyone who visits Minsk or the contaminated eastern regions of Belarus can feel the general malaise. It is palpable, this state that we would call depression rather than radiophobia and treat with small blue-and-white capsules. Like hunger and cold and deprivation, depression lowers the body's resistance to diseases, perhaps especially to the one that makes people seek solace by crawling into a bottle of vodka.

Still, it's not that Belarus hasn't tried to take care of its own. According to the Ministry of Emergencies, they decontaminated 500 settlements. Sixty percent of those they decontaminated two or three times. They removed 7,300,000 cubic meters of topsoil and buried it, but could either find or afford only 1,570,000 cubic meters to replace it. They asphalted dirt roads, streets, and sidewalks so that radioactive particles were not sent swirling in dust that would find its way into human lungs. They dismantled objects, removed roofs, and buried them. They shattered contaminated stones and bricks into powder so that no one could carry them away to use again.

But eventually the ministry admitted defeat, declaring, "it proved unreal [sic] to fully decontaminate settlements, agricultural and industrial facilities with a view to creating normal living and working conditions, since needs significantly exceed opportunities and resources."

Before giving up their efforts to mitigate Chernobyl's pollution, conscripts entirely demolished 110 settlements, some of which had thousands of residents. They buried 3,200 farms, and abandoned to weeds and decay 14,500 others they knew they should have buried. They decontaminated 1,300 pieces of industrial equipment and 529 ventilation systems in twenty-three enterprises. And then they had to contend with the nuclear waste. Bury it? Burn it? Store it in metal containers on the acres covered with abandoned clean-up vehicles around the Chernobyl plant itself? They did all this and more.

But by 1998, twelve years after the catastrophe, the Belarusans had re-settled only 260,000 of the 2.2 million people living on contaminated land. They had built schools with places for 33,700 students (130,000 had been displaced), preschools with 11,500 places, hospitals with 3,500 beds, and dozens of outpatient health clinics for treating a population that develops more radiation-related illnesses each day. In many places, they provided electricity, water, sewage, heat, natural gas, roads, and transportation systems, but not in all. They just couldn't afford it.

Driving the fourth truck in Den Kindern von Tschernobyl's annual winter convoy, I follow my leader and pull over onto the side of a snow-covered but freshly paved road in one of the newly built settlements. The houses are made of "clean" imported brick, often creamy white, trimmed in bright blue. Old radioactive wooden fences confine what little livestock remains.

Waiting for word to make its way down the convoy explaining why we're stopping here—we're completely out of food parcels, but perhaps we're picking up a wish list for the June convoy—I get down from the high cab to stretch my legs and watch a man pumping water at a newly mechanized village well. In the time it takes him to fill the bucket, one of the masons building the house across the road gathers his courage, leaves his job site, and approaches me. Like all Belarusans, first he makes deep eye contact. Then, he mimes his hunger: raw, chapped fingers in open mouth, hand on stomach. When he sees that I understand, he looks across the road at two companions studying me, their ungloved hands holding trowels motionless in the snow-filled December air. I have to get back in the truck to get my backpack, and I don't want him to go away, so I take him by the shoulders and kiss his rough cheek.

I'm thirty-six nonstop hours from Germany. Driving across winter-barren Poland tomorrow in the coming snowstorm, I'll wish I had snacks to keep me awake. But after ten days of moments like this I'm so ashamed of creature comforts, complacency, my ignorance about the plight of these people, that I want him to have whatever is in the truck. He's waiting when I return, and I unload the contents of my backpack on him: apples and oranges, sesame-honey bars tucked into his high coat pockets, cashews into the low ones. With a smile, I balance a wedge of cheese atop the fruit. The cheese makes him cry. He kneels in the slush and kisses my hiking boot.

Across the road, the man collecting water at the well tosses it on the blood-covered snow in his back yard, where he has just finished butchering the town's last pig.

"Could it happen here?" I asked a nuclear engineer in Iowa shortly after September 11, 2001.

"Depends upon what you mean by 'it,'" he said. "We have better containment systems, and our commercial plants don't use graphite to moderate reactors." (The fire that burned for days after the explosion at Chernobyl was fueled partly by the graphite that Soviet RMBK reactors use as insulation.) "It wouldn't be exactly like Chernobyl. But a containment dome, or the lack of graphite, doesn't make a reactor inherently less dangerous. If you mean, would a disaster at an American plant something like the explosion at Chernobyl contaminate as much land, contaminate it with the same kinds of radioactivity—yeah, it could happen here."

"Let's say," I postulated, "that I disconnect the moderating rods from the source of electricity and blow up the back-up generators?"

He looked at me for a quiet moment. "Yeah," he said, "you could make it happen here."

Cherikov is 140 miles from Chernobyl. In similar range of the Duane Arnold Energy Center are Madison, Wisconsin; Rockford-Freeport, Illinois (with a nearby nuclear power station and two reactors of its own to worry about); Rochester, Minnesota, home of the Mayo Clinic; Iowa's capital city, Des Moines, with three hundred thousand residents. And amid them all, this nation's richest, most productive farm lands; the ground that grows the cesium-greedy grains we feed to America's poultry, pork, and beef stock, the corn we turn into sweeteners for pop and processed foods, the soybeans our vegetarians depend on, the grains we bake into cereals in the Quaker Oats factory across town.

Whether they are Belarusan or American, two million people cannot be resettled, I think. At home, I get out an atlas and look at my country. Mentally, I draw 155-mile-radius circles around some of the 104 nuclear reactors sprinkled around the map. I consider the prevailing wind directions and imagine the inhabitants who would be living under those air currents. I wonder how we, the wealthiest nation on the face of the Earth, would ever cope with such a disaster, not why the Belarusans can't.

Recently a letter came from Irene. "We have been informed that now, suddenly, we live on a clean territory," she wrote. "Can you imagine such a thing? We are not paid for radiation anymore, and all government aid stops."

The radiation counter that stood in the middle of Cherikov like some nightmare version of a time and temperature clock disappeared the day after the announcement. Would that the radionuclides buried in the bones and muscles of Irene and Sasha and their children could so easily be removed.

(2004)

Moving Mountains

The struggle for justice in the coalfields of Appalachia

"YOU KNOW I USED TO NOT THINK MUCH OF BAIL BONDSMEN," SAID activist Matt Noerpel as we leaned against a chain-link fence outside the Campbell County Jail on a sticky August night in eastern Tennessee. "I mean, there's a social stigma about them. But we couldn't have done this thing without them." He meant bailing out thirty-four fellow activists who had trespassed, locked down, and otherwise disturbed the peace over the previous three months. "They even give us an Earth First! discount," he added.

"Really?" I was incredulous.

"Yeah, because they know we won't run. Our whole goal is to get arrested."

Noerpel and the others were part of Mountain Justice Summer, a four-month campaign against a radical form of strip mining called mountaintop removal that is ravaging the coalfields of central Appalachia. Early that morning, ten activists had blocked the entrance to the Zeb Mountain mine, one of the largest strip mines in Tennessee. They had been arrested for trespassing, and though their bail had initially been set at $10,000 each, a judge later whittled that down to $18,000 for all ten. The Tennessee Mountain Justice chapter was working the phones to raise 7 percent of that to pay a bonding company.

A steady stream of women passed by us, heading into the jail to retrieve husbands and other embattled males. An older bondsman, wearing an all-out bonding cap, had arrived and was chain-smoking next to Matt and me. "You with those protesters?" he wanted to know. Matt nodded. "Well you sure picked a bad place to get arrested."

"What do you mean?" Matt asked.

"You ever see that movie *Deliverance*? Well that's what all of Campbell County is like. Around here, they never heard of Miranda rights."

Unfortunately, phone calls from the protesters inside the jail were starting to confirm this grim assessment. And when they were finally released around midnight—drained and dazed—we got the whole story.

At three thirty that morning, around twenty Mountain Justice activists had parked an old station wagon across the haul road that leads to a large strip mine on top of Zeb Mountain. They removed its wheels and Sarah Shapero chained herself to the car with her arms stretched through PVC tubes and lock boxes. Others erected a forty-foot-high wooden tripod, and Ian Burton climbed to the top of it, where he wedged himself into a hammock, locked his wrists to the beams, and waited. An hour later, a security guard appeared and called for reinforcements. Another hour passed before five National Coal vehicles arrived on the scene. One irate driver sped toward the blockade, slamming on his brakes two feet from Shapero. Then he backed up and did it again. And again.

"He had this wild-eyed, I'll-never-be-held-accountable look to him," said activist Hilary Hosta, who by that point was on her cell phone, pleading with the police to come and restore some order.

When members of the Campbell County Police Department did arrive, they arrested all of the protesters who had gathered around Shapero to protect her from the charging truck. Then they towed the station wagon out of the road with Shapero still chained to it, causing heavy bruising up and down her arms. Meanwhile, the guard who had charged Shapero turned his attention to the tripod. He and several other National Coal employees began to pull all three beams apart at once. When protester Daniel Lee tried to stop them, the ringleader started kicking Lee in the stomach while the police watched. Some, the protesters said, were laughing.

Ian Burton, the young man in the hammock, crashed to the ground. One of the beams crushed his knee. "The cops did not once tell them to back off or stop what they were doing," he said outside the jail. "I was just lucky I didn't land on my head."

The protesters had not imagined things turning out like this. They had hoped to shut down the Zeb Mountain site for a day. And they had hoped that National Coal would respect, if not their intentions, at least the physical presence of their bodies. "I was expecting some aggression," said twenty-one-year-old Lisa Smith, who was taking part in a direct action for the first time. "But I really did believe that they would have some concern for whether we lived or died. They did not care. And realizing that was frightening."

Not since the glaciers pushed toward these ridgelines a million years ago have the Appalachian Mountains been as threatened as they are now. But mountaintop removal has not seen much press beyond the region; the media research group Project Censored recently listed it as one of the top ten underreported stories in America. The problem, in many ways, is one of perspective. From interstates and lowlands, where most communities are clustered, one simply doesn't see what is happening up there. Only from the air can you fully grasp the magnitude of the devastation. If you were to board, say, a small prop plane at Zeb Mountain, Tennessee, and follow the spine of the Appalachian Mountains up through Kentucky, Virginia, and West Virginia, you would be struck not by the beauty of a densely forested range older than the Himalayas, but rather by inescapable images of ecological violence. Near Pine Mountain, Kentucky, you'd see an unfolding series of staggered green hills quickly give way to a wide expanse of gray plateaus pocked with dark craters and huge black ponds filled with a toxic by-product called coal slurry. It appears as if a meteor shower had pummeled these mountains. The desolation stretches like a long scar up the Kentucky-Virginia line, before eating its way across southern West Virginia. The Environmental Protection Agency estimates that 7 percent of these mountains have been lost, which amounts to almost 320,000 acres, and if current mountaintop mining practices continue, 1.4 million acres—an area the size of Delaware—will be leveled by the end of the decade.

Central Appalachia provides much of the country's coal, second only to Wyoming's Powder River Basin. In the United States, one hundred tons of coal are extracted every two seconds. Around 70 percent of that coal comes from strip mines, and over the last twenty years, an increasing amount comes from mountaintop removal sites. In the name of expedience, coal companies have turned from excavation to simply blasting away the tops of the mountains. To achieve this, they use the same mixture of ammonium nitrate and diesel fuel that Timothy McVeigh employed to level the Murrow Building in Oklahoma City—except each detonation is ten times as powerful, and thousands of blasts go off each day across central Appalachia. Hundreds of feet of forest, topsoil, and sandstone—the coal industry calls all of this "overburden"—are unearthed so bulldozers and front-end loaders can more easily extract the thin seams of rich, bituminous coal that stretch in horizontal layers throughout these mountains. Almost everything that isn't coal is pushed down into the valleys below. As a result, 6,700 "valley fills" covering almost 84,000 acres were approved in central Appalachia between 1985 and 2001. The Environmental Protection Agency estimates that over 700 miles of healthy streams have been completely buried by mountaintop removal and thousands more have been damaged. Where there once flowed a highly braided system of headwater streams, now a vast circuitry of haul roads winds through the rubble. From the air, it looks like someone had tried to plot a highway system on the moon.

Serious coal mining has been going on in Appalachia since the turn of the twentieth century. Back then, men would disappear underground each morning with only a pick and a shovel. The narrator of the famous folk song "Sixteen Tons" was boasting about the amount of coal he could load in one day with his primitive tools, but a modern front-end loader can scoop up sixteen tons from a strip mine in a matter of minutes. Ever since World War II veterans climbed down from tanks and up onto bulldozers, the extractive industries in America have grown more mechanized and more destructive. In Kentucky, coal-related employment has dropped 60 percent in the last fifteen years; it takes very few men to run a strip mine operation, with giant machines doing most of the clear-cutting, excavating, loading, and bulldozing of rubble. And all strip mining—from the most basic truck mine to mountaintop removal—results in deforestation, flooding, mudslides, and the fouling of headwater streams.

That such reckless resource extraction could happen anywhere is alarming; that it is taking place in the most diverse ecosystem of North America only compounds the tragedy. The mixed mesophytic forest of central Appalachia is home to over seventy tree species and two hundred fifty birds. But two-thirds of all songbirds are now in decline across eastern Kentucky's Cumberland Plateau. Mountaintop removal has turned once contiguous forests into small, wooded islands that can no longer support many of their former inhabitants, from flying squirrels to bears and bobcats. Sedimentation from the valley fills, along with heavy metals leaching down from mine sites, have destroyed nearly all species of macroinvertebrates that live in headwater streams and provide key nutrients to downstream species.

Alongside this ecological devastation, an Eastern Kentucky University study found that children in Letcher County, Kentucky, suffer from an alarmingly high rate of nausea, diarrhea, vomiting, and shortness of breath—symptoms of something called blue baby syndrome—that can all be traced back to sedimentation and dissolved minerals that have drained from mine sites into nearby streams. Long-term effects may include liver, kidney, and spleen failure, bone damage, and cancers of the digestive track. Erica Urias, who lives on Island Creek in Grapevine, Kentucky, told me she has to bathe her two-year-old daughter in contaminated water because of the mining around her home. In McRoberts, Kentucky, the problem is flooding. In 1998, Tampa Energy Company (TECO) started blasting along the ridgetops above McRoberts. Homes shook and foundations cracked. Then TECO sheared off all of the vegetation at the head of Chopping Block Hollow and replaced it with the compacted rubble of a valley fill. In a region prone to flash floods, nothing was left to hold back the rain; this once forested watershed had been turned into an enormous funnel. In 2002, three so-called hundred-year floods happened in ten days. Between the blasting and the flooding, the people of McRoberts have been nearly flushed out of their homes.

Consider the story of Debra and Granville Burke. First the blasting above their house wrecked its foundation. Then the floods came. Four times, they wiped out the Burkes' garden, which the family depended on to get through the winter. Finally, on Christmas morning 2002, Debra Burke took her life. In a letter published in a local paper, her husband wrote: "She left eight letters describing how she loved us all but that our burdens were just getting too much to bear. She had begged for TECO to at least replace our garden, but they just turned their back on her. I look back now and think of all the things I wish I had done differently so that she might still be with us, but mostly I wish that TECO had never started mining above our home."

In the language of economics, Debra Burke's death was an externality—a cost that simply isn't factored into the price Americans pay for coal. And that is precisely the problem. Last year, American power plants burned over a billion tons of coal, accounting for over 50 percent of this country's electricity use. In Kentucky, where I live, 80 percent of the harvested coal is sold and shipped to twenty-two other states as far away as Arizona, Michigan, and Florida. Yet it is the people of Appalachia who pay the highest price for the rest of the country's cheap energy—through contaminated water, flooding, cracked foundations and wells, bronchial problems related to breathing coal dust, and roads that have been torn up and turned deadly by speeding coal trucks. Why should large cities like Phoenix and Detroit get the coal but be held accountable for none of the environmental consequences of its extraction? And why is a Tampa-based energy company—or Peabody Coal in St. Louis, or Massey Energy in Richmond, Virginia—allowed to destroy communities throughout Appalachia? As my friend and teacher the late Guy Davenport once wrote, "Distance negates responsibility."

The Mountain Justice Summer activists wanted to bring some responsibility back to the mountains and to mining. Seizing on Mississippi Freedom Summer as a model for their campaign, they were looking to instigate the same tensions that forced a segregated Birmingham into the national headlines in 1963 and exposed for the nation the vicious tactics of southern lawmen like Birmingham public safety commissioner Bull Connor. And, like the early civil rights activists, they were trying to turn regional injustices into a national crisis.

The specific injustice that had drawn the Mountain Justice folks together was the violent death of three-year-old Jeremy Davidson. At two thirty in the morning on August 30, 2004, a bulldozer, operating without a permit above the Davidsons's home, dislodged a thousand-pound boulder from a mountaintop removal site in the town of Appalachia, Virginia. The boulder rolled two hundred feet down the mountain before it crushed to death the sleeping child.

A month later, activists from West Virginia, Virginia, Kentucky, and Tennessee gathered in the child's hometown to protest the environmental and social destruction that is spreading across the region. Davidson's death is hardly an isolated incident. In West Virginia, fourteen people drowned in the last three years because of floods and mudslides caused by mountaintop removal, and in Kentucky, fifty people have been killed and over five hundred injured in the last five years by coal trucks, almost all of which were illegally overloaded.

After the rally in Appalachia, Sue Daniels, a biology professor from West Virginia, took some of the out-of-state activists to see a large mountaintop removal site that straddled the Virginia-Kentucky border. One was Erin McKelvy, a young woman who drives a rusting Mercedes powered by used vegetable oil. "We were all chipping away at our own little regions fighting mountaintop removal," McKelvy told me. "But I think standing up there, everybody sharing Sue's binoculars, looking out at the site, it really hit us all that we had to do something big." It was then that Daniels suggested something along the lines of Mississippi Freedom Summer or Redwood Summer, a 1990 campaign against corporate logging. Quickly, a group of core organizers from four states came up with a platform and a plan that had as its centerpiece a series of direct, nonviolent actions to be carried out from May through August. Forty-one years after Mississippi— and during the same summer that Edgar Ray Killen was finally convicted of murdering three civil rights workers there—Mountain Justice Summer was born.

On the third of July, I set out to meet up with some of the Mountain Justice Summer activists. I drove across ten thousand acres of boulder-strewn wasteland that used to be Kayford Mountain, West Virginia—one of the most hideous mountaintop removal sites I've seen. But right in the middle of the destruction, rising like a last gasp, is a small knoll of untouched forest. Larry Gibson's family has lived on Kayford Mountain for two hundred years. And most of his relatives are buried in the family cemetery, where almost every day Gibson has to clear away debris known as "flyrock" from the nearby blasting.

Last year, Kenneth Cane, the great-grandson of Crazy Horse, came to this cemetery. Surrounded by Gibson and his kin, Cane led a prayer vigil.

Then he turned to Gibson, put a hand on his shoulder, and said, "How does it feel to lose your land?"

"What was I going to say to him?" Gibson asked me, sitting at the kitchen table of his small, two-room cabin beneath a single, solar-powered fluorescent bulb. Certainly an Oglala Lakota heir would know something about having mountains stolen away by men in search of valuable minerals.

After a long pause, Gibson said, "For sixteen years people have been coming to my place, and here I am telling them what they don't see. I've never had so many people come to see what they don't see."

One of the people who came to see the desolation was Kentuckian Dave Cooper. At that time, he was working at a 3M factory, making Post-it notes. "I realized then how pointless it was," Cooper said of his job. So he quit, and started traveling nonstop on what has become known as The Mountaintop Removal Road Show, educating large and small crowds about this rapacious form of mining.

The view from Kayford Mountain has had that transformative effect on a lot of people. Last year, 756 people from twenty countries signed a large legal pad that functions as Gibson's guest book. Many went on to become part of the Mountain Justice Summer movement, for which Gibson has been both a mentor and a guiding force.

The day I visited, he was holding his annual family reunion, and since Gibson defines family as anyone who has joined the fight against mountaintop removal, the place was filled with older mountain people and younger urban activists. There were rebel flag license plates beside bumper stickers that read: I WENT TO THE MOUNTAINTOP AND IT WASN'T THERE. Gibson had lined up speakers and singers to perform throughout the day, and from time to time, he would take to the stage and deliver an impromptu speech.

A short, muscular man, Gibson is easily given to emotion when he starts talking about his home place—both what remains of it and what has been destroyed. And despite his stature, he is easy to spot in a crowd because of the brightly colored T-shirts he constantly wears, all of which read:

> WE ARE THE KEEPER OF THE MOUNTAINS
> LOVE THEM OR LEAVE THEM,
> JUST DON'T DESTROY THEM

Forty seams of coal lie beneath his fifty acres. Gibson could be a millionaire many times over, but because he refuses to sell, he has been shot at and run off his own road. One of his dogs was shot and another hanged. A month after my visit, someone sabotaged his solar panels. In 2000 Gibson walked out onto his porch one day to find two men dressed in camouflage, approaching with gas cans. They backed away and drove off, but not before they set fire to an empty cabin that belongs to one of Gibson's cousins. This much at least can be said for the West Virginia coal industry: it has perfected the art of intimidation.

Gibson knows he isn't safe. "This land is worth $450 million," he told me, "so what kind of chances do I have?" But he hasn't backed down. He travels the country telling his story and has been arrested repeatedly for various acts of civil disobedience. When Gibson talks to student groups, he asks them, "What do you hold so dear that you don't have a price on it? And when somebody comes to take it, what will you do? For me, it's this mountain and the memories I had here as a kid. It was a hard life, but here I was equal to everybody. I didn't know I was poor until I went to the city and people told me I was. Here I was rich."

Just down the mountain from Larry Gibson's home, in the town of Rock Creek, stands the Marsh Fork Elementary School. Back in 2004, Ed Wiley, a forty-seven-year-old West Virginian who spent years working on strip mines, was called by the school to come pick up his granddaughter Kayla because she was sick. "She had a real bad color to her," Wiley told me. The next day the school called again because Kayla was ill, and the day after that. Wiley started flipping through the sign-out book and found that fifteen to twenty students went home sick every day because of asthma problems, severe headaches, blisters in their mouths, constant runny noses, and nausea. In May 2005, when Mountain Justice volunteers started going door-to-door in an effort to identify citizens' concerns and possibly locate cancer clusters, West Virginia activist Bo Webb found that 80 percent of parents said their children came home from school with a variety of illnesses. The school, a small brick building, sits almost directly beneath a Massey Energy subsidiary's processing plant where coal is washed and stored. Coal dust settles like pollen over the playground. Nearly three billion gallons of coal slurry, which contains extremely high levels of mercury, cadmium, and nickel, are stored behind a 385-foot-high earthen dam right above the school.

In 1972, a similar coal impoundment dam collapsed at Buffalo Creek, West Virginia, killing 125 people. Two hundred and eighty children attend the Marsh Fork Elementary School. It is unnerving to imagine what damage a minor earthquake, a heavy flash flood, or a structural failure might do to this small community. And according to documents that longtime activist Judy Bonds obtained under the Freedom of Information Act, the pond is leaking into the creek and groundwater around the school. Students often cannot drink from the water fountains. And when they return from recess, their tennis shoes are covered with black coal dust.

Massey responded to complaints about the plant by applying for a permit to enlarge it, with a new silo to be built even closer to the school. It was this callousness that led to the first major Mountain Justice direct action on the last day of May. About a hundred out-of-state activists who had just finished a week-long training course at the Appalachian Folklife Center in Pipestem, West Virginia, where they participated in workshops on nonviolence, water-testing, and tree-sitting, drove straight to Marsh Fork Elementary School. Alongside another hundred local citizens, they gathered in the school auditorium and sang Woody Guthrie's "This Land Is Your Land" and Florence Reece's "Which Side Are You On?" Then they marched next door to the processing plant.

Inez Gallimore, an eighty-two-year-old woman whose granddaughter attended the elementary school, walked up to the security guard and asked for the plant superintendent to come down and accept a copy of the group's demands that Massey shut down the plant. When the superintendent refused, Gallimore sat down in the middle of the road, blocking trucks from entering or leaving the facility. When police came to arrest her, they had to help Gallimore to her feet, but not before TV cameras recorded her calling Massey Energy a "terrorist organization."

Three other protesters took the woman's place and were arrested. Three more followed. In the end, sixteen people were taken into police custody. Some were local people; others came from as far away as California. "You had urban freaks hanging out with rural America. That's what the whole protest was like," said Tennessee activist john johnson, who doesn't capitalize the first letters of his name "because I don't believe in capitalism." Indeed, if one were casting a film and needed a Russian anarchist, johnson would be the man. Wearing camo pants, a cavalry-style black hat, and a Prince Kropotkin beard, he cuts an impressive figure. But like many of the Mountain Justice people, he doesn't exactly blend in with rural Appalachia. All summer long, letters appeared in the *Charleston Gazette* demanding that the "outsiders" leave West Virginia alone. However, just as many letter-writers, like Kathryn Stone of Charleston, supported the "out-of-staters who are learning an early lesson in how power operates with impunity" in the coalfields of Appalachia.

Whatever the outsider status of Mountain Justice, all of the urban activists I talked with shared johnson's respect for the culture of the mountains. There was no patronizing solicitousness and certainly none of the condescension that outsiders have historically shown mountain people. "We brought a bunch of activists down here to build relationships with people in the coalfields, people who are still connected to the land," johnson said. "That's something that has been lost in this country." And Dave Cooper told me, "I don't think we can stop mountaintop removal just with the people in Tennessee, Kentucky, and West Virginia. We need everybody. It's got to be people from California and Washington, and I don't care what they look like."

In the end, the media coverage at the Marsh Fork rally prompted West Virginia governor Joe Manchin to promise he would put together an investigative team to look into the citizens' concerns. However, seven days after that promise, on June 30, Massey received its permit to expand the plant.

Three days later, when I got to Kayford Mountain, the mood was both defiant and discouraged. "It's easy to get overwhelmed by the power of the coal companies," admitted Jeff Winder, a Mountain Justice organizer from Virginia who had just performed a song he had written about Jeremy Davidson. "But the alternative is to do nothing and let them go unchecked."

The history of resource exploitation in Appalachia, like the history of racial oppression in the South, follows a sinister logic—keep people poor and scared so that they remain powerless. In the nineteenth century, mountain families were actually doing fairly well farming rich bottomlands. But populations grew, farms were subdivided, and then northern coal and steel companies started buying up much of the land, hungry for the resources that lay below. By the time the railroads reached headwater hollows like McRoberts, Kentucky, men had little choice but to sell their labor cheaply, live in company towns, and shop in overpriced company stores. "Though he might revert on occasion to his ancestral agriculture," wrote coalfield historian Harry Caudill, "he would never again free himself from dependence upon his new overlords." It was in a very real sense that the miner narrating "Sixteen Tons" felt that he owed his soul to the company store.

Like southern blacks, miners often lived in fear of crooked cops—deputy sheriffs that they called "gun thugs." Most coal states have one county that has earned the designation "bloody." In Kentucky, that distinction goes to Bloody Harlan County, where company thugs brutalized pro-union miners throughout the '30s in an effort to prevent collective bargaining. The Harlan County Coal Operators Association paid the salaries of all the sheriff's 164 armed deputies. Not until a deputy sheriff fired into the home of union representative Marshall Musick, killing his teenage son, did the governor step in to stop the mayhem. And though Harlan County miners were finally allowed to organize, their plight didn't improve much. As in nearly every county across central Appalachia, King Coal had gained control of the economy, the local government, and the land.

In the decades that followed, less obvious tactics kept Harlan County one of the poorest places in Appalachia. Activist Teri Blanton, whose father and brother were Harlan County miners, has spent many years trying to understand the patterns of oppression that hold the Harlan County high school graduation rate at 59 percent and the median household income at $18,665. "We were fueling the whole United States with coal," she said of the last hundred years in eastern Kentucky. "And yet our pay was lousy, our education was lousy, and they destroyed our environment. As long as you have a polluted community, no other industry is going to locate there. Did they keep us uneducated because it was easier to control us then? Did they keep other industries out because then they can keep our wages low? Was it all by design?" That question, I believe, deserves serious consideration. But whether one detects motive or not, this much is clear—forty-one years after Lyndon Johnson stood on a miner's porch in adjacent Martin County and announced his War on Poverty, the poverty rate in central and southern Appalachia stands at 30 percent, right where it did in 1964. What's more, maps generated by the Appalachian Regional Commission show that the poorest counties—those colored deep red for "distressed"—are those that have seen the most severe strip mining and the most intense mountaintop removal.

There is a galling irony in the fact that the Fourteenth Amendment, which was designed to protect the civil liberties of recently freed African slaves, was later interpreted in such a way as to give corporations like Massey all of the rights of "legal persons," while requiring little of the accountability that we expect of individuals. Because coal companies are not individuals, they often operate without the moral compass that would prevent a person from contaminating a neighbor's well, poisoning the town's drinking water, or covering the local school with coal dust. This situation is compounded by federal officials who often appear more loyal to corporations than to citizens. Consider the case of Jack Spadaro, a whistle-blower who was forced out of his job at the U.S. Department of Labor's Mine Safety and Health Administration (MSHA) precisely because he tried to do his job—protecting the public from mining disasters.

When the Buffalo Creek dam in West Virginia broke in 1972, Spadaro, a young mining engineer at the time, was brought in to investigate. He found that the flood could have been prevented by better dam construction, and he spent the next thirty years of his career at MSHA investigating impoundment dams. So when a 300-million-gallon slurry pond collapsed in Martin County, Kentucky, in 2000, causing one of the worst environmental disasters this side of the Mississippi, Spadaro was again named to the investigating team. What he found was that Massey had known for ten years that the pond was going to break. Spadaro wanted to charge Massey with criminal negligence. There was only one problem. Elaine Chao, Spadaro's boss at the Department of Labor, is also Kentucky Republican Senator Mitch McConnell's wife, and it is McConnell, more than anyone else in the Senate, who advocates that corporations are persons that, as such, can contribute as much money as they want to electoral campaigns. It turns out that Massey had donated $100,000 to a campaign committee headed by McConnell. Not surprisingly, Spadaro got nowhere with his charges. Instead, someone changed the lock on his office door and he was placed on administrative leave. After lawsuits and countersuits, Spadaro retired from MSHA, rather than accept a transfer far from his family in West Virginia.

Spadaro's story seems to validate what many coalfield residents have been contending for years—that the very agencies that should be regulating corporations are instead ignoring the law, breaking the law, and at times even rewriting the law in their favor, as when deputy secretary of the Department of the Interior and former coal lobbyist Stephen Griles instructed his staff to rewrite a key provision of the Clean Water Act to reclassify all waste associated with strip mining as merely benign "fill material." A federal judge rejected that change, arguing that "only the United States Congress can rewrite the Act to allow fills with no purpose or use but the deposit of waste," but the change was upheld in 2003 by the U.S. Fourth Circuit Court—on which sat John Roberts, the recently appointed chief justice of the Supreme Court.

What is a person—a real person—to do in the face of such a powerful collusion of money, law, and politics? Ed Wiley decided to take his case straight to the steps of the West Virginia capitol. On Tuesday morning, July 5, Wiley, a slim, soft-spoken man, unfolded a lawn chair in front of the capitol in Charleston and refused to leave until Governor Joe Manchin agreed to meet with him. As state workers filed up the steps, Wiley showed them a poster of an aerial view of the Massey processing plant and the huge sludge pond that threatened his granddaughter's elementary school. After a few hours, one of the governor's lawyers invited Wiley inside. In his office, Manchin promised Wiley that he would meet with state education officials the following day to discuss a way to move the school, and would meet with Rock Creek residents on Thursday. That's what Wiley wanted to hear. There was just one more thing. The governor had to repeat those promises to the news cameras waiting outside, or Wiley would stay put. So a reluctant Manchin joined his intrepid constituent for a press conference on the capitol porch. By noon, Wiley's work was done.

Three days later, I was standing in Richmond, Virginia's Monroe Park, next to a pretty girl with pierced lips and colorful yarn braided into her blond hair. On a flag made from a bedsheet, she had spray-painted the circle-A anarchy sign, then added orange flower petals all around it. The flag brushed across my face as we and about two hundred others listened to fiery speeches condemning mountaintop removal. On the same day that the G-8 summit protests were held in Scotland, these Mountain Justice activists were preparing to march ten blocks to the headquarters of Massey Energy to demand the closure of the prep plant behind Marsh Fork Elementary School.

Erin McKelvy had run an electrical cord from her vegetable oil–burning Mercedes to a small PA system. No fossil fuel would power this event. Short, gray-haired Judy Bonds stepped to the mike and told the crowd of mostly young, heavily tattooed, black-clad protesters, "I'm honored to be here with you. You're the only ones so far that really care about us hillbillies. We're an endangered species, we hillbillies. Massey Energy is terrorizing us in Appalachia. Little old ladies in their seventies can't even sit on their porches. They have to cut their grass wearing respirators. That's how these people have to live. The coal companies are the real terrorists in America. And we're going to expose them for the murdering, lying thieves that they are."

With that, the marchers started down Franklin Avenue, behind a long banner stretching across the street that read: INDUSTRIAL CAPITALISM KILLS OUR LAND AND PEOPLE. In front of the sign, Larry Gibson waved his arms like a conductor, slowly leading a throng he had spent sixteen years trying to muster. A band of drummers crowded together in the middle of the pack, beating out a furious tempo on spray-painted plastic buckets. Behind them loomed a large papier-mâché icon of King Coal. Someone with a megaphone shouted, "King Coal," then everyone else replied, "Off with his head!" over and over. About ten young women raced up and down the sidewalks, handing leaflets to everyone who had come out of the air conditioning to see what all the noise was about. It was really an impressive sight—all of these committed people dancing, shouting, waving signs, having some righteous fun. It's too bad, I thought, that this fight couldn't be decided with a dance contest. These guys would win hands down.

The protesters marched on past blooming crepe myrtle trees and exclusive clubs. Then they hung a right, and suddenly we were all standing in front of a granite-and-concrete monolith that had been cordoned off with yellow tape. Three policemen stood stoically in front of the four-story Massey Building. Employees were leaning out their windows, taking pictures of the marchers with their cell phones and offering them the inevitable advice to "get a job."

Down in the street, everyone was shouting, "Shame, shame, shame!" and "Come on down . . . Blankenship." Don Blankenship is the CEO of Massey, a man that many feel has dubious access to the Bush administration. Records show that from 2000 to 2004, whenever MSHA assistant secretary David Lauriski weakened a mine safety standard, it usually followed a meeting with Blankenship.

The stated goal of the Richmond march was to get Blankenship to personally accept Mountain Justice's demand that Massey shut down the prep plant next to the Marsh Fork Elementary School. Of course, everyone knew that wasn't going to happen. So several protesters lay down on the sidewalk, their arms locked inside PVC tubing covered with green papiermâché mountains, and waited to be arrested. The protesters lay in the heat for over an hour, until around four P.M., when word came down from an office worker that all of the Massey executives had left the building, using the side exit of their underground parking garage.

"We've shut down the operation of Massey coal company for a day!" Jeff Winder announced triumphantly through a megaphone. It was a minor victory, but in truth, everyone in the street had just about run out of chants and water. Bonds and Gibson soon convinced the crowd that it was time to head back to Monroe Park, that a front-page picture of nonviolent marchers would serve their cause better than one of the protesters tangling with riot police. So the young activists unlocked their arms and gathered up their props. There would be other days to get arrested.

A much larger victory came seven days later when, acting on information from *Charleston Gazette* reporter Ken Ward Jr., West Virginia's Department of Environmental Protection found that Massey had altered the permit maps of the processing plant beside the Marsh Fork School. After covering the Mountain Justice rally there in June, Ward had pulled the maps and found that Massey was no longer operating three hundred feet from a school as required by law. Engineers had redrawn one boundary line seventy-five feet closer to the school, right where Massey had just received the June 30 permit to build a new 168-foot-high coal storage silo. The DEP rescinded the new permit and ordered Massey to demolish work that had already begun on the silo's foundation.

"I don't think that's ever happened before," john johnson said of the revoked permit. "We brought massive citizen pressure to bear in a state that is bought and sold by the coal industry." As johnson, Dave Cooper, and Judy Bonds all told me, it was the persistence of the protesters that forced state regulators to act. Mountain Justice Summer was too big and too loud to be ignored.

On April 9, 1963, snarling police dogs pinned a black protester to the ground on a Birmingham, Alabama, street. The *New York Times* was there to report it. Martin Luther King Jr. and the Southern Christian Leadership Conference were ecstatic. "We've got a movement, we've got a movement!" one member exclaimed. "They brought out the dogs." Without the arrests in Birmingham, and the press that followed, John Kennedy would not have pushed for the Civil Rights Act, and without daily attempts to register black voters in Selma, and the violence that followed, Lyndon Johnson would have dragged his feet for years on the Voting Rights Act. King and the SCLC knew they needed numbers and they needed confrontation. They needed Bull Connor's dogs and Selma sheriff James Clark's police batons coming down on the heads of older African Americans. They needed to call out, for all to see, the men who enforced brutal oppression every day in the South.

In their own way, Mountain Justice activists worked hard to expose the injustice spreading across the coalfields of Appalachia. Through nonviolent actions and demonstrations, they attempted to show the nation how coal companies break the law with a pathological consistency and operate with little regard for the human consequences of their actions. Unfortunately, they never attracted the national attention that Mississippi Freedom Summer did. On that stage, Mountain Justice Summer couldn't compete with high gas prices and a foreign war, even though it is precisely that war over oil that is driving coal demands higher and laying mountains lower faster. That plus the fact that U.S. energy consumption increased 42 percent over the last thirty years. Urban affluence and this country's short-sighted energy policy are making Appalachia a poorer place—poorer in beauty, poorer in health, poorer in resources, and poorer in spirit.

"This wouldn't go on in New England," Jack Spadaro told me last July, up at Larry Gibson's place. It wouldn't go on in California, nor Florida, nor along the East Coast. After the '60s, America and the mainstream media seemed to lose interest in the problems of Appalachia. Though the Martin County slurry pond disaster was twenty times larger than the *Exxon Valdez* spill, the *New York Times* ignored it for months. But the seeming invisibility of the people in Appalachia does not make their plight any less real.

That the civil rights movement happened so recently in our country's history can seem dumbfounding, but not to the people who still live in the shadow of oppression. Those who live in the path of the coal industry— beneath sheared-off mountains, amid unnatural, treeless landscapes, drinking poisoned water and breathing dirty air—are fighting their own civil rights battle. And, as in the past, justice may be slow coming to the mountains of Appalachia. But justice delayed could mean the ruin of a place that has sacrificed much for this nation, and has received next to nothing in return.

(2006)

CHARLES WOHLFORTH

On Thin Ice

Climate change is a matter of life and death for Iñupiaq whaling communities

THE BRINK OF THE SHOREFAST SEA ICE CUT THE WATER LIKE THE edge of a swimming pool. A white canvas tent, several snowmachines and big wooden sleds, and a sealskin *umiaq* whale boat waited like poolside furniture on the blue-white surface of the ice. Gentle puffs rippled the open water a foot or two below, except near the edge, where a fragile skin of new ice stilled the surface. Sun in the north reached from the far side of the lead, backlighting the water and highlighting the imperfections in this clear, newborn ice with a contrast of yellow orange and royal blue. It was after midnight on May 6, 2002, three miles offshore from the NAPA auto parts store in Barrow, Alaska.

A hushed voice urged me on toward the edge. "Come on, there's a fox. They follow the polar bears."

The fox ran past the camp, beyond the ice edge, danced as it ran upon that new skin of ice floating on the indigo water. An hour or two earlier there had been no ice there at all and now it looked no thicker than a crust of bread. The fox used tiny, rapid steps. Its feet disappeared in motion. Its back arched high and its tail pulled up tall, as if strings were helping suspend it on that insubstantial film of hardened water. Somehow it knew how much weight a brand new sheen of ice could hold, and knew how to calibrate each step within that limit. The Iñupiaq whalers of Oliver Leavitt's crew watched and muttered with admiration as the fox pranced out of sight. All were experienced hunters, even the younger ones, but they were impressed by this skill. This animal knew something valuable, something they would like to know, something that could help them survive.

As a non-Native (but a lifelong Alaskan), I still felt uncertain standing on ice miles out on the ocean. I hadn't expected research on climate change to bring me to a whaling camp. But having set out to follow scientists studying dramatic warming in the Arctic, I discovered that those who knew this world best were the Iñupiat. A thousand years of hunting the bowhead whale from floating ice had instilled in them both a profound understanding of this environment and a special ability to perceive its changes.

The ice was bad that year. It had been bad for a decade and seemed to grow steadily worse. The shore ice should form in the fall as bergs left over from the previous year float near the beach and are sewn together by new ice that freezes in the cooling temperatures. These big bergs are chunks of the previous year's ice pack that never melted over the summer. They usually form out of old pressure ridges, mountains of ice built by the collisions of huge ice sheets, becoming fresh-water ice as warm spring temperatures drain pockets of brine trapped inside. The surface becomes rounded and smooth and the ice becomes dense, hard, and brittle. The Iñupiat call it *piqaluyak,* or glacier ice. Under the surface whiteness it glows iridescent blue. Iñupiaq travelers use the fresh water for making tea far from home.

Whalers seek out multiyear ice because it provides a strong platform for pulling up whales and it anchors the shorefast ice in place with its great mass. In the winter of 2001–2002, however, as for several years prior, little multiyear ice appeared at Barrow. The shore ice didn't form as solidly as it should, and it lacked the big, solid anchors that multiyear ice, or even new ice with large pressure ridges, would have provided. And on March 18, something strange and unsettling had happened. The ice went out, leaving open water right up to the beach in front of Oliver Leavitt's house. No one could remember the ice going out that early. Normally, it goes out in July. A dozen seal hunters floated out to sea on the ice. Search and Rescue helicopters went out to find them and bring them home. Some didn't know they were floating off into the Arctic Ocean until the helicopter showed up. You can't tell you're moving when your whole world starts to drift away.

Later, ice returned and refroze to the shore, but it wasn't sturdy ice and it still lacked good anchors. As whaling season began, a strong west wind pushed the ice against the shore for several days, then a strong east wind tested it and cleared away some of the junk ice. Oliver's theory now was that these events had cemented the ice adequately for safe whaling. He had chosen a flat area of ice with a color and height above the water that told him it was strong enough to pull up a whale. But every so often he sent someone to look at the watery crack that was a little behind us, or to check the dark ice—weak, brand new ice—that lay a mile or two back between us and dry land.

Morning came (not dawn, for the sun had rolled lazily along the northern horizon all night instead of setting) and Oliver sat, as he had since the previous day, on a long wooden sled next to his thermos and VHF marine radio, silently gazing on the water and the ice chunks and bergs drifting by slowly on the calm surface. Besides the danger of breaking off, another threat occupied his mind: a big mass of ice we could see across the lead, which was moving very slowly by toward the southwest, but also seemed to be getting closer at an imperceptible pace. Oliver said, "That's the dangerous ice. If people start noticing it's coming in we'll be out of here in five minutes flat."

The momentum behind an ice floe, even if moving only slowly, is stupendous; when it hits the unmoving shore ice, the collision can be like an immense, mountain-building earthquake, a terrifying event called an *ivu*. Oliver was young at the time of the big ivu in 1957, but he remembered how the ice went crazy, with big multiyear floes standing up on end and shattering far from the edge, forcing the crews to scramble for their lives over miles of cracking, piling ice, leaving camps, boats, and dog teams behind—their entire means of supporting their families. He had told such cautionary stories to the younger members of his crew, including his harpooner son, Billy Jens Leavitt.

In traditional spring whaling the umiaq perches on the ice edge. If a whale surfaces nearby, the crew launches as quickly and quietly as possible and paddles to the whale or to a spot where the captain expects the whale to resurface. For the harpooner to hit the whale's vulnerable spot, just behind the skull, the captain has to maneuver the boat right onto the whale's back or within touching distance alongside. The whale can move much faster than a boat driven by canoe paddles, so most of whaling is waiting quietly for a whale to come close enough to launch. That morning we saw only one whale, a far-off black back rolling across the surface, and heard another, a roaring blowhole exhalation from somewhere we could not see. Normally at this time of year, a crew would be seeing whales every few minutes. Crews farther down the lead were paddling in search of one, thinking the migration might be passing by on the other side of big ice across the lead.

Iñupiaq chatter on the marine VHF radio began to flow with comments from nervous captains up and down the lead. They saw the big pressure ridges across the open water growing noticeably closer. Oliver uttered a few words of Iñupiaq on the radio and the discussion stopped. "You got to talk to them quick before they scare themselves," he said. Each captain's experience and expertise were well known, an important factor in how whalers evaluated conditions and safety. Oliver Leavitt's name carried unquestioned authority.

The radio box was a sturdy plywood case with a car battery and a tall boat antenna. Each camp could hear its "base," usually the captain's home, and other camps spread out along twenty miles of the lead. Channel 72 was for whaling and channel 68 for routine in-town communication. VHF sets seemed always close at hand near kitchen tables and under the dash of pickup trucks. In the morning people said, "Good morning, good morning," to announce they were on the air, and the NAPA auto parts store—which carried harpoon parts and other whaling supplies—let everyone know when they were open for business. In the evening, each person said "Good night" when turning off the radio, and the children and grandchildren of whalers said good night to their fathers and grandfathers out in camp—sweet broadcasts of kisses and love names that the whole town could hear. During times of peril, the VHF allowed whalers to act almost as one, sharing observations about ice and water movement and dynamics from many perspectives.

The whalers handled these technical conversations in Iñupiaq, even though many younger people are not fluent. Some handy words don't exist in English, such as *mauragaq,* to cross open water by jumping from one piece of ice to the next, or *uisauniq,* an ice floe that breaks off with people on it. But more important, and untranslatable, are the meanings derived from the very structure of Iñupiaq, a language developed to deal with situations in a moving landscape without landmarks or any visible distinction between ocean and shore. In the absence of physical reference points, the speaker can position objects and events using movement, the relative locations of speaker and listener, and the directional orientation of the ocean and rivers. For example, *pigna* indicates that the thing you are talking about is above, has a length less than three times its width, is visible and stationary, and stands at equal distance between speaker and listeners. *Pagna* contains all the same information, except that the subject's length is more than three times its width. Iñupiaq word endings also aid coordination by allowing speakers to pass on oral information without losing nuances about the quality of the knowledge and how it was obtained. They cover a gradient roughly ranging from "I saw it myself and it is certain" to "Someone saw it and it might be true." (Contrary to popular belief, however, the Eskimos do not have 100 words for snow.)

As afternoon progressed the sun was bright and unseasonably warm. The ice reflected brilliantly while the deep, dark water swallowed light. The details of the pressure ridge mountains across the lead were clearly visible. The radio grew lively again. Oliver stood and watched the ice across the water intently. Everyone else stood too, waiting for what he would say. Then, calmly, "We better start packing up."

The younger men began by emptying the tent. Oliver worked on disabling the weapons and putting away the radio. Now you could see the ice moving through the water directly toward us. Everyone knew his job without a word, but Oliver said, "Better hurry up, Billy." When speaking to the younger part of the crew, he addressed only Billy Jens, like an officer giving orders to a sergeant. Things not fitting in right, the boys started throwing stuff on the sleds haphazardly. "Better hurry up, Billy," the tone this time a little higher.

Billy Jens had too much to do. I tried to tie down one of the sled loads for him, using half-hitch knots for speed rather than the quick-release knots the Eskimos prefer. The load came loose—I had tied the lashing line to the wrong rope. Billy Jens came around to retie it, but my tight half hitches were tough to untie. The boat was ready to go on the sled. The ice was a hundred feet away and closing fast. Oliver said, "Billy, pick up the boat." Billy was still trying to fix my mistake, without saying a word. I tried to help with the boat, but I didn't know where to grab it. Billy Jens grabbed the gunwale, and we heaved the boat onto the sled and started strapping it down. I could see the crystal-thin rims of ice from each side approaching, with the lead of water almost closed. We needed to escape before a possible ivu could break our ice free from the shore. "Better hurry up, Billy." Miscellaneous gear was thrown in the boat. Oliver told me to grab the back of a sled, where I stood, holding the handles. The snowmachines moved into place to hitch up.

As I was jerked into motion behind a snowmachine, I could see the collision begin. The glassy film of new ice from each side made contact and the delicate tracery that had supported the fox shattered and disappeared into the ocean.

We bounced wildly down the ice road, the boats pitching up to crazy angles on their sleds before they topped the ridges and raced down behind the snowmachines. Then we stopped on a big flat pan of ice near town. Crew after crew filtered in from the trails and joined us, until rows of sleds and boats stood side by side as if in a big parking lot. It was sunny and warm and a good time for friends to meet—teens with teens, captains with captains—and to talk of guns, snow machines, and ice conditions. No fear, no sense of relief. These days, with the bad ice and warm weather, an escape like this was routine.

Scientists predicted that global climate change would come first and strongest in the Arctic. They went there to learn how the sky, ice, snow, water, and tundra interact to drive changes in the world's environment. Scientists have measured Barrow more extensively than any other Arctic research site in the world. You can hardly turn around without bumping into a science project. Fascinating discoveries accumulated along that path. But the

Iñupiat already knew the patterns in the system and how they changed through time.

Arnold Brower, Sr., one of Barrow's most successful whaling captains, now in his eighties, had watched as the Arctic climate changed. "Unusually changed," he said. "And the pattern of animals, as to how they behave, like caribou and the fish, the seasons of spawning and seasons of ice forming on the surface.

"The current has been kind of unpredictable, because the current would change then it would change back, and sometimes it would quiet down and form into like a big pool of water, a lake out there in the ocean. And all of us sat there and without hardly any warning the current would shove out to one side and run for a week and then change over again. But in younger years it used to be two-way, and it would take time, and the wind wouldn't change it at all. . . . So it's not predictable at all what it's going to do next."

Whaling captain Harry Brower, Jr., said, "It's hard to find a place to pull up the whale. If you have this first-year ice, it's not really thick enough to hold the whale, pulling it out of the water. With that multiyear ice, if you have a large pan identified, you could pull up a whale there. We had an area specifically last spring where one big pan had fastened itself to that first-year ice and it probably was grounded because of that weight. And I think we butchered like seventeen whales on that ice pan. It was the only one heavy enough to pull up the whales."

Elder Thomas Itta, Sr., saw many differences while hunting, ranging far afield from the village of Atqasuk on his snowmachine. Hunting was no longer possible in June and July because the weather was too warm to keep the meat from spoiling. Far more seagulls and jaegers were flying in the area, and hawks appeared for the first time. Even the snow had changed. The snow on the tundra was thin and hard but in the bushy willows it built into soft, deep drifts, as deep as six feet. There never used to be so many willows. "They started growing here, there, and all over now," Thomas said.

Oliver Leavitt took longer to convince than some others that the climate had warmed. He kept hoping the difference lay in the way people were perceiving the weather, or that the changes were part of a cycle that would finally swing back to normal. But if it was a cycle, it was such a long one that no one could remember conditions like these.

The Iñupiat had developed a collective body of knowledge over a thousand years of subsisting from their environment. They were trained observers and they knew how to process their disparate observations into useful information for making decisions. In a language perfectly suited to the problems it addressed, they held long talks that synthesized what many people had seen over broad spans of time and space.

Every Native home was an information node. It could be disorienting: the VHF competed with the local radio station, a pinochle game, a TV, and sometimes a computer; kids ran around and elder family members sat at the table sipping coffee and telling stories. At the Volunteer Search and Rescue base, many of those elements were present, plus a pool game in progress, a hunk of walrus boiling, a big wall map to coordinate rescues, and various conversations in two languages. Everyone seemed to share information all the time, from around town, out on the tundra or the ice, and around the world. As wildlife biologist Craig George observed, "There's conversation, conversation, conversation back and forth, and then there's this statement that comes out. 'We know this.'"

One whaling captain's intuitive understanding of the ice was the product of many minds over many centuries. But the word intuition could get you in trouble. Oliver Leavitt went out of his way to say intuition had nothing to do with how he handled himself on the ice. His skills were based on experience. I think he was responding to a pseudospiritual use of the word. Some Alaska Natives believed that indigenous people were born with environmental knowledge; that they were essentially better than whites down in their bones. Scientists and practical people like Oliver naturally steered clear of such beliefs, which were contradicted every time a rural white trapper knew more about the environment than a TV-bound urban Alaska Native.

But even without drawing on the supernatural, the success of the Iñupiat in their environment did suggest a spiritual foundation. "The biggest connection between traditional knowledge and the spiritual way of life is about respect; respecting the environment, respecting the land, respecting the animals," said Oliver's friend Richard Glenn. A geologist by training, Richard had grown up in California but decided to take his place among his mother's people in Barrow. Now he was cocaptain of a whaling crew. "Traditional knowledge to me is centuries of trial and error. So what looks like an elegant solution is something that has only been learned because we've tried to do it in the wrong way in the past and this way works better. And that is also built around respect. Safety is built around respect. Survival is built around respect. You think you're better than the weather? Let's see what the weather has got in store for you."

On May 8, 2002, Oliver Leavitt's crew went on the ice again. The ice collision that had prompted our escape had not caused an ivu, and the campsite was intact. The sun blazed, surrounded by sun dogs, and the temperature was too warm for parkas, up to thirty-four degrees. The snow was melting and water stood in puddles in dips all over the sea ice. It was unnerving to run a snowmachine through water sitting on top of ice that was sitting on top of 130 feet of water.

Oliver had kept a haunch of caribou meat frozen in snow that was now disappearing. It was a traditional hunter's food: kill a caribou in cold weather, let it freeze, then carry the frozen haunch and snack on it, cutting chunks out with a sharp knife whenever energy flags or you feel cold. Techniques like these, using the Arctic cold to preserve food, helped the Iñupiat survive through long times of shortage and over journeys of great distance. But in this warm weather, Oliver's caribou had thawed. It was spoiled.

As the evening wore on, Billy Jens checked the ice crack behind us. He prepared to pack up for a quick escape. At 1 A.M., the entire ice sheet we were sitting on dropped a little with a jolt. Soon the camp was packed again and we were retreating, back down the trail with the sleds bouncing, crashing, and splashing over pressure ridges and through the slush and expanding pools.

The following day was warm again. The water was bright and motionless. The ice pack had receded dozens of miles from the shorefast ice. Many whalers on our part of the lead had given up. According to rules agreed to by the Barrow Whaling Captains Association, only the traditional, quiet style of whaling with the umiaq was allowed on the portion of the lead south of the tip of Point Barrow. North of there, whalers were permitted to use motorized aluminum boats—boats around fourteen feet long with thirty-five-horsepower outboards, about as large as could be fit on a sled and dragged to the ice edge. The motor allowed whalers to range far afield to find a whale, but the noise chased the whales away from the shore. They called it "boating," and called the boats "the aluminum." With so few whales near the ice, there was a movement to allow the aluminum all along the lead. Oliver was one of very few still camped along the lead with an umiaq. He said he'd rather quit and go hunting upriver than whale with the aluminum.

"I'm out here whaling," he said. "To me, that's not whaling."

At 5:15 P.M. a prayer of thanksgiving came over the VHF, the harpooner of George Ahmaogak's crew thanking God for a safe and successful hunt—they had killed a whale from their aluminum boat far to the north. The prayer came through the little radio with a tone as thin as wrinkled paper. It concluded, "In Jesus's name." Then a cheer came up from their boat, so many miles away across the water.

In accordance with tradition, the prayer not only announced the kill, it alerted everyone in town to come help pull the animal up with block and tackle and butcher it. All the whaling crews and the entire community would converge on the ice for a task that would take eighteen hours of continuous labor. Everyone helping would receive a share of the whale, as would elders and the infirm in town, and anyone who attended a public banquet at the captain's house or at the summertime Nalukataq festival, as well as relatives far away, who would get theirs in packages through the mail. A captain and crew win honor and respect for a successful hunt, but no one can own a whale.

The Ahmaogak boat gave coordinates from their GPS receiver and called for more fuel and more boats to pull the whale. Billy Jens and two other younger crew members would go up and help with the butchering and claim a share of the whale for Oliver's crew, but there was no rush. It would take all night to tow in the whale.

Clouds blanketed the sky as night fell. It began to rain. The crew put a tarp over Oliver's seating area on the sled. Oliver was disgusted. He recalled as a young man wearing two pairs of snow pants for spring whaling, standing night watch in temperatures twenty degrees below zero.

"Here's your global warming," he said. "It never rains this time of year. It melts the snow real fast."

The weather station in Barrow gives forecasts over the VHF during whaling season so crews can ask questions at the end. On May 10, not long after the rain, the meteorologist announced in disbelief, "There is officially no snow on the ground." A foot-deep snow pack had disappeared in three days. As always, after the question-and-answer session, someone said, "Thank you, weatherman." And the weatherman said, "You're welcome."

Since 1940, Barrow's snowmelt had come ever earlier on an accelerating line. Adjusting for the human-caused changes around the weather station (road dust in town enhances snowmelt) and using conservative statistical analysis, scientists estimated that the snowmelt had gotten eight days earlier, moving from about June 18 to June 10. Snowmelt on May 10 was off the charts.

Barrow whaling crews butchered only one more bowhead that season. Those crossing the ice to help with the final whale had to drive their snowmachines through deep water. Soon the last whalers gave up hunting. Normally whaling goes on into June and the ice doesn't go out until July. The season's total catch of only three whales was far too little to sate the community's appetite; some years, they brought in twenty or more.

At least Barrow, unlike other villages, still had fall whaling to look forward to. The geography of Point Barrow brought the bowhead migration near shore in both directions. But fall whaling was different, because there was no ice from which to ambush passing whales. Crews patrolled the ocean in larger boats with powerful outboard engines looking for a spout and counting on horsepower to get them to the whale before it could escape. Some Barrow whalers claimed they had already adapted to climate change by acquiring bigger boats and engines for fall whaling. Knowledgeable white men foresaw the next step of adaptation as phasing out spring whaling to hunt only in big boats in the fall. Richard Glenn cringed when I suggested that prospect to him. He loved camping out on the ice.

When I had stood with Richard on the sea ice that warm spring, he admitted that climate change appeared to be a fact. But when I returned to Barrow in the fall he still clung to the possibility that this appearance, with its dreadful implications, would prove misleading. "I was always looking forward to a back side of this cycle," he said. "I'm still hoping that that back side is coming. And if it doesn't, then we have to change. If it's part of a one-way progression, then life is really going to change."

"What kinds of things do you think about that would change?" I asked.

"If we start losing the spring season we have to totally rethink ice safety. The rules change. . . . Things that were true for fathers won't be true for sons, and so it will always be experiencing something new."

"That's kind of been the case for the last 150 years anyway," I said.

"Oh yes, the culture has changed, always. But there's always been some things: the ice on the lake will get five to six feet thick every year. Or ice that's accreted to the shoreline with enough pressure ridges is probably going to stick around. Those kinds of things, those little rules of thumb, are going to change. And that will change how you travel, how you hunt, how you stay alive."

Climate change that happens gradually is difficult for people to perceive. Even in Barrow, where the Iñupiat depend on wildlife, ice, and the timing of the seasons for their livelihood, some hunters fought the realization until faced with the terrible spring whaling season of 2002. By then, the ice, the Earth, and the elders were all telling the same story. A new and fundamental change was underway. Understanding climate change, as well as responding, happens inside individual human beings, in their minds and in their bones, through judgment and trial and error, in the way the Iñupiat, and all people, learn the truth by living it.

(2004)

The Black Mesa Syndrome

Indian lands, black gold

Black Mesa

Black Mesa is not black and it is not a mesa. It is four thousand square miles of ginger-colored plateau land in northern Arizona, a distinct elevated landmass the shape of a bear's paw. On a map, the Black Mesa coalfield looks like an inkblot on a Rorschach test, following the contours of the Pleistocene lake it once was. Over thousands of years the vigorous forests and plant life embraced by the lake decayed into a bog which in turn hardened to coal—some twenty-one billion tons of coal, the largest coal deposit in the United States.

Until 1969, the coal lay untouched and so close to the surface that the walls of the dry washes glistened with seams of shiny black. With a long-term value estimated as high as $100 billion, it lies completely under Indian reservation lands, for Black Mesa is also home to some sixteen thousand Navajos and eight thousand Hopis. In 1966 the Hopi and Navajo tribal councils—not to be confused with the general tribal population—signed strip-mining leases with a consortium of twenty utilities that had designed a new coal-fired energy grid for the urban southwest. Under the umbrella name WEST (Western Energy Supply and Transmission), the utilities promised more air conditioning for Los Angeles, more neon lights for Las Vegas, more water for Phoenix, more power for Tucson—and for the Indians, great wealth.

Today, thirty years after the strip-mining for coal began, the cities have the energy they were promised, but the Hopi and Navajo nations are not rich—that part of the plan proved ephemeral. Instead, Black Mesa has suffered human rights abuses and ecological devastation; the Hopi water supply is drying up; thousands of archeological sites have been destroyed; and, unbeknownst to most Americans, twelve thousand Navajos have been removed from their lands—the largest removal of Indians in the United States since the 1880s.

In the following pages, I want to untangle what went wrong on Black Mesa. Enormous political and economic powers have shaped the contemporary reality of this region, and yet, for twenty-five years, the American press, with few exceptions, has presented the Black Mesa story as a centuries-old land dispute between two tribes. The story that has not yet emerged is about the syndrome in which transnational corporations take and exploit indigenous lands, with the cooperation of host governments. I want to hold up Black Mesa as an example of that global syndrome, and I want to ask why our free press has largely been unable to tell the truth about Black Mesa.

Chester Arthur's Square

Surrounding the inkblot of the coal deposit is an almost perfect square of land—one cartographer's minute by one cartographer's minute—drawn by President Chester Arthur in 1882. His Executive Order created a reservation for Indians as the government might "see fit to settle therein."

Why would Arthur, a New Yorker and a product of political patronage, give a land grant three-fourths the size of Connecticut to a population that consisted of eleven hundred Hopis, three hundred Paiutes, and a few hundred Navajos? The answer has far less to do with safeguarding Indian residency than with timber, copper, and coal.

Chester Arthur was a rich man with rich tastes and no stranger to the alchemy of transforming government service into economic wealth. As far as we know, he never visited the West, but he was knowledgeable about Western railroad charters, land grants, and mineral exploration leases. He understood the trick of transforming wilderness into public domain lands, and then into prospecting leases. He understood how business and government worked hand-in-glove. In those days, land development companies were frequently subsidiaries of the railroads, and several years before the transcontinental railroad reached Arizona in 1881, the U.S. government had already explored, surveyed, and mapped the mineral riches of the Arizona Territory. Also in advance of the railroads, the government sent the Army to subdue the "savage tribes," such as the Navajos in the north and Apaches in the south, who blocked access to Arizona's resource-rich lands.

"The only minerals discovered in this region are coal and copper," wrote surveyor A. M. Stephen in 1879 to his superior, General Howard, who also held the title of Indian Inspector. "The coal deposit is lying between Oraibi and Moenkopi," the report continues. "The only white people . . . are about twenty families of Mormons at MoenKopi [sic] and Tuba City." Stephen accompanied his survey with a map of the coal deposit location.

Arthur understood immediately the implications of the map. If the Mormon families were allowed to continue to settle and improve their lands, they would, according to the provisions of the Desert Lands Act of 1877, be able to buy 160 acres at $1.25 per acre. They would also gain title to whatever mineral resources lay beneath those acres. But if the same lands were removed from the public domain and designated as Indian reservation lands, they would no longer be open to white settlement. On December 17, 1882, Arthur signed the Executive Order Reservation of 1882 "for the use and occupancy of the Moqui [Hopi] and such other Indians as the secretary of the interior may see fit to settle therein." By this act, Arthur kept control of the mineral resources of the region, and set them aside for another day.

The West, American myth tells us, was a place where there was real freedom—where you came with what you could carry and you made a life from it. The government was meddlesome, an intrusion, an invasion into the individual resourcefulness of the Western pioneers. That is the myth. In reality, the government and big business made it all happen.

John Boyden and the Peabody Leases

Chester Arthur's square remained untouched for seventy-five years, into the 1950s, when a Utah lawyer named John Boyden found a way to transmute the coal of Black Mesa into gold. A bishop in the Mormon Church and a former U.S. attorney, Boyden's dapper, modest appearance masked a fierce ambition and the hardball skills of a trial attorney. Beginning in 1957, he began to craft the legal, political, and economic strategy which would open up the coal deposit of Black Mesa to major energy development.

As a first step in his plan, Boyden needed the cooperation of the tribal council of one of the Indian tribes on Black Mesa. He approached the Navajo, who turned him down. He then went to the Hopi, whose leaders were bitterly factionalized between traditionals and progressives. Lacking a governing tribal council since 1938, the Hopi had no legal entity to hire Boyden, but as a law partner of the man who wrote the 1946 Indian Land Claims Law, Boyden was knowledgeable about both tribal council politics and Bureau of Indian Affairs policies. Accompanied by the government Indian agent, he set about traveling to all the Hopi villages, and talking to all the Hopi men who spoke English and who had been to government boarding schools. In the process, Boyden created a new tribal council.

Boyden was controversial from the minute he assumed his new role. One of his first actions was to introduce a bill in Congress creating a special court to allow the Hopi to sue the Navajo to clear title for the coal lands. Thousands of Navajos had settled on Black Mesa, and no energy company would take a chance on a lease that could be contested. Of the bill, Hopi leader Dan Katchongva wrote prophetically in 1956, "If [this bill] becomes law, it will destroy our Hopi way of life, religion and law. . . . The majority of the Hopis are against him as a lawyer."

The traditional Hopi were furious with Boyden's role and saw his presence as an intrusion from Washington. Caleb Johnson, a Hopi student at Princeton Theological Seminary writing to the Senate on behalf of traditional Hopi priests, made the astute observation that leadership of the Hopi and the boundary issue were linked. He added that leadership had a religious component and that the man Boyden had chosen as Hopi chairman was not respected. "The chairman of the tribal council," he wrote, "is a man who does not have a good record and has been convicted of a felony in a Federal court."

Others opposed the bill too, including the U.S. Attorney General William Rogers, on grounds that Indian land issues and reservation boundaries derived from treaties that were outside American property law. But in 1962, the special court did clarify title to the subsurface mineral estate and divided the surface rights. The Supreme Court declined to hear an appeal, and in 1966 the leases were signed.

At the top of the 1882 boundary are two irregular rectangles. These represent some sixty-five thousand acres leased by the Hopi and Navajo tribal councils to the Peabody Coal Company of Kentucky, the largest coal producer in the United States. The leases were signed secretly by the tribal councils and the company in 1966, with no larger tribal referendum on either side. The Navajos tried to block the mining equipment by setting up blockades in the road. The Hopi priests eventually sued their own tribal council, claiming the leases were illegal because they had been signed without a quorum.

John Boyden remained the Hopi's lawyer for thirty years. Although he presented himself as a humble country lawyer working for the Hopi pro bono, his fees—paid by the government out of monies held in trust for the Hopi—totaled $2.7 million, a figure revealed only after a Freedom of Information suit filed by the Native American Rights Fund.

Kennecott Copper and Strip-mining

Today at Black Mesa, buckets the size of a four-story building peel the topsoil off in mile-long strips—a technique called strip-mining. Instead of burrowing into the earth to find the mineral seam, the land over the mineral deposit is removed. Bulldozers shape the underlayers into enormous slag heaps, workers dynamite the exposed mineral bed, and steam shovels load the coal into massive transport trucks. By the time the coal is extracted, the land has turned gray, all vegetation has disappeared, the air is filled with coal dust, the groundwater is contaminated with toxic runoff (sulphates particularly), and electric green ponds dot the landscape. Sheep that drink from such ponds at noon are dead by suppertime.

In 1966, Kennecott, an international mining company seeking to diversify, bought Peabody Coal. Four years later, John Boyden moved his law offices to the tenth floor of the Kennecott Building in Salt Lake City, overlooking the Mormon Temple. As Boyden leveraged this land issue into a huge case, he violated a basic tenet of legal ethics: he represented two sides in the same case, working simultaneously for the Hopi tribe and for Peabody Coal. Although his former partners maintained it was "a mistake" that *Martindale Hubbell,* the national legal directory, listed Peabody Coal as one of Boyden's firm's clients, legal scholar Charles Wilkinson published an article in a 1996 issue of *Brigham Young University Law Journal* reproducing Boyden's correspondence with both parties. When Boyden wrote to the Peabody vice president as a Peabody attorney, he addressed him as "Dear Ed"; when he wrote to him as a Hopi attorney, he called him "Dear Mr. Phelps."

Not surprisingly, Boyden had not done particularly well for his Hopi client in the lease provisions: Low royalty rates (the two tribal councils split a royalty rate of thirty cents a ton at a time when the government royalty rate for coal extracted on public lands was $1.50 a ton), few environmental safeguards, and no provisions for renegotiation. The worst, however, was the provision that allowed Peabody to pump four thousand acre-feet (approximately a billion gallons) of water a year to run a coal slurry line.

The Black Mesa Coal Slurry Pipeline

The only operating coal slurry line in the United States extends 273 miles from Black Mesa to the Mohave Generating Station. A slurry, for those who have never seen one, operates like a giant garbage disposal, grinding huge chunks of coal into nugget-size pieces through enormous steel blades, mixing them with water, then sluicing the batter through a pipeline. For this operation, Peabody Coal has pumped a billion gallons a year for almost thirty years from the Black Mesa aquifer, the sole water source for the Hopi and Navajo peoples of the region. In these three decades, groundwater levels have dropped, wells and springs have dried up, and the entire ecology of Black Mesa has changed: plants have failed to reseed and certain vegetation has died out.

"The water has become more valuable than the coal," exclaimed Hopi Marilyn Masayesva at the government's environmental hearings. "The water is priceless. No amount of compensation can replace the source of life for the Hopi and Navajo people. It is absolutely immoral and irresponsible for the federal government to support a continuation of mining activities." Ms. Masayesva was one of hundreds of Hopi and Navajo who testified in 1989 about the negative effects of mining on their lands and against the government's extension of the mining permit. Thousands of years of water had been used up in a few decades. The government's environmental impact report concluded, however, that water "was outside the scope of their study" and the mining continued.

One cold March day in 1990, I visited the office of Black Mesa Pipeline, Inc. A dusting of snow still lay on the ground. In the distance, a weak sun illuminated the drag lines and I glimpsed cone-shaped piles of coal waiting to be fed into the conveyer belt. Lowell Hinkins, the operations manager, assured me that there was no connection between the Indian wells going dry and the operations of the slurry. The pipeline wells went a thousand feet deeper than the shallow wells of the Hopi and Navajo, he told me. He also confirmed that, yes, "Black Mesa is the only operating coal slurry line in the United States. The others are being built in China and Russia." I had just seen a company video that claimed coal was bringing economic prosperity and the "finer things of life" to the Hopi and Navajo. But it is hard to define prosperity.

The effects of coal slurry pipelines on water tables are known, and in all-white communities where such pipelines have been proposed, citizens have had enough political voice to defeat them. The larger truth about the Black Mesa pipeline must include the fact that it was built in part as an experiment—to test and improve technology primarily intended for other countries, like China and Russia. The Bechtel corporation had designed the pipeline in conjunction with a new design for an electrical generating station—the Mohave Generating Station of Laughlin, Nevada—which was also a test of technology for dewatering coal slurry. The owners of the new plant were Los Angeles Water and Power, Southern California Edison, Nevada Power (Las Vegas), and the Salt River Project (Phoenix)—all members of the energy consortium, WEST. In terms of population served by the utilities, their combined political power represented seven state governors, fourteen senators, and at least forty-eight congressmen.

The Mohave Generating Station

When the Mohave plant was completed, Bechtel's company magazine saluted it as "1.5 million megawatts for the West." Twenty-eight years later the *Los Angeles Times* observed, "The Mohave Generating Station is the biggest uncontrolled source of sulfur dioxide in the Southwest—a prime contributor to the gaseous haze that clouds visibility over the Grand Canyon."

Bechtel, of course, is famous for its multibillion dollar projects, and for shaping the politics and technology of the markets in which it does business. With forty thousand employees, Bechtel has built the three largest government-funded projects in U.S. history—the Hoover Dam, the Central Arizona Project, and the Central Artery Project in Boston.

When the Mohave plant opened in 1970, it raised new questions of strategic planning. A second plant, the Navajo Generating Station near Page, also engineered by Bechtel, was due to go on line in 1974. The two plants combined would require twelve million tons of coal a year for at least fifty years. Black Mesa would become home to the largest strip mine in the United States. What to do about the thousands of Navajos who lived in the way of this mining?

John Boyden was up to the challenge. He went back to Congress with new legislation to divide Black Mesa and give almost a million acres to the Hopi. By transferring land to the Hopi, who lived far away from the strip-mining, Navajo residents would become trespassers on the newly designated Hopi land, and the cost of removing them would be borne by the government. To frame the issue for Congress, Boyden hired a public relations firm that created a largely fictitious range war between the cattle-ranching Hopi, and the sheepherding Navajo.

In 1974, Congress, somewhat distracted by Watergate, passed Boyden's bill and granted the Hopi 900,000 acres. The law also provided for the physical removal of the Navajo (by the Indian Relocation Commission), but the problem, of course, was that there was nowhere for the Navajo to go.

Congress had no plans for alternative lands, no provisions for housing or health care or social services to acclimate the Navajo to an urban environment. Suicide and alcoholism became endemic among the displaced Navajo, but by the 1980s, when the Navajo and their supporters came to Congress to protest their situation, they had a hard time finding listeners. Peabody Coal had a new parent, a private holding company which included Bechtel. And by then, Bechtel was entrenched in government: Bechtel's former president George Shultz was Secretary of State; its former legal counsel, Caspar Weinberger, was Secretary of Defense; and former director of Bechtel Nuclear, Ken Davis, was Assistant Secretary of Energy. The president of Peabody Coal served on Reagan's Energy Advisory Board.

The Navajo Generating Station at Page

While the Mohave Generating Station is a model of bad technology in the service of terrible land use, the Navajo Generating Station, at the Arizona-Utah border, is a case study of a political process out of control. As soon as the Mohave plant was completed, Bechtel moved its construction crews to the tiny town of Page, Arizona, overlooking the scenic Glen Canyon Dam, to begin construction on a second electrical generating station—another giant at 2,250 megawatts, the second largest utility station in the U.S. Somebody named it the Navajo Generating Station, a name rich in irony, since fewer than half of Navajo families have electricity.

The U.S. government was the single largest owner. The Department of the Interior needed the electricity to run a federal water project, the Central Arizona Project, locally known as CAP. CAP is a concrete highway for water—infrastructure that lifts the waters of the Colorado River over three mountain ranges in order to carry it to Phoenix and Tucson. This engineering feat involves siphons, tunnels, dams, reservoirs, and fifteen electrically powered pumping stations. "With enough money, anything is possible," an engineer told me when I asked about the economic rationale for growing crops by means of the most expensive subsidized water in the world. The power to run the fifteen pumping stations comes, of course, from Black Mesa coal.

The political issues raised by the Navajo Generating Station are unique. The majority owner of the plant is the Bureau of Reclamation in the Department of the Interior. Within the same interior department is the Bureau of Indian Affairs, the agency legally entrusted with safeguarding Indian lands and resources. Questions immediately arise: How can the U.S. government exercise its trusteeship responsibility toward Indians when one of its agencies is benefiting directly from the coal leases that it encouraged the Indians to sign, negotiated by lawyers that it had appointed? Did the BIA exercise its fiduciary responsibility in negotiating the leases on Black Mesa? Who reviews conflicts of interest within the government?

In an era of transnational corporations operating all over the globe, the methods of separating indigenous peoples from their lands and natural resources have outstripped the capacity of any agency or nongovernmental organization to monitor or regulate. In what forum can we debate and redirect such dealings, which have such profound effects on life itself?

The line on the map that runs from Lake Havasu south to Tucson represents 335 miles of the most expensive water in the world. Phoenix and Tucson are located in the Sonoran desert, the hottest desert in North America, and the day I toured the control room of the Central Arizona Project, in August 1991, was a typical summer Phoenix day—113 degrees in the shade. I chatted with the operations manager, a retired Navy man who told me how they had built special bridges for wildlife crossings, fenced the aqueduct so that animals wouldn't drown, and implemented other engineering feats of environmental sensitivity. Looking at the pulsing computer screens and the operators who, with a few key strokes, could release millions of gallons of water from the Colorado River into grapefruit orchards and cotton fields hundreds of miles away, I wondered if it wouldn't be more sensible to farm in regions with a better water supply—like rain.

The Line That Isn't There

The line that *isn't* on the map is formed by a barbed-wire fence: The new boundary of the Hopi reservation follows no known topographical feature. Shaped a bit like a thumb, it was drawn by John Boyden in 1974, the same year that the Navajo Generating Station came on line and the same year that his little-noticed bill passed Congress. The Hopi Land Settlement Act divided Chester Arthur's 1882 reservation between the Hopi and Navajo. Boyden drew the line so that it gave approximately nine hundred thousand acres to the Hopi, who did not live over the coal, and relocated, at taxpayer expense, the twelve thousand Navajos (and sixty Hopi) who did. The Hopi Land Settlement Act also renamed the newly delineated land as the Hopi Navajo Joint Use Area, Hopi Partition Land, and Navajo Partition Land. The final version was introduced by Utah Congressman Wayne Owens (who, when defeated in reelection, became a partner in Boyden's law firm).

In Los Angeles, air conditioners hummed. Las Vegas embarked on an enormous building spree to make gambling a family vacation. Phoenix and Tucson metastasized out into the desert—building golf courses and vast retirement developments with swimming pools and fountains. Few realize that much of the energy that makes the desert "bloom" comes from the Black Mesa strip mines on an Indian reservation. Even fewer know the true costs of such development.

The Syncline and Roberta Blackgoat

Over thousands of years the Black Mesa coalfield was subjected to tectonic pressures and extrusions of molten rock hundreds of feet below the surface that caused the coal bed to fold and curve. Geologists call the curvature that comes close to the surface a syncline.

Roberta Blackgoat lives over a syncline. A Navajo who has lived on Black Mesa all her life, Roberta's cosmology tells her that she is inseparable from the land that surrounds her. When each of her children was born she buried his or her umbilical cord in her sheep corral to connect them to the land from which they come and the sheep who support them. (With sheep, the older Navajo say, "you've always got food on the table and clothes on your back.") When I visited her in February of 1991 I asked about the new boundary line and her view of the forces that dictated her relocation from land her family had lived on since the 1860s.

"The coal," she answered with a shrug. She was sitting at her loom in the back of her hogan weaving. I sat on a sheepskin spread over a dirt floor. I had placed my tape recorder next to her loom. As we talked she repeatedly referred to the altar. Finally I asked, But where is the altar? Here. Here, she answered impatiently. Eventually I understood that the altar was the spot where she was sitting, the hogan itself.

When I looked at the frame, I saw large logs, all placed in the direction they grew and in relationship to the sacred mountains of Dinetah, the land of the Navajo. A hogan, Roberta explained, is sung into place. Is there also a carpenter? I wanted to know. She shook her head. No carpenter. Songs. A ceremony brings a hogan into being. As we talked, I began to understand that a hogan replicates the Navajo universe in miniature, and that all human activity is directed toward remaining in balance with the earth and universal forces. Many Navajo people who move into the city often build a hogan in their back yards as a place to reestablish spiritual connection with the earth and to bring their lives into balance.

Roberta, whose grandmotherly appearance belies her forceful, astute leadership of the Big Mountain resistance, described to me a paradigm in which the earth is a sacred and living organism, in which human beings and the earth exist in a reciprocal relationship. This reciprocity is the foundation for her life. We are the people of the earth's surface, she told me, and no more important than the winged creatures or four-legged beings. The day before, as we rode to Keams Canyon, she tried to translate this concept into Anglo terms. The church is everywhere, she said. Land is the repository for religion, economics, sociology, history, science. And that is why she couldn't leave her land. And what about the coal, I asked, in the hogan. The shuttle stopped. Roberta spoke very clearly. "The coal is the liver of the earth," she said. "When you take it out, she dies."

It was my turn to sit in silence. Separated by only five feet of space, we were occupying two different models of reality. I had been taught that land was a kind of primal flooring for human beings, of value only when prodded into productive use. Roberta was describing the earth as the living host for all life. She was talking about earth's sustaining properties in a way that we, educated in the world of Western science, have only recently begun to call the biosphere.

How does one calculate the true costs of extinguishing such a complex culture?

True Costs and New Stories

Divide and conquer has a long history in America as a technique of removing Indians from their lands, a situation that is being replicated by transnational corporations throughout the world. As former United Nations Secretary General Boutros Boutros-Ghali observed about the struggles of indigenous peoples, "Cultures which do not have powerful media are threatened with extinction. The instruments of mass communication remain in the service of a handful." Over the past twenty-five years over twelve thousand Americans have been removed from their lands. Over a billion dollars of taxpayers' money has been spent to accomplish this human rights abuse.

Yet this story has never made it onto the six o'clock news. Today's news must be presented simply, and dramatically—with plot, character, scene, motivation. A complex story that blends economics, politics, anthropology, history is hard to tell in our free press. And a story that examines fundamental corporate activities is hard to tell in a corporate-owned media. As recently as 1996, the *New York Times* called the struggle between the Hopi and Navajo "a centuries-old tribal dispute." In April 1997, the *Boston Globe* devoted thirty-three column inches to a story on the Hopi and Navajo boundary issue without once mentioning the word "coal" or stating that the largest strip mine in the United States operated on those same lands. In February 1998, the *Los Angeles Times* presented a new spin: it is better to keep polluting than to deprive the Indian tribes of their coal royalty checks. Cleaning up the Mohave plant (actually it is the Navajo plant that is the prime polluter) "pits the interests of the environment against the economic needs of some of the nation's poorest citizens—the Native Americans of the Southwest." The implications of that debate, as the Los Angeles Department of Water and Power general manager told us, are "a sneak preview of the dilemmas to come as we try to grapple with the implications of global warming and air pollution in developing nations that depend on the energy industry."

Hopefully, that false syllogism will be refuted when the real story of how the Mohave plant was developed finds a public. To date, the news of events at Black Mesa has been shaped into the preferred narratives of corporate America—stories of corporate might grappling with economic progress, technological innovation, entrepreneurial capitalism, the settling of the American West, making the desert bloom. In the age of global capitalism in which corporations have bought the media, it is not surprising we see few stories about effective political resistance. Journalists look for a smoking gun in the corporate energy development on Black Mesa and, finding none, abandon the story. It is difficult to tell a story of legal theft, a story in which corporations have the political power to pass laws. But as the Navajo and Hopi have tried to explain, Black Mesa, once destroyed, will not come back. And we are all impoverished by the forces operating at Black Mesa, which degrade both culture and nature, and offer us instead a pseudoreality—a version of events that prevents clear analysis and creative thinking. We need new tools, new narratives, new stories—including stories about an economics that involves morality, an economics that helps us create the world we want to inhabit.

A year ago a delegation of Hopis and Navajos traveled from Arizona to the London stockholders meeting of Hanson's Ltd. (which had purchased Peabody in 1991) to protest the company's role in the devastation of Black Mesa lands and water. Lord Hanson called his security guards to throw the visitors out, but not before the *Daily Telegraph* reported their presence and took a photograph of Roberta Blackgoat offering a prayer. The prayer, she said, was crucial.

(1998)

Boundaries

Faux Falls

The unnatural wonder at Niagara

IN THE SPRING OF 2006, I GO SEE NIAGARA FALLS GET TURNED ON for the tourist season. I get there a day early, on March 31, and head straight for the Three Sisters to see the diminished river. The best thing in New York's Niagara Falls State Park, the Three Sisters are a mini-archipelago off the edge of Goat Island, the chunk of land splitting the Niagara River into the American Fall and Canadian Horseshoe Fall. I stop on the bridge to the First Sister and look upstream at the "Hermit's Cascade," a river ledge depicted on the island's interpretive marker as a surging mini-Niagara. Today it's a few freshets splashing over a flaky slice of rock.

Things perk up on the Second Sister and, by the Third, the river's in a frenzy. Even at low water, the Third Sister feels like what it is—a rocky outcropping in the middle of the Horseshoe rapids. Water rushes and swirls furiously around its edges. It's loud. Just downstream, the river surges over the Horseshoe Fall and disappears. A misty abyss marks the spot.

I am not alone. A middle-aged couple, sneakered and stout, pick their way along the path. They regard the rapids with the dull resignation of people beaten into subjection by miles of Thruway. Dutifully, they take turns posing for snapshots before the man approaches me.

"Do you know where the really big waterfall is?" he asks.

"See that mist over there?" I say, pointing. His face falls.

"The Horseshoe Fall? We saw that." His eyes go to the Canadian bank, a jumble of generic hotels, franchise restaurants, and kitschy attractions that make up Niagara Falls, Ontario. Canada's mind-numbing spectacle of monoculture on one side, the shuttered factories and potholed brownfields of Niagara Falls, New York, on the other: the two Niagaras wink at each other across the river like the complementary faces of globalism. And we are standing right in the middle, surrounded by natural wonder.

"I thought there was a bigger waterfall," he says.

"Come back tomorrow," I say.

Of course it's an exaggeration to say Niagara Falls is turned off and on for the tourists. It is actually turned up for the tourists. In the international Niagara Diversion Treaty of 1950, the U.S. and Canada agreed to go half-sies on one of the world's largest natural sources of hydroelectric power. The nations also agreed to let no less than 100,000 cubic feet of water per second—about half the natural volume—go over the Falls between the hours of 8 A.M. and 10 P.M., April 1 to September 16. This was so that the 22 million or so tourists who flock to Niagara annually, most in the summer, don't all walk away wondering where the big fall went.

But that's unlikely. In fact, most people are surprised to learn just how much of Niagara's water never goes over the Falls. Water diversions for hydropower are enormous, but their effect on the scenery is limited by massive engineering projects that keep everything looking the same. Even as one-half to three-quarters of the Niagara River is drawn off into four hydro tunnels and one canal, the waterfalls spread across the same crestline, look the same depth, and shimmer with the same emerald green. The end result is an environment that elides any conflict between landscape enjoyment and resource expenditure. You see? it cheerfully declares: we can have our lake and use it too.

I imagine the spring increase of water as a kind of local festival: they're turning the Falls back up! I call the New York Power Authority with visions of electro-geeks dialing up the water and watching it rip in a celebratory mood. Maybe champagne would be involved, or pizza. Donuts, at the very least. On the phone, however, Joanne Willmott, regional manager for community relations, assures me there's little fanfare around treaty implementation.

"What if I buy the pizza?" I ask. In the end, we arrange to meet at the Robert Moses Niagara Power Plant, a monster dam built right into the face of the Niagara gorge four and a half miles downstream from the Falls. The Moses plant collects all of the water diverted to the American side and runs it through 13 turbines in the main plant and 12 more in the supplementary Lewiston Pump-Generating Plant, producing, at top capacity, 2.4 million kilowatts of nonstop electricity. The Power Vista—the Authority's visitor center—is a huge, sunny room suspended over the river at one end of the looming plant. When you step onto the exterior deck, there's a constant low hum. Inside, kids scramble around a roomful of displays about electricity while their parents try to read them the interpretive signs. Joanne walks me to the centerpiece, a vast miniature replica of the region, highlighting the Authority's intakes, tunnels, generating stations, and reservoir. The Falls, in one corner, are represented by an inch-high clear plastic mold. Tiny white lights behind the plastic are meant to produce the illusion of frothy water.

Joanne introduces me to Norm Stessing, supervisor of operations, the man—in my mind—who can dial Niagara's thundering deluge down to a pathetic dribble. He doesn't look like a Power King; he looks like a Norm. He's medium height, stocky but trim and tanned, with even teeth and a quick, easy smile. His crisp shirt is tucked in perfectly. Norm grew up in the Niagara region. In the late '50s when the power plant was being built, his parents would bring him to see the massive project under way.

Norm dives into explaining how his power plant works with the vigor of a high school physics teacher who really believes in those kids.

"Our generator capacity is 100,000 cubic feet per second," he tells me, explaining the treaty implementation that starts again tomorrow. "But during the day our stream share is about 50,000." Before I know it, we've launched into a heady conversation about turbine efficiencies, pump storage, voltage step-ups, and price differentials. Luckily, I've read enough to have a basic understanding, because Norm, pointing to the model switchyard and explaining how voltage gets there through a mile of underground tunnels, is like a twelve-year-old boy who has been given a really, really cool toy.

In 1910, 10 percent of American homes were wired for electricity. By 1930, 70 percent were. It's easy to forget how radical electrification was. But if there's a main difference between our lives and those lived in Edith Wharton novels, it has less to do with carriages, corsets, and the sorely missed fish course than it does with turbines and megawatts. Electrification automated industry, deskilled labor, industrialized agriculture, depopulated rural areas, invented suburbs, and enabled a nonliterate mass media. Our fabulous modern lifestyle—Chicken McNuggets to *American Idol*—all began with electricity.

The change was more than infrastructure; it was a nationwide behavioral modification. And it required re-education. Americans had to be trained to stop fearing electricity and instead consume it, preferably—at least to the companies who generated and sold kilowatts—in large quantities. Major players General Electric and Westinghouse quickly decided to manufacture demand by inventing a lot of nifty electric appliances. But first they had to get average Americans to adopt what they called the "wedge" product— electric light—because it opened households to everything else. They had to sell the idea of electricity, and in this Niagara was key.

The Falls helped electricity get what marketing consultants today call "mind share." Average folks had only a vague notion of what electricity was. But they knew it was deadly. Thomas Edison had proved that. In the 1880s, striving to promote the direct current and discredit Nicola Tesla's brainchild, alternating current, Edison staged road shows meant to discredit AC by using it to electrocute dogs. This can't have made people eager to wire up their homes, especially those with pets. Nor did it help that New York State quickly saw a good use for high voltage alternating current, switching the murder penalty from hanging to electrocution in 1888, and dispatching its first killer by Old Sparky two years later. Electricity really needed a spokesmodel. In 1895, when a group of industrial barons began developing Niagara's hydro potential, the PR campaign had its mascot.

Beginning in the 1890s, a flood of articles about Niagara power hit newsstands. *Harper's, Nature, Collier's, McClure's, Blackwood's, The Saturday Review,* and *Cassier's* all printed articles describing Falls power projects and promoting the image of Niagara as unending bounty. *Harper's Weekly* was typical in calling it "an illimitable supply of cheap power."

Compared with coal, getting power from a waterfall was cleaner, safer, more renewable, and easier to understand—a Constable waterwheel writ large. A booklet printed in 1895 to promote Buffalo real estate bragged that Niagara created limitless power "without consuming an atom of the world's store of fuel, without destroying in the slightest degree the grandeur of the cataract and its environments." Go ahead and buy that toaster, the message ran; we've discovered a source of endless clean energy. Niagara was America's best-known site of natural splendor. Electricity would simply harness that splendor for man's use.

Brand Niagara launched for real at the 1901 World's Fair, the Pan-American Exposition in Buffalo. There, visitors were ushered into an electric utopia, featuring electric trolleys, rides, fountains, and appliances; a working miniature power plant; and row upon row of electric incubators holding live premature babies—all of it lit by 200,000 incandescent bulbs. At the center was the Electric Tower, a skyscraper featuring a seventy-four-foot artificial waterfall lit by ninety-four searchlights. On top of the tower was another searchlight, pointing toward the real Niagara Falls.

Before the fair, Lord Kelvin was quoted in *Literary Digest* gleefully predicting the day when men would turn Niagara off and on at will.

Here is what happens. Gravity constantly draws water into the hydraulic tunnels from the upper river, before the rapids start their descent. Once it goes into the tunnels, the water travels underneath the city of Niagara Falls, paralleling the river's course for four and a half miles. But the river drops—not only in the 176-foot Falls, but in the rapids above and below them. By the time the diverted water reaches the power plant's holding pool, or forebay, it is about 300 feet above the lower river. The increased drop means the water comes through the turbines with more pressure, generating more power than it would at a mere 176 feet.

At the forebay, the water can flow down through the main plant's penstocks, where it spins the turbines and passes out into the lower Niagara River, or it can be pumped as much as 120 feet up into the nineteen-hundred-acre Lewiston reservoir. The reservoir lets the Power Authority collect extra water at night, when tourists are sleeping and stream share is greater, for use during daytime, when power demand is up. Since the deregulation of electricity, the reservoir also creates an opportunity to optimize financials. As prices vary throughout the day, the Lewiston plant can pump water into its reservoir during periods of low demand for electricity, then release water through the generator when demand is high—in essence spending cheap power to make expensive power.

All of this is regulated by River Control, an arm of the International Joint Commission that manages the Falls. River Control measures the river hourly, and as its volume varies, calculates the amount each nation can draw down. River Control calls the power facilities—in the U.S., the NYPA Energy Control Central in Utica—every hour to dictate their stream shares.

At 7 A.M. on April 1, Norm explains, River Control will call Utica with a new stream share, reduced by the amount required to let 100,000 cubic feet per second go over the Falls by eight. Utica will call Niagara, and the workers in Norm's control room will sit down at their computers and begin turning off reservoir pumps. Each shutdown decreases the flow of water out of the forebay, thus decreasing the flow of water into the tunnels from the river by 4,000 cubic feet per second. When the water coming into the forebay equals the Authority's stream share, the water going over the Falls should be the amount required by the treaty, and tourists should be oohing and aahing at the sublime power of nature.

"You couldn't really turn off all of Niagara Falls, could you?" I ask Norm, my enthusiasm for the brute strength of it getting the best of me. "If you and the Canadian plant both just sucked as much water as possible out of the river and ran it through your generators at top speed?"

"We don't like to talk about it that way," he says, cracking an involuntary grin, "but in fact, yes, we could."

On the morning of the first, photographer Lisa Kereszi and I plan to hit the Three Sisters early and watch the water rise. I oversleep and wake at 6:30 to the sound of Lisa banging on my hotel-room door. Fifteen minutes later, we're parking near the Three Sisters. The river volume has already increased dramatically.

"Norm told me it wouldn't start until seven!" I wail. The Hermit's Cascade has gone from a lacy tablecloth to a billowing comforter, pouring over its small shelf with glee. Rock flats from yesterday are a rushing river, and a cascading mini-fall between the first and second islands has doubled in size. On the Third Sister, the previous day's boisterous rapids have sprouted jubilant geysers. Everything is louder, faster, greener.

I park myself on a rock and sulk. Maybe the water is still rising, I tell myself. I choose a large rock to stare at. Two Canada geese are holding their ground on top of it. Is the water getting higher? It's hard to say—stare long enough and the volume seems to grow. I imagine pumps shutting down, sluice gates upstream opening. The rapids seem to get more furious. White explosions shoot higher; the white ring around the rock boils harder. The geese turn around, looking perplexed. Geysers erupt around them. Finally one goose, then the other, lifts itself into flight.

Niagara is not the tallest waterfall in the world. It's not even the tallest waterfall in New York. As for volume, it's sixth in the world, and at least twelve of the world's waterfalls are wider. But stand at the brink of the Horseshoe for a few minutes and you'll hear someone murmer, *That's a lot of water.* Niagara's comparatively narrow width accentuates the feeling of volume: 100,000 cubic feet of water plunge over less than 4,000 feet of brink. Furthermore, Niagara is not actually a river, but a strait connecting two giant inland seas. One-fifth of the world's fresh water crowds itself into the narrow channel between Lakes Erie and Ontario, rushing—half of it, anyway—over the waterfall's drop, year in, year out, with little seasonal variation. The impression you get from the resulting hypnotic downrush is less about size than continuity. That's a lot of water, and it just keeps coming.

We like to think of electricity, too, as continuous. Flip a light switch, plug in a hair dryer, and a stream of electrons rushes out. Blackouts shock Americans because they undercut the illusion of an unending, ever-ready resource, a waterfall of power right there in the wall. Early hydro promoters played up the connection. "After all is said and done, very few people ever see the falls," declared Thomas Commerford Martin, president of the American Institute of Electrical Engineers in 1896: "Now the useful energy of the cataract is made cheaply and immediately available every day in the year to hundreds and thousands, even millions of people, in an endless variety of ways."

In this view, generating electricity isn't an imposition on the waterfall—it's the distribution of that natural resource to the general population. Your electrical outlet is your own private Niagara, just waiting to be turned on.

Controversy over water diversions raged throughout the early twentieth century. By 1900, a handful of corporations dominated the generation, distribution, and sale of electricity, including hydro. Park commissioners and high-minded citizens argued that in giving these private companies unlimited charters to river water, New York was pouring Niagara's splendor into the pockets of robber barons.

In Canada a similar state of affairs gave rise to a grassroots movement demanding public takeover of the rapidly developing private power industry. The result—after years of protest—was Ontario Hydro, a publicly owned utility that managed province water resources. Predictably, this did not happen in the U.S. Instead, American protectors of Niagara became obsessed with the waterfall itself. The Niagara question became not who had a right to the river water, nor how they should use it, but rather, how to keep the Falls looking pretty. And, with the help of industry spin doctors, keeping Niagara pretty was quickly reinterpreted as taking more water away.

A typical pamphlet issued by the Buffalo, Niagara and Eastern Power Corporation in 1927 posed the question, "Why is the Horseshoe Fall eating itself to ruin?" The answer, according to power company engineers, was clear: there was too much water! Silly nature. Only bigger drawdowns could save the Falls.

Furthermore, the pamphlet declared, Niagara benefited everyone by providing the cheap, dependable power needed for the "many electro-chemical products which are being manufactured at or near Niagara . . . and bestowed upon mankind." This host of goodies was bestowing something else upon mankind—a cataract of toxic waste. In spite of the power companies' emphasis on residential electrification, Niagara power—then as now—was mostly going to the heavy industries whose factories lined the riverbank. The American power plant's first customer was aluminum manufacturer Pittsburgh Reduction—later ALCOA. It was soon joined by dozens of electro-process industries. By 1925, Niagara Falls was a leading center for the production of abrasives, graphite and graphite derivatives such as electrodes and anodes, dry cell batteries, caustic soda and chlorine, and a wide range of ferro-alloys—metal compounds made by mixing iron with metals such as zirconium, chromium, manganese, and silicon.

As industry ramped up, focus on the waterfall intensified.

A 1931 report of the Special International Niagara Board anatomized its aesthetic value in painstaking detail, calculating how much of its beauty depended on volume, width, height, clarity, and color, going so far as to point out that the "actual volume" of the waterfall was not critical to beauty, though the "impression of volume" was. The report estimated how much water could be removed while maintaining the emerald green, the seeming depth and velocity. Charts, graphs, and a special set of color chips were adduced. The report concluded by recommending reshaping the riverbed to raise the water level just above the fall, boosting the appearance of volume. Although the report was shelved until adoption of the 1950 treaty, the theoretical transformation of Niagara from sublime natural wonder to engineering feat had begun. Nature would be saved by technology. Or at least the part of it people came to see would.

Why were Niagara preservationists so worried about the waterfall's beauty? They claimed it was an uplifting spectacle, the birthright of every American. But even as they sought to prettify the cataract while simultaneously encouraging electricity consumption, the dark undercurrents of cheap power were beginning to make themselves known. The American riverbank was lined with ugly factories. Disposing of electrochemical by-products was an increasing problem. And in 1935, twenty workers filed suit against ALCOA. They were dying of the lung disease silicosis.

At the Power Authority, I ask Norm how much electricity an average household draws in a day. About a thousand watts, he tells me. There might be stretches of time—when everyone's asleep, or at work, say—when a home is drawing only 100 watts—only the fridge is running, or the air conditioning. But in the evening, when you add in lights, fans, television, computers, microwave, hot-water heater, dryer, and cell-phone chargers, just for starters, that home draws a lot more watts. Averaged out over twenty-four hours, it's an ongoing kilowatt. I ask if that number is on the rise. Norm tells me it has doubled in recent memory.

The U.S. gets about 7 percent of its electricity from hydro power. Most people are surprised by that, because hydro is still the smiling public face of electricity. The New York Power Authority has visitor centers at several hydro plants. There are no visitor centers at nuclear or coal-burning power plants.

In the Northeast blackout of 2003, a widely circulated rumor held that the massive loss of power resulted from a lightning strike at Niagara. When he tells me this, Norm bristles, as if personally offended. He did not, he declares, lose power for a single second. How much that helped was pretty clear, even in the dark.

It's easy to forget that electricity—70 percent of which comes from burning fossil fuels—takes an environmental toll, because we don't see the plants that make it. It arrives in the socket clean and odorless. And even with recent price hikes, it's still relatively cheap. I have neighbors who leave their air conditioner on when they leave town in the summer, so their cats won't get too hot.

What if we had to look at a waterless Niagara as a testament to our greed for watts? I ask Norm if there are people who say we should turn off the Falls completely. After all, compared to burning coal, hydro is relatively benign. If we can't conserve, shouldn't we maximize power's cleanest sources?

Norm and Joanne glance at each other, and I sense I may have crossed the line into things the Power Authority doesn't like to discuss.

"There are some people who say that," he says, "but they're not serious."

What about the reverse, I ask. Are there people who want the Power Authority to stop diverting water and return the Falls to their natural state?

"Oh sure," he says, shrugging. "There are always people who think that."

"They should let it rip," declares Paul Gromosiak. "If I had my druthers, that's what they'd do." A well-known Niagara historian and author of such books as *Nature's Niagara, Daring Niagara,* and *Zany Niagara,* Gromosiak is an affable, white-haired man with the face of a Norman Rockwell schoolboy. He's been haunting the Falls since his age matched his face. I meet him at the visitor center of Niagara Falls State Park on the afternoon of April 1. The waterfall has swelled to full tourist volume, but Gromosiak is not impressed. He liked it better before the treaty.

"I used to go to Goat Island and sit on my favorite log and think," he tells me. Before water diversions began, the entire island was said to tremble with the force of the pounding water. Gromosiak says he remembers that himself.

"The ice coming over the Falls would hit the water below with a sound like cannon fire," he says wistfully. Now the Power Authority has installed an ice boom across the mouth of the strait at Buffalo, to keep ice from clogging the hydro intakes.

"They say it's a natural wonder, but they're lying," Gromosiak says, shaking his schoolboy head.

After adoption of the 1950 treaty, New York State moved to utilize increased water diversion allowances. Construction of the Robert Moses plant started in 1958. But a report by the International Joint Commission pointed out that, under the new treaty's terms, the river above the Falls would drop by four feet, the flow over the American Fall would shrink to next to nothing, and even the great Horseshoe would dwindle, its flanks going completely dry at times. Thus, as the power plant was being blasted out downstream, the U.S. Army Corps of Engineers and the Hydro-Electric Power Commission of Ontario addressed the waterfall. Two working models of the Falls were built, one by each nation, and plans were drawn up for a massive engineering project to guarantee "a very satisfactory scenic spectacle" during the day's 100,000 cubic feet per second, and "an impressive scenic spectacle" during the night's 50,000.

The works undertaken by the Army Corps and Ontario Hydro are still in place today. The most visible is a large control structure in the river just above the Falls, with eighteen sluice gates that open and close to enable precise changes in water flow over the brink. There are also weirs—submerged dams—upstream to raise the river level above the Falls, and weirs and riverbed excavations immediately upstream on both flanks of the Horseshoe, to draw water toward its edges and make it spread into "an unbroken curtain shore to shore." While they were at it, the Corps blasted off overhangs, braced up Goat and Luna Islands with dowels, bolts, and cable tendons, installed drains to reduce water pressure that might encourage rockfalls, and backfilled dewatered flats at the edges of the Horseshoe to disguise shrinkage and make new viewing platforms. They reshaped the American riverbank with excavated earth and added eight and a half acres of land to Goat Island's eastern end, enough for a helicopter pad, parking lot, concession stand, and roadway. Combined with the new water drawdowns, the engineering measures slowed erosion to a crawl. Niagara Falls was stabilized and almost completely man-made—and it looked better than ever.

This was boom time at Niagara. Lots of building was going on. Reading scrapbooks from the era at the Niagara Falls Public Library, I come across a *Niagara Falls Gazette* article about a 1957 Board of Education meeting. Four years earlier, Hooker Chemical had deeded some land to Niagara Falls; the city had built a school on it and wanted to subdivide the rest. Hooker attorney Arthur Chambers came to the meeting to stop them. No basements, waterlines, or sewers should be built on the site, he told the school board, because "you're apt to hit something we buried there." Wesley Kester of the Board of Ed remarked to the *Gazette,* "There's something fishy someplace." Indeed. After the buried "something"—pesticides, dioxin, and chlorobenzenes, among eighty-two identified chemicals—began leaking into nearby basements and surfacing to contaminate playgrounds, residents would develop nervous and blood disorders, and miscarriage and birth defect rates in the neighborhood would rise to appalling levels. A baby would be born with two rows of teeth, another with three ears. A housewife named Lois Gibbs would make the plight of the neighborhood's working-class families a national cause, and the idea of environmental justice an international issue.

Eventually the federal government would step in, with President Carter de-claring the site a federal disaster area, evacuating 950 families and creating Superfund to pay for remediating Hooker's toxic mess. But the struggle to make that happen would not begin for twenty years. And when Niagara Falls received the dubious honor of being named America's first man-made disaster, it wouldn't be called Niagara Falls, but would be named after the neighborhood Hooker chose for its dump: Love Canal.

Paul Gromosiak was there for all of it. He worked for Hooker Chemical as a young man, and later, when Love Canal was making the nightly news, he taught at a middle school in that very neighborhood. Children who lived near the site sometimes asked him if they were doomed to die.

The environmental problems in Niagara didn't start with Love Canal, nor did they end there. Today, about half of the city of Niagara Falls is EPA-designated brownfields, and there are currently nineteen active Superfund sites in Niagara County, three of them on the National Priorities List. Not much cleanup is likely to happen, because the current administration has bankrupted Superfund. But none of that can be seen by the tourists. The water doesn't smell as bad as it did in the '70s, and the waterfall, well, it looks great. Last May, the Falls provided a great backdrop for *Live with Regis and Kathie Lee*.

If a waterfall is, as Thomas Cole once proposed, "the voice of the land-scape," Niagara's sparkling, carefree roar is an outright lie.

Toward the end of our interview, I ask Gromosiak how it makes him feel that water is diverted from the Falls. He seems surprised by the ques-tion, and takes a moment to think about it.

"Insulted," he says at last. "I'm not getting a chance to see what I should be seeing—the full flow that would cause this natural wonder to do what it should be doing—cut out a gorge. The natural world doesn't stay the same—it changes all the time. Look at us: do we look the same as we did twenty years ago?"

I assure Gromosiak that I do, in fact, look the same as I did twenty years ago. He laughs.

"I like change," he tells me. "Change has natural beauty. It's unpredictable. There could be a big rockfall right now, and I would be so honored to be here for it. Erosion is a bad word to some people. We're so afraid of the natural world. But we're still at nature's mercy. And I hope we always will be."

After I leave Gromosiak, I drive back into Niagara Falls, today the sorry spectacle of a boomtown gone bust. Industry here peaked in 1953: the lat-ter half of the century was a steady decline as manufacturers decamped for lower-wage, regulation-free pastures. The upwards of 150,000 jobs lost in Erie and Niagara counties alone hover like rueful ghosts over Main Street, a strip of boarded-up storefronts and foreclosure notices, signposted with the fading names of defunct stores. Kresge. The Gaslight Lounge. Hart to Hart Furniture. Slipko's Food King. Two businesses are open: the Center City Neighborhood Development Corp. and, across the street, an establishment that appears to be known only as "Adult Videos."

I head east on Buffalo Avenue, the street where many of the chemical factories once stood. Only a couple remain: less than a mile from the Falls sprawls the massive complex of Occidental, the folks who bought Hooker. Factory buildings line both sides of the road, storage tanks and pipelines and smokestacks and a couple odd bathysphere-like structures whose purpose I can only guess, all of it threaded with electrical transmission towers.

I continue east, with the river on my right. This is the poor end of town. The street numbers go up, and the houses grow smaller. An unassuming little marina appears—Niagara Boat Docks. Just beyond it I see what you always come to eventually if you drive aimlessly in Niagara Falls: a huge mesa, raised in that telltale landfill form, landscaped, fenced, barbed-wired, and dotted with exhaust pipes. At its edge sits a playground, kid-free. I pull into the small parking lot.

The fence has an address on it—9829 Buffalo Ave. It's the Hooker 102nd Street Superfund site—the less publicized outfall at the other end of William T. Love's canal. Like Love Canal, just across the expressway, its fake mountain shape ominously suggests a landscape pregnant with monstrosity. How did I end up here? I think of Norm at his power plant, proudly describing turbine upgrades, and H. G. Wells in 1906, rapturously describing Niagara dynamos as "will made visible." I think of my own giddy thrill at the Power Vista, hanging over the edge of the deck to admire the massive penstocks. Who wouldn't be awed by the prospect of harnessing such a giant organic machine? Niagara full-force is a fantastic natural spectacle. Niagara turned off is another kind of spectacle, just as fantastic—and just as natural, since we too are part of the natural world. Somehow, it's the in-between Niagara—the harnessed waterfall pretending to be wild—that leads to the landscape I'm parked at now. Because if we don't admit that the things we do to enable our lifestyle even have a cost, how can we ever know when that price is too high?

I get out of my car and walk to the playground. The jungle gym is shaped like a ship, and topped by an American flag. A light rain is falling, but the flag is flying high, because it's not an actual fabric flag. It's a fake flag, made of stiff plastic so it stands there, always unfurled, always undulating in just the right way, and pointing in the direction of the Falls.

(2006)

The Edges of the Civilized World

Tourism and the hunger for wild places

I RECENTLY HAD THE GOOD FORTUNE TO BE SENT TO THE SEA OF CORTEZ by *Islands* magazine with a more or less carte blanche assignment to return with a story about my sense of several remote, uninhabited islands near the tip of the Baja Peninsula. I traveled with the landscape photographer, George Huey, and the skipper of our chartered yacht, a capable and amiable expatriate who liked to play "Sgt. Pepper's Lonely Hearts Club Band" with his morning coffee. The skipper said he felt like the Maytag repairman, because unlike most of his customers, George and I didn't care that much about the yacht's amenities. I did not once try out the snorkeling equipment, donned my bathing suit only once, and found my hiking boots to be the most useful items in my duffel. The vessel was simply our taxi from one cove to the next. We were primarily interested in gaining a sense of the flora and fauna of the islands, and understanding what was unique to the natural history and local customs—at least what could be gleaned from a hasty tour, a paltry few guide books, sparse encounters with fishermen and tourists encamped on the beaches, George's photographic lenses and plastic sacks full of film, my blank notebooks and binoculars.

George favored the angular light of dawn and dusk, so he would take the dinghy to shore before sunrise, getting in several hours of work while I dallied on board with coffee, trying to tune out Sgt. Pepper while perusing field guides and the previous day's notes. In the afternoon we'd go ashore, hike up an arroyo flowering with sea lavender, prickly pear, and wild fig, or perch on a coastal bluff recording particularities of wind and light on the water. While the larger islands near La Paz—Isla del Espiritu Santo and San Jose—kicked me into that alert state of reverie for which I eagerly trundle the wilds, nothing surprised me more than my response to Los Islotes.

Two steep-sided rocky outcrops joined by a reef, a bent archway cutting through the smaller of the two, these islets are smeared and dripping with the whitewash of frigate birds and pelicans. Blue-footed boobies preen in nooks of the high ledges, their cartoon-colored feet making George speculate, "What could be adaptive about that?" I tried to think of something. "Their feet blend in with the sky, so that sharks don't notice them when they float on the water." The theory seemed a bit far-fetched. A latticework light tower protrudes from the plateau on top of the larger islet, several ladders scaling the cliffs on the south side. The dominant species on this piece of land, for once, is not ours, but the California sea lion. This bifurcated hunk of rock serves as their rookery.

As we passed by, dozens of the creatures lounged on the rocks, the fur dark brown when they first climb up out of the water, then turning shades of gray and gold as they dry. A big golden bull reared up, his head thrown back, as he bellowed and bellowed into the sky. Most of the sea lions were sprawled out on rocks. The skipper said it was breeding season, but it looked like sleeping season to me. I saw a pair of them draped on rocks twenty feet above the waterline. The heftier of the two had a large wound on his back, perhaps from a propeller cut—the blank of black skin looking like a jagged cattle brand, the Bar-Z.

But the sea lions were not alone at Los Islotes. In addition to our sightseeing craft, a Special Expedition tour boat was anchored off the southeast point, and two Zodiacs filled with red-vested high-tech emissaries were off-loading into the water with snorkels and masks. A dozen or so were already dog paddling close to the rocky shore. A few sea lions were swimming near them. The people kept their voices hushed, and a guide on one Zodiac leaned near his charges to give quiet instructions before easing them over the side. There was an air of tenderness and caution in their motions. But rather than sharing the ecotourists' obvious reverence and joy as they moved in closer to the rocks, I found myself enraged and disgusted at the sight. Why so visceral a reaction on my part, I wondered, to people so passionate to be intimate with nature?

I had the same response one evening when we anchored alongside another charter yacht, this one loaded with six young professionals from Los Angeles who told us, with euphoria as hyped as if it had been drug induced, of their encounter with a massive herd of dolphins swimming with energetic purpose in the middle of nowhere. The Californians were amazed to see several hundred dolphins packed close together, arcing energetically in and out of the water as they made their way toward whatever notion of "destination" inhabits a dolphin mind. They launched their dinghy into the midst of the animal turbulence and were thrilled, they reported, when the dolphins began to play around their boat. Wanting to get closer to the wild thing from which they still felt separate, they suited up with snorkels, masks, and fins and dove in the water. The dolphins scattered like mercury.

Why do people always have to push the limits? Why wasn't it good enough to witness the dolphins from a respectful distance that didn't disrupt the mission on which the animals were bound? Why the hunger to get closer and closer? But trying to play with dolphins seemed fairly benign compared to the ridiculous extremes to which commercial ecotourism has grown to meet the ever-escalating desires of thrill-seeking nature lovers. One now can make a supervised dive among black-tipped sharks in the Caribbean, kneeling on the ocean floor while the monstrous ones rip at a frozen ball of chum the tour boat has suspended over their heads. "Professional shark handlers" in the Bahamas hitch rides on the pectoral fins of tiger sharks while the paying customers gawk with wonder through their divemasks. Am I just becoming another loudmouth in a nation of cranks, or does this trend suggest that we look for somewhat more civilized ways to connect with the nonhuman wild?

A few weeks after my trip, I met a field biologist who works as a guide on Special Expedition tours, including swims with sea lions in the Sea of Cortez. I asked him why he thought people needed these encounters with animals. "It's not a need," he said, "it's a desire. They want to be approved of by another species. It's a kind of penance for all the wrongs we've done against animals." I took him to mean not any personal transgression against beasts, but a collective guilt and grief about the extinction of the bison, the passenger pigeon, and the countless lost species we meet only in the daily news. People hunger to be close to a nonhuman world, or at least to a place in the world where humans are benign. I asked him if he thought that the boatloads of tourists swimming with the sea lions at Los Islotes were invasive or disruptive to the animals. He said he didn't think so and recounted that the sea lions become quite friendly. The cows and pups will come out to swim with the visitors and blow bubbles around them. Mothers actually push their babies closer to the humans.

But I was not convinced that the practice was harmless. What about disrupting their reproductive cycle? What would the cows be doing if they weren't out swimming around with humans? What happens to animals, who learn from such encounters that humans are harmless, when hunters or powerboat joyriders come churning into their midsts? And what about the ospreys, I hammered on, telling how I'd seen a string of twenty naturalist-led tourists make a landfall on Isla San Francisco and traipse directly up to the ridge where a nesting osprey did its best to protect a little airspace. "Well," he conceded, "there's not really any regulation out there." Ahh, I have my purchase on his attention now, I thought, though a more sober inner voice cautioned, There you go again, a loose-tempered poet mouthing off to a sober scientist, having nothing but questions to back up your case. My anger seemed out of proportion to the situation, until it made me realize that I was responding to something emblematic of our wounded relationship with nature, our species' imperialism—as if it were our goal to domesticate every habitat on the planet, to turn every wild creature into a safe and innocent expression of human desire—the Bambification of the wild.

So I began asking my friends what they thought it meant to be civilized. "To live in harmony with your fellow man," said one. "To live, like the animals, in harmony with the earth," said another. "Basically it comes down to Tupperware," said the third. "To drink from a silver cup when riding in a stagecoach," said one who'd been perusing the celluloid mythology of the Old West. Tohono O'odham poet Ofelia Zepeda said, "Our people don't really have a word for it. My mother just used to say, 'Keep your hair out of your face and don't be like the enemy.'" For centuries the word has been associated with the life of cities, with building communities and defending them against barbarians, with manifest destiny and domesticating the wild. But what can it mean to be civilized now when the perils of global warming, a heat-trap sky, shrinking wildlands, and cascading extinctions are waking us up to the idea that the earth is a global commons, the future of which is in our bumbling hands?

It seems obvious to me that to be civilized at this point in history must mean to set limits, to understand when our comfort and freedom exacts too extreme a cost on the overall well-being of others and on the planet that sustains us all, and to understand that certain possibilities, such as rediscovering faith in humankind, depends on setting limits, just as our freedom of movement in cars depends on occasional red lights. If we could see the entire webbed sphere of life on earth as the commons and ourselves as being responsible for maintaining its habitability, then citizenship would no longer be considered in terms merely of our local human community. Citizenship would mean learning to live in responsible relationship with all the people, plants, and animals on earth.

I suspect that a hunger for just such an experience of citizenship drives many of us to become tourists. We long to see foreign places and cultures, exotic flora and fauna. We long even more ardently to see those that are imperiled, because we don't want to pass up the last chance to see the [fill in the blank]. We long to get close, as close as the zoom lens has taught us we deserve to be. We want to look around, observe local traditions and wildlife, take a few photos, and go home feeling that we have learned anew something about the world's complexity, beauty, and trials. We want to discover our own innocence as reflected in a foreign place. With such good intentions, how can we see our presence in another's community as invasive or disruptive?

But ask locals what it is like to be on the other side of the tourist equation, and too often the word "tourist" becomes an expletive. What once was a history full of suffering, dignity, and hard-won survival becomes a parody of itself—cowboys, Indians, and mountain goats depicted on T-shirts and jockey shorts. Native ceremonial ritual with centuries of tradition to give it meaning becomes the latest three-minute show on MTV. Public land gets trashed and private land gets bought by outsiders, escalating property values so that locals can no longer afford to own, or even rent a home. Rather than being the center of town, locals become a service class devoted to meeting the needs of visitors who have a very short attention span for the needs and problems of the place. Everyone knows that the passers-through, and probably even the new settlers, won't be there to help when the local fishery or pulp mill is shut down. Locals, even those who have wooed in tourists, come to resent those on whom their economic well-being depends.

We who love to travel do not mean to harm the quality of other people's lives. We do not mean to contribute to the erosion of other creatures' land or other people's cultures. But human hunger is robbing the earth of its future. The rich rob the earth out of their greed, the poor rob the earth out of necessity, and those many of us in the economic middle flounder in despair and ambivalence. We simply are too numerous. Nevertheless our hunger to experience other places and ways of life does not abate. Our confidence that lives somehow more authentic than our own are out there waiting to teach us the meaning of life does not fade no matter how many strip malls and burger barns we find on our journeys. And the good that can come of travel continues to be real and enticing.

By the year 2000, tourism will become the world's biggest industry, according to predictions by the World Tourism Organization (a United Nations affiliate). One of the fastest growing branches of the industry is ecotourism, a phenomenon that has evolved out of the popularity of wild and exotic places, and the growing concern about environmental degradation. As more and more people have wanted to see big game in the Serengeti or the rainforest in Brazil, the travel industry has responded with bigger and more frequent tours. One industry estimate holds that four to six million Americans travel overseas for nature each year; nature tourists from Europe and Japan further swell the stream. The most popular destinations (according to a 1987 study) are Nepal, Kenya, Tanzania, China, Mexico, Costa Rica, and Puerto Rico. I suspect that Brazil, Rwanda, and the Galápagos would be likely candidates to add to this list in the '90s. And ecotourism is very popular within the United States; in 1989, there were 265 million recreational visits to the national park system alone. Many communities, from Alaska to Wyoming to West Virginia, in which natural resources are so depleted that logging, mining, ranching, or fishing are no longer economically viable ways of life, are looking to ecotourism as a future.

The *principle* of ecotourism seems wise. Promote educational trips aimed at increasing the tourist's appreciation of the natural world and local cultures, while making economic success dependent on the preservation of that very biological and cultural diversity. Cut down the rainforest, and the tourists won't come. Bring the fat tourist dollar into lean communities, and the global commons will stand only to gain. The old utopian conservation approach of closing off wilderness in order to protect it has largely given way to the belief that the better a wilderness is known, the less likely it will be destroyed.

But there are problems. Mass tourism, no matter what the intention, may hasten environmental degradation by adding further stress to natural resources, wildlife, and cultural integrity. One former ecotourism leader, who left the field due to her disillusion with its promise, spoke to me of her concerns: huge resorts plunked down on the beach displacing local people; cruise ships dumping waste offshore; safari vans rushing cheetahs for photos; hordes of camera-toting invaders gawking and snapping shutters at tribal people as if at Mickey and Minnie Mouse.

In addition, the nature of ecotourism makes its economic promise a gamble. One needs to look closely at where the ecotourism dollar ends up. A World Bank study estimated that over one-half of gross tourism revenues in the developing countries ends up back in developed countries. And while many travelers may be seeking penance with the wild, the intent of others is less noble. "I remember," the former ecotour leader reported, "a French family at a rather questionable rainforest camp off the Rio Negro in Brazil telling me that they hated humidity, didn't like boat travel nor sleeping in hammocks but felt that they had to get a few photos of the Amazon before it was gone." Even if the revenue from such tourists does go into the local economy of a disadvantaged area, what happens to that place when the fad to acquire such memorabilia of the wild dies out and a new market takes tourists elsewhere?

The Ecotourism Society (TES) was established in 1991 to address some of these concerns. Their definition of ecotourism is "responsible travel to natural areas which conserves the environment and sustains the well-being of local people," emphasizing that responsible ecotourism addresses both ecological and economic concerns. TES is a valuable resource for international research and planning, and if their guidelines for travelers and tour operators were adhered to, ecotourism might indeed heal the ills of exploitation and trivialization that tourism can create, and integrate conservation and development. On a hopeful note, the tourism industry's profile of an eco-tourist is a person interested in making a contribution to conservation, is well educated, an experienced traveler with dispensable income, and tends to be "amicable," "broad minded," "intelligent," "self-assured," and "sociable." Such people, it seems reasonable to conclude, will do their best to make this kind of travel a virtue.

At a recent visit to the Alaska Raptor Rehabilitation Center in Sitka, I was reminded by a naturalist of the correct procedure of handling an injured bird. "Our first impulse," she said, "is to pick it up, bring it close to our faces, cuddle and talk to it. But that amount of visual input can terrify the bird so that its heart will speed up and it will die." The proper technique is to cover the bird's eyes, thus quieting its alarm prior to further handling. I cite this example because it illustrates so well how the results of our actions are not always as benign as our intentions—and Lord knows we have plenty of examples to suggest that this axiom might be a useful one. Given the inordinate human capacity for blindness to the consequences of our actions, how might we exercise more care when trying to get closer to nature? It is as foolish to think that our presence does not upset the behavior and metabolism of wild animals, as it is to think that tourists will not change the character of a community. If we don't know whether our snorkeling up to the sea lion rookery will interrupt the animals' reproductive cycle, then why risk it? If we don't know whether tour boats chasing gray whales off the Baja coast will harm the leviathans, then why risk it? The same principle might be applied to cultural tourism in which travelers from uprooted cultures visit remote villages to gawk at "authentic" indigenous people.

Some of my "green" colleagues are fond of saying, "We must stop trying to control nature." But I have come to feel that such a position denies how powerful a force the human species is on the planet. We will control nature, often without even being aware that we are doing so. Sure, there will be microbes and hurricanes that will get the better of us. If one has faith in the profound and mysterious process of evolution on Earth, one must also have faith in the power that process has invested in us, as the dominant and determining species on the planet. One must also have faith in our ability to rise to the astonishingly difficult challenges we face in preserving the global commons.

Perhaps it seems absurd to think in terms of a global commons when we haven't yet learned how to be citizens of a human community without war, domestic violence, rapacious waste, and that trivialization of human suffering that passes for entertainment in our homes known as "the talk show." I've always thought that if the world suddenly faced marauding alien imperialists from another galaxy who give us a thirty-day ultimatum to stop our warring ways or else—we'd learn fast how to unify and protect each other. And we do face a common enemy capable of destroying the life we love on Earth. As Pogo said during the Vietnam War, "We've seen the enemy and it is us." Suddenly we are both the invading barbarians and the only ones around to protect the city. Each one of us is at the center of the civilized world and on its edge.

After leaving Los Islotes, George and I talked about the work we do and wondered whether, for all of our good intentions and love of the wild, we were merely shills for the worst of the tourist industry, the harbingers of the hordes that would despoil the delicate islands we were privileged to see in their innocence. We talked about Robinson Jeffers, whose radiant poems celebrating the natural world became so misanthropic late in his life that he suggested nuclear war would be a good thing, because it would purge the earth of our ruinous kind. We talked about the idea of "eco-porn"—the way idealized photographs of animals may foster the idea that creatures exist for our pleasure, rather than for the inherent dignity of their own existence. Still, it's hard to feel anything but admiration for a man who gets up before the sun, lugging a heavy tripod and backpack up the side of a mountain, then waiting, and waiting some more, for the light and the wind to be exactly right in order to hold onto a split second of the world's beauty. And it's hard to believe that my own attention to wild beauty is anything less noble than a healing of the soul. The human desire for wildness is strong and deep, we feel so distant from that source and its unconscious movements in our bodies and minds.

But, given that the hunger for the wild too often means that we love nature to death, I began to wonder how else I might feed that hunger. I began to think about how, collectively, we who love to travel might be more gentle, more thoughtful, more willing to redefine what gives us a wild thrill. For one thing, we might look for and nurture what's exotic and wild in ourselves—our imaginations and complicated emotions. We might come a bit closer, physically closer, to the most terrifying wilderness of all, our own mortality, the awareness of which makes us unique among animals while at the same time making us equal to all creatures that suffer birth and death. To understand our own animal nature, we might sit at the bedside of the dying or attend the birth of a child.

For another thing, we might understand that our hunger to be thrilled and frightened by nature's fierceness suggests our need to be humbled by the powers that have given us our lives. We might abandon the notion once and for all that we can know the world as it might be without human presence. That seems to be what we long for when we are saddened about going to a wild place and finding other people already there. This might lead us, when we travel, to be interested in what is at stake for local people in their relationship with their place, and to experience some exchange other than a monetary one. We might soften our alienating presence in another's community by traveling alone or in small groups, by having a single leisurely conversation with a stranger who has nothing to sell us. And we might be certain that the money we spend as tourists, especially when we visit economically deprived places, goes to those who most need it, rather than to the glitzy corporate resort that employs locals as parodies of a dying way of life—waiters and maids dressed as their peasant ancestors, while the resort's very construction may have displaced the last remnant of a local peasant culture. We might decide not to visit the most popular nature tour sites, or those where delicate conditions would be harmed by our presence. Rather than going and taking a snapshot, we might stay home and send a check. We might improve our position in the biological community by informally apprenticing ourselves to another species, slowly developing a deep understanding of one small corner of the biological world as an antidote to the overwhelming tide of superficial information about everything on Earth that threatens to drown our imaginations.

These are not prescriptions for what we should do to save the world. I don't really know what we should do. I do know that my sense of urgency about protecting the world's beauty and bounty has grown too keen for me to offer merely poetic ambivalence, or despair, or yet another plea to write to Congress. Perhaps, as Audubon once pointed out, it is not the world that needs saving, but our character.

After leaving the Sea of Cortez, I traveled, as an ecotourist, to the Mexican state of Michoacán to visit the monarch butterflies. There, on five forested mountaintops, the entire population of monarchs living east of the Rockies spends the winter. They migrate from as far away as Ontario, and though not all of the hibernating animals will live long enough to re-migrate back to their starting place, some will. The feat seems even more heroic when one learns that the migrating animals may be two or three generations removed from those making the previous migration from the north. The monarch migration is one of the most impressive natural phenomena on the planet. And the monarch reserve, established in 1986, is one of the more successful ecotourism sites.

The area to which the monarchs migrate is poor, having been farmed by local residents living for centuries on steep, now largely deforested, hillsides.

It looks a bit like a peasant California—rolling grassy hills, a few peaks topped with evergreen forest. The homes are mostly adobe, ramshackle, except for the care shown in the hanging planters made from aluminum cans that deck the outside walls. Fencerows are marked with agaves farmed for making tequila or *pulche,* a fermented drink with a nasty reputation. Cornfields are worked with oxen, children, and hands.

Until one has experienced walking in a wind caused by flapping butterfly wings, it is difficult to convey the power of the monarchs' aggregate presence. Millions of the animals are packed into the trees, hanging like huge colonies of mistletoe, or sacks of laundry. On warm days, many will flutter loose from the mass, the air becoming a blizzard of delicate, papery bodies, as they lower to sip water from a pool or to nectar on wildflowers dotting the forest floor. It is the largest gathering of a single animal anywhere in North America. This year between one-half and one billion monarchs are gathered in an area of less than fifty acres. They will live through the winter by metabolizing stored fat. So rich are these fat bodies that, if this forest were to burn, the trees would flame like whale oil lamps. Those monarchs fluttering to the flowers in midwinter are ones whose fat supply is too low to sustain them. They are unlikely to survive the cold. The forest floor is carpeted with dead monarchs. This is their sanctuary and their mortuary.

Of the five protected sites, only two are open to tourists, and these, only under the guidance of *vigilantes,* retrained loggers whose job it is to protect the forest from black market logging, disruption, and noise. GUARDA SILENCIO, read the signs posted along the trail—PROTECT THE SILENCE. The remaining three sites will not be opened until naturalists, both U.S. and Mexican, have a better understanding of the impact of tourism on the butterflies. As the *vigilantes* led our group through the forest, they leaned down and swept the dirt with their hands in order to clear the path of animals that had fallen in our way and did not have the energy to rise. At first I thought the action was a superfluous ritual—the scattering of bodies on the trail looked dead. But then I saw a man take one of the creatures in his palms and blow on it with his warm breath until the wings loosened and the frail one staggered into the air.

We may not know yet the impact of tourists on the monarchs, but I can say a thing or two about their impact on me. I left that ground with a quiet sense of the holiness of what has transpired on this planet as it has transformed from a ball of flaming rock to all this living complication. In an open-air stall with a wood-fired cookstove, I bought a meal from a sturdy woman with a braid that reached the back of her knees—*pollo con mole y tortillas azules y arroz,* the sweetest meat I'd ever tasted, flavored with marigold blooms fed to the local chickens to make their yolks more yellow and their flesh more fragrant.

Another woman pressed out handfuls of blue cornmeal—the primary crop grown on these steep depleted hills. She lay the dough between sheets of wax paper, flattened it in a wooden tortilla press to form the dark imperfect circles I would eat and eat until I could eat no more.

(1996)

JOHN LANDRETTI

On Waste Lonely Places

I have gone into the waste lonely places
Behind the eye; the lost acres at the edge of smoky cities.

—Theodore Roethke

I LIVE IN AN OLD NEIGHBORHOOD NEAR A SMALL DOWNTOWN, JUST beyond the reach of the last parking meters. Any of the houses here would look stately and haunted perched on a hill somewhere, but as it is they're all serried together down the long city blocks: most gables and bay windows look out on the bay windows and gables of one's immediate neighbor. I've given up a country view for convenience; the university where I work is just a half-mile away—and five hundred feet up—at rest on a stack of sea bottoms some 350 million years old. From that height the view affords a wilderness of hanging valleys and dramatic clouds that typify the Finger Lakes region of central New York. But at my home in the lowlands, where I occupy a second-story flat, I must content myself with a more modest vista: that meager scrap of landscape as seen from a small window in the back bathroom. You work with what you've got. Using the toilet as a chair I'll occasionally ponder that unextraordinary horizon of roofs, wires, and trees. The best viewing occurs at dusk, especially after a rain, when the sky is red and newly washed, when the clouds reflect on the wet glass of old garages and in the watery sheen of gardens.

Years passed by before I realized that the awe I sometimes felt among grandeur (the peaks of mountains, say) was really no different from the awe available to me in places as prosaic as the view from a bathroom window. It all seems to be a matter of keener seeing, of opening oneself to a degree of perception that Rilke suggests is not simply an aesthetic consideration, but an issue of personal responsibility: "All this was mission. / But could you accomplish it? Weren't you always / distracted by expectation, as if every event / announced a beloved? . . ."

I certainly know that hindsight marks *me* as distracted, a person so given to introspection that I've slid through countless days announcing beloveds left and right. To be sure, nobody could possibly devote all attention to every thing encountered—we would go mad—but it could be argued, successfully I think, that as a nation we Americans trend too far in the other direction, toward inattention, and if this is taken to be true we might do well to reconnoiter our aesthetic prejudices, especially those that shape our definitions of what we call "ugly" and even more so, "mundane."

As a boy I believed the only sights that deserved my undivided attention, simply because they were places, were those bastions of grandeur, our national parks. A national park was the high art of topography. Its purpose was to inspire and edify, the way we're told that a symphony is supposed to foment our finer sensibilities. This I learned from the adults that populated my childhood, well-meaning small-town folks who once or twice a year approached national parks the way they might attend a big-city concert: dressed for the occasion, they bought tickets and arrived with programs and an air of reverent uncertainty. Meanwhile the rest of their world, all those rural and urban scrapscapes that circumfused their days, received for the balance of the year that glazy attention usually given to music at supermarkets.

At the end of each spring in my old neighborhood, many of the families used to load up their cars and head west. Yosemite, Death Valley, Yellowstone—all through the summer and until the leaves dropped, they rolled out of the suburbs toward the geysers, the mesas, and peaks. During this collective absence I ran a profitable traffic in yard work; on those long afternoons of high summer I'd watch my reflection pacing a lawn mower in their vacant windows, and I'd wonder about the world they were bound for. What were they seeing and feeling in the presence of those topographical icons? In our kitchen my mother kept a nature calendar; occasionally I'd touch the picture (a split-rail fence before a mountain, a whale breaching at dusk) as if those images alone could charge my blood with a moment of "real" living.

When the families returned, their cars were always dusty, the windshields plastered with stickers. Though the children had a lot to say, I can no longer recall their stories. What stays in my mind is the parents, how so many of those people returned spent of language, how wearily they unpacked their luggage. Far from revitalized, they shuffled with the slump-backed, long-throated look of citizens returning from exile. While the wife implored after the kids, the husband would take me aside and press some cash into my hand—often with an appreciative, if perfunctory compliment, one that rarely followed any sort of inspection.

How was the trip, I'd say. Some husbands murmured about the expense, while others said "Fine." A few winked and told me to stay single. Most simply rubbed their faces and said they were glad to be back.

When I finished college I went west myself, finally passing through those majestic places encapsulated on the bumpers of my neighbors' station wagons. Now and then I traveled as a hitchhiker, musing over landscapes the whole way; headed nowhere special, I was pacing on a continental scale. At first I made a point to tramp through every national park in my path. A time or two I got into backcountry, but most often I simply glimpsed the grandeur from the edge of a park road, or the lip of a scenic overlook. Usually I shared the view with a host of other tourists, and I recall—of the more congested overlooks—that as time passed and more people arrived, these crowds always seemed to enact a common dynamic: they became a sort of microcosm, one that in a curious way acted out the whole of our moiled and imploring immigrant history.

Imagine a scenic turnoff at the Great Divide. Beyond the pay binoculars the view is magnificent, striated with glaciers and peppered with hawks. Say it's July Fourth, the dawn's early light. For a while the turnoff is unoccupied, save for a few orbiting flies and perhaps a marmot at rest on the base of its elongated shadow. Then a Winnebago sails in with flapping flags. These new arrivals dock near the edge and gape from stickered windows, bringing to this solitary view a sense of wonder and privilege. Then others begin to arrive; they park their RVs and stake places along the stone fence. Kids eye one another from the safety of parental legs. Animals mull in the dust and people walk around with pop cans and cigars. Still more arrive, and eventually the little overlook becomes as crowded as a steerage deck drawing up to Ellis Island. A line of people flute the line of the fence, and as they vie for a private audience, there grows among them an air of burgeoning annoyance and polite restraint. As the group continues to swell, so does the general uneasiness. The old timers feel entitled to the spot they had claimed; the newcomers feel the pie ought to be shared. The very latest arrivals sense this, as much as they note the lack of space, and grimly press on.

The worst aspect of this crowding is not the hostility or desperation, but the collective embarrassment. It's present in the flinching eye contact, in the contrast between the bright cheery clothes and that tight-lipped bumping around with cameras. Crowded as they are, they understand that something is amiss, that though they are physically close to the object of their journey, they remain as spiritually distanced as they were the day they left home. Despite all the gaping, the glaciers retain their cool and fragrant secrets and the hawks circle away out of sight. From high above, those turnoffs must be quite a view: each a little bump off a road where a crowd of tiny hands flail like cilia at time immemorial. It was during moments like these that I began to understand the why of that devitalized look which had marred the faces of so many of my childhood neighbors just back from grandeur.

As interactive an enterprise as I've found hitchhiking to be, it is also a study in solitude. Often it is life on a desert island. Check out the guard rails near Gillette, Wyoming; Altoona, Pennsylvania; El Paso, Texas and you will find home states scratched into the steel; you will see the hours tallied and crossed out, the names of lovers cut in with nubs of shale. This is the archaeology of the stranded. Perhaps it's more accurate to say that as the hitchhiker's day passes, his or her life is lived out on a string of desert islands—an archipelago of crossroads and on-ramps. It was this solitary aspect of hitchhiking, more than anything, that led me to reconsider the way I measure the worth of a place.

During all that "island hopping," with hours and sometimes days to kill in a single spot, I found myself forced to acknowledge, and later to admire, that meager terrain upon which I was repeatedly stranded. I refer to those places we pass every day: our interstate weed beds and chemical sloughs; the cinder narrows of our commuter tracks; the hard yellow fields around our tank farms; the industrial fairways and caged waterfalls of power plants; our pits of kudzu and piss elm; our dump-edge wallows with stumps and tires nested in ponds of green oatmeal. These are our other parks, our marginalized and unnoticed acres, grandeur's doppelgänger, with a doppelgänger's disturbing wisdom and equivocal hospitality.

The places I came to know best were the ones in which I found myself at dusk. I'd have traveled all night if I'd been assured safe passage, but it was too violent and unreliable a time, and so I would head for the margins, throw my hat to the ground and call it home. When I began to take these places into account, when I acknowledged that every such place was not mere background music between topographical symphonies, but that *any* patch of ground was special all to itself and worthy of consideration—then a curious reciprocation occurred: these places began to notice me.

What occurs is a kind of situational coalescence. As the taillights of that last ride grow small and wink out, the horizon gathers itself to your singular perspective. There is no grandeur to bait expectation, no promise to invite distraction, only the quiet of ditch and litter and grass and self; without preconceptions you begin to see your place in a different way, from the ground up. You warm to how consummate this place is in its becoming: the perfect pattern of stones along the shoulder; the fast food wrappers, their logos clinging just so to the sage; there at long rest in the shadows, that old trilobite of the highway, the fallen muffler. And so you become consummate yourself; instead of a face lost in an embarrassed crowd, you become unique and necessary to that moment, your perspective creating, for better or worse, this one place in the world. It is a time to whistle.

I recall a night in Ohio spent in the loop of a cloverleaf. The grass was tall and as I lay on my back, it rose up around me and created an intimacy of panicles and thistles that in their complete stillness seemed to touch against the stars. Meanwhile the trucks moaned around me, each executing in that curve of sound a profound change of course, from dead south to due east.

That circle of earth is named somewhere on a map; like all our land it is endowed with coordinates. Yet no traveler would have cause to set a course for such a place, and so its representation gathers dust somewhere—in a library perhaps, or among some courthouse archive—of interest only to civil engineers and road crews. Offering your attention to a waste place is like finding a book in the library, a book nobody reads. Or perhaps a book harboring a single due date, one purple smudge thirty years old. And there it is in your hand by the effortless design of coincidence. You look over its pages and before is effort and presence; whether the contents have appeal is another matter, but the book does exist and is open before you, full of its telling. And so it is with these shelves and sheaves of world that daily surround us: every rock, blade, and bottle, every leaf, an invitation to an understanding.

Keep in mind, lolling in a waste place will perplex and even disturb those who catch you at it. Once some time ago I was traveling back east when dusk came and I made camp just outside a large city, near the end of a runway. I sat in the sooty, blown-down grass and watched the jets rush through the goldenrod and lift away. Behind me was a road and beyond that the backwash of an industrial park. In the distance, lights strobed on a smokestack and powerline scaffolds marshaled along an oily black slough. I left my camp to wander along the slough. I counted box turtles, submerged appliances, watched the tiny shadow of a jet slide across the polished sludge. Meanwhile the cars shot by, one after the other, every driver glancing at me, askance. What in God's name, they seemed to wonder, was that man doing out there without a vehicle? A few bowed toward the other lane, giving me more than enough room. It was a sobering observation, to see that there are places in our cities so completely dismissed of our consideration that when one of us finally stops to poke around, the spectacle invites puzzlement and even alarm.

In my earliest days as a hitchhiker, when I was still inclined to grumble while stranded on my desert islands, I found myself, one evening, waylaid on a patch of Nebraska hardpan. There were train tracks along the road, and I remember how faraway and straight they went. Stuck for four hours, I was forced finally to give up any hope of night camped in full view of the Rockies. Wearily, I climbed the bank and tossed my hat on the ground. It was a five-star waste place, with beer cans at rest in the ditch and old cattails crippled against the sky. I chewed on some wheat bread and morosely watched as hundreds of small birds gathered on the power lines across the road. After dusk I crawled into my tent to wait out the night.

Some time later, when I was nearly asleep, my tent brightened, became a sort of nylon membrane shaking with light. I sat up, bolt straight, still half in a dream. The ground was trembling along my legs. There was an explosion and the light vanished. Another explosion, then a third. Following this came a bombardment of noise so loud and relentless that in my fright I believed the noise alone would kill me. It went on for ten minutes, a flash flood of axles and bed springs slamming down an iron coulee.

When it quieted I crawled from my tent, bewildered. I watched the caboose retreating, a speedy clickety-clack with a red light low at the terminus. That freighter must have been doing eighty. I went the five feet over to the tracks and grasped the rail still ringing and warm. From far away came a mournful whistle, then the child's play of a passing semi. A crescent moon was just up, lifting its hooks through those power lines of sleeping birds. This is what I am, it all seemed to say; now let's review.

I was not quick to go back to sleep. Instead I lowered myself onto the edge of that humming rail and stared awhile at the moon in the power lines. Here was not the grandeur of glaciers and massifs. But neither was it void space, a mere window blur from which to bounce a cigarette. It was *somewhere*, a place full of its own knowing, and it had shaken me to the core. I sat quietly for a long while, feeling the incredible reach of silence around me. It is a sobering thing, and strange, to live in a country so lathered with dreams and to find yourself in a place where nothing, absolutely nothing, is promised. I drew a breath and then for a long while looked out on all the different darknesses. By noon the next day I was among the mountains, among aspens and snow and alpine light; all that grandeur seen from a new perspective, seen walking as if walking anywhere, dazzling in its own place in the world.

(1994)

A Word in Favor of Rootlessness

I AM ONE OF THE CONVERTED WHEN IT COMES TO THE CULTURAL AND economic necessity of finding place. Our rootlessness—our refusal to accept the discipline of living as responsive and responsible members of neighborhoods, communities, landscapes, and ecosystems—is perhaps our most serious and widespread disease. The history of our country, and especially of the American West, is in great part a record of damage done by generations of boomers, both individual and corporate, who have wrested from the land all that a place could give and continually moved on to take from another place. Boomers such as Wallace Stegner's father, who, as we see him in *The Big Rock Candy Mountain,* "wanted to make a killing and end up on Easy Street." Like many Americans, he was obsessed by the fruit of Tantalus: "Why remain in one dull plot of Earth when Heaven was reachable, was touchable, was just over there?"

We don't stand much chance of restoring and sustaining the health of our land, or of perpetuating ourselves as a culture, unless we can outgrow our boomer adolescence and mature into stickers, or nesters—human beings willing to take on the obligations of living in communities rooted in place, conserving nature as we conserve ourselves. And maybe, slowly, we are headed in that direction. The powers and virtues of place are celebrated in a growing body of literature and discussed in conferences and classrooms across the country. Bioregionalism, small-scale organic farming, urban food co-ops, and other manifestations of the spirit of place seem to be burgeoning, or at least coming along.

That is all to the good. But as we settle into our home places and local communities and bioregional niches, as we become the responsible economic and ecologic citizens we ought to be, I worry a little. I worry, for one thing, that we will settle in place so pervasively that no unsettled places will remain. But I worry about us settlers, too. I feel at least a tinge of concern that we might allow our shared beliefs and practices to harden into orthodoxy, and that the bathwater of irresponsibility we are ready to toss out the home door might contain a lively baby or two. These fears may turn out to be groundless, like most of my insomniac broodings. But they are on my mind, so indulge me, if you will, as I address some of the less salutary aspects of living in place and some of the joys and perhaps necessary virtues of rootlessness.

No power of place is more elemental or influential than climate, and I feel compelled at the outset to report that we who live in the wet regions of the Northwest suffer immensely from our climate. Melville's Ishmael experienced a damp, drizzly November in his soul, but only now and then. For us it is eternally so, or it feels like eternity. From October well into June we slouch in our mossy-roofed houses listening to the incessant patter of rain, dark thoughts slowly forming in the cloud chambers of our minds. It's been days, weeks, *years,* it seems, since a neighbor knocked or a letter arrived from friend or agent or editor. Those who live where sun and breezes play, engaged in their smiling businesses, have long forgotten us, if they ever cared for us at all. Rain drips from the eaves like poison into our souls. We sit. We sleep. We wait for the mail.

What but climate could it be that so rots the fiber of the Northwestern psyche? Or if not climate itself, then an epiphenomenon of climate— perhaps the spores of an undiscovered fungus floating out of those decadent forests we environmentalists are so bent on saving. Oh, we try to improve ourselves. We join support groups and twelve-step programs, we drink gallons of cappuccino and café latte, we bathe our pallid bodies in the radiance of full-spectrum light machines. These measures keep us from dissolving outright into the sodden air, and when spring arrives we bestir ourselves outdoors, blinking against the occasional cruel sun and the lurid displays of rhododendrons. By summer we have cured sufficiently to sally forth to the mountains and coast, where we linger in sunglasses and try to pass for normal.

But it is place we are talking about, the powers of place. As I write this, my thoughts are perhaps unduly influenced by the fact that my right ear has swollen to the size and complexion of a rutabaga. I was working behind the cabin this afternoon—my summer residence—cutting up madrone and Douglas fir slash with the chainsaw, when I evidently stepped too close to a yellow-jacket nest. I injured none of their tribe, to my knowledge, but one of them sorely injured me. Those good and industrious citizens take place pretty seriously. Having no poison on hand with which to obliterate them, I started to get out the .22 and shoot them each and every one, but thought better of it and drank a tumbler of bourbon instead.

And now, a bit later, a spectacle outside my window only confirms my bitter state of mind. The place in question is the hummingbird feeder, and the chief influence of that place is to inspire in hummingbirds a fiercely intense desire to impale one another on their needlelike beaks. Surely they expend more energy blustering in their buzzy way than they can possibly derive from the feeder. This behavior is not simply a consequence of feeding Kool-Aid to already over-amped birds—they try to kill each other over natural flower patches too. Nor can it be explained as the typically mindlessly violent behavior of the male sex in general. Both sexes are represented in the fray, and females predominate. It is merely a demonstration of over-identification with place. Humans do it too. Look at Yosemite Valley on the Fourth of July. Look at any empty parking place in San Francisco or Seattle. Look at Jerusalem.

When human beings settle in a place for the long run, much good occurs. There are dangers, though. Stickers run the substantial risk of becoming sticks-in-the-mud, and sticks with attitude. Consider my own state of Oregon, which was settled by farmers from the Midwest and upper South who had one epic move in them, across the Oregon Trail, and having found paradise resolved not to stir again until the millennium. The more scintillating sorts—murderers, prostitutes, lawyers, writers, other riffraff—tended toward Seattle or San Francisco. And so it happens that we Oregonians harbor behind our bland and agreeable demeanor a serious streak of moralism and conformism. We have some pretty strict notions about the way people should live. We were among the first to start the nationwide spate of legal attacks on gay and lesbian rights, and we annually rank among the top five states in citizen challenges to morally subversive library books, such as *Huckleberry Finn, The Catcher in the Rye,* and *The Color Purple.*

This pernicious characteristic is strongest, along with some of our best characteristics, where communities are strongest and people live closest to the land—in the small towns. When my girlfriend and I lived in Klamath Falls in the early 1970s, we were frequently accosted by our elderly neighbor across the road, Mrs. Grandquist. She was pointedly eager to lend us a lawn mower, and when she offered it she had the unnerving habit of staring at my hair. Our phone was just inside the front door, and sometimes as we arrived home it rang before we were entirely *through* the door. "You left your lights on," Mrs. Grandquist would say. Or, "You really ought to shut your windows when you go out. We've got burglars, you know." Not in that block of Denver Avenue, we didn't. Mrs. Grandquist and other watchful citizens with time on their hands may have kept insurance rates down, but the pressure of all those eyes and inquiring minds was at times intensely uncomfortable. Small towns are hard places to be different. Those yellowjackets are vigilant, and they can sting.

Customs of land use can become as ossified and difficult to budge as social customs. The Amish, among other rural peoples, practice responsible and sustainable farming. But long-term association with a place no more *guarantees* good stewardship than a long-term marriage guarantees a loving and responsible relationship. As Aldo Leopold noted with pain, there are farmers who habitually abuse their land and cannot easily be induced to do otherwise. Thoreau saw the same thing in Concord—landspeople who, though they must have known their places intimately, mistreated them continually. They whipped the dog every day because the dog was no good, and that's the way no-good dogs had always been dealt with.

As for us of the green persuasions, settled or on the loose, we too are prone—more prone than most—to orthodoxy and intolerance. We tend to be overstocked in piety and self-righteousness, deficient in a sense of humor about our values and our causes. Here in the Northwest, where debate in the last twenty years has focused on logging issues, it's instructive to compare bumper stickers. Ours say, sanctimoniously, STUMPS DON'T LIE or LOVE YOUR MOTHER. Those who disagree with us, on the other hand, sport sentiments such as HUG A LOGGER—YOU'LL NEVER GO BACK TO TREES, or EARTH FIRST! (WE'LL LOG THE OTHER PLANETS LATER).

I don't mean to minimize the clear truth that ecological blindness and misconduct are epidemic in our land. I only mean to suggest that rigid ecological correctness may not be the most helpful treatment. All of us, in any place or community or movement, tend to become insiders; we all need the outsider, the contrarian, to shake our perspective and keep us honest. Prominent among Edward Abbey's many tonic qualities was his way of puncturing environmental pieties (along with almost every other brand of piety he encountered). What's more, the outsider can sometimes see landscape with a clarity unavailable to the native or the longtime resident. It was as a relative newcomer to the Southwest that Abbey took the notes that would become his best book, in which he imagined the canyon country of the Colorado Plateau more deeply than anyone had imagined it before or has imagined it since. His spirit was stirred and his vision sharpened by his outsider's passion. I don't know that he could have written *Desert Solitaire* if he had been raised in Moab or Mexican Hat.

Unlike Thoreau, who was born to his place, or Wendell Berry, who returned to the place he was born to, Edward Abbey came to his place from afar and took hold. More of a lifelong wanderer was John Muir, who we chiefly identify with the Sierra Nevada but who explored and sojourned in and wrote of a multitude of places, from the Gulf of Mexico to the Gulf of Alaska. I think Muir needed continually to see new landscapes and life forms in order to keep his ardent mind ignited. Motion for him was not a pathology but a devotion, an essential joy, an ongoing discovery of place and self. Marriage to place is something we need to realize in our culture, but not all of us are the marrying kind. The least happy period of Muir's life was his tenure as a settled fruit farmer in Martinez, California. He was more given to the exhilarated attention and fervent exploration of *wooing*, more given to rapture than to extended fidelity. "Rapture" is related etymologically to "rape," but unlike the boomer, who rapes a place, the authentic wooer allows the place to enrapture him.

Wooing often leads to marriage, of course, but not always. Is a life of wooing place after place less responsible than a life of settled wedlock? It may be less sustainable, but the degree of its responsibility depends on the authenticity of the wooing. John Muir subjected himself utterly to the places he sought out. He walked from Wisconsin to the Gulf Coast, climbed a tree in a Sierra windstorm, survived a subzero night on the summit of Mount Shasta by scalding himself in a sulfurous volcanic vent. There was nothing macho about it—he loved where he happened to be and refused to miss one lick of it. In his wandering, day to day and minute to minute, he was more placed than most of us ever will be, in a lifetime at home or a life on the move. As followers of the Grateful Dead like to remind us, quoting J. R. R. Tolkien, "Not all who wander are lost."

Muir's devoted adventuring, of course, was something very different from the random restlessness of many in our culture today. Recently I sat through a dinner party during which the guests, most of them thirty-something, compared notes all evening about their travels through Asia. They were experts on border crossings, train transport, currency exchange, and even local art objects, but nothing I heard that evening indicated an influence of land or native peoples on the traveler's soul. They were travel technicians. Many backpackers are the same, passing through wilderness places encapsulated in maps and objectives and high-tech gear. There *is* a pathology there, a serious one. It infects all of us to one degree or another. We have not yet arrived where we believe—and our color slides show—we have already been.

But if shifting around disconnected from land and community is our national disease, I would argue—perversely perhaps, or perhaps just homeopathically—that it is also an element of our national health. Hank Williams and others in our folk and country traditions stir something in many of us when they sing the delights of the open road, of rambling on the loose by foot or thumb or boxcar through the American countryside. Williams's "Ramblin' Man" believes that God intended him for a life of discovery beyond the horizons. Is this mere immaturity? Irresponsibility? An inability to relate to people or place? Maybe. But maybe also renewal, vitality, a growing of the soul. It makes me very happy to drive the highways and back roads of the American West, exchanging talk with people who live where I don't, pulling off somewhere, anywhere, to sleep in the truck and wake to a place I've never seen. I can't defend the cost of such travel in fossil fuel consumption and air befoulment—Williams's rambler at least took the fuel-efficient train—but I do know that it satisfies me as a man and a writer.

Such pleasure in movement—the joy of hitting the trail on a brisk morning, of watching from a train the towns and fields pass by, of riding a skateboard or hang glider or even a 747—must come from a deep and ancient source. All of us are descended from peoples whose way was to roam with the seasons, following game herds and the succession of edible plants, responding to weather and natural calamities and the shifting field of relations with their own kind. And those peoples came, far deeper in the past, from creatures not yet human who crawled and leapt and swung through the canopies of trees for millions of years, evolving prehensile hands and color binocular vision as a consequence, then took to the ground and learned to walk upright and wandered out of Africa (or so it now seems) across the continents of Earth. Along the way, lately, we have lost much of the sensory acuity our saga evoked in us, our ability to smell danger or read a landscape or notice nuances of weather, but the old knowing still stirs an alertness, an air of anticipation, when we set out on our various journeys.

The value of the traveler's knowing figures considerably in native cultural traditions. In Native American stories of the Northwest collected by Jarold Ramsey in *Coyote Was Going There*, I notice that Coyote doesn't seem to have a home—or if he does, he's never there. "Coyote was traveling upriver," the stories begin. "Coyote came over Neahkanie Mountain. . . ." These stories take place in the early time when the order of the world was still in flux. Coyote, the placeless one, helps people and animals find their proper places. You wouldn't want to base a code of conduct on his character, which is unreliable and frequently ignoble, but he is the agent who introduces human beings to their roles and responsibilities in life. Coyote is the necessary inseminator. (Sometimes literally.) He is the shifty and shiftless traveler who fertilizes the locally rooted bloomings of the world.

Maybe Coyote moves among us as the stranger, often odd or disagreeable, sometimes dangerous, who brings reports from far places. Maybe that stranger is one of the carriers of our wildness, one of the mutant genes that keep our evolution fresh and thriving. It is for that stranger, says Elie Wiesel, that an extra place is set at the Seder table. The voyager might arrive, the one who finds his home in the homes of others. He might tell a story, a story no one in the family or local community is capable of telling, and the children who hear that story might imagine their lives in a new way.

It could be Hank Williams who stops in, and he'll sing to you half the night, and maybe yours will be the family he needs, and he won't die of whiskey and barbiturates in the back seat of a car. Or Huck Finn might be your stranger, on the run from "sivilization," dressed as a girl and telling stupendous lies. It could be Jack Kerouac and Neal Cassady, on the road with their Beat buddies, hopped-up on speed, and they never *will* stop talking. It might be Gerry Nanapush, the Ojibwe power man Louise Erdrich has given us, escaped from jail still again to slip through the mists and snows with his ancient powers. Or it might be Billy Parham or John Grady Cole, Cormac McCarthy's boy drifters. They'll want water for their horses, they'll be ready to eat, and if you're wise you'll feed them. They won't talk much themselves, but you just might find yourself telling *them* the crucial story of your life.

Or yours could be the house where Odysseus calls, a still youngish man returning from war, passionate for his family and the flocks and vineyards of home. Just as likely, though, he could be an old man when he stands in your door. No one's quite sure what became of Odysseus. Homer tells us that he made it to Ithaca and set things in order, but the story leaves off there. Some say he resumed his settled life, living out his days as a placed and prosperous landsman. But others say that after all his adventures he couldn't live his old life again. Alfred, Lord Tennyson writes that Odysseus shipped out from Ithaca with his trusted crew. Maybe so, but maybe there was more to the story. Maybe Penelope, island bound for all those years, was stir crazy herself. Maybe they left Telemachus the ranch and set out together across the sea, two gray spirits "yearning in desire / To follow knowledge like a sinking star, / Beyond the utmost bound of human thought."

(1995)

WILLIAM CRONON

The Riddle of the Apostle Islands

How do you manage a wilderness full of human stories?

T HE APOSTLE ISLANDS ARE NOT ON THE WAY TO ANYWHERE. I MAN-
aged to grow up in southern Wisconsin, and even to fall in love with
the wild beauty of Lake Superior, without ever journeying to the northernmost tip of the state. There, the Bayfield Peninsula juts out into the cold
waters of the lake and an archipelago of twenty-two small wooded islands
lies just offshore. Not until a few years ago did I find myself, almost by
accident, gazing out at those islands and realizing I had found one of the
places on this good Earth where I feel most at home. I have been haunting
them in all seasons ever since.

There is nothing especially dramatic about the Apostles. In some places,
they meet the lake with narrow, pebble-covered beaches rising steeply to
meet the forest behind. Elsewhere, they present low sandstone cliffs, brown-
red in hue, that have been so sculpted by the action of wave and ice that
one never tires of studying their beauty. In a few places where the geology is
just right, the lake has widened crevices to form deep caves where kayakers
can make their way into darkness and listen to the rise and fall of water on
stone. Northern hardwood forest, swamp, marsh, and shore are the primary
habitats, with nesting bird colonies in the cliffs and a peripatetic population
of black bears that is surprisingly unfazed by the need to swim from island
to island despite the notoriously cold temperatures of the lake.

For nearly thirty-five years, these lands and waters have been protected
by the federal government as Apostle Islands National Lakeshore—a legacy of Wisconsin Senator Gaylord Nelson, father of Earth Day in 1970.
Sometime later this year, the National Park Service will issue recommendations for future management of the park. Although the NPS study recommending wilderness designation for the Apostles (spearheaded by another
Wisconsin senator, Russ Feingold) has not thus far attracted much attention, its implications reach far beyond the Apostle Islands. Anyone committed to rethinking human relationships with nature should pay attention
to its findings.

In the 1970 act that created it, the Lakeshore was dedicated to the "protection of scenic, scientific, historic, geological, and archaeological features contributing to public education, inspiration, and enjoyment." Since then, millions of Americans have come to appreciate the subtle, ever-changing beauty of the islands. Designating the Apostles as wilderness will be a milestone in the ongoing effort to protect them for future generations, and will constitute an important addition to our National Wilderness Preservation System in a region where far too little land has received such protection. Look at a map of legal wilderness in the United States, and for the most part you will see a vast blank expanse between the Appalachians and the Rockies. At a minimum, the Apostles can serve as a reminder that the Middle West also is a place of wildness, despite the common prejudice that nothing here deserves that label.

On the surface, there seems little reason to doubt that many of the Apostles meet the legal criteria specified by the 1964 Wilderness Act. Most visitors who wander these islands, whether by water or land, experience them, in the words of that Act, "as an area where the earth and its community of life are untrammeled by man, where man himself is a visitor who does not remain." Permanent improvements and human habitations are few, and those that do exist are often so subtle that many visitors fail to notice them. Whether one sails, kayaks, boats, hikes, or camps, opportunities for solitude are easy to find. Wild nature is everywhere.

And yet: the Apostle Islands also have a deep human history that has profoundly altered the "untouched" nature that visitors find here. The archipelago has been inhabited by Ojibwe peoples for centuries, and remains the spiritual homeland of the Red Cliff and Bad River Ojibwe bands whose reservations lie just across the water. Ojibwe people continue to gather wild foods here as they have done for centuries. The largest of the islands, Madeline, was the chief trading post on Lake Superior for French and native traders from the seventeenth century forward. Commercial fisheries have operated in these waters since the mid-nineteenth century, with small fishing stations scattered among the islands for processing the catch in all seasons. The islands saw a succession of economic activities ranging from logging to quarrying to farming. Most have been completely cut over at least once. The Apostles possess the largest surviving collection of nineteenth-century lighthouses anywhere in the United States. Finally, tourists have sought out the islands since the late nineteenth century, and they too have left marks ranging from lodges to cottages to docks to trails as evidence of the wilderness experience they came to find.

All of this would seem to call into question the common perception among visitors that the Apostles are "untouched," and might even raise doubts about whether the National Lakeshore should be legally designated as wilderness. But although most parts of these islands have been substantially altered by past human activities, they have also gradually been undergoing a process that James Feldman, an environmental historian at the University of Wisconsin-Madison who is writing a book about the islands, has evocatively called "rewilding." The Apostles are thus a superb example of a wilderness in which natural and human histories are intimately intermingled. To acknowledge past human impacts upon these islands is not to call into question their wildness; it is rather to celebrate, along with the human past, the robust ability of wild nature to sustain itself when people give it the freedom it needs to flourish in their midst.

Should Apostle Islands National Lakeshore become part of the National Wilderness Preservation System? Emphatically yes.

But to answer the question so simply is to evade some of the most challenging riddles that the Apostle Islands pose for our conventional ideas of wilderness. In a much altered but rewilding landscape, where natural and cultural resources are equally important to any full understanding of place, how should we manage and interpret these islands so that visitors will appreciate the stories and lessons they hold? If visitors come here and believe they are experiencing pristine nature, they will completely misunderstand not just the complex human history that has created the Apostle Islands of today; they will also fail to understand how much the natural ecosystems they encounter here have been shaped by that human history. In a very deep sense, what they will experience is not the natural and human reality of these islands, but a cultural myth that obscures much of what they most need to understand about a wilderness that has long been a place of human dwelling.

If this is true, then the riddle we need to answer is how to manage the Apostle Islands as a *historical* wilderness, in which we commit ourselves not to erasing human marks on the land, but rather to interpreting them so that visitors can understand just how intricate and profound this process of rewilding truly is.

Among my favorite places for thinking about rewilding is Sand Island, at the extreme western end of the archipelago. Most visitors today disembark at a wooden pier on the eastern side of the island, and then hike more than a mile to reach the lovely brownstone lighthouse at the island's northern tip, constructed way back in 1881. Built of sandstone from another island, it is an artifact of an earlier phase of Apostles history that has now vanished except for the overgrown quarries one still finds in the woods. Gazing out at the lake from atop the tower, it is easy to imagine that this is a lone oasis of civilization in the midst of deep wilderness.

But the path you walk to reach this lighthouse is in fact a former county road. If you look in the right place you can still find an ancient automobile rusting amid the weeds. Frank Shaw homesteaded the southeastern corner of Sand Island in the 1880s, and by 1910 more than seventy people—most of them Norwegian immigrants—were living here year-round. Sand Island had its own post office and general store. Island children had their own one-room school. There was even telephone service to the mainland, though it soon failed and was abandoned.

How did Sand Islanders support themselves in this remote rural settlement? Fishing was of course a mainstay. Logging went on occasionally, and from the 1880s forward the summer months saw a regular stream of tourists. But for several decades islanders also farmed. Few who visit this "pristine wilderness" today will recognize that the lands through which they hike are old farm fields, but such in fact they are. Indeed, look closely at the encroaching forest that was once Burt and Anna Mae Hill's homestead and you will quickly realize that the trees are not much more than half a century old. Indeed, some of the oldest are apple trees, offering mute evidence—like the lilacs and rose bushes that grow amid ruins of old foundations elsewhere on the island—of past human efforts to yield bounty and beauty from this soil.

The old orchards are in fact a perfect example of rewilding, since Burt Hill's farm still shapes the local ecology. As James Feldman describes the process, "In some areas of the clearing, willow, hawthorn, mountain ash, and serviceberry have moved into the sedge meadow in straight, regular lines, following the drainage ditches dug by Burt Hill when he expanded his farming operations in the 1930s." Nature alone cannot explain this landscape. You need history too.

The dilemma for the Park Service, then, is deciding how much of the Apostle Islands to designate as wilderness, and how to manage lands so labeled. More bluntly: should Burt Hill's orchard count as wilderness? And if it does, should park managers strive to erase all evidence of the Hills' home so visitors can imagine this land to be "pristine"?

What makes these questions so difficult is that the 1964 Wilderness Act and current National Park Service management policies draw quite a stark—and artificial—boundary between nature and culture. The implication of this boundary is that the two should be kept quite separate, and that wilderness in particular should be devoid of anything suggesting an ongoing human presence. Under the 1964 Act, wilderness is defined as a place that "generally appears to have been affected primarily by the forces of nature, with the imprint of man's work substantially unnoticeable." Strictly interpreted, this definition suggests that the more human history we can see in a landscape, the less wild it is. A curious feature of this definition is that it privileges visitors' perceptions of "untrammeledness" over the land's true history. It almost implies that wilderness designation should depend on whether we can remove, erase, or otherwise hide historical evidence that people have altered a landscape and made it their home.

Because this strict definition can exclude from the National Wilderness Preservation System too much land that might otherwise deserve protection, the less-well-known 1975 Eastern Wilderness Act offers an important counterpoint that is especially relevant to the Apostle Islands. It declares that wilderness areas can be designated east of the Hundredth Meridian even where land has been grazed, plowed, mined, or clear-cut—land, in other words, that the 1964 Act would emphatically regard as "trammeled." Unfortunately, the implications of the 1975 Act have still not been fully appreciated, so that federal managers continue to remove historic structures and artifacts in a misguided effort to fool visitors into believing they are experiencing a "pristine" landscape.

For instance, current NPS management policies adopt a strict definition of wilderness comparable to the 1964 Act in declaring that "the National Park Service will seek to remove from potential wilderness the temporary, non-conforming conditions that preclude wilderness designation." The bland phrase "non-conforming conditions" generally refers to any human imprints that diminish the impression that a wilderness is "untouched"— imprints, in other words, that constitute the chief evidence of human history. As Laura Watt has suggested in her valuable study of Park Service management at Point Reyes in California, "The Trouble with Preservation, or, Getting Back to the Wrong Term for Wilderness Protection," NPS efforts to create the appearance of pristine wilderness—even in a heavily grazed and logged area like Point Reyes—have included the following:

- intentionally demolishing historic structures;
- promoting natural resources at the expense of cultural ones;
- implying that dramatically altered landscapes are much more pristine than they truly are;
- privileging certain historic eras over others; and
- refusing to interpret for park visitors the human history of places designated as wilderness.

At both Point Reyes and Apostle Islands National Lakeshore, Park Service managers have ironically become the principal vandals of historic structures—tearing down ranches at Point Reyes, removing farms, fishing camps, and cottages at Apostle Islands—in an effort to persuade visitors that land remains untrammeled. Park visitors deceived by this carefully contrived illusion not only fail to see the human history of the places they visit; they also fail to see the many features of present ecosystems that are inexplicable without reference to past human influence. As Laura Watt points out, although the Park Service has long opposed the reconstruction of historic buildings and sites as inherently false and misleading, it shows much less compunction about false and misleading reconstructions of "natural" landscapes.

NPS management policies do call for the protection of "significant" cultural resources even on lands designated as wilderness, but such resources must meet very high standards of significance—generally, listing on the National Register—to merit protection. As a result, NPS generally forces managers to choose between two mutually exclusive alternatives, wild and nonwild. One either designates an area as wilderness and tries to remove "non-conforming conditions" so as to manage it almost exclusively for wilderness values; or one designates an area as a cultural resource and manages it for values other than wilderness. The heretical notion that one might actually wish to protect and interpret a cultural resource in the very heart of wilderness so as to help visitors better understand the history of that wilderness is pretty much unthinkable under current regulations.

All of this may seem abstract and academic, but it has very practical implications for how Apostle Islands National Lakeshore and other parks are managed when designated as wilderness. Under NPS policies, "improvements" are to be held to a bare minimum in designated wilderness. This means that even if historic human structures and artifacts are permitted to remain (most would typically be removed or destroyed), the best one could hope for them would be stabilization, not active protection, restoration, or interpretation. Trails would be kept to a minimum, and their routes would emphasize nature over culture to encourage visitors' perception of untrammeled wilderness—even when, as at Sand Island, the trail is in fact an old road. Perhaps most importantly from the point of view of human history, interpretive signs would be removed altogether, so that historic features in the landscape that most visitors might otherwise miss could not be marked. Although one might hope that brochures, guidebooks, and displays in visitor centers would encourage visitors to look for evidence of these historic features, wilderness designation under current NPS policies would prevent them from being interpreted on the ground.

Why does this bother me so much? Because I can't help seeing the straight lines along which willows and serviceberries are invading Burt Hill's orchard. I can't help caring about all the dreams and hard work with which he planted these apple trees so long ago. For me, Burt and Anna Mae's story makes this wilderness all the more poignant, and I cannot understand why we think we need to annihilate the record of their lives so we can pretend to ourselves—pioneer-like—that no one before us has ever stood here.

What alternatives do we have? How might we combine designated wilderness with an equal and ongoing commitment to interpreting the shared past of humanity and nature? If we can answer this question for the Apostle Islands, I believe we can also answer it for many other landscapes whose histories also combine wildness with human dwelling. Among the suggestions I'd make would be the following:

Most importantly, we should commit ourselves to the notion that Apostle Islands National Lakeshore is and always will be a historical wilderness: for centuries in the past, and presumably for centuries still to come, human beings have played and will play crucial roles in these islands. Visitors should come away from the park with a deepened appreciation not just for the wild nature they find here, but for the human history as well.

The interpretive framework that can best integrate the natural and cultural resources of this park is James Feldman's concept of rewilding. It should be at the heart of what the park offers to visitors. Here is a natural landscape that has been utilized for centuries by different human groups for different human purposes: first by native peoples for subsistence, then for fur trading, then in turn for fishing, shipping, logging, quarrying, farming, touring, and other activities. Natural resources here have long been exploited as commodities, and island ecosystems have changed drastically as a result. The shifting composition of the forest, the changing populations of wildlife on the land and in the lake, the introduction of exotic species, the subtle alterations of geomorphology: all of these "natural" features also reflect human history. Visitors should come away with a more sophisticated understanding of them all.

Furthermore, these changes have not all been in one direction, which is why Feldman's narrative of rewilding can be a source of hope for all who support efforts at ecological restoration. Although parts of the Apostle Islands have been drastically altered by activities like clear-cutting, wilderness is returning to such a degree that hikers can walk old logging roads and completely fail to realize that the woods through which they are traveling were stumps just half a century ago. I think they would learn more about restoration and rewilding if they could see those stumps in their mind's eye. We should be able to encounter an abandoned plow blade in the woods, or a rusting stretch of barbed-wire fence, or a neatly squared block of brownstone, without feeling that such things somehow violate our virginal experience of wilderness. We would do better to recognize in this historical wilderness a more complicated tale than the one we like to tell ourselves about returning to the original garden.

One of the most attractive features of Feldman's concept of rewilding is that it avoids the negative implication that past human history consists solely of exploiting, damaging, and destroying nature. As Feldman puts it, "rewilding landscapes should be interpreted as evidence neither of past human abuse nor of triumphant wild nature, but rather as evidence of the tightly intertwined processes of natural and cultural history." When we use words like "healing" to describe the return of wilderness to a place like the Apostles, we imply that past human history here should be understood mainly as "wounding" and "scarring." Such words do no more justice to the complexity of human lives in the past than they do to our own lives in the present. They implicitly dishonor the memories of those like Burt and Anna Mae Hill who once made their lives here and who presumably loved these islands as much as we do.

In keeping with the principle that the Park Service should not be in the business of promoting illusions about a pristine wilderness with no human history, the default management assumption should be that existing human structures and artifacts will not be removed even from designated wilderness. No erasures should be the rule except where absolutely necessary. Even in instances where there are safety concerns about a collapsing structure, other solutions for protecting visitors should always be sought before resorting to destruction and removal. In a rewilding landscape, old buildings, tools, fencerows, and other such structures supply vital evidence of past human uses, without which visitors cannot hope to understand how natural ecosystems have responded to those uses. Moreover, such artifacts today stand as romantic ruins, haunting and beautiful in their own right. Far from diminishing the wilderness experience of visitors, they enhance and deepen it by adding complexity to the story of rewilding.

Moreover, not all structures and artifacts should be permitted to go to ruin. The Park Service has already worked hard (with far too little funding) to preserve the beautiful historic lighthouses that are among the most popular destinations on the islands. But a grave weakness of current Park Service interpretation is its extreme emphasis on lighthouses and fishing as if these constituted the sum total of past human activities in the islands. Equally important phases of island history remain almost invisible. Ojibwa and other native histories are only beginning to receive the attention they deserve, and the histories of later island residents often go entirely unmentioned.

An NPS commitment to interpreting all phases of Apostle Islands history would mean more than just tolerating the presence of romantic ruins in an otherwise wild landscape. Certain structures and artifacts are so important to visitor understanding of island history that at least a few need to be stabilized or restored, and actively interpreted. Nowhere can visitors now explore a former brownstone quarry with the benefit of informed interpretation to help them appreciate how important this industry was to the built environment of the United States during the closing decades of the nineteenth century. Visitors would look with entirely different eyes at the brownstone buildings in nearby towns if they were encouraged to see where that stone originally came from. The same goes for logging sites and especially for old farms. Visitors almost surely leave Apostle Islands National Lakeshore with no appreciation for farm families like Burt and Anna Mae Hill who once raised crops and children on these islands, even though the remnants of their farms are still visible on the ground and are still reflected in the ecology of the forests that now grow on abandoned fields.

The bias of historical interpretation in the Apostle Islands, like many other historic sites in the United States, is generally toward earlier, "pioneer" periods. One crucial human activity that goes almost entirely uninterpreted for tourists in the Apostle Islands is tourism itself. Many mid-twentieth-century tourist cottages have already been torn down as "non-conforming." So far, there has been no effort to preserve any of these structures as cultural resources in their own right, to help visitors understand how tourism has emerged over the past two centuries as one of the most potent cultural forces reshaping landscapes all over the world. (The designation of wilderness in Apostle Islands National Lakeshore is inexplicable without reference to this cultural force.) Interpreting the history of tourism should be just as important as interpreting the history of lighthouses and fishing, and at least a few early tourist structures need to be preserved if this goal is to be accomplished.

If I had my druthers, I would also permit limited signage and interpretation as tools for educating visitors and managers alike that the presence of cultural resources such as fishing camps and cottages in the midst of wilderness does not automatically degrade wilderness values or the wilderness experience. Does Aldo Leopold's shack or Sigurd Olson's cabin diminish the wild lands surrounding it? I honestly believe such cultural resources can enhance visitor appreciation of the complex history of rewilding landscapes. If we're to tell stories about ecological restoration, as surely we need to do if we're to envision a sustainable human future, we need to leave evidence on the ground that will bear witness to such stories.

I'm nonetheless willing to acknowledge that standardized bureaucratic rules and regulations may not easily accommodate the kind of interpretive ambiguities that I prefer. So the wiser, easier strategy is probably to think of wilderness in the Apostle Islands as existing along a continuum, from areas that will be treated as "pure" wilderness (even though they are full of historical artifacts that should not be removed) to highly developed sites like the lighthouses that are managed almost entirely for nonwilderness values.

I would argue for a few locations outside of the designated wilderness which, although still managed to protect wilderness values, could be modestly restored and actively interpreted so as to help visitors understand the historic landscapes of logging, quarrying, farming, and early tourism. One might consider designating them as "historical wilderness areas" to signal that they should be managed with an eye toward balancing natural and cultural resources more evenly than would typically be true in "designated wilderness."

Sand and Basswood islands are the obvious candidates to be designated as historical wilderness, because their histories are so rich and varied—encompassing fishing, logging, quarrying, farming, and tourism in addition to Ojibwa subsistence activities—and so can serve as microcosms for the whole archipelago. These islands could be regarded almost as classrooms for historical wilderness, where visitors can learn about the long-term cultural processes that have in fact shaped all of the Apostles. Then, when they visit the designated wilderness where much less interpretation is permitted, their eyes will be trained to see the rewilding process they will witness there.

What are the chances that this new approach to protecting wilderness might actually succeed in the Apostle Islands? Surprisingly good. The park's superintendent, Bob Krumenaker, has been both visionary and eloquent in refusing to choose wilderness over history—or history over wilderness. "I don't think, if we do it right," he says, "that wilderness has to entail either balancing nature and culture—which suggests one gains while the other loses—or sacrificing one at the expense of the other. We can preserve both nature and culture at the Apostle Islands and should embrace the chance to do so."

Like Krumenaker, I favor educating visitors so they will recognize that wilderness can have a human history and still offer a flourishing home for wild nature. If we adopt such a strategy for managing wilderness in Apostle Islands National Lakeshore, the park can offer a truly invaluable laboratory, with implications far beyond its own boundaries, for rethinking what we want visitors to experience and understand when they visit a wilderness that is filled equally with human and natural histories.

Indeed, among the most precious experiences that Apostle Islands National Lakeshore can offer its visitors are precisely these stories. Management policy in the National Lakeshore should seek to protect wilderness values and historic structures, certainly, but it should equally protect stories—stories of wild nature, stories of human history. It is a storied wilderness. And it is in fact these stories that visitors will most remember and retell, even as they contribute their own experiences to the ongoing history of people and wild nature in the Apostle Islands.

(2003)

Reverence

Beyond Ecophobia

Reclaiming the Heart in Nature Education

JUST AS ETHNOBOTANISTS ARE DESCENDING ON TROPICAL FORESTS IN search of new plants for medical uses, environmental educators, parents, and teachers are descending on second and third-graders to teach them about the rainforests. From Brattleboro, Vermont to Berkeley, California, school children are learning about tapirs, poison arrow frogs, and biodiversity. They hear the story of the murder of activist Chico Mendez and watch videos about the plight of indigenous forest people displaced by logging and exploration for oil. They learn that between the end of morning recess and the beginning of lunch, more than ten thousand acres of rainforest will be cut down, making way for fast food, "hamburgerable" cattle.

The motive for all this is honorable and just: if children are aware of the problems of too many people utilizing too few resources, they will grow up to be adults who eat Rainforest Crunch, vote for environmental candidates, and buy energy-efficient cars. They will learn that by recycling their *Weekly Readers* and milk cartons, we can all save the planet. My fear is that just the opposite is occurring. In our zest for making them aware of and responsible for the world's problems, we cut our children off from their roots.

I confess to contributing money to the Children's Rainforest Project— a group that teaches kids about the rainforest and then funnels money raised from car washes and bake sales to the actual purchase of endangered lands in Costa Rica and Panama. At least this group doesn't just ring alarm bells—it gives kids a sense that they make a difference. But, what really happens when we lay the weight of the world's environmental problems on eight- and nine-year-olds already haunted with too many concerns and not enough real contact with nature?

If we fill our classrooms with examples of environmental abuse, we may be engendering a subtle form of dissociation. In response to physical and sexual abuse, children learn to cut themselves off from pain. In severe cases, children develop multiple personalities, other selves that aren't aware of painful experiences. My fear is that our environmentally correct curriculum similarly ends up distancing children from, rather than connecting them with, the natural world. The natural world is being abused and they just don't want to have to deal with it.

For *Childhood's Future,* a study of the changing nature of childhood at the end of the twentieth century, Richard Louv interviewed children, parents, community groups, and educators across the country. Visiting his own childhood neighborhood and elementary school, he talked with school children and noted that the relationship between children and nature has changed significantly in the last thirty years:

> While children do seem to be spending less time physically in natural surroundings, they also seem to worry more about the disappearance of nature—in a global sense—than my generation did. . . . As a boy, I was intimate with the fields and the woods behind my house, and protective of them. Yet, unlike these children, I had no sense of any ecological degradation beyond my small natural universe.

And in response to Louv's question of whether he liked to play indoors or outdoors better, one fourth-grader responded, "I like to play indoors better 'cause that's where the electrical outlets are." Children are disconnected from the world outside their doors, and connected with endangered animals and ecosystems around the globe through electronic media.

While children are studying the rainforest, they are not studying the northern hardwood forest, or even just the overgrown meadow outside the classroom door. Lucy Sprague Mitchell, educator and founder of Bank Street College of Education, spoke of the "here and now," the local forest or urban neighborhood, as the basis for her curriculum with six- through nine-year-olds. It is not until children are thinking logically and abstractly enough that she would embark on the "long ago and far away." It is hard enough for children to understand the life cycles of chipmunks and milkweed, organisms they can study close at hand. This is the foundation upon which an eventual understanding of ocelots and orchids can be built.

Some teachers can study both local forests and rainforests, and connect one to the other artfully, but many prefer rainforests because, from a curriculum perspective, they are much tidier to teach. To study the northern hardwood forest, you have to send a note home to parents reminding them that the kids have to wear boots next Tuesday. You have to deal with unruly kids and wind blowing the clipboard paper all over the place. To study rainforests, you can stay inside and look at all the pretty pictures of all those strange and wonderful animals, and make a miniature jungle.

In the face of this dissociation, children still try to make ends meet, to connect the far away and the close-by world. A mother recently shared an account of her eight-year-old daughter's afternoon project. Her daughter had been hard at work in the shed, her mom's studio, for more than an hour when she showed up in the kitchen with an elegant poster to be displayed at the general store across the street. Around an attractive illustration of a plump elephant, read the bold edict, conceived in all seriousness, SAVE THE ELEPHANTS. DON'T USE IVORY SOAP. Saving endangered species is just as much the rage as saving the rainforest these days, and so a recent school project on African wildlife had motivated this girl to take protective action. The mistaken connection between the killing of elephants for their ivory tusks and the ingredients of Ivory Soap illustrates the child's desire to make the world right. But wouldn't it make more sense to have this child feel protective of the muskrats in the pond across the street?

Rainforest curriculum may be perfectly appropriate in middle or high school, but it doesn't belong in the primary grades in elementary schools. When I was training to be an elementary school teacher, my professor in a math methods course speculated that if we waited until sixth grade, we could teach all of elementary school mathematics in eight weeks. He believed that if we wait until children's minds have developed more, mathematics would be easier for them to grasp.

Recently, the use of concrete materials (such as Cuisenaire rods, fraction bars, and Unifix cubes) and the grounding of math instruction in the stuff and problems of everyday life have improved the teaching of mathematics and helped reduce math phobia. Unable to connect the signs and symbols on the paper with the real world, many children were turning off to math. Adults describing their math phobia often date the beginnings of their problems to third and fourth grade when they just couldn't keep up anymore. Their math skills became frozen at the fourth-grade level. For adult math phobics, just the thought of long division can make them short of breath. As in any phobic reaction, the afflicted person feels anxiety and wants to flee from the situation. But with more child-centered math instruction, the problem of math phobia has diminished.

Perhaps to be replaced by ecophobia. Fear of rainforest destruction, acid rain, and Lyme disease. Fear of just being outside. If we prematurely ask children to deal with problems of an adult world, we cut them off from the possible sources of their strength. Let us consider some better ways to support children's biological tendency to bond with the natural world.

What's Important?

A graduate student of mine stumbled upon an intriguing discovery in his research with children last year. My assignment to the teachers in training was to conduct research that allowed them to open doors into the inner lives and thoughts of children. Steve Moore wanted to find out what was important to second-graders. He selected twenty-five magazine pictures of children on bicycles, people playing baseball, happy families, toys, dogs, eagles, pretty landscapes, farms, the earth from space, workplaces, and the like. Then he encouraged children to choose three pictures that seemed important and talk about them.

Moore conducted his interviews with 40 seven- and eight-year-olds in four different second-grade classrooms in adjoining towns. When he analyzed his results, he found a curious pattern. The children's responses fell into two distinct groups, despite the fact that all four classrooms seemed quite similar on the surface. In two of the classrooms, many children chose the picture of the earth from space, the eagle, and the deer. They talked about saving the planet, stopping pollution, and protecting eagles. They participated in the activity but didn't seem to really enjoy the process.

In the other two classrooms, the children chose pictures of Legos, playing baseball, homes, and families as the important things in life. In the interviews, the children seemed energetic and enthusiastic to participate in the discussions.

When Moore saw this pattern, he returned to the classrooms, spoke to the teachers and discovered a possible explanation for the differences. The first two classes had done an extensive Earth Week curriculum shortly before he conducted the interviews. Rainforest pictures were up on the walls, books and stories with environmental topics were in evidence, and one of the classes had just visited a new environmental education center. The second two classes had done very little for Earth Week and almost no environmental curriculum. These teachers were a little sheepish about their apparent avoidance of these issues.

When he looked again at his results from this perspective, he found another pattern. In his total sample he found:

• Eighteen comments of *concern for the environment* (pollution, extinction, etc.). All these comments were made by children in the Earth Week classes.

- Sixteen comments of *appreciation for the environment* (a place where we can live, I like birds, etc.). Seven of these comments were made by children in the Earth Week classes, nine by children in the non-Earth Week classes.
- Fifteen comments of *appreciation of families.* Fourteen of these were made by children in non-Earth Week classes and one by a child in an Earth Week class.

The result, from Moore's perspective, was a kind of despondency among the children in the Earth Week classrooms and a submerging of children's natural interests in a sea of problems:

> The whole issue of the Earth Week curriculum was a big eye opener to me. The interview patterns suggest that kids who had spent a week or more working on environmental issues were fully taken in by them. The Earth Week group made choices that were heavily weighted with concerns about the earth, the animals, homeless children. The non-Earth Week classes made choices about playing, about families, about having fun. I think we need to be careful about this kind of curricular brainwashing with children this age.

Though clearly not an exhaustive study, Moore's findings resonate eerily with a study conducted in West Germany during the 1980s, described to me by George Russell of Adelphi University. Concerned about acid rain effects on forests, the ozone hole, heavy metal pollution in European rivers, the aftermath of Chernobyl and other environmental problems, the Germans implemented a conscientious national curriculum endeavor. The intent was to raise the consciousness of the elementary student body throughout the country regarding environmental problems. By informing students about the problems and showing them how they could participate in finding the solutions, the education ministry hoped to create empowered global citizens. Follow-up studies conducted some years after implementation indicated just the opposite had occurred. As a result of the curriculum initiative, education officials found that students felt hopeless and disempowered. The problems were seemingly so widespread and beyond the students' control that their tendency was to turn away from, rather than face up to, participating in local attempts at problem solving.

If curriculum focused on saving the Earth doesn't work, what's the answer? One way to approach this problem is to figure out what contributes to the development of environmental values in adults. What happened in the childhoods of environmentalists, some researchers have asked, to make them grow up with strong ecological values? A handful of these studies have been conducted, and when Louise Chawla of Kentucky State University reviewed these studies she found an intriguing pattern. Most environmentalists attributed their commitment to a combination of two sources: "many hours spent outdoors in a keenly remembered wild or semi-wild place in childhood or adolescence, and an adult who taught respect for nature."

What a simple solution. No rainforest curriculum, no environmental action, just opportunities to be in the natural world with modeling by a responsible adult. Chawla noted that, "As Tanner has commented, not one of the conservationists that he surveyed explained his or her dedication as a reaction against exposure to an ugly environment." When the Sierra Club wants to raise money for saving old-growth forests, they send photographs of denuded, eroding hillsides with their donation requests. Defenders of Wildlife raises money by showing us the cuddly harp seal being bludgeoned to death. For adults with a commitment to preservation and a sense of self firmly in place, this technique appropriately motivates us to action.

For young children—kindergarten through third- or fourth-grade—this technique is counterproductive. Lurking beneath these environmentally correct curricula is the assumption that if children see the horrible things that are happening, then they too will be motivated to make a difference. But those images can have an insidious, nightmarish effect on young children whose sense of time, place, and self are still forming. Newspaper pictures of homes destroyed by California wildfires are disturbing to my seven-year-old New Hampshire daughter because she immediately personalizes them. "Is that fire near here? Will our house burn down? What if we have a forest fire?" she queries, because for her, California is right around a psychic corner.

What's important is that children have an opportunity to bond with the natural world, to learn to love it and feel comfortable in it, before being asked to heal its wounds. John Burroughs cautioned that, "Knowledge without love will not stick. But if love comes first, knowledge is sure to follow." Our problem is that we are trying to invoke knowledge, and responsibility, before we have allowed a loving relationship to flourish.

Bonding with the Earth

We often refer to those moments of wondrous happenstance as being in the right place at the right time. Curriculum often isn't, and it's usually too early. To get a sense of when to study rainforests or endangered species, or perhaps how to do environmental curricula at different ages, we need a scheme, a big picture of the relationship between the natural world and the development of the person.

For parents and teachers, it's most important to focus on the three stages of development that are the concern of elementary education: early childhood from ages three to seven, the elementary years from seven to eleven, and early adolescence from eleven to fifteen. The heart of childhood, from seven to eleven, is the critical period for bonding with the earth. Though these age frames need to be considered flexibly, my argument is that environmental education should be tangibly different during each period.

Over the past ten years, I have collected neighborhood maps from hundreds of children in the United States, England, and the Caribbean. From my analysis of these maps and interviews and field trips with these children, I have found clear patterns of development in the relationship between the child and her expanding natural world.

From age four until seven or eight, children's homes fill the center of their maps and much of their play is within sight or earshot of the home. Children often describe the worms, chipmunks, and pigeons that live in their yards or on their blocks and feel protective about these creatures.

From eight to eleven, children's geographical range expands rapidly. Their maps push off the edge of the page and they often need to attach extra pieces of paper to map the new terrain they are currently investigating. Children's homes become small, inconsequential, and often move to the periphery of the page. The central focus in these maps is the "explorable landscape."

From eleven to fourteen the maps continue to expand in scope and become more abstract, but the favored places often move out of the woods and into town. Social gathering places such as the mall, the downtown luncheonette, and the town park take on new significance. Annie Dillard captures this fascination with expanding horizons in her description of growing up in Pittsburgh in *An American Childhood*:

> I pushed at my map's edges. Alone at night I added newly memorized streets and blocks to old streets and blocks, and imagined connecting them on foot. . . . On darkening evenings I came home exultant, secretive, often from some exotic leafy curb a mile beyond what I had known at lunch, where I had peered up at the street sign, hugging the cold pole, and fixed the intersection in my mind. What joy, what

relief, eased me as I pushed open the heavy front door!—joy and re-lief because, from the trackless waste, I had located home, family and the dinner table once again.

At the same time as the child's home becomes less significant, forts and dens show up on children's maps. These special places of childhood, both found and built places, appear to be crucially important for many children from ages eight to eleven. Children of all landscapes find hidden places even in daunting circumstances, attesting to the importance of finding a place of one's own at this age. Kim Stafford describes this movement:

> Here was my private version of civilization, my separate hearth. Back Home, there were other versions of this. I would take any refuge from the thoroughfare of plain living—the dollhouse, the tree house, fur-niture, the tablecloth tent, the attic, the bower in the cedar tree. . . .
>
> There I pledged allegiance to what I knew, as opposed to what was common. My parents' house was a privacy from the street, from the nation, from the rain. But, I did not make that house, or find it, or earn it with my own money. It was given to me. My separate hearth had to be invented by me, kindled, sustained, and held secret by my own soul as a rehearsal for departure.

These new homes in the wilds, and the journeys of discovering, are the basis for bonding with the natural world. Children desire immersion, soli-tude, and interaction in a close, knowable world. We take children away from these strength-giving landscapes when we ask them to deal with far-away ecosystems and environmental problems. Rather we should be at-tempting to engage children more deeply in knowing the flora, fauna, and character of their own local places. The woods behind the school and the neighborhoods streets and stores are the places to start.

The Right Places at the Right Times

The challenge for parents and educators is to match activities and engagements with the periods of development in childhood. First, children need to develop emotional empathy for the creatures of the natural world. Next they need safe opportunities to explore their urban and rural landscapes, and finally, they need to have opportunities to work on problems in their local communities.

Empathy between the child and the natural world can be a main objective for children ages three through seven. As children move out into the natural world, we can encourage feelings for the creatures of the world outside. Children feel implicitly drawn to baby animals, so let us cultivate this empathy. This natural emotional connectedness is the foundation of the idea that everything is connected to everything else. Stories, songs, close encounters with animals, and seasonal celebrations are excellent activities.

Cultivating relationships with animals, both real and imagined, is one of the best ways to foster empathy during early childhood. Children love to run like deer, to slither along the ground like snakes, to be clever as a fox and quick like a bunny. There need be no endangered species here—there are more than enough common, everyday species to delight young children.

Take birds for example. How boring it is for children to try to identify birds by catching fleeting glimpses and then looking them up in books. Instead, consider what it is about birds that appeals to children: they fly and they make nests. Knowing that children like to become things rather than objectify them, why not make a set of wings for each child and set them out to experience life as a bird. After a few days of bird play, you might encourage children to paint their wings like one of the birds they'd seen nearby and this eventually can lead to looking at bird books and connecting names to the birds. By first becoming birds, children can slowly learn to step back and look at them without becoming separated from them.

Exploration marks the phase from ages seven to eleven. This is the time to immerse children in the stuff of the physical and natural worlds. Constructing forts, creating small imaginary worlds, hunting and gathering, searching for treasures, following streams and pathways, making maps, taking care of animals, gardening and shaping the earth are perfect activities during this stage.

School activities and family adventures can mirror the expanding scope of the child's significant world, focusing first on the surroundings of the home and school, then the neighborhood, the community, the region, and beyond. The Brookwood School in Manchester, Massachusetts has recently revised its science curriculum to focus on aquatic environments to take advantage of the range of watery places accessible from the school. Starting with a focus on woodland streams in first grade, the curriculum moves down the watershed to ponds in second grade, freshwater wetlands in third grade and eventually out to the ocean by eighth grade. The first graders' streams are right outside the classroom door, the ponds are a bit of a walk, the ocean is a half mile away, so the curriculum expands outward along with the scope of the children's interest and capabilities.

The water cycle isn't something to be taught in two weeks; it is best done over the six or eight years of elementary and middle school. The watercourses of the landscape are the circulatory system of the living earth, and we can only learn them by following them, literally and metaphorically. With this in mind, David Millstone, a fifth-grade social studies teacher in Norwich, Vermont recently began a local studies unit with a stream-following expedition. Recognizing the allure of stream following, he initiated a class expedition not knowing where the stream would lead. In a student newspaper about this expedition, one child's poem describes the passage through a long, unanticipated culvert encountered along the way.

Culvert

Cold, damp dark
rushing water
screams
yodels
splashes
suddenly a waterfall
spotlighted
like a gray and white curtain.
Finally light
sun
colors.

The children's writing for the newsletter fairly crackles with excitement about discovering something literally in their backyard. This project did not touch directly on acid rain, or ground-water pollution, or drinking water quality, or evaporation and condensation. It did, however, immerse children in exploring streams and understanding, in a personal way, where they go. Wet sneakers and muddy clothes are prerequisites for understanding the water cycle.

Social Action appropriately begins around age eleven and certainly extends beyond age fourteen. While woods, parks, and playgrounds are the landscapes of middle childhood, adolescents want to be downtown. Managing school recycling programs, passing town ordinances, testifying at hearings, planning and going on school expeditions all are appropriate activities at this point. Good school programs will also recognize the need for rites of passage towards the end of this period. Initiation signifies the transition into adulthood with the dual challenges of solitude and social responsibility.

When considering appropriate topics for elementary- and middle-school-aged children, I often suggest the maxim of, "No tragedies before fourth grade." Tragedies are big, complex problems beyond the conceptual and geographical scope of young children. Dealing with the nearby sadnesses of children's lives is a different matter. Parents getting divorced, pets dying, a favorite tree being cut down are necessary, tragic issues to cope with in the early elementary grades. But curriculum that focuses on environmental problems will be most successful when it starts in fifth and sixth grade and then focuses primarily on local problems where children can make a real difference. Community service programs can show students the relevance of the curriculum and gives local organizations a wonderful injection of youthful energy.

In Springfield, Vermont, a partnership program between the Riverside Middle School and the solid waste district is getting students into the community and solid waste managers into the school. After an overview of trash problems and how recycling can play a part in saving the town money and making it a safer place to live, groups of students are challenged to come up with a project that will contribute to the local effort. Kristin Forcier and Lauren Ellis, seventh graders in Pat Magrosky's class, conducted on-the-street surveys and found that only half of the people in the community recycled their car and household batteries. The rest of the batteries were either going into the landfill or getting incinerated, potentially causing groundwater or air pollution.

Lauren said, "I didn't really think that throwing away a can of Raid was that bad until we did this project. When I was little, I didn't really think about it. I just thought my water comes from the faucet and it's clean and it's perfect. *Unless,* it comes from near the landfill. Then it's just like spraying a can of Raid in your mouth."

So Kristin and Lauren decided to make recycling batteries easier. They got permission from downtown stores to set up battery collection sites at the Price Chopper market, the Citgo station, the Ames department store and the Bibens Hardware store. They presented the idea to the Springfield Recycling Committee and received a commitment to have volunteers collect the batteries from the collection sites. And they created large informational signs and brochures for each of the collection sites to explain why battery recycling is important for the community. When asked what she had learned from the project, Lauren commented, "A kid can do it, with the help of adults."

Though I have portrayed these stages separately, they are not mutually exclusive. Empathy doesn't stop when exploration starts. Rather, activities that encourage the evolution of empathy should continue throughout the elementary and middle school years. Exploration of the natural world begins in early childhood, flourishes in middle childhood, and continues in adolescence as a pleasure and a source of strength for social action.

After doing the weekly shopping with my seven-year-old daughter and four-year-old son last spring, we would put the groceries in the car and take a short walk across the meadow behind the shopping center to an unused railroad trestle. My children wanted to master their fear of walking on the deck of the bridge; they looked through the railroad ties at the moving water below and saw how far each of them could walk without holding my hand. On the way to and fro, we'd also fill up plastic bags with discarded garbage from along the side of the path. The kids named that activity "cleaning up Mother Earth." We probably only did five minutes of picking up but, week-to-week, it was easy to see the progress we were making. Such action seems fitting for children this age in the context of an engaging exploration. But let's watch out for the downward creep of our activist inclinations, and allow children the communion with nature that provides "intimations of immortality."

Taking Time

I went canoeing with my son Eli and his friend in early April. The plan was to canoe a two-mile stretch of the Ashuelot River, an hour in adult time. Instead, we spent a lot of time netting golf balls swept down from the upstream golf course off the bottom of the river. We hadn't planned this activity, but the boys were thrilled by it and it meant we spent a lot of time looking down into the shallows and depths of the river with a purpose. Which meant that we also wound up doing a lot of fish and bug watching too. We stopped at the mouth of a tributary stream for a picnic and went for a long adventure through a maze of marshy streams and abandoned flood plain oxbows. We tiptoed the tops of beaver dams, hopped hummocks, went wading (Eli called it "shallowing"), looked at spring flowers, tried to catch a snake, got lost and found. How fine it was to move at a meandery, child's pace.

The temptation to rush down the river is a trap waiting to catch parents and educators. Suffering from the time sickness of trying to do too much too quickly, we infect our children with our impatience. We make children do workbooks in kindergarten, we let seven-year-olds watch *Jurassic Park,* and we bombard them with tragic anxiety. After the Oklahoma bombing, a sixth-grade teacher asked his students what they thought of the television coverage and one student spoke for many of them when she said, "It's not good to show so much on television because kids see children all bloody and dead and it makes us scared about growing up in the world."

Some teachers are putting on the brakes. Jo Anne Kruschak, a first and second grade teacher in Thetford, Vermont, is spending a whole year doing a project on a local beaver pond and marsh. Most nature study or environmental education in American elementary schools lasts a matter of weeks. As a result, depth is sacrificed to breadth, and there's little opportunity for immersion in the landscape. But these first and second graders have visited the pond, about a quarter mile from the school, once a week through all kinds of weather. "In the beginning," Kruschak recalls, "I thought we'd run out of things to do and study by Thanksgiving. Now, I realize that there's no way we can follow up on all the neat opportunities by the end of the year."

The Harris Center for Conservation Education, located in the Monadnock highlands of southwestern New Hampshire, is one of the environmental education centers also taking the long view in designing its programs. Since Harris Center educators work with children and students throughout the elementary years, they have the time to let children bond with the natural world. Their school program brochure, entitled "Turning Science Inside Out," says:

> By the end of their journey with the Harris Center, students will have watched birds, searched for amphibians and insects, studied animal tracks, mushrooms and wild foods, surveyed wetlands, mapped local watersheds, learned the geological history of mountains in their area and tested the air and river quality. With one foot in snowshoe and the other in muck, we trek together learning the sweetness that comes with knowing the terrain.

If we want children to flourish, to become truly empowered, let us allow them to love the earth before we ask them to save it. Perhaps this is what Thoreau had in mind when he said, "the more slowly trees grow at first, the sounder they are at the core, and I think the same is true of human beings."

(1995)

Charlotte's Webpage

Why children shouldn't have the world at their fingertips

Thomas Edison was a great inventor but a lousy prognosticator. When he proclaimed in 1922 that the motion picture would replace textbooks in schools, he began a long string of spectacularly wrong predictions regarding the capacity of various technologies to revolutionize teaching. To date, none of them—from film to television—has lived up to the hype. Most were quickly relegated to the audiovisual closet. Even the computer, which is now a standard feature of most classrooms, has not been able to show a consistent record of improving education.

"There have been no advances over the past decade that can be confidently attributed to broader access to computers," said Stanford University professor of education Larry Cuban in 2001, summarizing the existing research on educational computing. "The link between test-score improvements and computer availability and use is even more contested." Part of the problem, Cuban pointed out, is that many computers simply go unused in the classroom. But more recent research, including a University of Munich study of 174,000 students in thirty-one countries, indicates that students who frequently use computers perform worse academically than those who use them rarely or not at all.

Whether or not these assessments are the last word, it is clear that the computer has not fulfilled the promises made for it. Promoters of instructional technology have reverted to a much more modest claim—that the computer is just another tool: "it's what you do with it that counts." But this response ignores the ecological impact of technologies. Far from being neutral, they reconstitute all of the relationships in an environment, some for better and some for worse. Installing a computer lab in a school may mean that students have access to information they would never be able to get any other way, but it may also mean that children spend less time engaged in outdoor play, the art supply budget has to be cut, new security measures have to be employed, and Acceptable Use Agreements are needed to inform parents (for the first time in American educational history) that the school is not responsible for the material a child encounters while under its supervision.

The "just-a-tool" argument also ignores the fact that whenever we choose one learning activity over another, we are deciding what kinds of encounters with the world we value for our children, which in turn influences what they grow up to value. Computers tend to promote and support certain kinds of learning experiences, and devalue others. As technology critic Neil Postman has observed, "What we need to consider about computers has nothing to do with its efficiency as a teaching tool. We need to know in what ways it is altering our conception of learning."

If we look through that lens, I think we will see that educational computing is neither a revolution nor a passing fad, but a Faustian bargain. Children gain unprecedented power to control their external world, but at the cost of internal growth. During the two decades that I taught young people with and about digital technology, I came to realize that the power of computers can lead children into deadened, alienated, and manipulative relationships with the world; that children's increasingly pervasive use of computers jeopardizes their ability to belong fully to human and biological communities—ultimately jeopardizing the communities themselves.

Several years ago I participated in a panel discussion on Iowa Public Television that focused on some "best practices" for computers in the classroom. Early in the program, a video showed how a fourth grade class in rural Iowa used computers to produce hypertext book reports on *Charlotte's Web*, E. B. White's classic children's novel. In the video, students proudly demonstrated their work, which included a computer-generated "spider" jumping across the screen and an animated stick-figure boy swinging from a hayloft rope. Toward the end of the video, a student discussed the important lessons he had learned: always be nice to each other and help one another.

There were important lessons for viewers as well. Images of the students talking around computer screens dispelled (appropriately, I think) the notion that computers always isolate users. Moreover, the teacher explained that her students were so enthusiastic about the project that they chose to go to the computer lab rather than outside for recess. While she seemed impressed by this dedication, it underscores the first troubling influence of computers. The medium is so compelling that it lures children away from the kind of activities through which they have always most effectively discovered themselves and their place in the world.

Ironically, students could best learn the lessons implicit in *Charlotte's Web*—the need to negotiate relationships, the importance of all members of a community, even the rats—by engaging in the recess they missed. In a school, recess is not just a break from intellectual demands or a chance to let off steam. It is also a break from a closely supervised social and physical environment. It is when children are most free to negotiate their own relationships, at arm's length from adult authority. Yet across the U.S., these opportunities are disappearing. By the year 2000, according to a 2001 report by University of New Orleans associate professor Judith Kieff, more than 40 percent of the elementary and middle schools in the U.S. had entirely eliminated recess. By contrast, U.S. Department of Education statistics indicate that spending on technology in schools increased by more than 300 percent from 1990 to 2000.

Structured learning certainly has its place. But if it crowds out direct, unmediated engagement with the world, it undercuts a child's education. Children learn the fragility of flowers by touching their petals. They learn to cooperate by organizing their own games. The computer cannot simulate the physical and emotional nuances of resolving a dispute during kickball, or the creativity of inventing new rhymes to the rhythm of jumping rope. These full-bodied, often deeply heartfelt experiences educate not just the intellect but also the soul of the child. When children are free to practice on their own, they can test their inner perceptions against the world around them, develop the qualities of care, self-discipline, courage, compassion, generosity, and tolerance—and gradually figure out how to be part of both social and biological communities.

It's true that engaging with others on the playground can be a harrowing experience, too. Children often need to be monitored and, at times, disciplined for acts of cruelty, carelessness, selfishness, even violence. Computers do provide an attractively reliable alternative to the dangers of unsupervised play. But schools too often use computers or other highly structured activities to prevent these problematic qualities of childhood from surfacing—out of fear or a compulsion to force-feed academics. This effectively denies children the practice and feedback they need to develop the skills and dispositions of a mature person. If children do not dip their toes in the waters of unsupervised social activity, they likely will never be able to swim in the sea of civic responsibility. If they have no opportunities to dig in the soil, discover the spiders, bugs, birds, and plants that populate even the smallest unpaved playgrounds, they will be less likely to explore, appreciate, and protect nature as adults.

Computers not only divert students from recess and other unstructured experiences, but also replace those authentic experiences with virtual ones, creating a separate set of problems. According to surveys by the Kaiser

Family Foundation and others, school-age children spend, on average, around five hours a day in front of screens for recreational purposes (for children ages two to seven the average is around three hours). All that screen time is supplemented by the hundreds of impressive computer projects now taking place in schools. Yet these projects—the steady diet of virtual trips to the Antarctic, virtual climbs to the summit of Mount Everest, and trips into cyber-orbit that represent one technological high after another—generate only vicarious thrills. The student doesn't actually soar above Earth, doesn't trek across icy terrain, doesn't climb a mountain. Increasingly, she isn't even allowed to climb to the top of the jungle gym. And unlike reading, virtual adventures leave almost nothing to, and therefore require almost nothing of, the imagination. In experiencing the virtual world, the student cannot, as philosopher Steve Talbott has put it, "connect to [her] inner essence."

On the contrary, she is exposed to a simulated world that tends to deaden her encounters with the real one. During the decade that I spent teaching a course called Advanced Computer Technology, I repeatedly found that after engaging in Internet projects, students came back down to the earth of their immediate surroundings with boredom and disinterest—and a desire to get back online. This phenomenon was so pronounced that I started kidding my students about being BEJs: Big Event Junkies. Sadly, many readily admitted that, in general, their classes had to be conducted with the multimedia sensationalism of MTV just to keep them engaged. Having watched Discovery Channel and worked with computer simulations that severely compress both time and space, children are typically disappointed when they first approach a pond or stream: the fish aren't jumping, the frogs aren't croaking, the deer aren't drinking, the otters aren't playing, and the raccoons (not to mention bears) aren't fishing. Their electronic experiences have led them to expect to see these things happening—all at once and with no effort on their part. This distortion can also result from a diet of television and movies, but the computer's powerful interactive capabilities greatly accelerate it. And the phenomenon affects more than just experiences with the natural world. It leaves students apathetic and impatient in any number of settings—from class discussions to science experiments. The result is that the child becomes less animated and less capable of appreciating what it means to be alive, what it means to belong in the world as a biological, social being.

So what to make of the *Charlotte's Web* video, in which the students hunch over a ten-by-twelve-inch screen, trying to learn about what it means to be part of a community while the recess clock ticks away? It's probably unfair to blame the teacher, who would have had plenty of reasons to turn to computers. Like thousands of innovative teachers across the U.S., she must try to find alternatives to the mind-numbing routine of lectures, worksheets, and rote memorization that constitutes conventional schooling. Perhaps like many other teachers, she fully acknowledges the negative effects of computer instruction as she works to create something positive. Or her instructional choices may have simply reflected the infatuation that many parents, community leaders, school administrators, and educational scholars have had with technology. Computer-based education clearly energizes many students and it seems to offer children tremendous power. Unfortunately, what it strips away is much less obvious.

When I was growing up in rural Iowa, I certainly lacked for many things. I couldn't tell a bagel from a burrito. But I always and in many ways belonged. For children, belonging is the most important function a community serves. Indeed, that is the message that lies at the heart of *Charlotte's Web*. None of us—whether of barnyard or human society—thrives without a sense of belonging. Communities offer it in many different ways—through stories, through language, through membership in religious, civic, or educational organizations. In my case, belonging hinged most decisively on place. I knew our farm—where the snowdrifts would be the morning after a blizzard, where and when the spring runoff would create a temporary stream through the east pasture. I knew the warmest and coolest spots. I could tell you where I was by the smells alone. Watching a massive thunderstorm build in the west, or discovering a new litter of kittens in the barn, I would be awestruck, mesmerized by mysterious wonders I could not control. One of the few moments I remember from elementary school is watching a huge black-and-yellow garden spider climb out of Lee Anfinson's pant cuff after we came back from a field trip picking wildflowers. It set the whole class in motion with lively conversation and completely flummoxed our crusty old teacher. Somehow that spider spoke to all of us wide-eyed third graders, and we couldn't help but speak back. My experience of these moments, even if often only as a caring observer, somehow solidified my sense of belonging to a world larger than myself—and prepared me, with my parents' guidance, to participate in the larger community, human and otherwise.

Though the work of the students in the video doesn't reflect it, this kind of experience plays a major role in E. B. White's story. *Charlotte's Web* beautifully draws a child's attention to something that is increasingly rare in schools: the wonder of ordinary processes of nature, which grows mainly through direct contact with the real world. As Hannah Arendt and other observers have noted, we can only learn who we are as human beings by encountering what we are not. While it may seem an impossible task to provide all children with access to truly wild territories, even digging in (healthy) soil opens up a micro-universe that is wild, diverse, and "alien." Substituting the excitement of virtual connections for the deep fulfillment of firsthand engagement is like mistaking a map of a country for the land itself, or as biological philosopher Gregory Bateson put it, "eat[ing] the menu instead of your meal." No one prays over a menu. And I've never witnessed a child developing a reverence for nature while using a computer.

There is a profound difference between learning *from* the world and learning *about* it. Any young reader can find a surfeit of information about worms on the Internet. But the computer can only teach the student *about* worms, and only through abstract symbols—images and text cast on a two-dimensional screen. Contrast that with the way children come to know worms by hands-on experience—by digging in the soil, watching the worm retreat into its hole, and of course feeling it wiggle in the hand. There is the delight of discovery, the dirt under the fingernails, an initial squeamishness followed by a sense of pride at overcoming it. This is what can infuse knowledge with reverence, taking it beyond simple ingestion and manipulation of symbols. And it is reverence in learning that inspires responsibility to the world, the basis of belonging. So I had to wonder why the teacher from the *Charlotte's Web* video asked children to create animated computer pictures of spiders. Had she considered bringing terrariums into the room so students could watch real spiders fluidly spinning real webs? Sadly, I suspect not.

Rather than attempt to compensate for a growing disconnect from nature, schools seem more and more committed to reinforcing it, a problem that began long before the use of computers. Western pedagogy has always favored abstract knowledge over experiential learning. Even relying on books too much or too early inhibits the ability of children to develop direct relationships with the subjects they are studying. But because of their power, computers drastically exacerbate this tendency, leading us to believe that vivid images, massive amounts of information, and even online conversations with experts provide an adequate substitute for conversing with the things themselves.

As the computer has amplified our youths' ability to virtually "go anywhere, at any time," it has eroded their sense of belonging anywhere, at any time, to anybody, or for any reason. How does a child growing up in Kansas gain a sense of belonging when her school encourages virtual learning about Afghanistan more than firsthand learning about her hometown? How does she relate to the world while spending most of her time engaging with computer-mediated text, images, and sounds that are oddly devoid of place, texture, depth, weight, odor, or taste—empty of life? Can she still cultivate the qualities of responsibility and reverence that are the foundation of belonging to real human or biological communities?

During the years that I worked with young people on Internet tele-collaboration projects, I was constantly frustrated by individuals and even entire groups of students who would suddenly disappear from cyber-conversations related to the projects. My own students indicated that they understood the departures to be a way of controlling relationships that develop online. If they get too intense, too nasty, too boring, too demanding, just stop communicating and the relationship goes away. When I inquired, the students who used e-mail regularly all admitted they had done this, the majority more than once. This avoidance of potentially difficult interaction also surfaced in a group of students in the "Talented and Gifted" class at my school. They preferred discussing cultural diversity with students on the other side of the world through the Internet rather than conversing with the school's own ESL students, many of whom came from the very same parts of the world as the online correspondents. These bright high school students feared the uncertain consequences of engaging the immigrants face-to-face. Would they want to be friends? Would they ask for favors? Would they embarrass them in front of others? Would these beginning English speakers try to engage them in frustrating conversations? Better to stay online, where they could control when and how they related to strange people—without much of the work and uncertainty involved with creating and maintaining a caring relationship with a community.

If computers discourage a sense of belonging and the hard work needed to interact responsibly with others, they replace it with a promise of power. The seduction of the digital world is strong, especially for small children. What sets the computer apart from other devices, such as television, is the element of control. The most subtle, impressive message promoted by the *Charlotte's Web* video was that children could take charge of their own learning. Rather than passively listening to a lecture, they were directly interacting with educational content at their own pace. Children, who have so little control over so many things, often respond enthusiastically to such a gift. They feel the same sense of power and control that any of us feels when we use the computer successfully.

To develop normally, any child needs to learn to exert some control over her environment. But the control computers offer children is deceptive, and ultimately dangerous. In the first place, any control children obtain comes at a price: relinquishing the uniquely imaginative and often irrational thought processes that mark childhood. Keep in mind that a computer always has a hidden pedagogue—the programmer—who designed the software and invisibly controls the options available to students at every step of the way. If they try to think "outside the box," the box either refuses to respond or replies with an error message. The students must first surrender to the computer's hyper-rational form of "thinking" before they are awarded any control at all.

And then what exactly is awarded? Here is one of the most underappreciated hazards of the digital age: the problematic nature of a child's newfound power—and the lack of internal discipline in using it. The child pushes a button and the computer draws an X on the screen. The child didn't draw that X, she essentially "ordered" the computer to do it, and the computer employed an enormous amount of embedded adult skill to complete the task. Most of the time a user forgets this distinction because the machine so quickly and precisely processes commands. But the intensity of the frustration that we experience when the computer suddenly stops following orders (and our tendency to curse at, beg, or sweet talk it) confirms that the subtle difference is not lost on the psyche. This shift toward remote control is akin to taking the child out of the role of actor and turning her into the director. This is a very different way of engaging the world than hitting a ball, building a fort, setting a table, climbing a tree, sorting coins, speaking and listening to another person, acting in a play. In an important sense, the child gains control over a vast array of complex abstract activities by giving up or eroding her capacity to actually do them herself. We bemoan the student who uses a spell-checker instead of learning to spell, or a calculator instead of learning to add. But the sacrifice of internal growth for external power generally operates at a more subtle level, as when a child assembles a PowerPoint slideshow using little if any material that she actually created herself.

Perhaps more importantly, however, this emphasis on external power teaches children a manipulative way of engaging the world. The computer does an unprecedented job of facilitating the manipulation of symbols. Every object within the virtual environment is not only an abstract representation of something tangible, but is also discrete, floating freely in a digital sea, ready at hand for the user to do with as she pleases. A picture of a tree on a computer has no roots in the earth; it is available to be dragged, cropped, shaded, and reshaped. A picture of a face can be distorted, a recording of a musical performance remixed, someone else's text altered and inserted into an essay. The very idea of the dignity of a subject evaporates when everything becomes an object to be taken apart, reassembled, or deleted. Before computers, people could certainly abstract and manipulate symbols of massive objects or living things, from trees to mountainsides, from buildings to troop movements. But in the past, the level of manipulative power found in a computer never rested in the hands of children, and little research has been done to determine its effect on them. Advocates enthuse over the "unlimited" opportunities computers afford the student for imaginative control. And the computer environment attracts children exactly because it strips away the very resistance to their will that so frustrates them in their concrete existence. Yet in the real world, it is precisely an object's resistance to unlimited manipulation that forces a child (or anyone) to acknowledge the physical limitations of the natural world, the limits of one's power over it, and the need to respect the will of others living in it. To develop normally, a child needs to learn that she cannot force the family cat to sit on her lap, make a rosebud bloom, or hurt a friend and expect to just start over again with everything just as it was before. Nevertheless, long before children have learned these lessons in the real world, parents and educators rush to supply them with digital tools. And we are only now getting our first glimpse of the results—even among teenagers, whom we would expect to have more maturity than their grade school counterparts.

On the day my Advanced Computer Technology classroom got wired to the Internet, it suddenly struck me that, like other technology teachers testing the early Internet waters, I was about to give my high school students more power to do more harm to more people than any teens had ever had in history, and all at a safe distance. They could inflict emotional pain with a few keystrokes and never have to witness the tears shed. They had the skill to destroy hours, even years, of work accomplished by others they didn't know or feel any ill-will toward—just unfortunate, poorly protected network users whose files provided convenient bull's-eyes for youth flexing their newfound technical muscles. Had anyone helped them develop the inner moral and ethical strength needed to say "no" to the flexing of that power?

On the contrary, we hand even our smallest children enormously powerful machines long before they have the moral capacities to use them properly. Then to assure that our children don't slip past the electronic fences we erect around them, we rely on yet other technologies—including Internet filters like Net Nanny—or fear of draconian punishments. This is not the way to prepare youth for membership in a democratic society that eschews authoritarian control.

That lesson hit home with particular force when I had to handle a trio of very bright high school students in one of the last computer classes I taught. These otherwise nice young men lobbied me so hard to approve their major project proposal—breaking through the school's network security—that I finally relented to see if they intended to follow through. When I told them it was up to them, they trotted off to the lab without a second thought and went right to work—until I hauled them back and reasserted my authority. Once the external controls were lifted, these teens possessed no internal controls to take over. This is something those who want to "empower" young children by handing them computers have tended to ignore: that internal moral and ethical development must precede the acquisition of power—political, economic, or technical—if it is to be employed responsibly.

Computer science pioneer Joseph Weizenbaum long ago argued that as the machines we put in our citizens' hands become more and more powerful, it is crucial that we increase our efforts to help people recognize and accept the immense responsibility they have to use those machines for the good of humanity. Technology can provide enormous assistance in figuring out *how* to do things, Weizenbaum pointed out, but it turns mute when it comes time to determine *what* we should do. Without any such moral grounding, the dependence on computers encourages a manipulative, "whatever works" attitude toward others. It also reinforces the exploitative relationship to the environment that has plagued Western society since Descartes first expressed his desire to "seize nature by the throat." Even sophisticated "environmental" simulations, which show how ecosystems respond to changes, reinforce the mistaken idea that the natural world conforms to our abstract representations of it, and therefore has no inherent value, only the instrumental value we assign to it through our symbols. Such reductionism reinforces the kind of faulty thinking that is destroying the planet: we can dam riparian systems if models show an "acceptable" level of damage, treat human beings simply as units of productivity to be discarded when inconvenient or useless, and reduce all things, even those living, to mere data. The message of the medium—abstraction, manipulation, control, and power—inevitably influences those who use it.

None of this happens overnight, of course, or with a single exposure to a computer. It takes time to shape a worldview. But that is exactly why it is wrong-headed to push such powerful worldview-shapers on impressionable children, especially during elementary school years. What happens when we immerse our children in virtual environments whose fundamental lesson is not to live fully and responsibly in the world, but to value the power to manipulate objects and relationships? How can we then expect our children to draw the line between the symbols and what they represent? When we remove resistance to a child's will to act, how can we teach that child to deal maturely with the Earth and its inhabitants?

Our technological age requires a new definition of maturity: coming to terms with the proper limits of one's own power in relation to nature, society, and one's own desires. Developing those limits may be the most crucial goal of twenty-first-century education. Given the pervasiveness of digital technology, it is not necessary or sensible to teach children to reject computers (although I found that students need just one year of high school to learn enough computer skills to enter the workplace or college). What is necessary is to confront the challenges the technology poses with wisdom and great care. A number of organizations are attempting to do just that. The Alliance for Childhood, for one, has recently published a set of curriculum guidelines that promotes an ecological understanding of the relationship between humans and technology. But that's just a beginning.

In the preface to his thoughtful book *The Whale and the Reactor* Langdon Winner writes, "I am convinced that any philosophy of technology worth its salt must eventually ask, 'How can we limit modern technology to match our best sense of who we are and the kind of world we would like to build?'" Unfortunately, our schools too often default to the inverse of that question: How can we limit human beings to match the best use of what our technology can do and the kind of world it will build? As a consequence, our children are likely to sustain this process of alienation—in which they treat themselves, other people, and the Earth instrumentally—in a vain attempt to materially fill up lives crippled by internal emptiness. We should not be surprised when they "solve" personal and social problems by turning to drugs, guns, hateful Web logs, or other powerful "tools," rather than digging deep within themselves or searching out others in the community for strength and support. After all, this is just what we have taught them to do.

At the heart of a child's relationship with technology is a paradox—that the more external power children have at their disposal, the more difficult it will be for them to develop the inner capacities to use that power wisely. Once educators, parents, and policymakers understand this phenomenon, perhaps education will begin to emphasize the development of human beings living in community, and not just technical virtuosity. I am convinced that this will necessarily involve unplugging the learning environment long enough to encourage children to discover who they are and what kind of world they must live in. That, in turn, will allow them to participate more wisely in using external tools to shape, and at times leave unshaped, the world in which we all must live.

(2005)

The Leadership Imperative

An interview with Oren Lyons

OREN LYONS, SEVENTY-SIX, IS A WISDOM CARRIER, ONE OF THE bearers of a variety of human tradition that can't easily be reduced to a couple of sentences. One reason he—and the tradition for which he is a spokesperson—isn't more widely known is that he doesn't actively seek forums from which to speak. If someone asks him, however, about the principles behind the particular Native American tradition of which he has, since 1967, been an appointed caretaker, he is glad to respond. He chooses his words carefully, and occasionally, these days, there is a hint of indignation in his voice, as if time were short and people generally willful in their distraction.

In an era of self-promotion, Oren Lyons represents the antithesis of celebrity. When he converses about serious issues, no insistent ego comes to the fore, no desire to be seen as an important or wise person. His voice is but one in a long series, as he sees it, and the wisdom belongs not to him but to the tradition for which he speaks. His approach to problems is unusual in modern social commentary because his observations are not compelled by any overriding sense of the importance of the human present. In place of a philosophy of progress, he emphasizes fidelity to a set of spiritual and natural laws that have guided successful human social organization throughout history.

The appeal of his particular ethics in the search for solutions to contemporary environmental and social problems can become readily apparent. It is importantly, however, not a wisdom anchored in beliefs about human perfection. It's grounded in the recognition and acceptance of human responsibility where all forms of life are concerned.

Oren is a Faithkeeper of the Turtle Clan among the Onondaga people of western New York. He sits on the Council of Chiefs of the Haudenosaunee, or the Six Nations as they are sometimes known. (In addition to the Onondaga, these would be the Seneca, Cayuga, Oneida, Mohawk, and Tuscarora.) The people of this "Iroquois Confederacy" share a philosophy of life given to them a thousand years ago by a spiritual being they call the Peace Maker. (He was named so partly because his instructions and warnings ended a period of warfare among these tribes, but his teachings about peace are understood to refer principally to a state of mind necessary for good living and good governance.)

When the Peace Maker came to the Haudenosaunee, he instructed them in a system of self-governing that was democratic in nature. (Benjamin Franklin and others, in fact, borrowed freely from this part of Haudenosaunee oral tradition and practice in formulating the principles of government upon which the United States was founded.) He emphasized the importance of diversity in human society to ensure sustainability and rejuvenation. And he urged a general tradition of thanksgiving.

The Peace Maker is sometimes called simply "the Messenger," someone sent by the Creator. The clan mothers among the Haudenosaunee, along with sitting chiefs such as Oren, are regarded as "runners," people responsible for keeping the precepts handed to them by the Peace Maker regenerating through time. As a council chief, Oren is said to be "sitting for the welfare of the people" and to be engaged in sustaining "the power of the good mind" in discussions with others on the council, all of whom are exchanging thoughts about the everyday application of the wisdom given them by the Peace Maker.

Oren has spoken often, recently, about a lack of will among world leaders, a failure to challenge the economic forces tearing apart human communities the world over, and the Earth itself. His response to the question of what society should do to protect life, however, is rarely prescriptive. Frequently what he says is, "It's up to each generation. There are no guarantees."

The Peace Maker's advice included an important warning for the chiefs and clan mothers. Some of his instruction, he said, would apply to life-threatening situations that would develop before the Haudenosaunee were able to fully grasp their malevolent nature. While the insights needed to manage such trouble would emerge among council members, the people might initially adamantly reject the council's advice. As decision makers, he said, the chiefs and clan mothers would have to be prepared to absorb this abuse. Oren recounts these words of the Messenger: "You must be tolerant [of harsh critics] and must not respond in kind, but must understand [their fear], and be prepared to absorb all of that, because it is not all going to be coming from your enemies. It is going to be coming from your friends and families. This you can expect."

In public, Oren Lyons carries himself with the unaffected manner of elders in many of the world's indigenous traditions—unpretentious, understated. His physical presence in a room, however, radiates authority. In conversations, you quickly sense that he takes life more seriously than most. He is an articulate and forceful speaker when it comes to discussing the worldwide movement toward civil society, a movement that would marginalize the sort of governance and commerce that today threaten life everywhere.

Oren Lyons, long a professor of American Studies at the State University of New York at Buffalo, is the publisher of *Daybreak,* a national Native American magazine. Before being appointed to the Onondaga Council by the clan mothers in 1969, he was successfully pursuing a career in commercial art in New York City. An All-American lacrosse goalie while a student at Syracuse University, he was later elected to the National Lacrosse Hall of Fame in both Canada and the United States, and named honorary chairman of the Iroquois Nationals lacrosse team. He is the recipient of many national and international awards, and for more than three decades has been a defining presence in international indigenous rights and sovereignty issues.

—Barry Lopez

Barry Lopez: Why is sovereignty such a crucial issue for Native American people today?

Oren Lyons: Well, sovereignty is probably one of the most hackneyed words that is used in conjunction with Indians. What is it, and why is it so important? It's a definition of political abilities and it's a definition of borders and boundaries. It encapsulates the idea of nationhood. It refers to authority and power—ultimate and final authority.

It's such a discussion among native peoples in North America, I would say, because of our abilities at the time of "discovery"—and I use that term under protest, as if to say that before the advent of the white man in North America nothing existed. Where does that idea come from? Well, it comes from the ultimate authority of the pope at the time. I'm talking 1492. The Roman Catholic Church was the world power. Now it's my understanding that in the Bible, both the Old Testament and the New Testament, there is no mention of the Western Hemisphere whatsoever—not the least hint. How could they miss a whole hemisphere?

So here we were in our own hemisphere, developing our own ideas, our own thoughts, and our own worldview. There were great civilizations here at the time. In 1492, Haudenosaunee—which is better known as the

Iroquois by the French, and Six Nations by the English—already had several hundred years of democracy, organized democracy. We had a constitution here based on peace, based on equity and justice, based on unity and health. This was ongoing.

As far as I know, all the other Indian nations functioned more or less the same way. Their leadership was chosen by the people. Leaders were fundamentally servants to the people. And in our confederation, there was no place for an army. We didn't have a concept of a standing army, and we had no police. Nor was there a concept of jails, but there were of course fine perceptions of right and wrong, and rules and law. I would say that in most Indian nations, because they had inhabited one place for so long and were *a people* for so long, the rules and laws were embedded in the genes of the people more or less, in the minds of the people certainly, but not written. Plenty of law, almost on everything, but unspoken. Unspoken unless transgressed. There was always reaction to transgression.

Across the water, in Europe, our brother was engulfed in great crusades. If you look at their histories and what is in their museums, no matter where you are—whether it's Germany or France or England or Holland or whatever nation—in their great halls you'll see paintings of battles. Always. That must have been a terrible way of life. Now I speak of Europe because they are the ones that came here. And when they came here, the pope said, If there are no Christians on these lands, then we'll declare the lands *terra nullius*—empty lands—regardless of peoples there. And the question arose almost immediately, Were the aboriginal people *indeed people*? That was the big discussion. Why? Well, you can say a lot of things, but the issue is land—always has been and always will be.

The ideas of land tenure and ownership were brought here. We didn't think that you could buy and sell land. In fact, the ideas of buying and selling were concepts we didn't have. We laughed when they told us they wanted to buy land. And we said, Well, how can you buy land? You might just as well buy air, or buy water. But we don't laugh anymore, because that is precisely what has happened. Today, when you fly across this country and you look down and you see all those squares and circles, that's land bought and sold. Boundaries made. They did it. The whole country.

We didn't accept that, but nevertheless it was imposed. They said, Let's make us a law here; we'll call it the law of discovery. The first Christian nation that discovers this land will be able to secure it and the other Christian nations will respect that. What does that do to the original people, whose land of course they are talking about? We just weren't included. They established a process that eliminated the aboriginal people from title to their own land. They set the rules at the time and we were not subjects, we were objects, and we have been up to this point. That's why indigenous people are not included in the Declaration of Human Rights of the United Nations. We are still objects in common law.

In today's courts, in New York and Massachusetts and Pennsylvania, they talk about the preemption rights of the law of discovery. Today. Land claims are being denied on the basis of the law of discovery. It has not gone away whatsoever. You really have to get the case law and look at it, because they not only say that we don't have land tenure, they say that we have only the right of occupancy. And they don't have to pay us anything, because we're part of the flora and fauna of North America.

No wonder Indians wonder about what sovereignty is.

BL: Native elders are often credited with being informed about the environment, or knowledgeable about spiritual issues, but rarely credited with expertise when it comes to governance. Why aren't native elders sought out for their wisdom about a good way to govern, a good way to serve people?

OL: Well, to put it simply, our worldview, our perspective, and our process of governance is contrary to private property. Private property is a concept that flies in the face of our understanding of life, and we would say of the reality of life. Private property is a conception, a human conception, which amounts to personal greed.

And then there's the spiritual side that you mention. You can't see the spiritual side . . . well, you get glimpses of it. Any hunter will tell you, you see it in the eyes of the deer, that bright spark, that life, that light in his eyes, and when you make your kill, it's gone. Where did it go? It's the same light that's in the eyes of children, or in the eyes of old men, old women. There's a life in there, there's a spirit in there, and when you die, when your body gives up the ghost, as Christians say, spirit leaves. We believe that.

We believe that everything we see is made by a Creator. Indeed that's what we call the ultimate power. *Shongwaiyadisaih.* The maker of all life. The giver of life. All powerful. We see the Creation—everything—as what the giver of life has produced here. And if we believe that, which we do, then we must respect it. It's a spiritual Creation, and it demands that kind of respect. So when I see people, they are manifestations of the Creator's work, and I must respect them. It doesn't matter what color they are—anything alive.

A thousand years ago, when the Peace Maker brought to us the Great Law of Peace, *Gayanahshagowa,* he set as our symbol for the confederation of Haudenosaunee a great tree, and he said, "This is going to be the symbol of your work and your law: a great white pine, four white roots of truth that reach in the four directions of the world. And those people who have no place to go will follow the root to its source and come under the protection of the Great Law of Peace and the great long leaves of the great tree." And then he admonished the leaders and the people, and he said, "Never challenge the spiritual law. Never challenge it because you cannot prevail." That's a direct instruction to leadership.

BL: It seems to me that the federal government in the United States is reluctant to invite Indian people to the table because, as you've just said, you can't have effective leadership without spiritual law, and you can't talk about good governance without environmental awareness. Yet we need—all of us need—the counsel of minds that successfully addressed questions of social justice long before Western culture, arguably, complicated them with the notion of industrial progress.

OL: After the Peace Maker gathered five warring nations—the Mohawks, the Oneidas, the Cayugas, the Senecas, and the Onondagas—and after great efforts and great cohesive work, the power of the unity of the good minds brought together this confederacy based on peace. And after he had taken the leaders and sat them under this great tree on the shoreline of Onondaga Lake and instructed them on the process of governance, on the principles of governance, on the importance of identity and the importance of rule and law, he said, "Now that we've planted this great tree, in your hands now I place all life. Protection of all life is in your hands now," and when he said all life, he meant literally, *all life.*

And it's an instruction that we carry today. We feel responsible for animals, we feel responsible for trees, and responsible for fish, responsible for water. We feel responsible for land and all of the insects and everything that's there. And when he spoke of the four white roots reaching in the four directions, I think he was talking to all people. Not just Haudenosaunee. This is an instruction for all people.

But after all of that, a woman said to him, "Well then," she said, "how long will this last?" And he answered, "That's up to you." So it's completely up to us if we want this Creation to continue, and if we want to be involved in it, a part of this whole recycling, this whole regeneration of life, and we want to be celebrating it, and we want to be enjoying it, and we want to be preserving it, carrying it on, protecting it for future generations.

In one of his many instructions he said, "Counselors, leaders," he said, "now that we have raised out here, now that you are who you are," he said, "when you counsel for the welfare of the people, then think not of yourself, nor of your family, nor even your generation." He said, "Make your decisions on behalf of the seventh generation coming. You who see far into the future, that is your responsibility: to look out for those generations that are helpless, that are completely at our mercy. We must protect them." And that's great counsel in today's times, if we want the seventh generation to be here, and to have what we have.

BL: What do you think is the great impediment to the implementation of that wisdom?

OL: Human ego is probably the biggest impediment—the amazing ability of any human to perceive themselves as almighty powerful, no matter what. That is a big problem. We were instructed long before the Peace Maker to be respectful, to have ceremonies, to carry out thanksgivings for everything. We have an enormous amount of ceremony and thanksgiving still going on in North America. Indian nations across the country are still carrying on those ceremonies in their languages and through their dances. We're trying.

And we're told, as long as there is one to speak and one to listen, one to sing and one to dance, the fight is on. So that is hope. To not give up. To try, and to use reason. Peace Maker said, "I'm going to throw your weapons of war into this hole." He uprooted that great tree and instructed all the men to bring their weapons of war and to cast them into this hole. That was the first disarmament. And he said, "I'm not going to leave you unprotected and helpless." And he gave us the great tobacco plant. And he said, "This will be your medium to speak to me when you need to." And he gave us a very special plant, which we still use, still speak to him with.

We believe. And I think as long as we're doing that, there is a chance.

BL: When you meet with people—Desmond Tutu for example, Gorbachev, other people who've sought your counsel and the wisdom of the Six Nations—do you sense a possibility that these cultures that are driven by issues of private property, social control, and capitalism can be guided by your example of how to conduct a civilization without warfare?

OL: Indian people have as much dissension among themselves as anybody. I think that our understanding is simply that dissension begins with each individual. You don't need two people to have that tension; you have it within yourself. As a human being, you have a spiritual center, and if you go too far to the right or too far to the left, you're out of balance. And that occurs every day.

In the creation story that we have, we talk about the twin brothers, one good, one evil, and we talk about the battles that they went through, enveloping the Earth itself. It's a story to the people, to explain that within each of us we have these tensions, and that on any given day any one of us can be the world's worst enemy.

And that's why you have councils, and that's why you have rule, and that's why you have community and law, because that is part of humanity. And there is no ultimate authority. But of course over time people have found standards of moral right, and I think that's where the real law lies. It lies in morality. A balance.

The only thing that you can do is have custom in usage, and a good example. That's why grandpas and grandmas are so important. They are the transition people. They move the children into the next generation. Peace Maker said, "Make your decisions on behalf of seven generations." He's telling you to look ahead, to not think about yourself. If you can stop thinking about yourself and begin thinking about responsibility, everything is going to get better. Immediately everything will change. But that is not the makeup of the human mind. There's always the evil twin. And there's always the good twin. It's a daily battle.

BL: My own problem at the moment is a frustration that my fate, the fate of the people I love, and the fate of my family are in the hands of men who see no reason to listen to counsel from outside the circumscribed world of their own knowledge. I live in a country in which people take pride in never having had any kind of experience with other cultures, who believe that they have perfected the ways of life to such a degree that forcing them down the throats of other people is an act of benevolence. They don't want people who speak for the integration of spiritual and material life at the table because these people are disruptive when it comes to issues of consumerism, economic expansion, and international cooperation. To me, this is fundamentally not only unjust, but stupid.

OL: I see it that way too. We're being placed in an untenable position by greed and force and authority. If I was sitting on the moon looking back on North America, on the democracy that was here when Haudenosaunee was meeting and the Peace Maker was bringing these ideas to us, I would have seen this light, this bright light. I'd see it grow. And then in 1776, when the Continental Congress came as close to Indian nations as they ever would in their style of thinking, that light was growing again. The idea of democracy and the idea of peace were there.

But it began to dim almost immediately, as they began to take away peoples' rights in the Constitution of the United States. The Constitution institutionalized the idea that only men with money or property could vote. They said it was okay to have a slave or two or three or ten or twenty. The light began to dim. Haudenosaunee chiefs shook their heads and they said, "You're courting trouble." And then it really got dim in 1863, and 4 and 5 and 7 and 8, when they had a great civil war in this country over the issues of power, authority, slavery. That was a very intense war. That was brother against brother.

And so it goes on, this idea of private property, this idea of accruement of wealth. And now we have corporate states, corporations that have the status of states—independent and sovereign, and fealty to no one, no moral law at all. President Bush has said, "Let the market dictate our direction." Now if that isn't about as stupid as you can get. What he said was, let the greed of the people dictate the direction of the Earth. If that's the basis of a country, then it's really lost what you would call a primary direction for survival.

This is really the danger today—this empty, senseless lack of leadership. But it doesn't mean that responsibility isn't in the hands of the people. To come down to the nut of the whole thing, it's the people's responsibility to do something about it. Leadership was never meant to take care of anybody. Leadership was meant to guide people; they take care of themselves. People should be storming the offices of all these pharmaceutical companies that are stealing money from them. They should be dragging these leaders, these CEOs, out into the streets and they should be challenging them. They're not doing that. They're just worried about how they're going to pay more.

It's the abdication of responsibility by the people. What was it that they said? By the people and for the people? That was the Peace Maker's instruction: *Of, by, and for the people.* You choose your own leaders. You put 'em up, and you take 'em down. But you, the people, are responsible. You're responsible for your life; you're responsible for everything.

People haven't been here all that long as a species on the Earth. We haven't been here all that long and our tenure is in question right now. The question arises, Do we have the wisdom, do we have the discipline, do we have the moral rule, the moral law, are we mature enough to care for what is our responsibility? That question can only be answered by the people.

This interview grew out of an Orion Society event called Artful Advocacy, which was hosted and funded by the Rockefeller Brothers Fund, with additional support from the Nathan Cummings Foundation and the Compton Foundation.

(2007)

Assailed

Improvisations in the Key of Cosmology

for Annie Dillard, in correspondence with
whom this essay first began to stir

Journal Entry

The countless things that fit in our minds and imaginations do so because
they are abstract. Abstraction is not just the corporatist's or ideologue's
friend and the artist's and nature lover's enemy: it's what makes memories and knowledge portable, stories and art possible, and experiences and
music had and heard by a "you" capable of moving through time and space
into a "me."

The trouble with abstraction is that the matter that surrounds us (including that which makes up living natural systems, living creatures, and
ourselves) is *not* abstract. Much of it is also not portable. And much of
the matter that is portable (redwood trees and wild salmon for instance) is
irrevocably altered or destroyed when humans move it, against its own will,
through time and space.

Each of our actions unleashes forces latent in abstract language upon the
realm of matter and living forms. This is why we need stories. Stories are
matter and spirit at play. Stories, though made of language, can honor matter via an implicit cosmology portable enough to carry around in our hearts
and heads. Just as a jazz pianist can pull trained instincts from his fingers
and abstract knowledge from his head, then improvise an interaction with
a keyboard to make music unique to time and place, so (I hope!) can a
workable cosmology be produced to guide our interactions with creation,
moment to moment, place to place.

I live in the extreme upper Columbia River system, in the Bitterroot
Mountains' rainshadow, in a cottonwood and willow creek bottom between
seven-thousand-foot ridges. We call the year 2002. I've just turned half a
century old. Do I possess such a cosmology?

Assignment to myself: sit down some day soon and see if you can improvise, jazz-pianist-style, a series of cosmological riffs based on what is portably you; what moves through time and space with your matter and spirit; what you have seen, heard, remembered, imagined, dreamt, and experienced to be true . . .

Improvisation #1: Stars, Cells, Snow

It's early March in Montana, and the door between winter and spring is swinging violently. For days, including this one, a sometimes breezy sometimes brutal southwesterly wind has been breaking over the Bitterroots, bringing walls of cloud so vast and near-black they look world-ending. Each wall dumps a load of snow. An impossibly blue sky breaks out. The snow grows blinding, melts, birds burst into arias, summer feels just round the corner. Then, tied to the balm like an anti-proverbial March lion to its lamb, the next cloud-wall appears, hurtling the world back an entire season.

Studying the weather as I drive my daughters to school, I return home, go to my desk, look round the room, and realize that after a winter of writing my study looks as if the same weather has been blasting through it. Setting aside the manuscript I'd planned to work on, I fetch a dustcloth and cardboard box and set out to restore order. An hour into this work I start to recycle two old magazines (a *Time,* a *National Geographic*), but first open the *Time* to save a grouse-feather "bookmark." The page the feather was marking stops me in my tracks.

It's a Hubble Space Telescope photo of clouds in the Orion Nebula. They're fifteen hundred light-years (that's 10,000,000,000,000,000,000,000 miles) from Montana and me. They're made not of ice crystals, like the clouds outside, but of superheated hydrogen that lights them from within. In color they range from orange to gold to rosewood brown, pierced here and there by tiny flares of bright pink. In form they're flagrantly phallic, and remind me of stalagmites, velvet moose antlers, coral formations, basalt columns on the lower Columbia River and, begging our pardon, one of the exceedingly odd parts of Everyman. In size, though, the Orion clouds annihilate all earthly analogy: *they are six-trillion miles long.*

There are projections coming off them. Shaped like animal ears, bean sprouts, the antennae of slugs (some artfully tipped by the pink flares), the protuberances are tiny compared to the masses out of which they grow. Yet even the smallest, the Hubble astronomers tell us, are as wide as our entire solar system. And even the smallest contain something astounding: stars.

Those piercingly pink flares? They're foetal stars, every one of them, caught by the Hubble camera in the very process of being born. What's more, the astronomers tell us, our Sun, solar system, Earth, its hydrogen, oxygen, water, life forms, you, me, are all the offspring of these same types of clouds.

For the first time it hits me: the Sun, Earth, and I are siblings. Despite our obvious endless differences, we're each the progeny of just such stupendous clouds. As I sit by my Montana window, I am seated in the light of an Ancient Brother, on the lap of an Ancient Sister, looking, as if in a family album, at a photo of three Heavenly Father/Mothers. This gives me a feeling so paradoxical it makes me dizzy. I am so tiny and short-lived compared to the Orion parent-clouds! Yet I share a progenitive shape with them, I have conceived offspring as have they, and my offspring shine like stars to me.

A strange fact from a book I've been reading (Sara Maitland's *A Joyful Theology*): the number of cells in the human body is almost exactly the same as the number of stars in the Milky Way. Is this meaningless coincidence or a purposeful symmetry devised by our Creator? I have no idea. I only know that some facts make me happy and that a flurry of such facts have begun to whirl through me now.

Fact: the spring day has darkened and snow is swirling and falling again.

Fact: a contradictorily bright feeling is sweeping through me.

Facts: I am sitting amid mountains, pondering a celestial cloud whose "snow" is stars and a terrestrial cloud whose "stars" are snow; my children and I each have a Milky Way's worth of cells burning in our bodies; and our galaxy has a human being's worth of star-cells shining in its vast swirl.

Improvisation #2: True Wilderness

This dusty old *National Geographic* at my feet? I remember now why I saved it: another Hubble Space image: as I recall, the most cosmologically inspiring space photo I've seen.

Opening to it, I'm sure enough struck dumb. To capture this image the telescope was aimed, as the astronomers describe it, at one of the darkest parts of space, focused on an interstellar region "the size of a grain of sand held at arm's length," and 276 exposures were taken over ten days "to gather as much distant light as possible." The result is a photograph not of layers of stars, but layers of entire *galaxies,* "as far as the Hubble's eye can see."

I walk slowly back through all this. Here's a mere *speck* of our universe, a sand-sized grain of it, yet when a 276-exposure jury turns in its verdict, the grain is seen to contain a vast field of jeweled galaxies glittering in blankness and blackness. The physical gaze of this photo has penetrated so deep it's become spiritual. It tells a story too vast for thought or word, yet here it sits on a page, speaking a beyond-language of spheres, swirls, colors, light. Even the tiniest points in this image, the astronomers say, are not stars but galaxies. The light from some, traveling at 186,000 miles per second, takes *eleven billion years* to reach Earth. This is what I call a *Roadless Area*! This is true Wilderness. The number of stars, star-birthing nebula-clouds, solar systems, planets, moons, mineral-forms, life-forms, dead-forms, implied by this single photo stops my mind and leaves me hearing music. If we could look back toward ourselves from some bright point here pictured, the entire Milky Way would be a shining dot, our Sun a nothingness lost in that dot, our Earth and selves a dream within nothingness. Lacking some sci-fi miracle such as "warp speed" that lets us travel millions of times faster than light, not a molecule of this vastness will ever be disturbed, colonized, globalized, debated, exploited, degraded, or touched by that strangely greedy animal, the human being.

What strikes me, what consoles me here, is that Earth is at one not with our greed but with the multigalaxied swirl. Industrial folly has knocked some of our planet's systems out of balance; it has created extinctions that have thrown the evolution of forms aeons backward in time. But bacteria are patient creatures, and evolution's an indestructible process. Earth will swirl on. It's only a speck known as "humanity" that may not. The wilderness in this photograph contains us the way a shoreless ocean contains a drop. Even at our grandiose worst, we are a negligible jot of darkness in a universe filled with beauty and light.

Improvisation #3: Assailed

On a five-foot shelf within reach of my desk I keep forty or so volumes I've read so many times that their imaginative flights and insights now bleed into my own. One is Annie Dillard's *For the Time Being*. I vaguely remember a sentence in this book filled with the same music the multicolored galaxies have me hearing. I seem to recall it having been written not by Annie but by her hero, the French paleontologist, priest, and mystic, Teilhard de Chardin. I grab the book and flip through pages till the swirl of galaxies and de Chardin's words mesh. The music turns out to have been coming from two sentences. They run:

> By means of all created things, without exception, the divine assails us, penetrates us, and molds us. We imagined it as distant and inaccessible, whereas in fact we live steeped in its burning layers.

These words somehow reverse the Hubble image, throwing the swirl of galaxies into my interior. It seems an unnecessary act of cosmic exhibitionism

when, out the window, sunlight bursts forth, the finches, crossbills, gros-
beaks, and siskins burst into song, and now-blinding snowflakes keep swirling down. Turning from snow to galaxies to embryonic pink stars to a desk
photo of my daughters, I am assailed. My youngest, in the photo, holds a
single petal of a living sunflower. The same flower's blind eye followed the
sun across the sky every day last summer, then in autumn bowed low, and
in winter fed its eye to the birds. The birds repaid it by planting bits of
eye in the dirt. Tiny green sprouts now unfurl all over the yard. The sun is
burning four million tons of itself per second to enliven this world of birds,
sunflowers, and melting snow. Aged suns explode like old blossoms, their
fragments scattering, falling into orbits, becoming planets. The seeds of future suns gestate in fiery phallus clouds.

The sunlit snow is a falling Milky Way. The cells of my brain and body
are another. We are born of and fed by a sacrificial burning. We live steeped
in and contribute to its layers. The brown eyes of my daughters burn so
serenely. Yet they burn. The music of de Chardin's words rises. Tears rise. I
turn from stars to sunlight to sunflowers to snow to my children's faces.
I feel us steep in the sacrificial layers.

Improvisation #4: Science & Reverence

I hold the thing we call "nature" to be the divine manuscript. I hold the
infinite wilds to be the only unbowdlerized book we possess of the Creative
handiwork that gives and sustains life. Human industry is shredding
the divine manuscript like an Enron document. The "President" and those
who appointed and control him call this shredding "economics" and "freedom." It's not quite a lie. But the freedom to shred the divine manuscript
is not an economics any lover of neighbor, self, or Earth wishes to practice.
When self-giving starts to give you joy, you grow bewildered by the spectre
of selfishness, fall out of the nationalist/capitalist loop, and limp about in
search of healthier hopes.

A new source of hope for me: the growing reverence for nature and its
mysteries among scientists. Though science itself never caged us, until recently the sciences were committed to mechanistic paradigms and an obses-
sion with the physically measurable universe that made reverence possible
only by disconnecting spirituality and scientific thought. The so-called
Enlightenment and its empirical thinking led, sans spirit, to the effective
naming of things, cataloging of things, dissecting, extracting, and reconstruction of things, to create the modern world as we know it. By the late
twentieth century, the same divorce between spirituality and science had

led to genetically warping even the most sacred living things, filing corporate copyrights on ancient living things, and raping, monoculturizing, extincting, and abstracting ourselves from living things as if we were not living things ourselves.

I see two chief causes for the countering outburst of reverence in science—one famous, the other infamous. The famous cause: the new physics. Quantum mechanics have changed the way we see the universe. The old proton/neutron/electron atom, for instance, is as unfit for describing matter as we now understand it as a horse and buggy are unfit for negotiating a contemporary freeway. Atomic particles are now said to derive from "immaterial wave packets"; space is now said to have had ten original dimensions that collapsed, at the beginning of time, to form the "superstrings" of which subatomic particles consist. Field theory. Morphogenesis. It's hard to keep up with all the ways that physics is telling us that Space, Time, and Matter derive from something infinitely subtler and greater than all three.

The infamous cause of the new reverence among scientists: suffering. How many biologists, botanists, ethnologists, anthropologists, have been forced to renounce their fields in mid-career because their living objects of study have died out before their eyes? How many more have been so dismayed by the world's barrios, biological dead or disease zones, slave job and oil war zones, that they've abandoned their disciplines to become peace activists or humanitarians? I'm not going to belabor these problems. I touch on them to introduce a sentence that strikes me as pivotal: "Problems cannot be solved," wrote Albert Einstein, "at the same level of consciousness that created them."

That emininently practical man, E. F. Schumacher, though famed for his book *Small is Beautiful,* ended his career with *A Guide for the Perplexed*— a meticulous, Thomist, tour de force on levels of consciousness and how to change them. De Chardin strikes me, in this context, as a person in whom humanity's problems have in a sense been solved—for a man whom the divine is "assailing, penetrating, and molding" is not living at a level of consciousness capable of shredding the divine manuscript in the name of "freedom."

The thoughts, words and deeds of men like Einstein, Schumacher, and de Chardin make me wonder what would happen if we would-be problem-solvers focused less exclusively on the problems coming at us. Einstein and de Chardin were renowned for the absentminded, daydreamy, walk-about states in which their great insights came to them. Mahatma Gandhi, too. I feel there's more to this than the eccentricities of three quirky men. What if our primary focus became the level of consciousness with which we greet the dawn, the day, our every breath, our burning, and *then* we turned to face the problems?

Improvisation #5: Toward Living Language

The human brain is the most complex physical object in the known universe. Its ten billion neurons, says scientist Gerald Edelman, can make a million billion interconnections. Our thoughts, dreams, imaginings, fire lucidly or weave drunkenly through our cortexes in patterns as complex as stars gyring through a galaxy. Yet Sir John Carew Eccles, the Nobel Prize-winning brain researcher, tells us that the brain is not itself the cause of its own synaptic convolutions. The brain doesn't *produce* energies: it merely receives them. Picking up invisible impulses, it transposes them into data that the ego-consciousness can translate. But the energies themselves, says Eccles, come from a realm inaccessible to any known method of measurement—a realm we could easily call "spiritual."

The Benedictine contemplative Willigis Jager, in his book *Search for the Meaning of Life,* describes many convergences between the new physics and metaphysics. The microelectromagnetic forces known as "L-fields," for instance, create, inform, and sustain literally everything in nature. Yet they are not a chemical process, not a mechanical sequence, not anything that pre-1960s scientific models described or believed in. L-fields, say those who study them, literally sculpt us and all lifeforms, yet they're not "literal" at all. They're intangible. To even explain how they're detected requires a treatise more reminiscent of Aquinas than of Newton.

Moving further into the transrational: morphogenetic fields are called "metafields" for the same reason metaphysics is called metaphysics. These fields are "above" (*meta*) the material realm, and can be neither seen nor measured. Indeed, in the words of scientist Rupert Sheldrake, they are "free of matter and energy" entirely (!). Yet morphogenetic fields, Sheldrake and others say, "shape and direct the entire animate and inanimate creation." When, for instance, a cut sprig of willow is jammed into the ground and watered, it is matterless, energyless morphogenetic forces *outside the matter and energy of the sprig* that cause an entire tree to grow from the cutting. Likewise, when a dragonfly egg is tied off in the middle, unseen fields outside the egg's own matter and energy cause an entire organism to grow from each fragment.

We have in my view entered another Roadless Area. We're still studying science, yet we stand amid energyless, matterless, invisible powers that "shape and direct the entire animate and inanimate creation," and these powers are no more graspable than the contents of the Hubble-glimpsed galaxies eleven billion light-years away. I'm not trying to deify morphogenetic fields here. What interests me is the fact that I'm speaking of things beyond my comprehension—but beyond science's as well. There is something poignant in this to me. We nature dweebs, fly fishers, imaginative writers, contemplatives, are used to the good company of things far beyond our comprehension. Many scientists are not. Is there anything we Uncomprehenders can do to help scientists feel more comfortable with swimming in the end where you never touch bottom?

That all things are shaped by "fields" that are "beyond energy and matter" is now what we can oxymoronically yet truthfully call "solid science." As a result, in the realm of language (my area of professional competence) the scientific facts of the matter are becoming impossible to express in spiritually neutral scientific terms. Science has moved in a generation from the easily stated but mistaken claim that we are mortal matter, chemical compounds, and little more, to the inspiring but linguistically problematic claim that we are living repositories of the invisible wisdom of primordial electromagnetic and morphogenetic fields. Scientists who disdain religion are horrified by the mounting pressure to deploy overtly spiritual terms such as de Chardin uses. But the use of such terms does not mean that you've turned into Pat Robertson or Jerry Falwell.

And what of science's own pet terms? It is no more defensible, empirically speaking, to believe in a universe created by "the Big Bang" than of one created by Shiva's lingam. "The Big Bang was not big, it was sub-atomic," writes Sara Maitland. "And it was not a bang, it was necessarily silent, since in the absence of time and atmosphere there was nothing to convey sound waves, and nothing to receive them either." I've read definitions of quarks and muons that sounded less believable than definitions of the Holy Ghost. My advice to scientists is: relax; accept this. If unseen fields beyond literary or scientific expression lie at the root of all life forms and matter—if these fields are invisible yet deducible, ineffable yet artful, indescribable yet powerful, and if in the attempt to speak of them science has never sounded so much like ancient myth or scripture—so be it. I realize that to many an old-school scientist, the words "ancient myth and scripture" translate "superstitious pap." But this is mere arrogance. Ancient thought as expressed in wisdom literature, myth, and scripture is unanswerably profound *and* poetic, and scientists who actually study the ancients know it. Cutting-edge physicists have been pondering India's five-thousand-year-old Upanisads for decades, stunned by their exacting observations of how unseen fields and mayavic forces create this world of forms.

If it is actual poetry that physics and fields are showing us, it's time scientists opened their minds to poetry. If *problems cannot be solved at the same level of consciousness that created them,* I suggest we contemplatives, scientists, writers, artists, teachers, activists, Earth-lovers, transcend petty discomfiture, acclimatize to the new-to-physics but in fact ancient, incomparably less mechanistic, intuitive way of sensing things, and bring a reverence for the unseen to bear on how we behave toward the seen. Because we have definitely got problems. The best science we have evinces increasing humility toward the unknown. But our worst science ignores the best and goes profitably a-whoring on behalf of the most greed-driven, life-squandering nimnams on Earth. Consider the "reverence" of the Department of Defense and the thousands of scientists it hires to perfect the deadliness of weapons. Consider the "reverence" of nuclear physicists and the nightmares they have helped spawn. Consider the "reverence" of scientists hired by industry leaders like Harry Merlo, CEO of Louisiana Pacific, who said: *"We need everything that's out there. We don't log to a ten-inch top or an eight-inch top or a six-inch top. We log to infinity. Because we need it all. It's ours. It's out there and we need it all. Now."*

Pick your science.

Einstein: *"In the new physics, there is no place for both field and matter, because field is the only reality."*

Willigis Jager: *"There aren't two kinds of laws: matter and mind. Rather, there is a single continuous law for both matter and mind. Matter is the domain of space in which the field is extremely dense."*

De Chardin: *"Concretely speaking, there is no matter and spirit. There exists only matter that is becoming spirit."*

Frederick Sommer: *"Spirit is the behavior of matter. Perception does not take spiritedness into a state of affairs that does not already have it."*

Stephen Hawking: *"What is it that breathes fire into the equations and makes a universe for them to describe?"*

St. John of the Cross: *"The fire! The fire inside!"*

Bhagavad Gita: *"Behind the manifest and unmanifest there is an Existence that is eternal and changeless. This Existence is not dissolved in the general cosmic dissolution. Fools pass blindly by it, and of its majesty know nothing. It is nearer than knowing . . ."*

Improvisation #6: Beyond-Language

The English word "mysticism" was unknown to me as a boy. My child mind excelled at acceptance, declined categorization, embraced spirit, matter, and contradictions without judgment, and everything that happened simply was.

The word "mysticism" still means little to me as an experiencer, since everything I experience continues to simply be what it is. But as the beneficiary of certain inner experiences that have guided my life, and as a writer in love with a world in which much of what is visible is abused and much of what is life-giving is unseen, my respect for the word "mysticism" grows if only because, by definition, it shepherds us toward realms in which "what is" is much more than physical. I am therefore stepping, this fine March day in my fiftieth year, out of a closet in which I've spent my writing life happily hidden, and openly confessing myself (with a blue-collar, rednecked blush) to be the experiential mystic I have in fact always been.

My long love for rivers is partly to blame. In visiting the same streams year in and year out as Earth tilts on her axis, causing foliage, insects, fish, birds, seasons to arrive out of seeming nowhere, things occasionally tilt on some kind of interior axis, causing invisible yet artful, imperceptible yet detectable forces to arrive out of nowhere inside me. I have so far used fiction alone as a repository for these unexpected falls into inwardness. But as I grow older I notice the way great nature-probing nonfictioneers from Rumi to Blake to Thoreau, Dickenson, Whitman, Muir, Jeffers, de Chardin, Gary Snyder, Wendell Berry, Pattiann Rogers, Mary Oliver, Jane Hirshfield, and on and on, unapologetically leap now and then in their writing, as they must leap in their lives, from discursive language and the outer world into "beyond-language" and inner realms. My friendships with a few people on this list, and my own life, have together convinced me: these linguistic leaps are based on simple fidelity to experience. When experience flies into realms that language cannot touch, simple honesty of narration demands beyond-language.

Consider Henry David Thoreau. In a letter to one H. G. O Blake, Thoreau unapologetically avers that humans can participate in the same kind of creative acts as the Creator Himself:

Free in this world as the birds in the air, disengaged from every kind of chains, those who practice the yoga gather in Brahma the certain fruits of their works. The yogi, absorbed in contemplation, contributes in his degree to creation. He breathes a divine perfume, he hears wonderful things. Divine forms traverse him without tearing him, and united to the nature which is proper to him, he goes, he acts as animating original matter. . . . Depend upon it that, rude and careless as I am, I would fain practice the yoga faithfully.

I have no rational idea what Henry is saying here. But I am struck by this:
Thoreau: *"Divine forms traverse him without tearing him . . ."*
De Chardin: *"The divine assails us, penetrates us, molds us . . ."*

What sort of experience might create such similar sentences?

Though famed for an astute midwestern groundedness, Aldo Leopold too leapt, now and again, from natural history into outright mystical testimony. In *Round River,* for example, he writes:

> The song of a river ordinarily means the tune that waters play on rock, root and rapid. This song of the waters is audible to every ear, but there is other music in these hills, by no means audible to all. To hear even a few notes of it you must first live here for a long time, and you must know the speech of hills and rivers. Then on a still night, when the campfire is low and the Pleiades have climbed over rimrocks, sit quietly and listen for a wolf to howl, and think hard of everything you have seen and tried to understand. Then you may hear it—a vast, pulsing harmony—its score inscribed on a thousand hills, its notes the lives and deaths of plants and animals, its rhythms spanning the seconds and the centuries.

Reason protests such assertions. "A *thousand* hills!" it huffs. "Is this *science*? Is Aldo's *vast harmony* supposed to be audible? Then why can't *I* hear it? How can he claim to have heard something that spans *centuries* when he himself died in less than a century? This is a buncha late-night campfire woowoo. His editors should've cut it."

Reason makes all such leaps sound foolish, because they *are* foolish—to unadorned reason. But from boyhood through manhood it has been my experience that trying to grasp an insight, a deep mystery, a transrational experience, or any act of love via reason alone is rather like trying to play a guitar with one's butt. As E. F. Schumacher more politely puts it, "Nothing can be perceived without an appropriate organ of perception." This is not to demean reason. It's only to say that, unless trained like a bird dog to heel in the presence of love and mystery, reason lunges forth barking, scaring off meta-meanings that only the heart could have hoped to embrace. When a superb reasoner like de Chardin says that "the divine assails us, penetrates us, and molds us," he has not left his sanity behind: only his reason. He is exposing matter to spirit. He's using beyond-language to do it. We can go with him. Our reason can't.

In the late-medieval classic, *The Cloud of Unknowing,* the anonymous author states that no evil can touch, and no reasoning make an impact upon, the divine creativity that proceeds from the depths of the soul. Spiritually speaking, nothing's changed since those words were set down. And the same words can be said of the symphony of forces woven through galaxies, unseen fields, synapses, ecosystems, subatomic particles and cells. The physical universe as we now understand it cannot be accurately described via static modes of thought, for that which enlivens all things is dynamic, imperceptible, and—I believe with all the science of my heart—*holy*. We are steeped in and assailed by it even as we "study it." We have no objective distance from it and never shall. Our study of the infinite wilderness involves us in mystery, steeps us in ignorance, inspires awe, and demands humility and reverence. The notion that we can stand apart from all things, infer the existence and true properties of all things, and solve the dire problems we have created for ourselves, with reason alone, is what I would call rationalist woowoo.

Improvisation #7: Music of the Spheres

Another de Chardin declaration cited by Annie Dillard: "It is precisely because he is so infinitely profound and punctiform that God is infinitely near."

The first time I read this I had no idea what it meant, so I looked up the word "punctiform." Seldom has a dictionary had a more powerful effect on me: the instant I read that "punctiform" means "of the nature of a point or dot," de Chardin's sentence smote me with yearning. I was amazed. I still understood next to nothing, yet my intuition sensed something incredible.

Tying my reason by its leash to a tree, I began creeping up on possible meta-meanings without it.

Pondering de Chardin's sentence in *For the Time Being*, Annie Dillard asks, "Is it useful to think of God as *punctiform*?"

Her question sounded so odd and rhetorical that I expected a joke to follow.

Instead, she wrote, "I think so."

And I suddenly had goose bumps.

Next Annie cites a scientific study on sand, of all things—informing us that the oldest grains of sand on Earth are the most perfectly spherical, and that a river takes a million years to move a spheroid grain a mere hundred miles.

Back at the tree, my reason howled. "What's any of that got to do with *anything*? These supposed observers of Earth are no longer *on* Earth! They're lost in space! And now you've tied me to a fuckin' tree and are wandering off with them! Come back! You need me!"

I answered my poor panicked doubting organ in this way: "Yadda yadda yadda, my reason. I know I need you—to do stuff like my taxes. But who needs Earth or its objects to speak of certain experiences we humans enjoy while on Earth? Sit. Stay. I'll be back in a while—hopefully."

My reason sank into a sulk. What was left of me sank into reflection:

The references to "punctiformity," to "the nature of a point or dot," to "nearness," all smote me with yearning. So did Annie's sentence: *The oldest grains of sand on Earth are the most perfectly spherical.* Why did she "answer" de Chardin with such a crazy fact? Why did that fact sing inside me?

Sitting quiet amid these questions—not trying to answer them, just enjoying their odd company—I suddenly fell through a floor inside myself and landed amid an intensely recollected experience. I would speak of this. To do so will be to speak of a mystery intelligible to me only as mystery. I have no language with which to approach that mystery but beyond-language. I know before writing it that my description will leave me sounding like a fool to my reason. But I'm not getting any younger. The thought of dying without having described this wonder makes me feel like an ingrate. I prefer fools to ingrates. So here goes:

In the thirteenth century, Rumi spoke a spontaneous poem in Persian, which a disciple set down, scholars later translated into English, and the poet Coleman Barks recently reconstructed to sound like this:

> *Don't go to sleep one night.*
> *What you most want will*
> *come to you then. Warmed*
> *by a sun inside, you'll see*
> *wonders. Tonight, don't put*
> *your head down. Be tough,*
> *and strength will come.*
> *That which adoration adores*
> *appears at night.*

Beginning in boyhood but lasting well into manhood, I had a recurring experience, always at night, of what Aldo Leopold might call a *vast, pulsing harmony* and de Chardin an *infinite punctiformity.* Beginning when I was about twelve—always after long, vigorous outdoor days—I'd lie down in the dark, so dazzled by the wonders of the day that I would consciously swear off sleep in order to keep pondering all I'd seen and done.

While conducting these reviews I'd eventually enter a state wherein my body felt as though it was buzzing, and my eyes would see vividly in a waking dark. What normally followed this state was a clean fall into dream and sleep. My boyhood trick, though, was to fiercely resist that falling and just keep gazing at what the night and my state let me see. I would "be tough." And sure enough, strength would come.

The beyond-language experience began when the vibration of my body was joined by an exquisite sense of density: of massive physical weight. This weight felt both vastly greater and vastly *other* than that of my body. It seemed a physical visitation by something heavy and huge—something a physicist might call "a field." The only reason the weight didn't crush me, it seemed, was that it permeated me the way colors permeate vision, or water permeates a sponge: I grew so absorbed that there was no "me" left to crush.

Shortly after the density grew palpable I'd hear an oceanic hum: a single note, majestically deep and simple. To hear this was to desire to hear nothing more. Any question I might have thought to ask about who made it, where it came from, how it was produced, felt answered without speaking by its music.

Simultaneous to the sound I would see, as plainly as I'd seen the light and objects of the day, an enormous sphere. This sphere, I knew instantly, was the source of the music, the density, the weight. It floated in a sea of black. I hovered before it, its motionless satellite—though once the experience began, pronouns became impossible: "I" was now an invisible perceiver consisting of the senses of feeling, hearing, and sight. Body and mind were gone. Yet "I" was doing just fine without them.

The enormous sphere was beautiful to see, to hear, and to feel—a swirling mass of reds and oranges, lit from within, vast as a close-up star, though not at all hot. My being pulsed in tune with its massive hum, a sensation indescribably blissful, yet peaceful. Fear was not possible in this musical state. I had no ego to be afraid with, no body to be afraid for. The sphere was not just the largest thing in existence, it was the *only* thing, and I watched, felt, heard it in a state I can only call *adoration*.

But the experience grew richer. Every time I beheld the sphere the encounter had movements, like a symphony. Every time, the movements were the same:

First Movement: After "I" had adored the sphere for a time, "I" would move toward it. Anticipation would fill me. My effaced self would ease closer to the sphere till its dimensions seemed impossibly vast, its note capable of singing a universe into existence. Despite this potency, the sphere was all-gentle. The intimacy between us, when I could approach no closer, was as delicate as when we touch, with a cautious fingertip, the surface tension of still water. "I" remained on one side of this tension. *Infinitely profound and punctiform, infinitely near,* the sphere's music, light, and power reigned on the other.

Second Movement: When proximity to the sphere could not be closer, my point of view would suddenly turn inside-out. I'd feel this hugely—a thrill like when a jet plane hits an air pocket and drops a thousand feet, only not frightening. Once this inside-outing occurred I'd find that I could see, feel, and hear in the opposite direction. What I beheld brought bliss:

A second sphere had been born. The very twin of the first. Precisely as magnificent. Precisely as vast and profoundly close. The beautiful hum had doubled. It seemed as though the original sphere had divided, like a cell creating two of itself, but that I'd been too close to see it. The discovery of the second sphere, the feelings it stirred, were off the charts. *Cataclysms* of pleasure passed through me. (I'm trying hard to avoid sexual terms.) Lodged between an orb so vast I'd experienced it as all-encompassing, and now a second "all-encompass-ingness," I'd turn my being one way, then the other, and adore them both.

Third Movement: Anticipation rose again. I drew slightly away from the vast spheres in order to be able to see them without shifting perspective. Then, as I watched, felt, listened, they simultaneously and this time *visibly* divided, like cells, giving me a double "inside-out" feeling, creating four of themselves, the oceanic music a fourfold harmony now.

The plot thickened, grew fruitful, multiplied. I watched/felt/heard the spheres create eight of themselves, then sixteen, then 32, 64, 128, every orb glowing, lit from within, the music, bliss, sense of density and mass coming in waves, a vast, pulsing harmony. They *loved to divide,* they *loved to be fruitful.* At each division I felt their love as if it were my own. Awash in this geometrical, musical mode, I watched the spheres go on dividing, grow incalculable in number, pour forth color, hum their multitudinous song, till they'd become so numerous that I had to draw away from the "surface tensions" and interfaces in order to behold them all.

Still dividing, still self-generating, they came to look like a vast wall of spheroid fruits, growing smaller with each division—first melons, then grapefruits, then oranges, apricots, wrong-colored grapes, then blueberries, then currants, till they became something too small for fruition, tiny seeds perhaps, or a sea of thrumming, internally lit grains of sand. (*"The oldest grains of sand on Earth are the most perfectly spherical . . ."*)

Final Movement: Anticipation dawned again—the most blissful dawning of all—and I saw that each grain of the infinity of spheres had become so small that they were no longer separate: they had divided into an infinity of orbs so miniscule that they had merged back into a single vast unity, their incalculable harmony, too, had become a single *basso profundo* note, till I realized that,

Da Capo: I was back in the Beginning, gazing at the smooth, *infinitely punctiform* surface of the Original Vast Sphere. It floated in a sea of black. I hovered before it, its motionless satellite, in a state I can, again, only call *adoration*. With which the entire "symphony" commenced movement by movement, exactly as before, till I fell asleep in an exhaustion of density, division, creation, music, bliss.

Improvisation #8: Fruits

There it is: a mystery intelligible to me only as mystery. I don't know beans about the "meaning" or "utility" of this thing. Such experiences don't care if they're comprehensible, useful, apropos, politic, polite: such experiences *assail*. But I've always loved and trusted the line: *By their fruits ye shall know them.* And in applying it to the spheres I realize that, mysterious as they remain to me, they have created tangible fruit.

When, for instance, I first heard of medieval cosmologists referring to a "music of the spheres," my faithful dog, Reason, howled, but the heart of me thought, *Why not?* And when I read the *Upanisadic* description of a state in which the soul perceives infinite hugeness and infinite smallness as one and the same, and came across the Quranic statement, "All Creation in the hands of the Merciful One is smaller than a mustard seed," and learned of the mathematician Georg Cantor and his followers proving that infinities come in an infinite range of sizes, and read Paul Davies's discussion of Cantor ("any [Infinity], being a unity and hence complete within itself, must include itself. . . . If it is One, then it is a member of itself and thus can only be known through a flash of mystical vision") I thought, *Beautiful Spheres, Final Movement.* When I opened the dusty *National Geographic* this morning and saw galaxies swirling in a jot of universe "the size of a grain of sand held at arm's length," when de Chardin's words then flipped these galaxies into my interior, tears rose because, for an instant, I heard the *profundo* hum of a glorious old nighttime companion. And when I dreamed the other night, after watching *Captain Corelli's Mandolin,* that I was shot dead by a hundred machine guns, shot so many times that a dark bullet-driven wind blew my soul irrevocably away from even my dead body and I was invisible and afraid and had neither breath nor voice with which to call out to my God, I called out in bodiless desire anyway, and a spheric point pierced the wall of the grim gray world in which I drifted, the point expanded, tore that world's wall apart like so much wet Kleenex, a light poured through, and I saw my Beloved's cheek and brilliant eye peeking at me through the hole, just that much of Him, yet there was such love in that eye, such *What-a-trick-I've-pulled!* glee, that a posthumous existence without need of this body felt not just possible but certain, and I woke with a jolt of joy. And when, looking for de Chardin's "assailed" sentence this morning, I reread Annie Dillard's writing—

> There is no less holiness at this time—as you are reading this—than there was the day the Red Sea parted. . . . There is no whit less might in heaven or on Earth than there was the day Jesus said, "Maid, arise" to the centurion's daughter, or the day Peter walked on water, or the night Mohammed flew to heaven on a horse. . . . In any instant you may avail yourself of the power to love your enemies; to accept failure, slander, or the grief of loss; or to endure torture. . . . "Each and every day the Divine Voice issues from Sinai," says the Talmud. Of eternal fulfillment, Tillich said, "If it is not seen in the present, it cannot be seen at all"

—I felt nothing but an urge to shout: *Go Annie! You're singin' the morphogenetic gospel now!*

The sensations of weight, of palpable presence, of *hum*, still come over me now and again walking the mountains or cities, wading the traffic or trout streams. I don't seek such sensations. (How would one even begin?) They just check in now and then, unlooked for, in the course of what comes. A spring aspen leaf might brush my face, and I'll close my eyes and find myself feeling the tiny, self-contained universe that is a spring-green aspen cell suddenly making two of itself, and thus growing, *because it loves to.* I witness "fruitful multiplication" in our Montana-winter-blighted fruit trees or the year's brood of Bantam chicks, the creek's insects or the river bottoms' whitetail fawns, the newborn wood-ducks, the kingfishers, the kill-deers, and wonder comes upon me in the form of music as the densities, unions, and divisions of love are made palpable. I've stood by the ocean, seen the slight curve of horizon, felt the ocean's hum, and seen: *the very seas are a single sphere.* I've had the sense, standing in running water, that I've been not just close to the molecules flowing round me but *inside* them: that I've experienced, in the womb or aeons earlier, the coming together and breaking apart of spheric particles of H and of O. I've witnessed the aging, sickness, and deaths of plants, animals, family, friends, self, the migrations to new climes, transmigrations into unknowns, jolts into new awareness or bodies, slow breakdowns by organic or industrial attrition, transformations of earth, water, matter, energy, clouds, leaves, souls—and the *thousand hills* feeling and a vast pulsing harmony and an anguish of joy have filled the bit of me left unabsorbed.

It's time I stopped building sentences now and stepped down to the creek, as I've done half my life come evening. This time of year I'll look for the rainbows that migrate up from the bigger rivers to spawn. And I'll find a pair, if this spring is like the last eight, in a tiny side channel a quarter mile downstream. As I approach them on my belly I'll be crawling across spheroid grains of white granitic sand. I'll then lie like a Muslim, watching a female trout, an arm's length from my eyes, beat her body against gold-colored pebbles, build a stone nest, and fill it with a thousand lit-from-within orange spheres. I'll watch the male ease over like one of the gray-black snow clouds above. And when the milt pours down, each nested sphere will suddenly love to divide and divide till it's a sphere no longer but a tiny, sphere-eyed trout. I'll encounter the same trout over the slow course of summer, drifting down toward the rivers, growing by dividing, defeating time; I'll catch them now and then, release most, eat a few, and the survivors will return in twelve or sixteen seasons, bearing the milt clouds, glowing spheres, and hidden fields that carry the genius of trout toward my children's children's world.

There's not much more to discuss here. Either I'm crazy or I'm not, and the kingdom of heaven is within us or it isn't, and a divine punctiformity exists or it doesn't, and we sense it or we don't. If we do, God help us. And if we don't, God help us. Because if inner kingdoms and morphogenetic truth are delusions, where's the harm? You think Congress isn't deluded? If the punctiform spheres I've glimpsed are sheer delusion, then Congress, the spheres, and I are just three phantasms amid a chaos of delusions and nothing matters so hey ho, let's run out and express our "freedom" by "voting" for one of them nifty, interchangeable, Earth-eating plastic Lego units with names like Trent Cheney, Newt Army, and Dick Lott till the galaxies abort us, amen.

But if the punctiformities I've glimpsed in some sense *do* exist—if each and every day the Divine Voice *does* issue from Sinai, and if every inch of Creation is pierced by Its song and every dot, point, cell, particle, field is so moved by the Music that it loves to sing, swell, shrink, leap, divide, transform, and bear all fruit and all life in response—well then *ahhhhhhhhhhhhh!* How grateful I am to be here! And how carefully and attentively I want to live!

I still have no rational idea what I mean when consciousness revs up and perceives mystery or field amid mind, amid life, amid matter. But oh do I have *images* of what I mean! I can't lend logical credence to Annie's sense that punctiformity is "helpful in sensing God." But man can I lend a bit of Beyond-Credence! I don't know beans about beans let alone about God, but if we are ever to rise to new levels of consciousness or to the Beauty that is Truth, we've gotta call 'em as consciousness Truly sees 'em.

I therefore confess my lifelong love for a wilderness found outside myself, normally, till once in a while I encounter it within. It's a wilderness entered, it seems, through agendaless alertness at work, rest, or play in the presence of language, rivers, mountains, music, plants, creatures, rocks, moon, sun, dust, pollen grains, dots, spheres, galaxies, grains of sand, stars, every sort of athletic ball, cells, DNA, molecules, atomic particles, and immaterial forces. It's a wilderness that occasionally "inside-outs" me, leading to the adoration of a Chardinian burning and Leopoldian pulsing harmony that leaves my mind wondrous happy but far, far behind. It's a wilderness my dog, Reason, will never succeed in sniffing out, chomping up, or rationally defining, yet a wilderness I've been so long and gratefully assailed by that I've lost all but comic interest in my dog's endless sniffing and suspect that even the dog begins to enjoy itself when the wilderness flips us inside itself.

I believe—based on phallic clouds giving birth to stars, spring storm-clouds to snow, snowbanks to rivers, orange orbs to trout; I believe based on punctiform dots melting into vastest spheres, spheres dividing their way back into dots, lives collapsing into ashes and dust, and dust bursting back to life; I believe based on spheric shapes singing, dividing, creating cells, plants, creatures, creating my children, sunflowers, sun, self, universe, by constantly sacrificing all that they are in order to be reconfigured and re-born forever and ever—that when we feel Love's density, see its colors, feel its pulse, it's time to quit worrying about reason and words and cry: *"My God! Thanks!"*

If I stake my life on one field, one wild force, one sentence issuing from Sinai it is this one: *There is no goal beyond love.*

(2002)

The Rise and Fall of Natural History

How a science grew that eclipsed direct experience

IN THE EARLY SUMMER OF 1912, MY GRANDMOTHER BOARDED AN eastbound train in Seattle to take her first job. Grace Phelps earned her teachers' credentials in the embryonic University of Washington, then just a handful of buildings plunked down among old-growth forest. Once certified to teach in the young state, Grace easily obtained a position at Lake Chelan, a remote town at the foot of a glacial lake set deep in Washington's Cascades.

The journey involved a Great Northern locomotive through the mountains, a river steamer on the undammed Columbia River, and a stagecoach for the steep and rocky passage around a gorge below the lake's outlet. When she finally arrived in Chelan, the school board was there to meet her, all three of them. As Grammy told it, she stepped down from the stagecoach, directly onto the hem of her long traveling skirt. Her stern employers looking on, the young woman went down, scraping her knees. But she was obliged to smile as she was helped up by her principal, who told her there was no need to show such obeisance upon arrival at her post. Miss Phelps would meet that grim visage at least once more during her year in Chelan: when she was chastised for leading botany walks on Sundays.

The problem, of course, was the Sundays, not the subject. In those tight-laced times, the Sabbath was not to be broken for purposes of instruction, unless it was for Sunday School. But as for botany walks—well, they were commonplace, practically anywhere in the country. For those were the times when the subject of nature study was ubiquitous in American schools. Naturalists such as John Burroughs and Asa Gray were among the most respected people in society, and natural history was considered a high and worthy calling. The notion that an educated person would have a basic acquaintance with local flora and fauna was widely held, and broadly practiced.

My grandmother, though interested in nature all her life, would not have been described in those times as a "naturalist." Though always extraordinary in my memory, she was just an ordinary teacher in this respect: along with the other standard subjects, she taught the close and direct study of nature. This was completely in tune with the times. Gram's period on the U.W. campus was barely after the heyday of the Young Naturalists' Society—a band of pioneer Seattle men and women dedicated to the study of natural history in all its forms. Their patron was Arthur Denny, cofounder of the university; Orson Bennett "Bug" Johnson, the sole professor of science, led their field studies and forays.

Leap forward now to the fall of 1965, when I arrived at the University of Washington in search of a fundamental education as a naturalist. Now there were many more buildings, and the old growth had retreated far away. I made my way to Johnson Hall, long the home of botany and zoology on campus, in search of what might remain of "Bug" Johnson's legacy. As a lad of arid eastern Colorado, I might as well have landed on a new, unexplored planet, a would-be naturalist's paradise. Nearby ravines and marshes, the Olympics and Cascades on either horizon, all promised endless immersion in natural history.

But I needed an academic framework for the studies I had in mind. My first intoxicated look at the university catalog revealed a plethora of natural history classes: birds, mammals, insects, local flora, lichens and mosses, mushrooms, marine invertebrates, paleontology, astronomy, on and on. The only problem was, you couldn't actually take those courses; at least, not many. And you certainly couldn't major in them. They were intended for "dessert": after you'd filled your plate with "hard" sciences such as math, physics, chemistry organic and inorganic, physiology, cell and molecular biology and the like, you might be able to squeeze in one or two field-based classes as electives. The first year I nearly flunked out of the university as I skipped chemistry labs to bird Union Bay in a canoe. Two or three times I changed majors before I finally found a way through the Byzantine university apparatus and a sympathetic dean who helped me dowse a degree out of the place. All along, I got to know the professors who signed my way into the courses I longed for. They became life-saving mentors, coconspirators in erecting my illicit major, and lifelong friends.

For starters, there was Melville Hatch, "Bug" Johnson's legatee as keeper of the museum's insect collections, master of the region's vast beetle fauna, and scholar of Darwiniana. I took the last courses of his half-century teaching career. The professor's great jowls wagged beneath a puzzled grin, as he lectured on the very changes that would ensure he was the last of his kind. Another zoologist, Frank Richardson, taught splendid bird and mammal classes. His pipe and white Hemingway goatee were traits shared with a close friend and colleague in botany, Arthur Kruckeberg, founder of the Washington Native Plant Society and sponsor of our ecology action club. Down the hall from Art in Johnson Hall dwelled Daniel Stuntz, kind and gentle professor of mycology who specialized in psychedelic *Psilocybe* but would never take them. His laboratory was packed instead with edible mushrooms and French pastries for the benefit of hungry students. These and other professors in geography, geology, forestry, and elsewhere gave me exactly what I needed.

And they were on their way out. Most were older, or being encouraged to retire early. The only young naturalist on the faculty, shortly after receiving the outstanding teaching award for his magnificent classes in field natural history, was denied tenure; the department wanted superstar lab candidates who published frequently in all the right journals. A few profs interested in complete organisms survived by being strong on theory. But the majority of new appointments had little connection with the field, and as they came in, the old courses disappeared one by one from the catalog. Soon it would have been impossible to assemble a curriculum such as I had gleaned.

The University of Washington experience was not unusual. Throughout the country, the attrition of academic naturalists has been progressive over the past half-century. It would be easy just to call it a shift in pedagogic styles and a predictable development toward an always elusive modernity. But this is too facile, especially when the full consequences of the purge of the naturalists are considered. Two main concerns seem evident to me.

First, a populace less familiar with its nonhuman neighbors is one whose own impacts are unlikely to be noticed and moderated by choice. Ecological ignorance breeds indifference, throttling up the cycle I call the extinction of experience: as common elements of diversity disappear from our own nearby environs, we grow increasingly alienated, less caring, more apathetic. Such collective anomie allows further extinctions and deeper impoverishment of experience, round and round. What we know, we may choose to care for. What we fail to recognize, we certainly won't.

Second, many of the naturalists were systematists and taxonomists—the very men and women who recognize, describe, and catalogue the organisms of the earth. At a time when taking account of biodiversity has never been more urgent, we have lost much of our capacity for training and employing such people. Along with the naturalists went most of the courses and jobs in systematics, leaving the great institutional collections that sustain and contain our store of knowledge in grave jeopardy. Taxonomy grew unfashionable as laboratory research brought more prestige, glamour, and grant money—especially grant money—to the universities. Biologists David Wilcove and Thomas Eisner consider the institutional rejection of natural history to be one of the biggest scientific mistakes of our time.

But this isn't the whole story. To see what happened to natural history, we must revisit the time when botany walks were de rigueur and butterfly nets wouldn't rate a second look on a campus where half the students today have cell-phone implants and the other half wouldn't know a Douglas fir from a dogwood.

Natural history came to the New World with the colonists, who brought an educated and needful interest in the products of the earth. Of course it was already here, since native populations everywhere have been superb naturalists, or else perished. But that native knowledge was soon dispersed and eradicated, leaving a once well-known biota to be rediscovered by the likes of the Bartrams, Clark, Townsend, Nuttall, and their vigorous ilk, trained in the Linnaean tradition. George Washington and Thomas Jefferson were both excellent naturalists. A lively, experimental curiosity in plants and animals was nothing unusual, it was simply one component of the engaged citizen's life.

The nineteenth-century Naturalist reached its apogee in the person of Jean Louis Rodolphe Agassiz, a Swiss geologist and zoologist who developed the comprehensive Museum of Comparative Zoology at Harvard University. Agassiz liked to say, "If you study nature in books, when you go out-of-doors you cannot find her." According to a later naturalist of acclaim, David Starr Jordan, Agassiz brought about "a complete revolution in natural history study in America . . . not a category of facts taken from others, but the ability, through contact, to gather the needed facts. As a result of his activities, every notable teacher of natural history in the United States for the second half of the nineteenth century was at some time a pupil of Agassiz or of one of his students." In 1873, in Buzzard's Bay, Massachusetts, he initiated the very first summer field station for natural history study and teaching, the model for hundreds of institutes since.

The close study of nature had its economic and exploitative side: the various state Natural History Surveys that sprang up in the 1800s were not concerned solely with an intellectual interest in the kindly fruits of the Earth. The agricultural depression in New York State in 1891–1893 drove many people off the land and into New York City. A program in nature study was begun at the Cornell College of Agriculture as a first step in interesting children of the country in better farming. For fifteen years the director was Professor Liberty Hyde Bailey, a student of Agassiz's and a well-respected zoologist. In 1903, Anna Botsford Comstock took this over, writing leaflets for teachers and students, organizing Junior Naturalists Clubs and correspondence courses. She would bring the Nature Study Movement to its fullest degree of development over the next thirty years.

The program received heartening response from thousands of students all over New York. Comstock's goals clearly went far beyond the initial hopes, amounting to no less than an ecological context to general education for all students. She believed "the reason why nature-study has not yet accomplished its mission, as thought core for much of the required work in our public schools, is that the teachers are as a whole untrained in the subject." To remedy this lack, in 1911 Comstock published a large book called the *Handbook of Nature-Study*, replete with hundreds of lessons as well as relevant poems, photographs, and vignettes.

Nature study on the New York plan, now that its manifesto was everywhere available, took off all over the country. Anna Comstock's *Handbook* became one of the most universal texts in the American classroom, and it was not the only one of its kind. I have collected dozens of titles, mostly published between 1890 and 1940. They take different approaches, some more didactic than others, others baldly emulating Comstock's form and style but seldom as well written. What they share is a devotion to the idea of first-hand experience with the animals and plants under study. Clifton Hodge, in *Nature-Study and Life*, called this kind of direct contact "the sheet anchor of elementary education, all the more necessary as modern life tends to drift away from nature into artificialities of every sort." And that was in 1902! What would he think a hundred years later, when children are more likely to recognize a Palm Pilot than a palm tree?

The implicit goal of all these books and the movement that inspired them, along with the Audubon Nature Clubs that followed, the novels of Gene Stratton Porter, the philosophy and writings of Theodore Roosevelt, the essays of Joseph Wood Krutch and Edwin Way Teale, and an entire culture of nature study, is just this: *essential nature literacy*. In a shocking line that seems hyperbolic today but may have been quite true in 1911, Comstock claimed that her weighty work "does not contain more than any intelligent country child of twelve should know of his environment; things that he should know naturally and without effort, although it might take him half his life-time to learn so much if he should not begin before the age of twenty."

And that's where things stood between the World Wars. Not that every citizen came out of public school a naturalist, nor every teacher a gifted guide. But there was a time in this country—the time when my grandmother led botany walks in Chelan—when a general familiarity with the fauna and flora around us was considered by consensus to be a worthwhile educational goal, and the naturalists were still highly respected in the universities.

So what happened? The answer isn't simple, but I believe it has to do with three main developments: the rise of highly quantitative, experimental, and specialized scholarship—the so-called "hard sciences;" the depopulation of the countryside and rise of the cities and suburbs; and World War II and the subsequent Cold War. The signs that nature study was on the defensive are already apparent in the Publisher's Foreword to the 1939 (24th) edition of the *Handbook,* which would still be printed into the late forties: "Some readers of the *Handbook* have suggested that the new edition be oriented away from the nature-study approach, and be made instead to serve as an introduction to the natural sciences. . . . But the nature-study approach has been preserved. The kernel of that method of treatment is the study of the organism in its environment, its relation to the world about it, and the features which enable it to function in its surroundings. . . . The promising science of ecology is merely formalized nature-study. . . . The truth is that nature-study is a science, and is more than a science; it is not merely a study of life, but an experience of life."

Science, however, did not agree. As mathematics penetrated deeper into every province of science, the descriptive and empirical nature of natural history began to look subjective to its critics. The fact that Mrs. Comstock and her followers admitted poetry and, horror of horrors, emotion, into their range of responses to the natural world planted them firmly beyond the pale of objectivity. The catchword that arose was "rigor" (and more recently, "robust"). How could an observation be robust, possess rigor, if it was merely "anecdotal" (the final condemnation) instead of experimental and statistically significant? In the end, what doomed the naturalists was exactly what Anna Comstock celebrated in her work: in her long experience as a nature-study teacher, she wrote, she had "never been able to give a lesson twice alike on a certain topic or secure exactly the same results twice in succession." Since repeatability is a fundamental canon of the modern scientific process, this admission is anathema. "Natural history" became not only unfashionable, but derogatory; "naturalist" came to be a pejorative, or at best a quaint condescension.

It is worth examining the charges against the naturalists. Indeed, many of them permitted personal impressions into their work. Others attempted to minimize this, like Joseph Grinnell at U.C. Berkeley, who required field notes to be kept in a prescribed manner to reduce bias. This brought a degree of observational rigor to field studies, but there was also plenty of slop and cheap sentimentality in the less thoughtful precincts of the genre. Since nature study was oriented toward the young, anthropomorphism was often employed. Sometimes, as in Thornton Burgess's *Bedtime Stories,* this was done with great skill alongside observation to convey the actual behavior of the animals. But all too often, nature stories descended into moralizing or emotional pandering, with animals as handy foils, wholly out of character with their namesake species. A vigorous debate arose over purported "nature faking" when John Burroughs and Theodore Roosevelt accused Ernest Thompson Seton, Rev. William J. Long, and others of setting up wildlife dramas in their books that never actually occurred in the wild, just for commercial effect. While Burroughs himself, Enos Mills, John Muir, and others were keen and careful observers, their high-flown language nonetheless turned off the more hard-headed natural scientists in the academies who conflated honest sentiment with sentimentality.

The fact that many university naturalists rebelled at the increasingly quantitative nature of academic science and did not possess the tools for performing multivariate analyses and other tests of statistical significance inevitably furthered the gap. This allowed their modernist colleagues to portray them as soft and hopelessly outmoded, if not outright unreliable. The scientists had a point. A better kind of science had become available, at least as far as demonstrating the reality of perceived results. When the old guard failed to embrace these techniques (often for lack of the necessary math, and later computer skills) they appeared to be fuddy-duddies or dilettantes, treating the natural world in a popular or superficial way. Many of the newer generation rejected the notion that results of value could be gained through observation of organisms in their habitats in the absence of experiment, manipulation, or statistics. They came to regard the old school as stuffy and intransigently old fashioned, to be rooted out if unable to adapt to the new terms.

However, the blame cut both ways, and the revolution threw out the best with the worst. The fact that the lab scientists frequently knew next to nothing about the organisms they studied as molecular or cellular "systems" or mathematical models made them defensive and unnecessarily hostile toward the naturalists, whose knowledge they sorely could have used. Just as the scientists saw the naturalists as oversimplifying amateurs, the field people saw the new professionals as reductionists ignorant of the actual ways of field and forest. As one teacher with a foot in both camps put it, how sad to have lost a healthy collegiality between the young bloods on the cutting edge and the old farts with all the facts.

Things might have gone differently. The highly respected biologist Marston Bates, in his 1950 book *The Nature of Natural History,* argued that natural history and the erudite-sounding term "ecology" both "apply to just about the same package of goods." He rejected neither, and felt that the most important task confronting natural history was to find "appropriate experimental methods." But as experimental biology complexified too far for anyone to be a successful generalist in the Jeffersonian manner, specialization ruled. Medicine and genetics helped to drive research away from the whole organism and into the cell and the molecule, thus out of the field and into the lab. Natural history was placed on a high, dusty shelf as a romantic artifact.

When the Second World War arrived, resources shifted to support a kind of science that had to deliver specific results: bombs capable of precise mayhem seemed a higher priority than classifying beetles. Children learned to identify aircraft profiles instead of songbirds. The aftermath left science in thrall to the national purpose of winning the Cold War. And then came *Sputnik,* the first Russian satellite and the coup de grace for the nature study movement. After 1956, advanced math programs arose around the country. Biology classes shifted toward the microscope and away from the field. Meanwhile, urban flight left a much-depleted population of rural residents in close daily contact with the countryside, even as the Victorian popularity of collecting the artifacts of nature was fading. The objective of a nature-literate citizenry was quietly forgotten.

So is natural history really dead? Certainly not. Only one member of the University of California system still retains the title Emeritus Professor of Natural History, but there have always been fine scientists who were also professed naturalists—people such as Rachel Carson, Loren Eiseley, Paul Ehrlich, Jane Goodall, Bernd Heinrich, Gary Nabhan, and E. O. Wilson, who entitled his memoir *Naturalist.* Many fine ecologists of lesser renown have invigorated universities today, men and women who know that basic, real-world observation can be undertaken with rigor; they just can't teach much natural history as such, or call themselves naturalists too openly. Some departments where natural history may be performed at a safe remove from the old field's associations, and with more numbers involved, have adopted the ungainly label "organismal biology." Other schools buck the trend. Evergreen State College in Washington offered the best of natural history and field instruction for its first thirty years, though this may be fading as the first wave of faculty retires. The University of Vermont has a field natural history masters program, and Texas Tech offers such a major.

But overall, few classes in field natural history are available. Though statistical cladistics and DNA studies are breathing new life into classification, pure systematics is as outré as ever. Unpaid adjuncts and amateurs perform much of the curatorial and classificatory labor in the museums, where a serious crisis looms in the apprehension of biological diversity. The main lepidopterist on "Bug" Johnson's old turf today is a truck driver, and the primary authorities on West Coast earthworms are a mother and son who receive no support for their important work. Who will tell us what we are losing, when we can no longer name the pieces—most of which have not even been described?

As for the children, some think environmental education has taken up the slack for the long-extinct nature study movement, but I don't believe that's the case. I have taken part in a great many E.E. programs, attended lots of conferences, observed numerous facilities. This is some of the most important work being done today, and the level of dedication is off the scale. I have only praise for the professionals involved. Yet there are fundamental differences between the old way and the new, and the new is by no means always better. For starters, nature study always and fundamentally stressed direct contact between student and organism. The point was to emulate the discoveries that country children would make on their own, enhanced by information to put the finds in context. Anna's lessons were meant to get children out, or to get the actual materials into the classroom. Nowadays, second-hand connection is the rule, via games, lab specimens, and computers. Enter the Internet, its vastness of information making vicarious field-tripping instantly available. This can be a good thing, in proportion. But most teachers agree that no Web site can substitute for a spiderweb, while scintillating pixels on a screen will never replace the scintillant scales on a butterfly's wing. The virtual is even more remote from real life than cells and molecules. Still, all too often, teachers see no choice. That one-on-one, kid-and-creature chemistry largely went out with the slate board.

Second, nature study at its best happened regularly, often daily, and at every level. Environmental education, if funded at all, frequently takes place only during certain grades for brief times. Typically, sixth graders will have an outdoor education experience for one week—and that's that, except for bits and pieces fitted into other studies here and there. Standardized testing further marginalizes E.E., since it doesn't figure into the all-important test scores. Few schools expose students to frequent and regular nature studies these days. And if they do, the outings and materials are likely to be sponsored by a timber company or resource agency and consist largely of propaganda.

Third, and of great importance, is the difference in approach to plants and animals today. Nature study premised itself on the assumption that boys and girls would become acquainted with their local flora and fauna, by name, features, and habit. What birds flew and nested near the school, and how did they feed? What plants sprang up, outside the garden? Who sang in the spring chorus at dusk? But today, I see students coming out of school with no appreciable knowledge of their non-human neighbors: every evergreen is a pine, all brown birds are sparrows; a frog is a frog is a frog. Instead of the names and traits of other species, E.E. tends to concentrate on the "big picture" of ecological roles, functions, habitats, relationships, and patterns. Laudable goals, except it is like watching a play with no cast list! And is therefore liable to seem meaningless.

I generalize, of course. Splendid, knowledgeable teachers and exceptional facilities and programs do exist. However, many field trips more resemble recess in the woods than wood lore. Kids at one E.E. camp I visit each spring are so hyped to get out that they run and yell much of the time, while wildlife makes itself scarce and teachers resort to quasi-military and summer-camp routines to keep them (literally) in line. The few kids I find eager to learn a little natural history are swamped by the escapee tumult of the rest. Ropes courses and Ritalin are not what Anna Botsford Comstock had in mind. But then, as she found, uninformed teachers cannot teach nature with passion or results; few teachers today know any natural history at all, because they had none in high school or college.

The unavoidable facts that available habitats have retreated from the vicinities of most schools; that field trips have been truncated for reasons of liability, distance, and budget; and that students are so many, all make it much more difficult to ensure direct contact today. Consider too the hugely reduced access of children to wild places in their free time, whether because of safety concerns, Nintendo, or sprawl, and the conclusion seems inescapable that we are farther than ever from a vision of a people on intimate terms with its cohabitants. While naturalist activities such as bird and butterfly watching grow in popularity as leisure pursuits, summer field institutes proliferate, and the National Audubon Society is investing in new nature centers all over the country, these still involve trivial numbers compared to mall-hopping, football, or NASCAR racing.

We are not likely to return to nature study as it once was. Human society has become vastly more complex, even as the natural world has been simplified. During our nation's two previous fins de siècle, naturalists sat as president, and were admired for it. This is patently not the case now, when the relevance and rightness of good natural history teaching has never been greater but its estate never more distanced from the main affairs of the land and its leaders.

Our environmental professionals are superbly trained in engineering, management, and theory, yet seldom have any intimate knowledge of the working parts of the systems they measure, monitor, and care for. Likewise, the quality of ecological research being done in the universities and field stations has never been higher, but its context has never been narrower for most practitioners. Even the nature interpreters in our parks and preserves tend to know far less about the denizens of their precincts than the practice of communicating about them. Anna Comstock said "it is absolutely necessary to have a wide knowledge of other plants and animals" in order to understand our relations to any one kind. As one kind of animal ourselves, in deep need of righting our relations with the rest, a fundamental acquaintance with flora and fauna should be common knowledge. But when the people we delegate to study, manage, and interpret the natural world are unversed in its parts and ways, how is the ordinary citizen supposed to achieve ecological literacy?

What I most fear is how direct experience flees before these winds of change, along with a nuanced, responsive awareness of the very earth we inhabit. In his 1908 book *Nature-Study,* Frederick L. Holtz wrote that "the child's interest in nature is the outcome of curiosity, wonder—and is the complement of the social interest in bringing him into right relationship with the world." As the distance grows between a tiny priesthood who know small parts of nature very well and a massive population who know next to nothing about the whole and not even the names of their neighbors, a right relationship with the world seems more and more elusive. Today, when children have all too many stimuli and all too few opportunities to experience bald wonder, many seem to lack any real interest in nature. Yet I believe, along with Carson and Wilson, that wonder is innate in the very young, waiting only to be ignited before the cheap tricks of modern life damp the fuse. Nothing can light the flame of fascination in a child like another living thing.

It may be the naturalists who save us in the end, by bringing us all back down to earth.

(2001)

"These Green Things"

The San Francisco Garden Project

H ER BOSS, THE SHERIFF OF SAN FRANCISCO SAYS, "CATHY HAS A magical ability to change people's lives." Cathrine Sneed has trained in the law and agroecology, studied biodynamic gardening at Emerson in England, and completed the Agroecology program at the University of California. Currently director of the Garden Project, Sneed is the founder of the horticultural program for the San Francisco County Jail where, in an eight-acre garden, prisoners grow produce using the biodynamic French intensive method. Weekly, the garden's organic produce is delivered to projects that supply food to seniors, homeless people, and AIDS victims. Above all, this organic, chemical-free garden is a living metaphor for the healthy lives the jail gardeners are trying to create.

After being released, many of the former prisoners choose to continue working with plants in The Garden Project, a series of programs that helps released prisoners re-enter their communities as good citizens. They begin at the Carroll Street training garden, a half-acre organic garden where they grow tender vegetables for sale to local restaurants, notably the legendary Chez Panisse run by the legendary Alice Waters. After training, students can join The Tree Corps, which plants and maintains trees in low-income areas of San Francisco. In addition to these programs, The Garden Project is establishing organic urban gardens that offer long-term jobs for program graduates. This model "ladder" towards employment and participation in the community is a wise, effective alternative to the more typical scenario for former prisoners. Often lacking skills, resources, and support, up to 80 percent of prisoners released from county jails return within three months. Financially draining to society, the pattern is also morally unacceptable—one gauge of the cycle of racism, injustice, poverty, and crime that has wounded the national soul.

In addition to her devoted attention to the jail garden and its offshoots, Cathrine Sneed is co-chair of the San Francisco Tree Advisory and a board member of Elmwood Institute. She has received many awards; most recently she was named a "Hero of the Earth" by the Eddie Bauer Corporation, and was honored by The Foundation for the Improvement of Justice. Looking on her works, it is easy to understand why Alice Waters has said of Cathrine Sneed: "I would do anything she asks me to do. Anything. When I look at her, I feel real hope for the world." About her transformative powers, Sneed herself will only say, "It is embarrassing to me when people say all of the different things they say about me because I don't really figure in the equation. It is the garden that changes people's lives. It is working with these green things."

This is the story of the San Francisco County Jail Garden and The Garden Project, told in the words of their founder and guiding spirit, based on talks she gave at the Aspen Design Conference and at Harvard College.

Cathrine Sneed speaks about her work with prisoners and gardens:

Hello. I always love to talk to people about what we're doing in San Francisco because hearing about it gives people ideas about what can happen in places other than San Francisco.

I have spent a lot of time in jail myself—as a counselor to women serving time there. It was my job to try to help these women find ways to do something with their lives other than what they had been doing. Most of them were in jail for drug use, drug possession, drug sales. Most of them had been and were prostitutes, and most of them had children. These women *wanted* to believe me when I told them there was something else they could do with their lives, but the reality was that they didn't have any education. In San Francisco, we test everyone that comes in our jail. The median reading level is fourth grade, fifth grade, sixth grade. Most of the people in our jail have never had jobs. And so as much as these women wanted to say, "Yeah, Cathy, we believe what you're saying, we *can* do something else with our lives," the reality was grim.

After several years working closely with these women, and despairing about their situation, I learned that I had gotten a serious kidney disease. I was twenty-eight and I had two little kids, and it was a shock when the doctor said, "Well, it doesn't look good. You're not responding to drugs and you can either stay here in the hospital and die or you can go home and die." Just before my doctor came up with that statement, a good friend of mine had given me *The Grapes of Wrath*. I read it, and what struck me was this—Steinbeck is saying that to be really alive, these people felt that they must be connected with the soil, with the earth. I grew up in Newark, New Jersey and I had not had much connection with the earth. Now, lying in the hospital, it occurred to me that since San Francisco's jail stands right on what was, in the 1930s, a 145-acre farm, it made good sense to bring prisoners outside of the jail buildings, onto the land, and try to grow things again.

I was fortunate, because I was supposed to kick the bucket any minute, and when my dear friend, Michael Hennessey, our sheriff, visited me in the hospital he said, "Yeah, Cathy, if you want to take them outside and garden, fine. Why don't you do that?" He said this thinking that I *was* going to kick the bucket, but that in the meantime I would feel good. Well, I didn't die, and when I got out of the hospital, I set out with four prisoners onto the old farm. I wish you could have seen their faces when they said, "We're going to do *what* here?" I said, "Well, first of all, we have to start by cleaning up this mess."

And so we started cleaning up. For twenty years, the sheriff's department had used the old farm as a storage area and it took us three years to clean up the mess. We did it without tools, without wheelbarrows. The jail gardeners literally tore down old buildings with their hands. They didn't have jackets or raingear. They had their T-shirts and their thin jail clothes and little thong shoes to clip-clop around in. What began to touch me was that I started to see these people care about something for the first time. I started to see them *care* that we were slowly cleaning up this mess, and *care* that I was so excited about it. And then I saw *them* get excited. From that point on we began to grow things.

One of the first people who came out into the garden with me was a man I'll never forget. His name is Forrest. Forrest was about forty-five then, with a criminal history that spanned three decades. He had ten arrests for assault with a deadly weapon, probably fifteen arrests for drunk driving, and related things. Not a nice guy. And yet Forrest came out with me initially, busted his butt to clean up this old dump, this old farm. Soon, a wonderful horticulture therapist named Arlene Hamilton joined us. We started to grow herbs. We started slowly with only $300 from the sheriff and his friends to buy a few things, and maybe ten gardeners in 1984. Today, 160 prisoners go out every day to an eight-acre garden. It is fenced for the deer, because we have lots of deer. We have tools now and we grow an amazing amount of food that we give to the soup kitchens, and to projects that feed seniors, the homeless, and people too sick with AIDS to feed themselves. A lot of people ask me, "Why do you *give* the food away?" We give the food away because it is important for the prisoners to have an opportunity to feel good about themselves.

People ask me, "What is it about gardening—getting your hands in the earth—that makes the connection with these people. Why couldn't it be getting them on a computer? What do you think is so good about the gardening?" Well, in fact it's important to say that gardening isn't for everyone, but growing things does give many people a sense of power. When the prisoners see a garbage dump turn into a garden and know that Alice Waters wants vegetables that are growing there, they get a sense of power. They made it happen with their hands! And also it is the experience of living things, green things, beauty, Mother Nature. This reminds me of something Wendell Berry said in *The Unsettling of America*. He talks about how, in America, anything done with your hands is looked down on. I look at the community I'm working with, and I think, "What's missing is nature and beauty, the beauty that can be made with our hands." I say to these guys, "Look, you guys, let's weed the baby lettuces, and then let's watch what happens. They're going to grow more, they'll be better. And people will pay top organic dollar for them." Growing things is a metaphor. I also say to them, "If we don't put chemicals on this stuff that we're growing, people are going to pay more for it. It's the same for you. If you don't put heroin into your arm, you are going to be better off. Your family will be better off." The experience of growing works in terms of healing, of my counseling. I can *show* them what I'm talking about. Many people here in the jail are substance dependent. One thing the garden shows them is how much better life is without chemicals. You can take chemicals and put them in the garden and get fast results, but look what it does to the soil.

My concern with farm programs in the jail is—well, I'm sure you all saw that movie with Paul Newman—*Cool Hand Luke*—in which prisoners were *forced* to do agricultural labor in chain gangs. I mean, there's been jail farms forever, and it is very, very important that our jail people have a *choice*. Either you can work in the farm and grow food for the soup kitchen, *or* you can go to computer class, *or* the literacy class. There has to be a choice. It's very, very important that you give people who have hurt people, who have killed people, an opportunity to be able to look in the mirror and say, "God, I can do something good."

People in our country do want solutions, and I have seen many, many people like Forrest go from all those long convictions to being a kick-ass radish grower. Now he is the first person to come up to you in the garden. At first, it is kind of menacing, because he looks kind of menacing. He's got tattoos everywhere, but what he wants to do is give you a bouquet of flowers, because he is very proud of the flowers. That is transformation.

This program makes people who have no hope have hope, which is a tremendously powerful thing. It is working with these green things that gives them a sense of life. And most of them have never had it from anywhere else. Another prisoner, named Danny, said to me, "I'd like to go work on a farm for somebody. And I want to be dedicated to the farm like I am here. I was like a dead tree when I first came here. And I've seen what watering does, if you water the tree and feed it nice, it grows up and it has fruit. I don't want to go back to the streets and just hang around, and waste, and die." And these women—who are almost all in here for prostitution—are *strong* women. Do you know how hard it is to stand on a street corner every night for hours, in the cold, with practically no clothes on? *Strong women,* only on the wrong path.

I want to tell you something because not many people like you get an opportunity to visit a jail—jails are bleak places. Our jail is so bleak, despite our beautiful garden, that I always wonder—*How can we keep people in this horrible situation in horrible cages, and then expect them to come back and be normal nice people, living with everyone?* That's not going to happen. The people I work with are the kind of people who, when you see them, you cross the street because they are scary people. But this garden program helps people understand that they aren't just scary, they are part of a community. They leave our jails all over the country and they come back and live in our communities, they ride the bus with us.

For many years I felt it was wonderful that we had this garden, that we were feeding people, that people's lives were changing. But it is frustrating to realize that for most of the people in our jail, being in the garden program is better than their life at home—*better* than living on the street, than living in hotels for homeless, than living in projects. It was devastating for me to realize that for many of these people, the garden program was the best experience of their adult life, of their whole life. And that, at the end of their sentence, many people came up to me and said, "Cathy, I don't want to go, I want to stay here." In fact, some of them ended up back in jail just because they wanted to be back in our garden. But most of them returned to selling their bodies and drugs because no one would hire them to do anything else. So I realized we needed another program to help them continue the experiences they had in our garden, but outside the jail.

I often bring people from the community to the jail to see what we are doing. One day, a local businessperson came, a man named Elliot Hoffman who has a large bakery named Just Desserts. He looked around and he said, "You know, I need so many strawberries. You could grow strawberries and I could buy them from you." Personally, I was hoping that this man would say, "Hey, I'll give you a check. You can buy tools." But he kept saying, "No, no, I would really like to buy strawberries from you." So he invited me out to his bakery in Hunter's Point. Behind his bakery was this old garbage dump, about a half an acre. And he said, "You could bring the people here and you could grow a lot of strawberries. " I kept looking at this garbage dump and thinking, to myself, "You know, I have enough to do here at the *jail,* I would really just like a check from this person."

Fortunately for us all, Elliot persisted, and finally after a couple of hours, when it became clear to me that he wasn't going to give me a check, we decided to start a post-release program for people leaving the jail. Today, people can leave our jail program and come to this half-acre garden and continue to grow food that we sell to Chez Panisse, which is a very fancy, wonderful restaurant in Berkeley run by Alice Waters. We also sell a lot of fruit to Just Desserts and we are involving other businesses. We're talking with The Body Shop, we're talking with Esprit. We're talking with any business that will listen about spreading this idea. We call this place in Hunter's Point "The Garden Project." After a while, Elliot got to know our people and hired some of them. Of course, that first guy Elliot hired disappeared with the Just Desserts truck. He had just gone to cruise his neighborhood and he didn't think anything about it because he had never had a job before. Elliot didn't get scared by that, and he has hired more people from our program for his bakery.

When we first started The Garden Project the land belonged to a certain huge corporation. I said to them, "Well look, you guys, you have a garbage dump in this poor neighborhood. Let us help you clean it up; we'll grow things on it, and your property won't be a wreck anymore." The huge corporation said to me, "Look, lady, we're not a charity. Give us $500,000 for the land." It seemed to me there was no way I was going to give them a dime. And so we climbed over their fence and made a garden. Now, this is felony trespassing, and remember on my little business card it says, "Special Assistant to the Sheriff." So I said to the sheriff, I said, "Michael, this huge corporation says I need $500,000 and what I'd like to do is clean up their dump and start a garden." Michael said, "Do it. And don't forget that not only are they going to have to put *you* in jail, they're going to have to put *me* in jail." I always encourage people to say *no* to anybody who says it can't be done.

What we have throughout this country is poor people and vacant land. I grew up in Newark, New Jersey, and when I left, twenty years ago, there were acres and acres of land where buildings were burnt down in the riots after Martin Luther King died. Now, instead of having people standing out on the corner, they could instead be growing fruit that Ben & Jerry's says they'll buy. They could do that in Newark; they could do that in Denver. What we're doing is finding ways to connect nature and people.

I go from feeling very hopeful to feeling extremely sad in my work. I feel very sad when I go to our jail and see so many African-American men, so many Spanish-speaking men and women who do not have a future, who do not have any hope. And, it's discouraging when I hear cops say, "Well, that's all they want," or when I hear people say, "They can make more money selling crack." That's so false. The people out there selling drugs for the most part are making barely enough to buy the crack they are using. They are on a path that is destructive—for all of us. Crime affects all of us, every day, and it's important that we start looking at what's happening in our country. We are producing millions of people who have no hope, who have nothing to lose, and if you have nothing to lose, you're a dangerous, dangerous person. What happened in Los Angeles is what happens when many, many people feel that they don't matter, that they don't count. The sadness that I feel about these human situations, and I'm sure all of us feel, in some ways numbs us. It makes us feel that it might be easier to protect the spotted owl or to protect land. With land, you know, you can buy it up and make sure that no one builds on it. But to help people to change, it doesn't take a year. It takes many years, many other people.

When I was asked to speak here [at the Aspen Design Conference] I thought, oh, what am I going to say to these people? They cannot know what I'm doing. But then I realized that you are the people who are *designing* our communities. And I feel very hopeful that you want to hear about this. I feel very hopeful that with your understanding and all your expertise, you can start designing an America that *includes* the men and women that I work with, the men and women who fill our jails. You know, California spends many millions of dollars building jails, and fewer millions of dollars educating children. It costs $25,000 a year to keep a person in a cage. They could go to Harvard! They could go a lot of places. What I see in our project is what happens when government, business, and community people join together. I'm asking you to help to redesign a new world. When I tell my students, "I went to Aspen and to Harvard and told the people what we're doing here in the garden, and they listened and they *cared*," my students know that it means that they *count*, that there's hope. They hold their heads up a little, and they think "God, we matter. We count."

When I told the San Francisco Unified School District that Alice Waters at Chez Panisse wants to buy all the vegetables we can grow, they said, "Well, we have land all over and we're spending to clear the weeds, so why don't you do something with it?" That's good, that's good. We can grow a lot of radishes for Alice on what used to be school district land. The Department of Forestry is also spending a lot of money trying to safeguard our forests. Now, the Angeles Forest is not so far from South-Central Los Angeles, so I said to them, "Let's pay the people that are standing around the streets in South-Central Los Angeles to plant trees. Let's pay them to maintain the trees." What we are talking about is putting people and the environment together. It starts with us saying, "We can do better," because we *can* do better.

Last Friday, I spoke at the funeral of Donnell, a man who was in my garden program four years ago. He had just turned eighteen. This man could not tell time. He could not read. So I asked Smith & Hawken, which is a fancy tool company, to hire this young man when he left our program in the jail, and they did. But after two months of him coming to work late, and a few times of him stealing clothes that they were trying to sell, they said, "Cathy, we really want to help your project, but, you know, this guy isn't working." I understood when they let him go. But when they did, he went back to the Sunnydale projects, back to selling drugs. He was killed by a young man with whom he had had an argument. The young man came back after the argument and blew his head off. This happens every day.

Donnell was one of those young men who did not want to leave our jail, the garden. He said, "Cathy, I don't want to go back out there. Can I stay here?" I said, "Donnell, you *cannot* stay in jail. It's, it's illegal!" Donnell said to me, "Cathy, you know a lot of people. You can pull some strings. The sheriff's your friend. Please ask the sheriff to let me stay here." I asked Sheriff Hennessey, who's a wonderful, wonderful man, "Michael, can we let Donnell stay? He's afraid to go back." Michael said, "Cathy, it *is* illegal, and our jail is overcrowded. People are sleeping on the floor. We can't keep Donnell in the jail." When I was talking at his funeral, I was aware that most of the people attending were young men, and most of the young men knew who I was, and it was not because they heard me on National Public Radio or read about me in the *New York Times*. Anywhere I go in San Francisco people come up to me and say, "Oh I know you." If they're African American, I know they know me from the jail. Something's very wrong.

People say, "You seem so passionate about this. It seems like more than a job to you. What keeps you going?" What keeps me going is that the young men and young women in our jail look very much like the young men and young women who live in my house—my children, my nieces and nephews. If you look at statistics, I know that my daughter and my son don't have a future. We are talking about reconstruction, redirecting, rebuilding. We are talking about hope and solutions. I look at these lupines and trees on the stage with us today, and I think—We could be paying somebody to be watering these plants. The somebodies could be people like the people in my program. When I see vacant lots and garbage dumps, I know who would love to have the opportunity to clean them up. We need to see that, despite the enormous obstacles these young women and men face, they are remaking their lives.

The people who have said, "This makes sense," come from all over. I got a letter not so long ago from California's attorney general. I have to say I was afraid to open the envelope; I thought maybe I was being indicted. The attorney general wrote to me to say, "Cathy, what you're doing is a model for law enforcement throughout this state. It is an inspiration to law enforcement and I'm sending information about it to all the attorney general's offices in the state and I am going to *make* them come visit you." And so many people hear of our program and we are getting more support and requests to help begin similar programs.

Last summer, we got a contract to plant trees for San Francisco. Since then we've planted over 2,000 trees in the city. The people planting trees are called The Tree Corps and are getting eight dollars an hour to plant trees. They used to be crack sellers. They used to sell crack to pregnant mothers, to their own mothers. Now they're selling hope because when they're out there planting trees in Hunter's Point and in The Mission, people look at them and say, "Wait a minute. I don't have to sell crack. I can do something else 'cause if my uncle and my cousin and my brother can plant trees, *I* can plant trees." I have a *waiting* list of people who want to plant trees, and wherever we go, people follow us. This one young man came, and he said, "Cathy, I'm sorry to come to you like this." He had an Uzi under his little jacket and crack in the pockets. He said, "I'm sorry to come to you like this, but I don't want to do this. I want to plant trees." I want to be able to give him an opportunity to plant trees because we need trees. You have heard of global warming?

Planting trees is super work and, for me, the most powerful thing is when you consider that the person doing it used to be selling drugs, hurting other people, and is now trying to figure out whether the tree pit is deep enough. When you give people an alternative to throwing their life away most people choose that. And I will never forget my first day when The Tree Corps and I began working with John, the Department of Public Works employee who was first assigned to work with us. His coworkers were teasing him, but John just puffed out his chest and said, "Wait a minute, these people are just like you. They are going to learn a skill." And then John proceeded to teach our students as much as he knew—and he has been a tree trimmer and planter for twenty years. But what he really taught our students is that people care. And that you can learn Latin names if you want to. It was a powerful relationship. John has since been transferred and we are doing it on our own. Now that The Tree Corps reflects the people in the neighborhood, people know that this tree in the ground means that their uncle, or brother, or sister has a job and so they protect the tree, whereas before they often cut it down. It is not weird, but quite wonderful.

One of our planters is Rumaldo. He is about fifty-three years old and he has been to jail six times. Rumaldo has four grown children and now he brings his children around and says, "I planted that tree" and then he tells them the Latin name for the tree and what the tree needs and he puffs out his chest and he doesn't hurt people anymore. Because he is too tired to—he is out planting trees. But it is a long, constant struggle. I got a message the other day from a man named Burl who was with us for about six months. When he started working with The Tree Corps he had just overcome his crack addiction. He came to work every day but he had nowhere to live and was living in his car, and he got back on the street and readdicted. I got a message the other day that he was asking whether or not I was too mad at him to consider allowing him to rejoin the program. And of course I am not too mad at him.

After her talks, members of the audiences asked Ms. Sneed questions:

Audience: I live in Washington Heights (in New York City) near an outdoor stairway where everyone used to congregate to buy crack. A woman in our neighborhood got the idea to develop this area into a garden. She made it with the help of children, ones who had just started to get into trouble. Do you ever work with children?

CS: On Earth Day, 900 people joined us at an elementary school. This school looked worse than our jail. All over the country we have schools that look like jails, where the children are treated like they're in jail. Anyway, I caused sort of a ruckus, and people came together to renovate this school—we painted it and made a garden. Every day I get calls from schools to make gardens. There is a real need in the schools, and people should not have to go to jail to get reconnected with the Earth! We must reclaim land and people together. Also, a garden can produce revenue, and for kids who have no way of getting money to buy sneakers or something they want—selling carrots beats the hell out of selling crack.

Audience: I work for a corporation that is doing a development in West Humboldt Park, a very heavy hit area in Chicago. The community concept is for employment training, a childcare center, and a school. We hear about what a long process it is to train welfare mothers, much more than two-years. Does your program teach other life skills and literacy?

CS: To be in The Garden Project, people have to agree to go to school. If they don't have a high school diploma, they must get it in jail. If they have a diploma, they go to community college. They garden four hours a day; go to school or do community service for another four hours. Some of my students have rap sheets [criminal arrest records] that go out this door, but when I say to them, "To be in the program you must go to college," they do it! The reason is that they're loving gardening and beginning to feel good about themselves. And, they want to be able to read the bean packets, to know *why* the beans are growing. You should *see* me teach a roomful of women in jail for prostitution the concept of asexual plant propagation. They are like, well, maybe here is a solution. The jail administrators used to feel that we had to *make* the prisoners do education. But the garden *inspires* people to learn.

(1994)

Monsters

Designer Genes

Lured by the prospect of making better babies, we stand on the threshold of changing forever what it means to be human

I GREW UP IN A HOUSEHOLD WHERE WE WERE VERY SUSPICIOUS OF dented cans. Dented cans were, according to my mother, a well-established gateway to botulism, and botulism was a bad thing, worse than swimming immediately after lunch. It was one of those bad things measured in extinctions, as in "three tablespoons of botulism toxin could theoretically kill every human on Earth." Or something like that.

So I refused to believe the early reports, a few years back, that socialites had begun injecting dilute strains of the toxin into their brows in an effort to temporarily remove the vertical furrow that appears between one's eyes as one ages. It sounded like a Monty Python routine, some clinic where they daubed your soles with plague germs to combat athlete's foot. But I was wrong to doubt. As the world now knows, Botox has become, in a few short years, a staple weapon in the cosmetic arsenal—so prevalent that, in the words of one writer, "it is now rare in certain social enclaves to see a woman over the age of thirty-five with the ability to look angry." With their facial muscles essentially paralyzed, actresses are having trouble acting; since the treatment requires periodic booster shots, doctors warn that "you could marry a woman [or a man] with a flawlessly even face and wind up with someone who four months later looks like a Shar-Pei." But never mind—now you can get Botoxed in strip mall storefronts and at cocktail parties.

People, in other words, will do fairly far-out things for less-than-pressing causes. And more so all the time: public approval of "aesthetic surgery" has grown fifty percent in the United States in the last decade. But why stop there? Once you accept the idea that our bodies are essentially plastic, and that it's okay to manipulate that plastic, there's no reason to think that consumers would balk because "genes" were involved instead of, say, "toxins." Especially since genetic engineering would not promote your own vanity, but instead be sold as a boon to your child.

The vision of genetic engineers is to do to humans what we have already done to salmon and wheat, pine trees and tomatoes. That is, to make them *better* in some way; to delete, modify, or add genes in developing embryos so that the cells of the resulting person will produce proteins that make them taller and more muscular, or smarter and less aggressive, maybe handsome and possibly straight. Even happy. As early as 1993, a March of Dimes poll found that 43 percent of Americans would engage in genetic engineering "simply to enhance their children's looks or intelligence."

Ethical guidelines promulgated by the scientific oversight boards so far prohibit actual attempts at human genetic engineering, but researchers have walked right to the line, maybe even stuck their toes a trifle over. In the spring of 2001, for instance, a fertility clinic in New Jersey impregnated fifteen women with embryos fashioned from their own eggs, their partner's sperm, and a small portion of an egg donated by a second woman. The procedure was designed to work around defects in the would-be mother's egg—but in at least two of the cases, tests showed the resulting babies carried genetic material from all three "parents."

And so the genetic modification of humans is not only possible, it's coming fast; a mix of technical progress and shifting mood means it could easily happen in the next few years. Consider what happened with plants. A decade ago, university research farms were growing small plots of genetically modified grain and vegetables. Sometimes activists who didn't like what they were doing would come and rip the plants up, one by one. Then, all of a sudden in the mid-1990s, before anyone had paid any real attention, farmers had planted half the corn and soybean fields in America with transgenic seed.

Every time you turn your back this technology creeps a little closer. Gallops, actually, growing and spreading as fast as the Internet. One moment you've sort of heard of it; the next moment it's everywhere. But we haven't done it yet. For the moment we remain, if barely, a fully human species. And so we have time yet to consider, to decide, to act. This is arguably the biggest decision humans will ever make.

Right up until this decade, the genes that humans carried in their bodies were exclusively the result of chance—of how the genes of the sperm and the egg, the father and the mother, combined. The only way you could intervene in the process was by choosing who you would mate with—and that was as much wishful thinking as anything else, as generation upon generation of surprised parents have discovered.

But that is changing. We now know two different methods to change human genes. The first, and less controversial, is called somatic gene therapy.

Somatic gene therapy begins with an existing individual—someone with, say, cystic fibrosis. Researchers try to deliver new, modified genes to some of her cells, usually by putting the genes aboard viruses they inject into the patient, hoping that the viruses will infect the cells and thereby transmit the genes. Somatic gene therapy is, in other words, much like medicine. You take an existing patient with an existing condition, and you in essence try and convince her cells to manufacture the medicine she needs.

Germline genetic engineering on the other hand is something very novel indeed. "Germ" here refers not to microbes, but to the egg and sperm cells, the germ cells of the human being. Scientists intent on genetic engineering would probably start with a fertilized embryo a week or so old. They would tease apart the cells of that embryo, and then, selecting one, they would add to, delete, or modify some of its genes. They could also insert artificial chromosomes containing predesigned genes. They would then take the cell, place it inside an egg whose nucleus had been removed, and implant the resulting new embryo inside a woman. The embryo would, if all went according to plan, grow into a genetically engineered child. His genes would be pushing out proteins to meet the particular choices made by his parents, and by the companies and clinicians they were buying the genes from. Instead of coming solely from the combination of his parents, and thus the combination of their parents, and so on back through time, those genes could come from any other person, or any other plant or animal, or out of the thin blue sky. And once implanted they will pass to his children, and on into time.

But all this work will require one large change in our current way of doing business. Instead of making babies by making love, we will have to move conception to the laboratory. You need to have the embryo out there where you can work on it—to make the necessary copies, try to add or delete genes, and then implant the one that seems likely to turn out best. Gregory Stock, a researcher at the University of California and an apostle of the new genetic technologies, says that "the union of egg and sperm from two individuals . . . would be too unpredictable with intercourse." And once you've got the embryo out on the lab bench, gravity disappears altogether. "Ultimately," says Michael West, CEO of Advanced Cell Technology, the firm furthest out on the cutting edge of these technologies, "the dream of biologists is to have the sequence of DNA, the programming code of life, and to be able to edit it the way you can a document on a word processor."

Does it sound far-fetched? We began doing it with animals (mice) in 1978, and we've managed the trick with most of the obvious mammals, except one. Some of the first germline interventions might be semimedical.

You might, say some advocates, start by improving "visual and auditory acuity," first to eliminate nearsightedness or prevent deafness, then to "improve artistic potential." But why stop there? "If something has evolved elsewhere, then it is possible for us to determine its genetic basis and transfer it into the human genome," says Princeton geneticist Lee Silver—just as we have stuck flounder genes into strawberries to keep them from freezing, and jellyfish genes into rabbits and monkeys to make them glow in the dark.

But would we actually do this? Is there any real need to raise these questions as more than curiosities, or will the schemes simply fade away on their own, ignored by the parents who are their necessary consumers?

Anyone who has entered a baby supply store in the last few years knows that even the soberest parents can be counted on to spend virtually unlimited sums in pursuit of successful offspring. What if the Baby Einstein video series, which immerses "learning enabled" babies in English, Spanish, Japanese, Hebrew, German, Russian, and French, could be bolstered with a little gene-tweaking to improve memory? What if the Wombsongs prenatal music system, piping in Brahms to your waiting fetus, could be supplemented with an auditory upgrade? One sociologist told the *New York Times* we'd crossed the line from parenting to "product development," and even if that remark is truer in Manhattan than elsewhere, it's not hard to imagine what such attitudes will mean across the affluent world.

Here's one small example. In the 1980s, two drug companies were awarded patents to market human growth hormone to the few thousand American children suffering from dwarfism. The FDA thought the market would be very small, so HGH was given "orphan drug status," a series of special market advantages designed to reward the manufacturers for taking on such an unattractive business. But within a few years, HGH had become one of the largest-selling drugs in the country, with half a billion dollars in sales. This was not because there'd been a sharp increase in the number of dwarves, but because there'd been a sharp increase in the number of parents who wanted to make their slightly short children taller. Before long the drug companies were arguing that the children in the bottom 5 percent of their normal height range were in fact in need of three to five shots a week of HGH. Take eleven-year-old Marco Oriti. At four foot one, he was about four inches shorter than average, and projected to eventually top out at five foot four. This was enough to convince his parents to start on a six-day-a-week HGH regimen, which will cost them $150,000 over the next four years. "You want to give your child the edge no matter what," said his mother.

A few of the would-be parents out on the current cutting edge of the reproduction revolution—those who need to obtain sperm or eggs for in vitro fertilization—exhibit similar zeal. Ads started appearing in Ivy League college newspapers a few years ago: couples were willing to pay $50,000 for an egg, provided the donor was at least five feet, ten inches tall, white, and had scored 1400 on her SATs. There is, in other words, a market just waiting for the first clinic with a catalog of germline modifications, a market that two California artists proved when they opened a small boutique, Gene Genies Worldwide, in a trendy part of Pasadena. Tran Kim-Trang and Karl Mihail wanted to get people thinking more deeply about these emerging technologies, so they outfitted their store with petri dishes and models of the double helix, and printed up brochures highlighting traits with genetic links: creativity, extroversion, thrill-seeking criminality. When they opened the doors, they found people ready to shell out for designer families (one man insisted he wanted the survival ability of a cockroach). The "store" was meant to be ironic, but the irony was lost on a culture so deeply consumer that this kind of manipulation seems like the obvious next step. "Generally, people refused to believe this store was an art project," says Tran. And why not? The next store in the mall could easily have been a Botox salon.

But say you're not ready. Say you're perfectly happy with the prospect of a child who shares the unmodified genes of you and your partner. Say you think that manipulating the DNA of your child might be dangerous, or presumptuous, or icky? How long will you be able to hold that line if the procedure begins to spread among your neighbors? Maybe not so long as you think: if germline manipulation actually does begin, it seems likely to set off a kind of biological arms race. "Suppose parents could add thirty points to their child's IQ," asks MIT economist Lester Thurow. "Wouldn't you want to do it? And if you don't, your child will be the stupidest in the neighborhood." That's precisely what it might feel like to be the parent facing the choice. Individual competition more or less defines the society we've built, and in that context love can almost be defined as giving your kids what they need to make their way in the world. Deciding not to soup them up . . . well, it could come to seem like child abuse.

Of course, the problem about arms races is that you never really get anywhere. If everyone's adding thirty IQ points, then having an IQ of one hundred fifty won't get you any closer to Stanford than you were at the outset. The very first athlete engineered to use twice as much oxygen as the next guy will be unbeatable in the Tour de France—but in no time he'll merely be the new standard. You'll have to do what he did to be in the race, but your upgrades won't put you ahead, merely back on a level playing field. You might be able to argue that society as a whole was helped, because there was more total brainpower at work, but your kid won't be any closer to the top of the pack. All you'll be able to do is guarantee she won't be left hopelessly far behind.

In fact, the arms-race problem has an extra ironic twist when it comes to genetic manipulation. The United States and the Soviet Union could, and did, keep adding new weapons to their arsenals over the decades. But with germline manipulation, you get only one shot; the extra chromosome you stick in your kid when he's born is the one he carries throughout his life. So let's say baby Sophie has a state-of-the-art gene job: her parents paid for the proteins discovered by, say, 2005 that, on average, yielded ten extra IQ points. By the time Sophie is five, though, scientists will doubtless have discovered ten more genes linked to intelligence. Now anyone with a platinum card can get twenty IQ points, not to mention a memory boost and a permanent wrinkle-free brow. So by the time Sophie is twenty-five and in the job market, she's already more or less obsolete—the kids coming out of college just plain have better hardware.

"For all his billions, Bill Gates could not have purchased a single genetic enhancement for his son Rory John," writes Gregory Stock, at the University of California. "And you can bet that any enhancements a billion dollars can buy Rory's child in 2030 will seem crude alongside those available for modest sums in 2060." It's not, he adds, "so different from upgraded software. You'll want the new release."

The vision of one's child as a nearly useless copy of Windows 95 should make parents fight like hell to make sure we never get started down this path. But the vision gets lost easily in the gushing excitement about "improving" the opportunities for our kids.

Beginning the hour my daughter came home from the hospital, I spent part of every day with her in the woods out back, showing her trees and ferns and chipmunks and frogs. One of her very first words was "birch," and you couldn't have asked for a prouder papa. She got her middle name from the mountain we see out the window; for her fifth birthday she got her own child-sized canoe; her school wardrobe may not be relentlessly up-to-date but she's never lacked for hiking boots. As I write these words, she's spending her first summer at sleep-away camp, one we chose because the kids sleep in tents and spend days in the mountains. All of which is to say that I have done everything in my power to try and mold her into a lover of the natural world. That is where my deepest satisfactions lie, and I want the same for her. It seems benign enough, but it has its drawbacks; it means less time and money and energy for trips to the city and music lessons and so forth. As time goes on and she develops stronger opinions of her own, I yield more and more, but I keep trying to stack the deck, to nudge her in the direction that's meant something to me. On a Saturday morning, when the question comes up of what to do, the very first words out of my mouth always involve yet another hike. I can't help myself.

In other words, we already "engineer" our offspring in some sense of the word: we do our best, and often our worst, to steer them in particular directions. And our worst can be pretty bad. We all know people whose lives were blighted trying to meet the expectations of their parents. We've all seen the crazed devotion to getting kids into the right schools, the right professions, the right income brackets. Parents try and pass down their prejudices, their politics, their attitude toward the world ("we've got to toughen that kid up—he's going to get walked all over"). There are fathers who start teaching the curveball at the age of four, and sons made to feel worthless if they don't make the Little League traveling team. People move house so that their kids can grow up with the right kind of schoolmates. They threaten to disown them for marrying African Americans, or for not marrying African Americans. No dictator anywhere has ever tried to rule his subjects with as much attention to detail as the average modern parent.

Why not take this just one small step further? Why not engineer children to up the odds that all that nudging will stick? In the words of Lee Silver, the Princeton geneticist, "Why not seize this power? Why not control what has been left to chance in the past? Indeed, we control all other aspects of our children's lives and identities through powerful social and environmental influences. . . . On what basis can we reject positive genetic influences on a person's essence when we accept the rights of parents to benefit their children in every other way?" If you can buy your kid three years at Deerfield, four at Harvard, and three more at Harvard Law, why shouldn't you be able to turbocharge his IQ a bit?

But most likely the answer has already occurred to you as well. Because you know plenty of people who managed to rebel successfully against whatever agenda their parents laid out for them, or who took that agenda and bent it to fit their own particular personality. In our society that's often what growing up is all about—the sometimes excruciatingly difficult, frequently liberating break with the expectations of your parents. The decision to join the Peace Corps (or, the decision to leave the commune where you grew up and go to business school). The discovery that you were happiest davening in an Orthodox shul three hours a day, much to the consternation of your good suburban parents who almost always made it to Yom Kippur services; the decision that, much as you respected the Southern Baptist piety of your parents, the Bible won't be your watchword.

Without the grounding offered by tradition, the search for the "authentic you" can be hard; our generations contain the first people who routinely shop religions, for instance. But the sometimes poignant difficulty of finding yourself merely underscores how essential it is. Silver says the costs of germline engineering and a college education might be roughly comparable; in both cases, he goes on, the point is to "increase the chances the child will become wiser in some way, and better able to achieve success and happiness." But that's half the story, at best. College is where you go to be exposed to a thousand new influences, ideas that should be able to take you in almost any direction. It's where you go to get out from under your parents' thumb, to find out that you actually don't have to go to law school if you don't want to. As often as not, the harder parents try and wrench their kids in one direction, the harder those kids eventually fight to determine their own destiny. I am as prepared as I can be for the possibility—the probability—that Sophie will decide she wants to live her life in the concrete heart of Manhattan. It's her life (and perhaps her kids will have a secret desire to come wander in the woods with me).

We try and shape the lives of our kids—to "improve" their lives, as we would measure improvement—but our gravity is usually weak enough that kids can break out of it if and when they need to. (When it isn't, when parents manage to bend their children to the point of breaking, we think of them as monstrous.) "Many of the most creative and valuable human lives are the result of particularly difficult struggles" against expectation and influence, writes the legal scholar Martha Nussbaum.

That's not how a genetic engineer thinks of his product. He works to ensure absolute success. Last spring an Israeli researcher announced that he had managed to produce a featherless chicken. This constituted an improvement, to his mind, because "it will be cheaper to produce since its lack of feathers means there is no need to pluck it before it hits the shelves." Also, poultry farmers would no longer have to ventilate their vast barns to keep their birds from overheating. "Feathers are a waste," the scientist explained. "The chickens are using feed to produce something that has to be dumped, and the farmers have to waste electricity to overcome that fact." Now, that engineer was not trying to influence his chickens to shed their feathers because they'd be happier and the farmer would be happier and everyone would be happier. He was inserting a gene that created a protein that made good and certain they would not be producing feathers. Just substitute, say, an even temperament for feathers, and you'll know what the human engineers envision.

"With reprogenetics," writes Lee Silver, "parents can gain *complete control* [emphasis mine] over their destiny, with the ability to guide and enhance the characteristics of their children, and their children's children as well." Such parents would not be calling their children on the phone at annoyingly frequent intervals to suggest that it's time to get a real job; instead, just like the chicken guy, they would be inserting genes that produced proteins that would make their child behave in certain ways throughout his life. You cannot rebel against the production of that protein. Perhaps you can still do everything in your power to defeat the wishes of your parents, but that protein will nonetheless be pumped out relentlessly into your system, defining who you are. You won't grow feathers, no matter how much you want them. And maybe they can engineer your mood enough that your lack of plumage won't even cross your mind.

Such children will, in effect, be assigned a goal by their programmers: "intelligence," "even temper," "athleticism." (As with chickens, the market will doubtless lean in the direction of efficiency. It may be hard to find genes for, say, dreaminess.) Now two possibilities arise. Perhaps the programming doesn't work very well, and your kid spells poorly, or turns moody, or can't hit the inside fastball. In the present world, you just tell yourself that that's who he is. But in the coming world, he'll be, in essence, a defective product. Do you still accept him unconditionally? Why? If your new Jetta got thirty miles to the gallon instead of the forty it was designed to get, you'd take it back. You'd call it a lemon. If necessary, you'd sue.

Or what if the engineering worked pretty well, but you decided, too late, that you'd picked the wrong package, hadn't gotten the best features? Would you feel buyer's remorse if the kid next door had a better ear, a stronger arm?

Say the gene work went a little awry and left you with a kid who had some serious problems; what kind of guilt would that leave you with? Remember, this is not a child created by the random interaction of your genes with those of your partner, this is a child created with specific intent. Does *Consumer Reports* start rating the various biotech offerings?

What if you had a second child five years after the first, and by that time the upgrades were undeniably improved: how would you feel about the first kid? How would he feel about his new brother, the latest model?

The other outcome—that the genetic engineering works just as you had hoped—seems at least as bad. Now your child is a product. You can take precisely as much pride in her achievements as you take in the achievements of your dishwashing detergent. It was designed to produce streak-free glassware, and she was designed to be sweet-tempered, social, and smart. And what can she take pride in? Her good grades? She may have worked hard, but she'll always know that she was spec'ed for good grades. Her kindness to others? Well, yes, it's good to be kind—but perhaps it's not much of an accomplishment once the various genes with some link to sociability have been cataloged and manipulated. I have no doubt that these qualms would be one of the powerful psychological afflictions of the future—at least until someone figures out a fix that keeps the next generations from having such bad thoughts.

Britain's chief rabbi, Jonathan Sacks, was asked, a few years ago, about the announcement that Italian doctors were trying to clone humans. "If there is a mystery at the heart of human condition, it is otherness: the otherness of man and woman, parent and child. It is the space we make for otherness that makes love something other than narcissism." I remember so well the feeling of walking into the maternity ward with Sue, and walking out with Sue and Sophie: where there had been two there were now, somehow, three, each of us our own person, but now commanded to make a family, a place where we all could thrive. She was so mysterious, that Sophie, and in many ways she still is. There are times when, like every parent, I see myself reflected in her, and times when I wonder if she's even related. She's ours to nurture and protect, but she is who *she* is. That's the mystery and the glory of any child.

Mystery, however, is not one of the words that thrills engineers. They try and deliver solid bridges, unyielding dams, reliable cars. We wouldn't want it any other way. The only question is if their product line should be expanded to include children.

Right now both the genes, and the limits that they set on us, connect us with every human that came before. Human beings can look at rock art carved into African cliffs and French caves thirty thousand years ago and feel an electric, immediate kinship. We've gone from digging sticks to combines, and from drum circles to symphony orchestras (and back again to drum circles), but we still hear in the same range and see in the same spectrum, still produce adrenaline and dopamine in the same ways, still think in many of the same patterns. We are, by and large, the same people, more closely genetically related to one another than we may be to our engineered grandchildren.

These new technologies show us that human meaning dangles by a far thinner thread than we had thought. If germline genetic engineering ever starts, it will accelerate endlessly and unstoppably into the future, as individuals make the calculation that they have no choice but to equip their kids for the world that's being made. The first child whose genes come in part from some corporate lab, the first child who has been "enhanced" from what came before—that's the first child who will glance back over his shoulder and see a gap between himself and human history.

These would be mere consumer decisions—but that also means that they would benefit the rich far more than the poor. They would take the gap in power, wealth, and education that currently divides both our society and the world at large, and write that division into our very biology. A sixth of the American population lacks health insurance of any kind—they can't afford to go to the doctor for a *checkup*. And much of the rest of the world is far worse off. If we can't afford the fifty cents a person it would take to buy bed nets to protect most of Africa from malaria, it is unlikely we will extend to anyone but the top tax bracket these latest forms of genetic technology. The injustice is so obvious that even the strongest proponents of genetic engineering make little attempt to deny it. "Anyone who accepts the right of affluent parents to provide their children with an expensive private school education cannot use 'unfairness' as a reason for rejecting the use of reprogenetic technologies," says Lee Silver.

These new technologies, however, are not yet inevitable. Unlike global warming, this genie is not yet out of the bottle. But if germline genetic engineering is going to be stopped, it will have to happen now, before it's quite begun. It will have to be a political choice, that is—one we make not as parents but as citizens, not as individuals but as a whole, thinking not only about our own offspring but about everyone.

So far the discussion has been confined to a few scientists, a few philosophers, a few ideologues. It needs to spread widely, and quickly, and loudly. The stakes are absurdly high, nothing less than the meaning of being human. And given the seductions that we've seen—the intuitively and culturally delicious prospect of a *better* child—the arguments against must be not only powerful but also deep. They'll need to resonate on the same intuitive and cultural level. We'll need to feel in our gut the reasons why, this time, we should tell Prometheus thanks, but no thanks.

(2003)

The Pirates of Illiopolis

Why your kitchen floor may pose a threat to national security

A FEW WEEKS AFTER 9/11, I GAVE A LECTURE ON ENVIRONMENTAL pediatrics at the New York Academy of Medicine. The talk had been planned months earlier, but it wasn't at all clear, in the days leading up to it, whether the event would take place. My host said, frankly, he could not guarantee an audience. I had misgivings of my own. The drive to Manhattan from my office at Cornell took five hours even before the George Washington Bridge was outfitted with security checkpoints, and I had a newborn who would be riding with me across that bridge.

In the end, we decided, as so many people did in those first dazed weeks, that since all possible actions felt wrong anyway, we should just get on with it. And so my husband paced marble corridors with our son on his shoulder while I addressed a half-filled auditorium. In the audience were a number of pregnant women and, as I was getting ready to leave, they approached me as a group. They wanted to know about that most toxic of all synthetic chemicals, dioxin, which, at vanishingly small concentrations, can cause developmental problems as well as cancer. Had the incineration and collapse of the World Trade Center sent a dioxin-filled plume over Manhattan? They had heard that the towers were filled with PVC plastic and that PVC makes dioxin when burned. Is that right? Were their babies in danger?

I tried to keep my voice calm. Yes, I said, PVC—or polyvinyl chloride, or vinyl—makes dioxin when it burns and yes, the Trade Center was surely full of PVC. It's used in electrical cables, flooring, wallpaper, and office furniture. I said I didn't know what health threats the smoke created for the people breathing it—or for the fetuses they might be carrying. Colleagues of mine at Mount Sinai Medical Center were, right now, researching those very questions. Unfortunately, the answers would be years away. Science takes time, especially when actual exposures are unknown and the outcomes, like subtle developmental deficits, can take years to manifest.

The pregnant women watched Elijah nurse. I looked down at their various-sized bellies. We all fell into silence.

The next morning, I left my sleeping son and spouse in the hotel and took a nearly empty subway downtown. The trains under lower Manhattan were not running, so at some point I got out and started walking. There were no towers to navigate by, a fact that seemed as surprising as it was obvious. I figured I was getting closer when the faces of the missing began appearing on every wall and pole. And then I rounded a corner near a closed-up barbershop, and there it was.

I felt as if I were looking at the ruins of some ancient civilization. There was the broken pillar. There was the curl of smoke before the crumbled facade. There was the scrap of cloth fluttering from the blasted window. There was the rubble. There was the gaping hole.

After a while, I noticed that my blouse was damp with milk. Somewhere uptown a baby was getting hungry. Fumbling with the buttons to my jacket, I dropped my book bag onto a sewer grate. Just then, in a surreal transaction, a cab appeared, a sobbing woman got out, and I got in.

Back in Ithaca later that evening, I saw that my green book bag had turned gray with Ground Zero ashes. Lying on my kitchen floor, it was still holding my breast pump and a couple of diapers, along with my lecture notes. I lifted the bag gingerly and carried it out to the porch. I'd deal with it tomorrow. For now, I focused on the floor. Around and around I went with the broom, until there was not a speck of dust or ash anywhere. The floor's vinyl beige squares and bland blue flowers seemed innocent and reassuring.

At 10:40 P.M. on April 23, 2004, a PVC plant in Illiopolis, Illinois, blew up. A village of about nine hundred souls, Illiopolis sits in the rural center of the state about an hour south of my hometown. You get to Illiopolis by driving down old Route 121, which, when I was a teenager, was the road favored by motorcyclists and the envied owners of Pontiac Firebirds. It was seldom patrolled. Along the highway was Keith's Truck Stop, an all-purpose establishment that included a string of rooms in back that we called a "no-tell motel."

A photograph of the explosion at the Formosa Plastics Plant in Illiopolis appeared in the *Ithaca Journal.* It was the first time in my memory that photographs from that part of the world appeared in the local paper here. Indeed, the disaster made headlines all around the globe, and it was spectacular by all accounts. The blast killed four workers outright—a fifth would die twenty days later—and sent into the night sky a hundred-foot fireball. This ball, once it faded from view, left behind a dark, hovering mass that drifted slowly over the landscape like some kind of evil UFO.

Four towns were evacuated, several highways closed, a no-fly zone declared, and three hundred firefighters from twenty-seven surrounding communities battled the flames for three days. Their efforts were complicated by the power outage—triggered by the shock wave—that disabled the water supply. Formosa Plastics ran the wells that provided the town's water.

The U.S. Chemical Safety and Hazard Investigation Board was summoned to determine the cause of the explosion. Its chairwoman, Carolyn Merritt, estimated that it would take a year to figure out why the plant blew up. Terrorism was ruled out. But beyond that, only two facts were known for sure. One: a large amount of vinyl chloride, the vaporous feedstock of polyvinyl chloride, had been released into the air immediately before the whole facility blew skyward. Two: the explosion originated in the reactors where vinyl chloride and vinyl acetate were being mixed together.

Meanwhile, a consortium of agencies began investigating the long-term health and environmental consequences of the explosion and the plume that wafted over the landscape in the days that followed. This investigation will take far longer than a year. Science is slow.

But politics, like fetal development, is not. Within a fortnight of the accident, Formosa Plastics vowed to rebuild, and Republican lawmakers pledged to help them find the money to do so. A business group in Springfield made plans to include the PVC plant in a special "enterprise zone" that would relieve the company from paying sales tax on building materials. These deals were being brokered before investigators could safely get within a quarter mile of the plant; its charred remains were structurally unstable and coated with "pyrolytic breakdown products"—otherwise known as soot—that, given the chemicals known to have detonated, very likely contained dioxin.

By early May, Illiopolis had vanished from the newspapers. I talked to a pediatrician friend who practices in the area to see what she knew. Gail had been vacationing when the explosion happened. "I read about it in the newspapers in Maui," she said. "And now I get back home, and it's like it never happened."

On the other hand, Illiopolis was still making headlines in the trade magazines. In May, the Web site ebuild.com disclosed the contents of a communiqué from Armstrong World Industries to the U.S. Securities and Exchange Commission. In it, Armstrong warned that the explosion might disrupt the manufacture of its vinyl floors and thereby impact financial results. Meanwhile, as reported in *Floor Covering Weekly,* the three kingpins of flooring—Armstrong, Congoleum, and Mannington—all announced price increases in vinyl composition tile due to the explosion-induced PVC shortfall. It turned out that, at 200 million pounds per year, the Illiopolis plant was a major supplier to these three customers of a particular kind of PVC resin needed to make vinyl floors. Who knew? Usually, chemical chains of custody, as they are called, are carefully guarded industry secrets. Who sells what chemical to whom is not a query public affairs officers are normally happy to answer. In order to trace the connections, it takes a disaster of some magnitude to break them.

I went to Illiopolis in June. I drove a rental car from my mother's house down what is now called I-155 and then took a series of blacktops through thigh-high corn until I crossed the railroad track.

If you've never seen a chemical plant up close, you should. It's not enough to gaze down at one from the air or glance over your shoulder while driving by. You have to walk up to the fence line and stand there for a while. Once you recover from the sheer size of it—these facilities usually command thousands of acres—see if you can figure out what goes on there. It's not as inexplicable as the maze of pipes and catwalks makes it seem. There has to be a source of water, often a river, and a method of transportation, often a rail line, and a source of power. The white orbs with spiral staircases snaking around them contain flammable liquid chemicals, as do the cylindrical tanker cars. The square hopper cars contain something solid, as does anything that looks like a silo.

I pulled off onto a gravel service road, got out of the car, and there it was. Twisted sheets of metal. Knotted piles of pipe. A blackened hull. A gaping hole.

The storage silos were still standing. The hopper cars were still on their tracks. A field of corn hissed in the wind. I checked to see which way its leaves were blowing to make sure I was upwind from what I was looking at.

The last worker to die from injuries sustained during the explosion was Randy Hancock, age fifty. Randy had clung to life in the Springfield Memorial burn unit for nearly three weeks until he heard the news that his wife, Linda, also a worker at the plant, was already dead. According to family members, he had, in his last days, repeatedly used his right hand to gesture toward his left, pointing to the place where a wedding ring would be. From this, they inferred he wanted news of Linda. When finally told that she was gone, Randy slipped into a coma, and then he was gone too.

The manufacture of PVC is a straightforward affair. The first step involves the generation of chlorine gas, which is created in chlor-alkali facilities through a process that has changed little in the past half century. It basically involves running electricity through brine. The result is caustic soda and chlorine gas. The chlorine is then combined with ethylene, which is derived from the refining of natural gas. After a couple of intermediate steps, the product is vinyl chloride, a sweet-smelling vapor that liquefies under high pressure and can be transported via train car to PVC plants. Once there, the small vinyl chloride molecules are bonded together in big vats to form long molecular chains called polyvinyl chloride. In so doing, the feedstock turns into a solid polymer called resin. All by itself, PVC resin is not very useful. It does, however, readily combine with other polymers and mixes easily with all kinds of additives, fillers, and stabilizers. In these ways, PVC can be made, for example, bendable, sticky, rigid, filmy, or heat resistant. The mixing of vinyl chloride and vinyl acetate—the activity that immediately preceded the Illiopolis explosion—is a means of creating a copolymer that works well for making floors.

One of the big debates raging within architecture and design circles these days is whether PVC is an inherently dangerous material. At face value, the very question seems queer. Some of the most banal household objects are made of vinyl. Garden hoses. Shower curtains. Bath toys. Sewer pipe. Carpet. Siding. And the credit cards with which to buy them all. But for all its apparent inertness, PVC has a number of menacing qualities, most of which can be attributed to the fact that it is one of the few common plastics to contain chlorine. PVC is 56 percent chlorine by weight, and it is this ingredient that makes vinyl an environmental wild card.

The risks begin with the first step of manufacturing. Chlorine gas, PVC's progenitor, is a wicked poison that turns into hydrochloric acid upon contact with moisture. It kills by burning the airways of those who inhale it. Victims suffocate in their own body fluids; those who survive are often incapacitated for life. This is why, after World War I, chlorine gas was outlawed by international agreement as a chemical weapon. But it's still prevalent in manufacturing, and accidents do happen. In January 2005, a ruptured chlorine tanker car in Graniteville, South Carolina, killed 9 people, hospitalized 500, and turned 5,400 residents into evacuees. That accident was eerily similar to one that occurred six months earlier near San Antonio, Texas, where a chlorine tanker car derailment killed 3 and sickened 49.

Once chlorine is combined with ethylene, the dangers multiply. The oily liquid so created, ethylene dichloride, is a probable human carcinogen that, when spilled, has a nasty habit of heading straight for groundwater. According to the National Toxicology Program, at least four Americans out of every hundred drink water containing traces of ethylene dichloride. Vinyl chloride—the next step along the manufacturing chain—is a potent carcinogen linked to liver, blood, and brain cancers. It possesses the additional quality of being explosively flammable. Vinyl acetate, another carcinogen, is also explosive. (Workers in the Illiopolis plant wore special nail-less shoes to avoid striking sparks on the concrete floors.) And, at several points along the way, vinyl production generates dioxin—a chlorinated pollutant that travels the globe on the jet stream, lasts for up to thirty-five years in human tissues, and reaches its highest concentrations in breast milk.

Nor do the hazards end once the toxic feedstocks of PVC eventually find their way into home furnishings. Fumes emitted from vinyl materials can degrade indoor air quality and contribute to respiratory distress among inhabitants. A new vinyl shower curtain, for example, can raise indoor air toxicity for longer than a month. A 2003 Finnish study that investigated complaints of adult-onset asthma among employees working in an office building revealed rates of asthma there to be nine times higher than expected. Researchers discovered that degraded vinyl floor covering had released volatile chemicals into indoor air. When the offending floor was removed, air quality improved, as did the respiratory health of the workers. Similarly, a large study in Sweden found that the combination of moisture and PVC flooring worsened asthmatic symptoms among children.

And there is no good way to dispose of vinyl. Vinyl is, for all intents and purposes, unrecyclable. The various additives and stabilizers—including heavy metals like lead—that are used to give PVC its myriad physical properties contaminate the recycling stream when mixed with other plastics. Thus, PVC dies one of three deaths, all of which have environmental consequences. It can be buried in a landfill where the various plasticizers used to make it flexible leach out and threaten air and groundwater. It can be shoveled into a trash incinerator, which destroys the plasticizers but creates dioxin and heavy metal-laden ash. Or it can burn up in an uncontrolled fire resulting from accidents, arson, or acts of terrorism. When a building burns, not only do the chlorine and carbon atoms in PVC rearrange themselves to form dioxin, but hydrochloric acid is also generated, along with black, choking smoke. Both hamper search-and-rescue operations and endanger fleeing occupants.

Add to all this the fact that PVC plants are leaky places. Take a look at the Toxics Release Inventory, the self-reported list of chemical emissions that manufacturers submit each year to the U.S. Environmental Protection Agency. If there is a PVC facility in your home state—there are twenty-one of them currently operating within nine states—it will appear among the state's biggest polluters. Taiwan-based Formosa Plastics Incorporated, "The Prince of PVC," has a laundry list of serious environmental violations in Cambodia, Texas, Louisiana, and Delaware.

Formosa's Illiopolis plant ranked within the top ninetieth percentile in the nation for air releases of carcinogens in 2001. This distinction was entirely attributable to the 41,000 pounds of vinyl chloride that it released that year. On top of this, Formosa released 40,000 pounds of vinyl acetate. In 2002, Formosa's vinyl chloride emissions fell to 31,000 pounds, while its vinyl acetate emissions rose to 45,000 pounds. In other words, for two years running, this facility released into the air *each day* about 200 pounds of cancer-causing chemicals.

On the Illinois prairie, the prevailing winds blow from west to east. Two miles east of the PVC plant sits the village of Illiopolis, where tiny bungalows share residential streets with formerly grand Victorians. The police station and the city hall occupy a small building under the grain elevator. There is a thriving downtown hardware store. On Matilda Street, at the very west edge of town, Illiopolis High School—"Home of the Pirates"—sprawls next to the middle school, the elementary school, and the pre-kindergarten. All that stands between the Pirates's playing fields and Formosa's daily two hundred pounds of known and suspected carcinogens is corn.

Two chemists have devoted their careers to understanding the community health threats created when chemicals from PVC plants drift to the far side of the fence line. One of them is Wilma Subra, who has studied air quality in the neighborhoods surrounding various PVC plants in Kentucky and Louisiana. Even in the absence of explosions and upsets—during times when the plants were operating normally—Subra has documented consistent patterns of dioxin and vinyl chloride exposure to area residents, including schoolchildren.

In February 2004, Subra presented her data at the first public meeting of the U.S. Green Building Council's vinyl task force in Washington, D.C. The council is in the midst of promulgating a rating system that can be used to certify buildings as "green," in much the same way that the U.S. Department of Agriculture now certifies food as organic. The council's system, called LEED—Leadership in Energy and Environmental Design—offers points toward certification to architects who incorporate energy-saving and environmentally friendly materials into their designs. The council's PVC task force is now charged with deciding whether a point should be given for "vinyl avoidance." (Full disclosure: my research for this article was carried out in part as a consultant to Healthy Building Network, a public-interest group that watchdogs the activities of the U.S. Green Building Council.)

The vinyl issue is complicated by the financial stakes held by some of the council's members. Armstrong, for example, is a corporate member of the U.S. Green Building Council. This is not a complete conflict of interest. Armstrong is not only a leading producer of vinyl flooring; it also makes linoleum flooring, which is considered an environmentally friendly alternative to vinyl. However, Armstrong has no domestic supplier for raw linoleum—which is made from linseed oil, cork, and jute—and so, for now, must import the material from Europe, which keeps the price high. (Including installation, an average-quality linoleum floor costs about the same as a floor made of high-quality sheet vinyl and about twice as much as one made from vinyl composition tile. But the longevity of linoleum exceeds vinyl tile by a factor of three, making it a more cost-effective flooring material in the long run.)

Subra, who won a MacArthur Award for her research, was warmly received by the council's vinyl task force in February 2004. Its members asked thoughtful questions and asked to see more data. After Subra's presentation, however, more than twenty different vinyl lobbyists spoke on the virtues of PVC. A year later, when the task force released the first public draft of its PVC assessment, Subra's work was largely ignored. By contrast, other institutions have taken more definitive action. The Australian Green Building Council has already rejected PVC as a green building material. So have the state of New York, the cities of San Francisco and Boston, and at least two major hospitals.

The other chemist investigating the public health effects of PVC is Pat Costner, a former industry scientist who now works for Greenpeace. Costner focuses on dioxin formation when PVC burns. Should you ever wonder exactly how much dioxin is generated when a shredded vinyl glove is incinerated in a laboratory combustor, Pat Costner would be the person to call. When I asked her to help me understand how much dioxin might be formed from the feedstocks of PVC under the conditions of an explosive fire, she said that it was hard to know. It all depended on the kinds of chemicals stored at the plant and the weather conditions during the three days the fire raged. Vinyl chloride does make dioxin when burned. But much of that gas, Costner said, should have risen above the flames once the top blew off the reactor, thereby avoiding combustion. The larger share of dioxin formation probably occurred during the later, smoldering fires, especially those involving solid PVC. To wit, I needed to find out how much resin was stored on-site.

Beverley Scobell looks like Betty Ford, only prettier. She has lived in Illiopolis for forty years, and her house is just behind the spire of the Catholic church—that's how she told me how to find it—and next to the post office. It's a foursquare Victorian that is not what you would call meticulously restored but it isn't shabby either. Even in the shimmering heat, it was cool and dark inside.

She and her husband, Hank, served as volunteer firefighters for more than two decades, although they were no longer active members the night Formosa blew up. They originally joined the firehouse, Bev said, for the social life. The firefighters' parties were the best in town.

Hank and Bev had gone to bed early the night of the accident. Hank was asleep and Bev was watching Leno when the power went out. Seconds later she heard the boom.

Hank went right to the firehouse. Bev went to the home of a disabled elderly neighbor, Connie, and helped her get dressed by flashlight, presuming that an evacuation order was imminent. In fact, there was already such an order, but few residents of Illiopolis knew about it. Because of the blackout, the emergency siren failed to go off.

When Hank came back from the firehouse, he reported that the wind, miraculously, was blowing to the south-southwest—away from the town. Nevertheless, and against a current of evacuees driving east, Hank, Bev, and Connie all got in the car and headed west, toward the cloud. The plan was to deliver Connie to her nephew's house in Mechanicsburg, but by the time they got there, that community was also under evacuation. So they doubled back. In the end, Connie spent the night in a sealed room at a firehouse in a nearby village. Bev and Hank went on to Springfield.

"We never believed or bothered to know what went on out there," said Bev of Formosa Plastics. "It was just a fact of life. We've lived with it for so long."

Around the corner from Bev lives Rayeanna Stacey, Illiopolis's coordinator for emergency services. A certified emergency medical technician, she drives the van that runs with the fire trucks. Rayeanna is also the village clerk and the school bus driver. Her husband, Dennis, is the superintendent of public works and first captain at the fire department.

Rayeanna was testy about the issue of the siren never going off. She had been complaining for years to Formosa about the need for an emergency siren that worked during a power outage. For that matter, Rayeanna added, she had also objected repeatedly—and to no avail—to the many vinyl chloride tanker cars that sometimes spent the night parked on the tracks right in the center of town. All it would take is a couple of teenage pranksters and nobody in Illiopolis would wake up in the morning.

The night Formosa blew up, Rayeanna and Dennis were at their cabin an hour south of Illiopolis. Alerted by pager, they made the trip home in much less time than that. Dennis joined the firefighters at the scene of the disaster. Rayeanna went to Christine's Diner, which had been turned into a command center for emergency responders. Before the weekend was over, she would transport four dead bodies in her van.

Rayeanna emphasized what a miracle it was that the initial blast did not set off a chain reaction of even larger explosions. Because some of the first responders on the scene were employees of the plant, they were familiar with the layout and could direct others to critical locations. In her professional opinion, if all the chemicals in and around the plant had detonated, there would be nothing living within a five-mile radius.

Rayeanna said, "We never trained for something like this." And then she cried.

Before I entered the Springfield Memorial burn unit, I had to pass through a windowless room containing a sink with a foot-operated tap and a list of instructions. Thorough disinfecting of hands was a requirement for entry. Anyone with a communicable disease was ordered to leave.

After washing up, I stepped inside. Directly in front of me was a glass wall with a bed on the other side. In the bed lay what appeared to be a gray, granite sculpture in the shape of a reclining man. A nurse approached and asked if she could help. I said I wished to see Bradford Bradshaw. The nurse said that decision would be up to Donna, his companion, who was in the cafeteria eating lunch. Brad had just come through surgery and was resting. Then the nurse looked through the same glass pane where I had looked, and I realized that the sculpture on the bed was in fact the man I had come to see. Bradford Bradshaw, age forty-seven, a longtime Formosa employee, was the last remaining blast survivor still hospitalized.

When Donna returned, she said Brad had just learned that he had permanently lost the vision in his right eye. He was burned over 60 percent of his body. He had not yet been told about Randy Hancock's death. I decided my visit was not appropriate.

Shelley Perry oversees the tiny but well-organized Illiopolis Public Library. According to a newspaper clipping taped to the front door, she was once named Librarian of the Year. When I told Shelley she looked exactly like her picture on the door, she laughed. When I told her I needed help locating the repository of explosion-related information that the Illinois Environmental Protection Agency had established here, she laughed again. She knew all about this claim but said the library had received nothing yet. She did show me a flyer for an upcoming event. On June 16, the Illinois

EPA was hosting a public availability session to be held in the high school cafeteria. The flyer indicated that the session would focus strictly on health and environmental concerns arising from the explosion at the Formosa Plastics plant and would offer no comment on the ongoing investigation regarding its cause.

I found this don't-even-ask clause chilling. More off-putting to the Illiopolians I spoke with was the "availability" concept. Shortly after the blast in April, the village had held a bona fide public meeting that drew five hundred people. It was a worthwhile event, said those who attended. The various investigators made speeches and answered questions from the audience. By contrast, officials at the upcoming venue would be stationed at tables, and individuals would have to approach them one on one. If you just wanted to go and listen, you wouldn't learn much.

When I pulled into the high school parking lot for the availability session, it was filled with overcoifed reporters standing in front of television cameras. Once inside, I realized why the interviews were taking place outside. Without air-conditioning, the cafeteria was besieged with swarms of gnats. Everyone was sweating and waving their hands around. Nevertheless, I thought the press was missing a great photo opportunity. Formosa's table was located adjacent to the "Home of the Pirates" banner that displayed the school's mascot: a one-eyed pirate in skull-and-crossbones regalia.

I approached the Formosa table first. It was staffed by Roe Vadas, the local plant manager, Peter Gray, an environmental engineer, and Rob Thibault, the manager of corporate communications. I wanted to know what chemicals were on-site when the explosion happened. I asked the question a variety of ways—What about those storage silos? Are they full or empty right now?—and received different versions of the same response. That's business information. We're not going to go into that. That's proprietary. Some are full. And some are empty. When I asked if anyone in Illiopolis knows what kind of chemicals are stored and used at Formosa— like, say, Rayeanna Stacey, emergency response coordinator—the answers got even murkier. I was told there was something called a "risk management plan" that had been written and submitted by Formosa, but it wasn't a document that I could have. Of course Emergency Response had a copy.

The Illinois EPA table was across the room, staffed by, among others, Joe Dombrowski, the designated project manager of the ongoing environmental investigation. Yes, a written list of chemicals stored on-site at Formosa had been supplied to the IEPA. No, I couldn't have a copy, but I could file a Freedom of Information Act request. Behind the table was a map of the county over which was superimposed a series of concentric rings and arrows, with the site of the Formosa plant as the bull's-eye. This was truly interesting. It depicted wind direction and speed during the first seventy-two hours after the explosion. Essentially, during the three days the fire burned, the wind made a complete 360-degree turn. It also rained during this time. When I asked if copies of this map were available to the public or if it were posted on a Web site somewhere, the answers were no and no. When I asked if the smoke plume itself had been mapped, I was told it wasn't done that night and couldn't be done now.

The second half of that sentence was simply untrue. There are several good computer models for mapping wind-dispersion patterns of toxic materials. Radioactive fallout can be mapped. So can dioxin.

On the far side of the room were the tables for the Illinois Department of Public Health. From its representatives, I learned that no one knew whether cancer rates in this community were higher than normal and that there were no immediate plans to conduct such a study. The department would be glad to run the numbers, I was told, if someone in the community asked for that analysis to be conducted. So far, no one had.

The public availability session was starting to feel like the Q and A after a college lecture—without the lecture. To learn something, you had to come up with exactly the right question, a task I myself was failing.

I looked over at the Formosa table and decided to give it one more try. "Let me make sure I have this straight. If someone in Illiopolis came up to you and asked what chemicals you store out at your plant, your answer would be what exactly?" I received another harangue about proprietary information and corporate competitiveness. I was told I should learn something about how vinyl is made. Read a chemical engineering book. Go to vinyl.org. At some point, I quit listening because the glowering scowl on the Formosa plant manager's face came to resemble so closely that of the pirate's above our heads that I got distracted. I was trying to remember what I knew about the Formosan pirates of yore. I dimly recalled that their ships had terrorized the coasts of Taiwan during the Dutch occupation.

Outside in the parking lot, I ran into Rayeanna Stacey. I asked if Formosa had ever provided her a chemical inventory. She said no.

The first dioxin test results were made public in July. They showed higher-than-normal levels in soil collected from twelve of thirteen sites located on and around Formosa's property. The highest had dioxin concentrations of fifty parts per trillion, which is ten to fifty times greater than average background levels. By way of reassurance, the Illinois EPA's report pointed out that "the findings were not unexpected, since dioxin is commonly found when certain chemicals are burned"—as though bad news that is predictable is somehow less alarming than the kind that is not. Formosa spokesman Rob Thibault was quick to say that Formosa may not be the source of the dioxin "given the history of the site." And about this, he is certainly correct. Munitions manufacturing can also generate dioxin, and the four-mile-by-eight-mile tract of land on which Formosa sits was once the Sangamon Ordnance Plant. Between 1942 and 1945, when Illinois was the nation's leading producer of ammunition, this plant turned out fuses, propellants, boosters, and ninety-millimeter rounds.

A second round of testing found dioxin in soil samples collected from nearby sites. But the public was assured that these levels were not "significantly elevated." Washing one's hands after gardening was said to be a good idea, though.

On July 13, Formosa began loading its unexploded stockpiles of vinyl chloride and vinyl acetate into two-dozen railroad cars for transfer to its other plants. The image of ninety-ton tanker cars full of liquid explosives rattling across the plains—to where? Texas? Louisiana? Delaware? New Jersey?—was deeply unsettling. It was a reminder that the low whistle of a freight train in the night is no longer just the sound of lumber, coal, and grain on the move. Although originally laid to carry such goods, the train tracks that traverse the back yards of countless small towns and big cities are now used to transport all manner of dangerous chemicals. Each year in the United States, 1.7 million carloads of hazardous materials travel the rails. These include the highly explosive feedstocks for America's floors. According to the Argonne National Laboratory, vinyl chloride ranks 8th among the top 150 hazardous materials most heavily shipped by rail. Vinyl acetate is 25th. Ethylene dichloride is 125th. (It's an eye-opening list; other items include "molten sulfur," "bombs," and "warheads, rocket.")

Clacking tanker cars. A nostalgic train whistle. Predawn darkness. Now insert into this picture a terrorist armed with a device of the kind once manufactured by the Illiopolis plant during its incarnation as a bomb factory. It's hard to write these words—as if the very act of describing horrific possibilities has the power to make them come true. (My young children believe strongly that this is so. If they knew what I was saying here, they would cover my mouth with their hands and whisper, "Don't speak it, Mama!") But I have stood at Ground Zero, and I can easily imagine a hijacked tanker train and a major metropolitan area. I can imagine a truck, a suicide bomber, and a vat of vinyl chloride. I can imagine a PVC plant used as a weapon of mass destruction.

Such scenarios are the motivation behind various congressional chemical security bills—none of which has so far passed. Two months after 9/11, New Jersey Senator Jon Corzine drafted the Chemical Security Act. Among other things, the bill would have compelled chemical plants to assess the availability of safer alternatives to inherently dangerous technologies. After intense lobbying by the chemical industry, the bill foundered. Subsequent attempts to regulate security at chemical facilities have also run aground.

In October 2004, the Paper, Allied-Industrial, Chemical and Energy Workers International Union (PACE) released a survey that attempts to pierce the secrecy surrounding antiterrorism initiatives at U.S. chemical plants. Based on the observations of workers in 125 such plants, the union reports that while three-quarters of facilities have added guards and fences in response to 9/11, fewer than 17 percent have made changes in the design of their operations that would make chemical processes inherently safer.

It's an easy bet that the Illiopolis plant was not among that 17 percent. The week after PACE released its report, the U.S. Occupational Safety and Health Administration announced that it was charging Formosa's Illiopolis facility with forty-eight federal workplace violations. Among them: failure to repair defective equipment, inadequate inspections of equipment, insufficient training in emergency response, and poor maintenance of fire-protection equipment. Formosa said it would appeal the ruling.

Back in New York, I sweep my kitchen floor. Bending down to separate the dropped crayons from the day's crumbs, I wonder if Bradford Bradshaw— or any of his five dead coworkers—might have had a hand in stringing together the molecules that make up this floor. It's not a remote possibility. Prior to April 23, 2004, the Formosa plant in Illiopolis made fully *half* of all the flooring-grade vinyl in the United States.

Now when I look at my floral-patterned floor I think of emergency sirens that fail to go off. I imagine the hushed urgency of evacuees taking to the roads. I see tanker cars rattling through towns where unsuspecting citizens sleep. My visit to Illiopolis was a vivid illustration of how the manufacture of PVC is an ongoing source of terror for the workers and the people living in the communities where it is made. And yet, phasing out chlorine-based chemical manufacturing, in which PVC plays a starring role, will require a federal government uncorrupt enough to place the chemical security of the nation, as well as the health of all its citizens, above corporate interests.

On this last front, we are moving in exactly the wrong direction. While the idea of making chemical processes inherently safer is still being discussed by some members of Congress, the substitution of alternative, less toxic materials is not even part of the dialogue. Instead, the biggest trend since 9/11 is growing secrecy about which chemicals are used where and how they are transported. In the name of homeland security, databases that were once available to me as a researcher—data, for example, on accidents at U.S. chemical plants—have been pulled off the Web. Public knowledge about chemical manufacturing is becoming increasing limited.

At the local level, by contrast, there are some hopeful signs. In January 2005, the Washington, D.C., city council voted to ban train and truck shipments of deadly chemicals within two miles of the Capitol. Other cities are considering similar bans. One railroad company has already filed suit, and others are likely to follow. Legislation that reroutes trains carrying explosives, extreme flammables, and cargo that is known in the transportation business as TIH—toxic by inhalation—will raise the cost of transporting such poisons and may encourage a shift toward alternative materials. It also may indicate that the public is beginning to wake up to the widespread risks of large-scale toxic production, which we have, so far, passively or unknowingly accepted.

There are signs of change at the international level, too. In May 2004, the Stockholm Convention became international law. Ratified by eighty-nine nation-states (but not the U.S.), this United Nations treaty targets twelve persistent, highly toxic chemicals—including dioxin—for worldwide elimination. Many thinkers and scholars in Europe believe that there is a sober, moral obligation under the Stockholm treaty to phase out PVC entirely. Chief among them is German chemist Michael Braungart, coauthor of *Cradle to Cradle: Remaking the Way We Make Things,* who has called the manufacture of PVC a form of chemical harassment.

In my own household, I am embracing the concept with which the U.S. Green Building Council is currently grappling: vinyl avoidance. I'll start with my kitchen floor, which I will soon replace with linoleum or sustainably harvested wood. This will be my personal contribution to homeland security. More to the point, my son, now three years old, has respiratory allergies. I am as invested in protecting his security of person as I am the security of his homeland. Therefore, I also plan to strip from the walls the vinyl wallpaper left behind by the previous family and tear out the PVC-backed carpet in the playroom.

As I ponder all this, Elijah drags his box of toy trains and wooden tracks into the kitchen and excitedly describes a plan to construct a great railroad across the floor. His engines pull tankers labeled flour, oil, and molasses. Derailments are frequent. Watching his engineering project take form, I feel my own resolve stiffen. The dangers posed by PVC are real, but they are not inexorable. We need not remain a nation of Illiopolians, living just downwind of potential catastrophe.

(2005)

Radioactive Roadtrip

*A fast-paced tour through the craters and gates of the
notorious Nevada Test Site*

THE DEPARTMENT OF ENERGY'S NORTH LAS VEGAS FACILITY ON LOSEE
Road doesn't look like much from outside the fence. There's the moth-
balled fourteen-story "high bay" tower, where they used to assemble the
instrument packages that would hold nuclear devices in place for detona-
tions, but it's a bland structure that doesn't look as large as it really is unless examined closely. There are office buildings with a variety of official
signs and guard posts, but it's not until you enter the property and meet
the gentlemen from Wackenhut that you begin to appreciate the difference
between this and, say, a university research park or a chemical plant.

The Wackenhut guards, many of them former Navy SEALS and U.S.
Army Special Forces personnel, are dressed in desert camo fatigues and
carry serious sidearms. Just speaking to these guys in a booth by the parking lot makes me nervous.

Visitation to the Nevada Test Site is down to forty to eighty people per
month, most of the traffic now going to Yucca Mountain, the controversial
nuclear-waste storage site proposed to start accepting high-level radioactive
materials possibly as soon as 2005. The NTS staff is down from 12,000 to
around 2,300 people since the 1992 moratorium on testing was passed, with
300 of those DOE and other federal employees. The rest are Wackenhut
personnel and other associated contractors. Apart from its ongoing "stewardship" of the nation's nuclear stockpile—which means the testing, maintenance,
and occasional upgrading of existing warheads—what the DOE is attempting
to do is convert the NTS mission into one of commercial usage.

I am here with Matt Coolidge, director of the Center for Land Use Interpretation, a nonprofit organization that catalogs sites of unusual land use
and makes them accessible through visual documentation. As a "research
organization dedicated to finding the common ground in issues of land
use," the Center takes a neutral stance, leaving it up to viewers to frame
their own judgments—a practice that gives it access to sites and materials

that would otherwise be off limits. The CLUI's *Guide to the Nevada Test Site* is a publication valued by the DOE because it saves them time and effort, showing people what's out here without proselytizing. Matt has come to verify information for the new edition of the guidebook, and I am along for the ride.

We are intrigued by the fact that a security authorization is needed to unlock the "visitor's" center. Once inside, we watch a twenty-minute videotape of excerpts from the twelve most recent additions to the ninety declassified government films now available to the public that depict nuclear-bomb tests and "Broken Arrow" incidents. It's with some amazement that I witness recovery crews combing wreckage in Spain, Greenland, and Yuba City, California, for parts from bombs accidentally dropped and/or lost in bomber crashes. Inside the visitor's center, we find everything from photographs of petroglyphs on the Test Site to blurbs for VentureStar, a private aerospace company hoping to launch the next-generation space shuttle, an operation that the NTS is attempting to lure onto the property. A gift shop, which is closed, offers T-shirts, hats, and mugs.

Back in the DOE parking lot, we're joined by Derek Scammel, who drives up in the white Jeep Cherokee that we'll use for our tour. Scammel has become well known as a guide to the Test Site, where he's been schlepping media people around for twelve years. After minor preliminaries, we load ourselves into the Jeep and drive north toward Mercury, the town that serves as the major entry point for the Test Site. We have a minute-by-minute itinerary of the locations we are to visit, which projects us finishing around nine tonight, but Scammel thinks we'll be able to accomplish everything by sunset. The Test Site, an area about the size of Rhode Island, resides entirely within the Nellis Air Force Range, which covers an additional 4,120 square miles, a total area larger than Connecticut and almost the size of Israel.

Derek has a standard spiel for visitors but gets only part way into it before Matt begins to query him on the status of certain valleys, such as the infamous Area 51, which he's heard has been ceded by the DOE to the air force in a trade for a small extension of the Test Site into the Nellis Range. The exchange reputedly was made in order to capture some ground contaminated by the 1968 Schooner shot, a shallow underground nuclear test that sent fallout as far away as Montreal.

"Groom Lake, you mean. Only civilians call it Area 51. Yes, it's Air Force now."

When we inquire politely about radioactivity, Scammel sets up his initial lines of defense. First, we won't be exposed to enough radiation to measure during the day, as most radioactivity diminishes relatively quickly over time. Furthermore, radioactivity tends to infect metal and topsoil, most of which has been scooped up and buried. The isolated areas that are still hot we're not allowed into. Matt adds that he's traveled across parts of the Site with a person carrying a Geiger counter, including multiple grounds-zero of bomb tests, and the only radioactive thing they encountered all day was an orange Fiesta dinner plate in a display case, a ceramic brand notorious for containing traces of uranium.

"There are 42 square miles of contaminated area on the Test Site, and 106 square miles disturbed by the test program—out of a total of 1,375," Derek offers. "It's clean compared to other DOE sites, such as Rocky Flats in Colorado and Hanford in Washington."

Fifty minutes out of Las Vegas, we pass a relatively small playa, or dry lakebed, to the east. Matt explains it's used for live-fire demonstrations several times a year. "VIPs are brought in to see how the military is spending its money, and aircraft fly in from all over the country, including B-1 bombers from South Dakota, all choreographed to arrive within a forty-five-minute period to drop bombs in time to rock 'n' roll music. People sit in bleachers and watch; there's even a Jumbotron© TV screen so they can catch instant replays. The computer-game company people are really anxious to come see this stuff." Maybe up close the playa would bear scars from this high-explosive exhibitionism, but from the road it looks level and pristine, just another screen for the media upon which entertainments are projected.

At 8:10 A.M. we pass the Indian Springs Auxiliary Air Field, a small Air Force base next to the highway, and Matt continues his rolling commentary. "Look at the hangars at the north end as we pass them. This is where they deploy UAVs, the unmanned aerial vehicles that they used in Kosovo." We don't spot any today, but I've seen pictures of the $25-million Global Hawk. It's a cockpitless craft that looks like a blind albino bat, but can fly for up to thirty-five hours and as high as 65,000 feet. Made by Northrop Grumman in San Diego, it may be used mostly for intelligence gathering. The unmanned vehicles still have an unfortunate tendency to veer out of control, however, and the desert remains the safest place to test them.

The synergy of all this—the electronic-game techies filming the military explosions in the Mojave for action backdrops on video screens, games that will be played by a generation of kids who will grow up to control the computer joysticks for unmanned vehicles bombing real targets in, say, a Middle Eastern desert—is more than a little disturbing.

Our first stop is the Wackenhut office, where we check in to receive temporary passes that we clip onto our shirtfronts and show to the guard at the gate as we drive through. Except for two guys driving a fuel truck later in the day, he's the last person we'll see while we cover more than 200 miles of dirt roads through hundreds of thousands of acres.

Mercury itself is a proverbial ghost town; its bowling alley, movie house, cafeteria, and gas station—where Derek fills the tank from a pump labeled "No Brand Gasoline"—are all intact but completely empty of people. The absence of personnel is partly owing to the severe reductions in staffing after the moratorium, and partly because it's Friday. People work from seven in the morning until five in the evening, and the commutes can run up to two hours each way from Las Vegas, because no one lives on the base—a safety and security precaution. Therefore, Test Site workers pull a four-day week, and Derek is working on what should be his day off, a convenient time to show visitors around while the area is devoid of activity.

Our route today will take us first to the Buckboard Mesa area in the west-northwest quadrant, then gradually work back to the south. We start by trying to locate the ground zero of the Little Feller I explosion, the last of the above-ground nuclear tests, which was conducted in 1962. Taking the Pahute Mesa Road, then turning off on a succession of increasingly less-maintained dirt tracks, Derek has trouble pinpointing the location of the test, as it's been eight to ten years since he was last in this corner of the Site.

Matt spots a tank sitting on a ridge nearby. At first Derek thinks it's a construction vehicle, but then he sees the turret, its gun barrel drooping toward the ground. We park as close as we can and walk up to a modest wire fence surrounding the small knoll. Derek stays with the Jeep, and I wonder if he's out here so much that he tends to limit his exposure.

As we troop around the exclosure, we can't help but step on black cables of varying thickness, all leading inward to ground zero. Typically, several miles of cable, over a million dollars worth, were used during each test. What makes it possible to measure the effects of a blast is the fact that whereas radiation and electricity travel at the speed of light, the heat and pressure waves travel much slower, enabling signals from test instruments located at ground zero to outrun the vaporization front of the blast by about a foot.

Little Feller was a very low-yield device, an atomic bomb fired from a recoilless rifle mounted on an armored personnel carrier. In pictures, the shell itself looks like the cartoon of a bomb, a stubby teardrop the size of a rural mailbox with fins. Lobbed at the site, it exploded about forty feet over the tank in what's known as a military effects test, an experiment to see what the blast and radiation would do to equipment—in this case, an M48 tank from the 1950s, and its theoretical crew. The tank, while definitely askew and put out of function, is surprisingly intact.

Here's the thing about the fence, however: its perimeter has been moved. The original exclosure, which is still visible, surrounded only a few hundred square yards, but, as Derek has pointed out, rain and wind move the soil around, plus the effects of radiation are better understood all the time. The more recent boundary includes ten times as much territory. This is not comforting. Not that the cases are exactly comparable, but the nuclear disaster at the Chernobyl power plant in 1986 initially killed thirty-one people, and Soviet authorities predicted that only a few thousand more might be affected by the contamination. As of spring 2000, the Ukraine Health Ministry has declared that 3.5 million people have fallen sick or will be adversely affected as a result of the reactor explosion.

It's not that people lie so much as that bureaucracies tend to remain collectively optimistic in the face of disasters. This is because their role is to protect vested interests, whether of capital gains or political power. So it takes a while for the fences to get moved farther out, whether it's at this scale, or expanding the boundary of the Test Site itself to enclose some ground that remains inexplicably hot and on the move.

The fence posts a sign that says radcon-5, which none of us can translate, including Derek, who claims not to know what it means. It seems obvious, though: a middle range of radiation contamination. I find it surprising that we're standing within a hundred feet of a small ground zero without so much as a dosimeter, or film badge, pinned to our shirts along with our passes, which would have been the case during previous decades.

We retrace our way out to Yucca Flat, passing by a fence surrounding ground zero of the Apple II shot and noting that it's posted as radcon-10, then bear north to the largest manmade crater in America, the site of the Sedan test. Yucca Flat is the most bombed landscape on Earth, the valley where the majority of the 928 nuclear tests carried out at the Site took place. In one aerial view of the flat, I once counted at least 135 subsidence craters from underground tests, where the below-surface explosions had imploded enough material to leave behind a pockmark on the surface. The density of the testing was so high that the rims of many craters almost touch each other, some only a few feet across, others dozens of yards across. The Sedan Crater, however—the most popular tourist attraction on the Site—is entirely something else.

Among the proposed peacetime uses of nuclear power was earthmoving for large construction projects, such as a harbor in Alaska and a new ditch across Central America, the "Panatomic Canal." The series of explosions called the Plowshare Program included shallow tests, such as the Schooner shot, and deep ones like Sedan. For the latter, a 104-kiloton device was lowered 635 feet below the ground; its detonation on July 6, 1962, moved twelve million tons of earth in a millisecond. The crater is 1,280 feet wide, 320 feet deep, and hosts a viewing stand on its lip where we stop for several minutes to take pictures.

Vigorous patches of tumbleweed grow on its steep slopes, and cables lead downward, remnants from lowering various test crews, the *Apollo 14* astronauts (who practiced maneuvering around in its lunarlike environment), and even a television news team who broadcast live from the bottom of the crater as a publicity stunt.

Once again back on the road, Derek plunging back and forth on the empty and crumbling asphalt at fifty to sixty miles an hour, we stop by the fence surrounding the atmospheric Smoky test. This is one of those sites that's never been mopped up, the soil contamination too massive for a cost-effective cleanup. To enter it, you have to be escorted by safety personnel and wear protective clothing that immediately becomes low-level nuclear waste and must be placed in a storage facility. Smoky, a 9,408-pound thermonuclear device yielding forty-four kilotons, was blown up on top of a 700-foot tower in front of a mountain to see how the proximity of a geophysical feature would affect the blast pattern. The mountain behind it is gray, instead of brown like the surroundings, its soil having been blown off clear down to bedrock. The blast headed up and out to where we're standing, hence we can't see ground zero directly. We're too far away, but not at all unhappy about it.

Our last stop before lunch is Japan Town, three wooden houses built with traditional materials so the effects of radiation on victims in Hiroshima and Nagasaki could be simulated. Handsome structures in various states of collapse, they were exposed to varying levels of radiation from a bare reactor mounted atop a 1,527-foot tower. The BREN (Bare Reactor Experiment Nevada) tower, which has since been relocated to Jackass Flats, was then the tallest manmade structure in the world, and it still holds the record in America west of the Mississippi.

A few minutes down the road and we're parked for lunch at one of the "typical American homes" built for the Apple II blast. Once an entire mock town sat here: a school, a library, fire and radio stations, even a small utility grid. Unlike the "Doom Town" that was blown away by the Annie test of 1953, the footage of which has been featured in everything from civil-defense films to the movie *Atomic Cafe,* several of these structures survived.

A site that we won't visit today, although we'll be skirting its edge, is Yucca Mountain. Within the Test Site's boundaries, it's nonetheless its own administrative entity, and I ask Derek why.

"Well, it's a bit controversial politically. Senators [Richard] Bryan and [Harry] Reid, for instance, couldn't stay in office if they didn't represent to their Nevada voters that they're against bringing radioactive waste to the state. But Bryan worked here, you know, and we're standing on top of 150 million curies of radioactivity that's underneath the soil from the tests. That's far, far more than would ever be stored at Yucca Mountain.

"Our budget is voted on by Bryan and Reid. If we were tied to Yucca Mountain, it would make it harder for them to help us. So we keep things separate as much as possible. But I don't think the repository will ever open up."

"Because Nevada will turn it down?" I ask.

"No, because the waste has to be shipped across the country, and every single state it would pass through will sue to stop it."

But it might take only a single disaster at a local storage facility to change peoples' minds. As Derek points out, the waste will flow along the "line of least political resistance," and Nevada has neither the population nor enough seniority in its congressional delegation to prevent the shipments to Yucca Mountain.

After lunch, we drive by Yucca Lake, which appears untouched compared to the majority of Yucca Flat with its hundreds of craters. Although inert dummies were dropped onto the playa to test the durability of bomb casings, none of the valley's 86 aboveground or 400 underground blasts cratered its surface. Down by its far end stands a rocky outcrop known as News Nob, at the base of which are the sagging wooden bleachers where correspondents sat to watch fourteen atmospheric tests from 1951 through 1962. We pull off the road, Derek once again waiting by the Jeep while we scramble up the rocks to take pictures. From where we stand to where the bombs were detonated—from where Walter Cronkite was made speechless for the only time in his life to those mushroom clouds we've all seen pictures of—was only about three miles. Less than 16,000 feet. It seems a preposterously small distance.

It was from here that the first atomic explosion was broadcast on live television in the 1950s, and all I can imagine is that the view across the playa to ground zero must have scared the shit out of the cameramen. Think of a blast so bright that you could see the bones in your forearms crossed over your closed eyes, as if you were Lot attempting to blot out the destruction of Sodom and Gomorrah. Envision a hot thundercloud boiling up so high over you that you would have to crane back your head as far as it would go to see it. Think of the shock wave passing through you on its way to Las Vegas, only twenty-two seconds away.

Derek beeps his horn at us politely, anxious to keep moving. From our tour of what were the earliest uses of the Test Site we move on to the latest, the storage of low-level nuclear waste. Yucca Mountain, should it open, will accept only high-level radioactive waste, the stuff so hot that it slowly cooks then fractures the very rocks in which it is entombed. But then there's all the low-level stuff, such as the protective clothing worn by visitors to the Smoky site, and the mid-level contamination of equipment used in subcritical bomb tests, which are allowed to continue under current international treaties. Not as dangerous as the spent fuel rods that Yucca Mountain might have to accept, these are still by-products of the military-industrial complex that have to be stored and monitored under controlled circumstances. The low-level pits that we visit in Frenchman Flat, the next valley south, are state of the art: a broad excavation in which waste is stored in drums and boxes, stacked eight to nine deep, then buried. That simple.

Each container is bar-coded and placed within a numbered grid so that specific items can be retrieved, should it be necessary. The difference between how this waste is being handled and what's proposed at Yucca Mountain points up a heated argument within the scientific community. Entomb the high-level waste so it can spread only minimally, and with a low chance that it will be dispersed more widely by a natural catastrophe, such as an earthquake or volcanic disruption, during the tens of thousands of years its radioactivity will remain lethal. Or keep it on or near the surface so that, should new disposal technologies arise, scientists can get at it easily.

All the time we're staring down into the pit, puffy white cumuli have been coalescing into dark rain clouds spreading toward us. On the other side of the pit, a dust devil kicks up. Thin gray curtains of virga, rain that falls but fails to reach the ground, are beginning to pull down the sky. Derek keeps us moving, this time to what he calls "the pièce de la résistance," the Frenchman Flat playa, which is the larger of the two dry lakes at the NTS.

Frenchman Flat is 123 square miles in extent and even from a distance it takes three photographs with a wide-angle lens to capture its breadth. It was chosen as the site for so many aboveground tests precisely because it was large and flat enough to provide a stage upon which to view and photograph the shots. Concrete industrial buildings, an underground parking garage doubling as a mock community shelter, steel bridge trestles, a glass house, parked aircraft, railroad equipment, automobiles, and military vehicles . . . even a grove of 145 ponderosa pine trees over 150 feet tall and anchored in cement were among the objects subjected to nuclear blasts at Frenchman's. The trees are long gone, but much of the other wreckage is scattered about.

A 12'x8'x8' Mosler bank vault from San Francisco was placed on the flat for the Priscilla test in 1957, its ten-inch-thick steel door set in a steel box weighing fourteen and a half tons, which was encased in reinforced concrete several feet thick. During the same year, some 1,200 swine were kept in pens nearby, pigs having skin that most closely approximates that of humans. Anesthetized and placed at eleven stations from 2,607 to 9,405 feet from ground zero, 719 of them were subjected to Priscilla. The vault is still there; its door swung from the blast. Of the pigs, only the pens remain.

The sky is getting much darker now, the wind picking up, and we instinctively head back to the Jeep, knowing that airborne particulate matter on the Site might not be the healthiest substance to inhale.

The third and final part of the Test Site we visit, Jackass Flat, is an area of moderate usage, but interesting for the variety of work carried out there, which ranges from the $6.6-billion Yucca Mountain Project to abandoned MX missile silos.

Nuclear power from the 1950s onward has always been thought of by some scientists as having uses other than military ones. The Plowshare Program was one example, beating swords into instruments of cultivation being the metaphor. Project Rover, the development of nuclear rocket engines for interplanetary space travel, was another, and was tested here, as was Project Pluto, in which rocket engines were designed for terrestrial travel. There were two primary reasons for abandonment of the contemporaneous engine programs. First, it was impossible to achieve a cost-effective power-to-weight ratio in the craft, given the amount of shielding needed between the reactor and the pilot to keep him alive. Second, there was the little public-relations problem should one of the reactors fall uncontrollably back to Earth. But the testing was carried out, nonetheless, and the radcon level posted on the fence is 15, the highest we've seen all day.

The dark skies, which we had left temporarily at Frenchman Flat, are now catching up to us, and as we drive deeper out onto Jackass Flat, I wonder if we'll get a thunderstorm. We pass by the BREN tower, relocated from where it held the bare nuclear reactor above Japan Town. It's so skinny and tall that it makes no sense visually, looking like your average 350-foot-tall radio transmission tower. But in reality it's almost five times taller, and there's an elevator that goes to the top, a trip that must be harrowing on a structure so slender in comparison to its height.

We drive almost to the Lathrop Wells gate of the Test Site, which leads out to Highway 95 and is the primary entrance point used by Yucca Mountain workers, before we head back to exit through Mercury, a retracing demanded by security. At our turn-around point, four immense concrete cylinders lie next to each other on the ground. They're so large that the Jeep could easily drive into them, and we hike inside one and down to its far end. It's more than eerie to be standing at the bottom plate of what was to be a silo for the proposed MX Missile Program, a steel plug more than a foot thick against which the flames of the rocket would have pushed during launch.

The MX was an idea promoted by President Reagan, and despite deep and lengthy adverse public reaction, abandoned for good only when he switched allegiance to its doppelgänger, the Star Wars Program, which is still under development. The MX system would have placed hundreds of underground silos spread out over 25,000 square miles of Nevada and Utah. Employing 100,000 people to build and costing an estimated $100 billion at the start of construction, much less the finish, it would have been the largest building project in the history of humankind. The missiles were to have been shuffled from silo to silo by rail and special trucks (on highways massively reinforced to handle the load)—a ponderous shell game.

The space-based Star Wars would have used lasers to shoot down missiles. Its problem was the obverse of the MX; instead of a shell game featuring a few missiles and many launching sites, lasers would have had to cope with many decoys launched from only a few sites. All such defensive systems, including the current scheme to erect a fixed land-based missile shield, have similar numerical deficiencies in their logic. Countries capable of launching large strikes against a missile or laser shield would deploy numerous decoys, thus watering down the success ratio of the defense. Countries with smaller numbers of missiles would be encouraged to build more.

Looking around us at the empty valleys, I think it's not just politics that drives leaders to push for illogical systems. It's also a severe disconnect from reality. If the visual nature of this landscape makes it hard to understand, do we suffer from a corollary dissonance in comprehending large populations in cities? When calculating the cost, efficacy, and misery of nuclear war, are we simply unable to understand the vaporization of millions of people?

Energy at that scale is meaningless to us unless we see its effects. Just as we reduce the desert to cartography in order to subdivide it and build houses, a mathematics that does not address the shortage of water, so we reduce large energies and aggregates of humanity into numerical physics and demography. When Derek talks about 150 million curies of radiation on the Test Site, it's not only a meaningless number to me, it does not bring individual suffering into the equation. Numeracy allows us to manipulate the world while abstracting ourselves away from the consequences.

By the time we finish mulling over the size of the MX weapons, it's almost five o'clock. Derek was right—we'll get back to Las Vegas about sunset. On our way out of Jackass Flat, I keep my eye on the BREN tower, the only major vertical structure visible for miles. The radio that Derek carries has just broadcast a blanket warning over the Test Site for lightning strikes, warning everyone out here—all four of us—to stay away from tall objects. Statistically it's far more likely that we'd be struck by lightning than receive a lethal dose of radiation, yet I find lightning, a natural and visible hazard, the more acceptable threat, easier to comprehend than the invisible man-made one.

As we drive back to hand in our badges to the Wackenhut people, I ponder how our society can come to grips with this ability to effect apocalypse, especially at a time when our politicians refuse to ratify the Comprehensive Test Ban Treaty. If Civil War sites are designated as national monuments and used to educate busloads of schoolchildren about the costly calculus of war, why not the Nevada Test Site? The Sedan Crater is already listed on the National Register of Historic Places, its viewpoint a deliberate analog of those provided by the National Park Service at other scenic climaxes, including that greatest tourist hole of all, the Grand Canyon.

If people are so entranced by the military sublime that they vie with one another to see explosions and their aftermath, nuclear or not, then why not turn the place into a park and charge admission? The NTS could use the money, and nothing could be more instructive than educating Las Vegas tourists about the largest gamble in the history of mankind—that we can survive our ability to destroy all life on the planet.

(2003)

Winged Mercury and the Golden Calf

Two elements, one economic theory, and a cascading torrent of collateral damage

I

For a while in the middle of the twentieth century, economists liked to model their subject as hydrology. They built elaborate systems of pipes, pumps, and reservoirs through which water traveled, allegedly modeling the movements of money, wealth, capital. They were funny devices, stuck halfway between literal-mindedness and metaphor, and they begged many questions about the nature of economies and the nature of water. Since that time, water contamination and scarcity have become global issues, and water privatization an especially heated one. But even if you left aside all the strange things we do to water, water was never exactly a good model for economies, since the implication was that the flow of capital is natural, that money moves like water.

Even water doesn't move like water in our systems. Our economies produce lots of strange uphill pumping (as Los Angeles does with the Colorado River's water, as the Bush tax cuts do with the nation's wealth), as well as hoarding, flooding, squandering, false droughts, and unnecessary thirsts unto death. What model explains the hundred-foot yachts and fifth homes U.S. captains of industry accumulate while hunger, homelessness, lack of access to medical care, and general precariousness overtake more and more of the population? Or Bechtel Corporation privatizing the water supply in a Bolivian town and jacking up prices to the point that the poor were expected to do without—what kind of economic model is that? Could we model as a flood the uprising that forced Bechtel out?

But there's another problem with the attempt to represent wealth as water, which is that wealth was for millennia embodied for monetary societies not by the two-hydrogen, one-oxygen molecule that makes life on Earth possible, but by a true element, a heavy metal, and a fairly useless one: gold. The real movement of wealth and poverty through an economy, or at least our economy, might better be modeled by the movement of gold out of the California ecosystem during the Gold Rush and by the release of deadly mercury into the same system during the same rush.

The gold was the point. The mercury was the secret. The former yielded a one-time profit and was thereafter mostly sequestered, made into coins or worn as ornaments, not even much of a speculative commodity during the century and more that the price of gold was fixed. The latter was dispersed in all the streams in which and near which gold was mined, mercury being useful in securing the gold with the old technologies of ore refinement. More than a century and a half later, the mercury continues to spread, per-vading thousands of miles of stream and river, continually flowing with the rivers of the Gold Rush into the San Francisco Bay, and moving out-ward into the great ocean. Mercury travels from other mining operations into other water systems too, including the Salmon River in Idaho and the Amazon in Brazil. In stream, river, bay, and ocean, it enters the bodies of aquatic creatures, moves up the food chain into bigger fish, and then into other predators, including our own species, where it particularly affects the mental capacities and nervous systems of young children and unborn chil-dren, so you can say that at least indirectly gold dims the minds and drains the futures of the youngest among us. The gathering of gold then and now is the spread of mercury. The making of wealth along this extractive model is often also a far more widespread and long-lived generation of poverty.

In the popular version of the California Gold Rush, every man is free to seek his fortune, and flannel-shirted miners panning for gold in moun-tain streams strike it rich. This picturesque vision of the bearded prospector with his pick and pan is still re-enacted at places like Knott's Berry Farm amusement park near Disneyland in Orange County and celebrated in tourist-dependent towns up and down Route 49, which runs through the old Mother Lode, the gold-bearing belt in the Sierra Nevada. It's a vision of natural riches naturally distributed, a laissez-faire and free-market system in which all start out even, with the implication that all thereby have equal opportunity to benefit. It was almost nearly briefly true, if you ignore the racist laws and the violence that deprived Asians and Latinos of mining ac-cess and basic rights. Non-Europeans were subject to special taxes, denied the right to stake claims or work them independently, intimidated, lynched, driven off the richest sites, and barred from legal recourse, but their lot was far more pleasant than that of the native Californians. Bounties were paid for their scalps or ears, and they had no legal or treaty rights. (Though they owned the mother lode from which the gold came, most received noth-ing from the rush but ruin.) Disease, deracination, starvation, despair, and outright murder reduced the indigenous population by about four-fifths during those early years of the Gold Rush. So if you imagine a world in which everyone is a young white man, you can picture the gorges, ridge-lines, and canyons in which the Gold Rush unfolded as the level playing field of which free-market enthusiasts sing.

Distinguished historians once endorsed this version of the Gold Rush as a paradise of opportunity: California historian and former *Nation* editor Carey McWilliams wrote in 1949, a century after the rush began, "Few could conquer with Pizarro or sail with Drake, but the California gold rush was the great adventure for the common man." McWilliams went on to say, "Since there was no 'law of mines' in 1848, the California miners adopted their own rules and regulations in which they were careful to safeguard the equality of opportunity which had prevailed at the outset." But within a decade of James Marshall's January 1848 discovery of gold on the American River, mining in the Mother Lode shifted from simple pans and sluice boxes to complex mechanical systems. The mining organizations built larger washing devices to get the gold out of the streams, introduced hydraulic mining—the use of high-powered jets of water—to hose it out of the nearby landscape, and launched hard-rock mining operations, whose tunnels and shafts still riddle the Sierra landscape, in order to get underground ore that could then be crushed and processed in a stamp mill.

The technological changes were paralleled by a shift from individual endeavor to increasingly industrialized large-scale processes requiring capitalization and eventually producing stockholders and distant profiteers, as well as bosses and employees. By that point, it took wealth to get wealth. Charles Nordhoff in his 1873 guidebook to California mentions a three-thousand-foot tunnel dug near the Yuba River at a cost of $250,000, completed before "a cent's worth of gold could be taken out of the claim"—not the kind of investment option available to everyone. Some of the earlier photographs are astonishing. Whole rivers were diverted so that men could pick more easily at the bed, and if the economy is imagined as flowing like water, these evicted rivers provide some interesting metaphors.

Many of the men who joined the scramble for gold spent much to get to California only to become destitute or die by malnutrition, disease, violence, suicide, accident, or other typical mining-camp misfortunes. Many others became ordinary laborers working for ordinary wages, with no chance of striking it rich. It was a colorful world, with lurid newspapers published seemingly in every small town, touring singers, theaters, and even opera in San Francisco, writers like Joaquin Miller and Bret Harte, a tsunami of alcohol consumed in taverns with concomitant brawls, delirium tremens, brothels—ranging from courtesan palaces to child-rape mills—and a lot of vigilante injustice. Maybe it's all evident in the names of their mining camps. Murderer's Bar, Hangtown, Rough and Ready, and Sucker Flat all existed by 1849.

Of course the division of labor and inequality were there from the beginning. Walter Colton, a Protestant minister who had settled in Monterey when it was still part of Mexico, wrote on August 12, 1848, "Four citizens of Monterey are just in from the gold mines on Feather River, where they worked in company with three others. They employed about thirty wild Indians, who are attached to the rancho owned by one of the party. They worked precisely seven weeks and three days, and have divided $76,844— nearly $11,000 to each." That is, if you leave out the thirty who likely worked for trade goods and food. Or leave out that the Feather River ran through the territory of the Maidu, who had not sold or surrendered their land by treaty, so that all riches extracted and lands ravaged were done so illegally. Today's equivalent, the gold rush that would make Nevada, were it an independent nation, the world's third largest gold producer, is taking place on land never quite obtained from the Western Shoshone.

Perhaps the terrain of gold rushes should be described as a level playing field riddled with mineshafts and poisoned waters.

II

Just as one of those useful commentators from another culture or galaxy might perceive the purpose of drinking heavily to be the achievement of a splitting headache and furry tongue in the morning, so she might perceive mining as a way of ravaging great swaths of the land, water, and air about as thoroughly as it is possible to do. For from an ecological point of view, mining produces large-scale, long-term poverty of many kinds while producing short-term wealth for a small minority. When it comes to iron, aluminum, copper, and other metals essential for industrial society, you can argue that the mining is necessary, but about 80 percent of the world's current gold production is made into jewelry destined for India and China. The soft yellow metal has had few practical uses throughout history. The U.S. government even now has 8,134 tons hidden away and recently recommitted itself not to sell, helping to buoy up the metal's current high price (after dropping to about $250 in the 1990s, it has recently soared to more than $700 an ounce).

Gold was itself money and money was gold throughout most of Near Eastern, European, and American history, right until August 15, 1971, when President Richard Nixon took the wartime U.S. off the gold standard for various then-expedient reasons, and most of the world followed. Until then the bills that circulated were essentially receipts for gold held in vaults, and the gold coins still in circulation into the twentieth century were literally worth their weight in gold. During the long era of the gold standard, the metal was the means by which all else was quantified, the measure of all other things. Its value when extracted and abstracted from the landscape was obvious. The difficulty of quantifying the true cost of extracting it is the basic environmental failure of accounting, or maybe of money.

Contemporary accounting does sometimes speak of "externalized costs," those borne by others than the profiteers, and by this measurement the Gold Rush was very expensive. Today's environmental and social justice advocates would like to see "true cost" accounting, in which the value or cost of an item takes into account its entire impact from creation to disposal or recycling. Moves to measure costs in this way are increasing as communities begin to recognize the ways that a corporation, industry, or enterprise may bring specific benefits to their region, but may also potentially wreak pervasive or long-term damage, social and ecological. Similar analyses could be performed on many enterprises previously framed as profitable simply by asking, For whom? And who pays? For how long? You can look at an individual automobile, for example, as conveying profit to the seller and usefulness to the buyer and noxious fumes and social ills to the larger community.

The California Gold Rush clawed out of the foothills of the Sierra Nevada considerable gold—93 tons or 2.7 million troy ounces in the peak year of 1853 alone, an estimated 973 tons or 28.4 million troy ounces by 1858, more than 3,634 tons or 106 million troy ounces to date. In the course of doing so, everything in the region and much downstream was ravaged. Wildlife was decimated. Trees were cut down to burn for domestic and industrial purposes and to build the huge mining infrastructure that was firmly in place by the 1870s. That infrastructure included huge log dams to make water available on demand—the photographer Carleton Watkins took some pictures of them, looking alarmingly precarious as they stoppered deep valleys full of water. According to environmental historian Michael Black, "Within its first five years of operation, California's hydraulic cavalry dismembered whole forests to construct five thousand miles of ditches and flumes. This figure was doubled by the close of the decade." The earth was dug into desolation and later hosed out so that some landscapes—notably the Malakoff Digging and San Juan Ridge near Nevada City—are still erosive badlands of mostly bare earth. But most of all, the streams and rivers were devastated. The myriad waterways of the Sierra Nevada were turned into so much plumbing, to be detoured, dammed, redirected into sluices high above the landscape, filled with debris and toxins. Water as an industrial agent was paramount, and water as a source of life for fish, riparian creatures, downstream drinkers, farmers, and future generations was ignored.

By 1853, the Sacramento River's once prodigious salmon run was in steep decline, and so were those of most of the rest of the streams and rivers that flow into the San Francisco Bay. Black continues, "Three years later, an exasperated commissioner reported that owing to mining, fish runs on the Feather, the Yuba, and the American rivers were dead." Also in 1853, an Indian agent wrote of the native peoples in the region,

> They formerly subsisted on game, fish, acorns, etc. but it is now impossible for them to make a living by hunting or fishing, for nearly all the game has been driven from the mining region or has been killed by the thousands of our people who now occupy the once quiet home of these children of the forest. The rivers or tributaries of the Sacramento formerly were clear as crystal and abounded with the finest salmon and other fish. . . . But the miners have turned the streams from their beds and conveyed the water to the dry diggings and after being used until it is so thick with mud that it will scarcely run it returns to its natural channel and with it the soil from a thousand hills, which has driven almost every kind of fish to seek new places of resort where they can enjoy a purer and more natural element.

There was no new place of resort; the fish mostly just died off.

At the time, the costs of the Gold Rush were perfectly apparent to its witnesses; only later was it reconfigured as a frolic. As Nordhoff said in 1873,

> At Smartsville, Timbuctoo, and Rose's Bar I suppose they wash away into the sluices half a dozen acres a day, from fifty to two hundred feet deep; and in the muddy torrent which rushes down at railroad speed through the channels prepared for it, you may see large rocks helplessly rolling along. . . . Of course the acres washed away must go somewhere, and they are filling up the Yuba River. This was once, I am told by old residents, a swift and clear mountain torrent; it is now a turbid and not rapid stream, whose bed has been raised by the washings of the miners not less than fifty feet above its level in 1849. It once contained trout, but I now imagine a catfish would die in it.

The volume of mercury-tainted soil washed into the Yuba was three times that excavated during construction of the Panama Canal, and the riverbed rose by as much as eighty feet in some places. So much of California was turned into slurry and sent downstream that major waterways filled their own beds and carved new routes in the elevated sludge again and again, rising higher and higher above the surrounding landscape and turning ordinary Central Valley farmlands and towns into something akin to modern-day New Orleans: places below water level extremely vulnerable to flooding. Hydraulic mining washed downstream 1.5 billion cubic yards of rock and earth altogether. "Nature here reminds one of a princess fallen into the hands of robbers who cut off her fingers for the jewels she wears," said one onlooker at a hydraulic mine.

The Gold Rush was a huge giveaway of public or indigenous resources to private profiteers, a mass production of long-term poverty disguised as a carnival of riches. Which is to say that the profit the mining operations made was contingent on a very peculiar, if familiar, form of enterprise it might be a mistake to call free: one in which nature and the public domain could be squandered for private gain, in which the many were impoverished so that a few could be enriched, and no one was able to stop them in the name of the public, or almost no one.

Only one great battle was fought against the mining, by downstream farmers. They too were invaders transforming the landscape, but in that pre-pesticide era of farming with horse and plough, their impact was at least comparatively benign and they had, unlike any miners anywhere, an interest in the long-term well-being of the place, not to mention a useful product. The farmers took the hydraulic mining operations of the central Sierra to court for polluting the rivers, raising their beds, and rendering farms extremely vulnerable to flooding, and they won in 1884. Robert L. Kelley, in his 1959 history of the lawsuit, called it "one of the first successful attempts in modern American history to use the concept of general welfare to limit free capitalism."

III

Gold is heavy, and it sinks to the bottom of a pan, a rocker, a long tom, or whatever device you might have used to get the metal out of the stream in the early days of the California Gold Rush. Some of the gold always slipped away—unless you added mercury, also known as quicksilver, to the water and silt in your pan. The mercury amalgamated with the gold, making it easier to capture, but then some of the mercury inevitably washed downstream. With hydraulic mining, the same methods were used on far larger scales. You hosed out riverbanks, hillsides, mountainsides, breaking the very landscape down into slush and slurry that you then washed for the gold.

Then you poured mercury, one flask—seventy-five pounds—at a time, into the washing device. This was one of the most extravagant uses of mercury during the Gold Rush, and much of it escaped into the environment. With hard-rock mining, as the 1858 *California Miner's Own Handbook* describes it, you put pulverized ore into "an 'amalgamating box' containing quicksilver, and into which a dash-board is inserted that all the water, gold, and tailings may pass through the quicksilver." Here too the mercury helped capture the gold. You dissolved the amalgamation by heating it until the mercury vaporized, leaving the gold behind, and then tried to capture the vapor in a hood for reuse. Inevitably some of it would be atmospherically dispersed, and breathing mercury fumes was one of the more deadly risks of the process.

During the California Gold Rush, an estimated 7,600 tons or 15,200,000 pounds of mercury were thus deposited into the watersheds of the Sierra Nevada. The U.S. Geological Survey estimates that placer, or stream-based, mining alone put ten million pounds of the neurotoxin into the environment, while hard-rock mining accounted for another three million pounds. Much of it is still there—a U.S. Fish and Wildlife biologist once told me that he and his peers sometimes find globules the size of a man's fist in pristine-looking Sierra Nevada streams—but the rest of it ended up lining the bottom of the San Francisco Bay. Some of it is still traveling: the *San Jose Mercury News* (named after the old mercury mines there) reports that one thousand pounds of the stuff comes out of gold-mining country and into the bay every year, and another two hundred pounds comes from a single mercury mine at the south end of the bay annually. Some of this mercury ends up in the fish, and as you move up the food chain, the mercury accumulates. According to the San Francisco Estuary Institute, "Fish at the top of the food web can harbor mercury concentrations in their tissues over one million times the mercury concentration in the water in which they swim." All around the edges of the bay, warning signs are posted, sometimes in Spanish, Tagalog, and Cantonese, as well as English, but people fish, particularly poor and immigrant people, and some eat their catch. They are paying for the Gold Rush too.

Overall, approximately ten times more mercury was put into the California ecosystem than gold was taken out of it. There is something fabulous about this, or at least fablelike. Gold and mercury are brothers and opposites, positioned next to each other, elements 79 and 80, in the Periodic Table of the Elements. And they also often coexist in the same underground deposits. Gold has been prized in part because it does not rust, change, or decay, while mercury is the only metal that is liquid at

ordinary temperatures, and that liquid is, for those who remember breaking old thermometers to play with the globules, something strange, con-
gealing into a trembling mass or breaking into tiny spheres that roll in all
directions, ready to change, to amalgamate with other metals, to work its
way into the bodies of living organisms. The miners called it quicksilver for
its color and its volatility. Half gold's goodness is its inertness; it keeps to
itself. Mercury's problem is its protean promiscuity.

Gold was never more than a material and occasionally a curse in the
old stories, but Mercury was the deity who shared with his namesake element the elusive fluctuant qualities still called mercurial, and it is as the
god of commerce and thieves that he encounters the "precious" metal gold.
Perhaps in tribute to the element's talent for engendering fetal abnormali-
ties, Mercury is also the Roman counterpart to the Greek god Hermes, father of Hermaphrodite, though mercury-generated birth defects are never
so picturesque.

At least from Roman times onward, mercury was critical for many of
the processes used to isolate both gold and silver from ore. Thus mercury
was a crucial commodity, not valued in itself, but necessary for obtaining
the most valued metals. Sources of mercury were far rarer than those of
gold, and so one of the great constraints on extracting wealth from the New
World was the limited supply of mercury (in forested parts of the world,
heat could be used in gold refining, but in the fuel-poor deserts, mercury
was the only means). The Almaden Mine in Spain and then the Santa
Barbara Mine in Huancavelica, Peru, were the two major mercury sources
in the Western world from the sixteenth until the mid-nineteenth century,
and when the Spanish colonies gained their independence, they (except for
Peru, of course) lost easy access to this supply of mercury.

So dire was this lack that the Mexican government offered a reward—
$100,000 by one account—to whoever could discover a copious supply.
In the northwesternmost corner of old Mexico, in 1845, a staggeringly
rich mercury lode was discovered by one Captain Don Andres Castillero.
Located near San Jose at the southern end of the San Francisco Bay, the
New Almaden Mine was well within the territory seized by the United
States by the time it was developed. And only days before the February 2,
1848, treaty giving Mexico $15 million for its northern half was signed, gold
was also discovered in California. Thus began the celebrated Gold Rush,
which far fewer know was also a mercury rush, or that the two were deeply
intertwined.

One anonymous 1857 visitor to the New Almaden Mine published his
(or her?) observations in *Harper's Magazine* a few years later. "One of the

most curious circumstances connected with the New Almaden Mine is the effect produced by the mercurial vapors upon the surrounding vegetation," said the report.

> Despite the lofty chimneys, and the close attention that has been de-voted to the secret of effectually condensing the volatile matter, its escape from the chimneys withers all green things around. Every tree on the mountain-side above the works is dead, and some of more sensitive natures farther removed exhibit the influence of the poison in their shrunken and blanched foliage. . . . Cattle feeding within half a mile of the hacienda sicken, and become salivated; and the use of waters of a spring rising near the works is guarded against. . . . The workmen at the furnaces are particularly subjected to the poisonous fumes. These men are only able to work one week out of four, when they are changed to some other employment, and others take their place for a week. Pale, cadaverous faces and leaden eyes are the conse-quences of even these short spells; and any length of time continued at this labor effectually shortens life and impregnates the system with mercury. . . . In such an atmosphere one would seem to inhale death with every respiration.

Without the torrent of toxic mercury that poured forth from this and a few smaller mercury mines in the Coast Range, the California Gold Rush would probably have been dampened by foreign monopolies on mercury. Though the New Almaden mining operation closed more than thirty years ago, the mercury there is still leaching into the San Francisco Bay. A series of Gold Rush-era mercury mines has gravely contaminated Clear Lake a hundred and twenty miles or so to the north, where the local Pomo people have seven times as much mercury in their systems as the regional nor-mal. In many places, mercury contamination of water forces native North Americans, who have traditionally relied on marine animals and fish as pri-mary food sources, to choose between tradition and health.

Gold is the paradise of which the bankers sang; mercury is the hell hid-den in the fine print. The problem is not specific to the California Gold Rush, which only realized on a particularly epic scale in a particularly lush and pristine landscape the kinds of devastation gold and mercury can trig-ger. The current gold rush in northeastern Nevada, which produces gold on a monstrous scale—seven million ounces in 2004 alone—is also dis-persing dangerous quantities of mercury. This time it's airborne. The forty-mile-long Carlin Trend on which the gigantic open-pit gold mines are situated is a region of "microscopic gold" dispersed in the soil and rock far underground, imperceptible to the human eye, unaffordable to mine with yesteryear's technology. To extract the gold, huge chunks of the landscape are excavated, pulverized, piled up, and plied with a cyanide solution that draws out the gold. The process, known as cyanide heap-leach mining, releases large amounts of mercury into the biosphere. Wind and water meet the materials at each stage and create windblown dust and seepage, and thus the mercury and other heavy metals begin to travel.

As the Ban Mercury Working Group reports, "Though cumulatively coal fired power plants are the predominant source of atmospheric mercury emissions, the three largest point sources for mercury emissions in the United States are the three largest gold mines there." The Great Salt Lake, when tested in 2004, turned out to have astonishingly high mercury levels, as did wild waterways in Idaho, and Nevada's gold mines seem to be the culprit. The *Reno Gazette-Journal* reported that year, "The scope of mercury pollution associated with Nevada's gold mining industry wasn't discovered until the EPA changed rules in 1998 to add mercury to the list of toxic discharges required to be reported. When the first numbers were released in 2000, Nevada mines reported the release of 13,576 pounds in 1998. Those numbers have since been revised upward to an estimated 21,098 pounds, or more than 10 tons, to make Nevada the nation's No. 1 source of mercury emissions at the time." Glen Miller, a professor of natural resources and environmental science at the University of Nevada, Reno, estimates that since 1985, the eighteen major gold mines in the state released between 70 and 200 tons of mercury into the environment.

Maybe some of this is already evident in the Greek myth of King Midas. Dionysus, the god of wine and revelry, gave Midas a single wish and regretted the mortal's foolish choice: the ability to turn anything he touched into gold. The rest is familiar. The king transformed all he touched so that what he tried to drink became gold when it touched his lips, and his thirst grew intolerable. Worse yet, he touched his daughter and his greed turned her to inanimate metal, and it was with this that he begged the god to take back his gift, resigned his crown and power, and became a rural devotee of the god Pan. In this ancient tale, gold is already associated with contaminated water and damaged children.

Midas is mythological, but true tales of gold-as-horror checker the history of the Americas. There is an extraordinary print from Girolamo Benzoni's 1565 *La Historia del Mondo Nuovo,* a report by an embittered witness to fifteen years of Spanish colonization. In the image, unclothed native men, tired of being savagely forced to produce gold, pour the molten metal down the throat of a captive Spaniard in pantaloons. Thus literal fulfillment of a hunger for wealth leads to death, and thus revenge for the brutality of the gold economy begins in the Americas. Another tale comes from the Death Valley Forty-Niners, seeking an easy and finding a hard route to the California gold fields. On their parched sojourn across the desert, one gold-seeker abandoned $2,500 in gold coins to lighten his load in the hopes that thus unburdened he might make it to water and life. Another of these desperados snapped at his companion that he had no interest in what looked like gold-bearing ore along the route through the dry lands: "I want water; gold will do me no good."

Gold is a curse in Exodus too, when the Israelites, having lost faith during their pilgrimage in the desert, come to worship the golden calf made out of melted-down jewelry. Moses comes down from the mountaintop, grinds the golden idol into powder, throws it into a stream, and forces them to drink it.

For us, perhaps the golden calf is the belief that the current economic system produces wealth rather than poverty. It's the focus on the gold to the exclusion of the mercury.

(2006)

In the Name of Restoration

M Y FIRST TIME IN PRINCE WILLIAM SOUND, I FELT AS JOHN MUIR must have when, one hundred years ago, he named it a "bright and spacious wonderland." I was filled with wonder at long fjords of clear cold waters threading between steep verdant mountains; at vast ice fields held in jagged peaks from which glaciers poured to the sea; at ancient ice calving like thunder from those glaciers; at the abundance of fish and marine mammals that thrived in this rich yet harsh landscape, the northernmost reach of the temperate rainforest.

And I was amazed at how untouched it seemed: so few people ventured into those waters; so few even knew of its existence. On those trips fourteen years ago, I spent days in the Sound without seeing any sign of humans. It was this place that compelled me to stay in Alaska, to settle here, find work and home and community. It is this place to which I return every summer, drawn to it as one is drawn to love.

It is also this place that, ten years ago, suffered the most damaging oil spill in history: forty thousand tons of crude oil spread along 1,500 miles of remote coastline. Now the mark of a decade is upon it, a decade of attempts to heal the place.

How well have we done? The focal point of public attention has been the billion-dollar natural resource settlement managed by the Exxon Valdez Oil Spill Trustee Council, state and federal agency representatives charged with restoration. This money was not to be used to compensate people harmed by the spill, but solely for the place and its wild inhabitants. To restore the wild, reverse the damage.

Eight years after the spill, I traveled to southwestern Prince William Sound to write a silver-lining story for a newspaper: $34 million of the restoration money had been used to protect sixty thousand acres of virgin rainforest from clear-cutting. I was elated to return to one of my favorite areas of the Sound, for good news, bright and shining news. This area was ground zero of the spill: first and hardest hit. The vast majority of the oil came ashore here, where most of the Sound's salmon pour into in spring, where millions of birds migrate through, where orcas and humpbacks and Steller sea lions congregate.

But on that trip to the heart of the spill zone my worst fears were realized: much of what has been funded has not been restoration. It has instead, as *Scientific American* put it, been a "scientific fiasco." We have not acted in the best interests of the place, but have instead fallen prey to short-term self-interest—the same self-interest that caused the spill in the first place.

When I arrived, Roger Stowell, my guide, took me to Ewan Bay, one of five watery fingers off Dangerous Passage, where a reversing waterfall links the bay to an oval lagoon. On an outgoing tide, the water pours into the bay, reaching a height of ten feet. When the tide turns, the water flow reverses, rushing to make the water level in the lagoon equal to that of the bay. Evening light sifted golden through tall spruce and hemlock, and a bloom of lion's mane jellyfish floated beneath our boat; on our way out we came upon a sea otter, mother with pup on her belly. I felt as if I had returned to paradise.

The next morning we headed to Sleepy Bay, a north-facing curve of beach on Latouche Island. The day was warm and the waters flat; we passed a pod of orcas feeding in Montague Strait. But at Sleepy Bay, the scene shocked and saddened me. Multicolored booms in three parallel half-circles cordoned off a beach. A dozen people, dressed in bright yellow raingear though there wasn't a cloud in the sky, milled around on shore, wielding buckets and long pipes. The intensity of human activity contrasting with all other beaches we had passed, was all too familiar. In 1989, nearly every beach looked like this.

Sleepy Bay has endured all attempts to get the oil out. In 1990, I watched bulldozers move rocks, digging into the beach to uncover oil for hot water to wash away. The beach wasn't cleaned so much as rebuilt, left scrubbed and sterile. And still it held oil. In the summer of 1998, when other wild salmon stocks finally returned to the Sound, the stream at Sleepy Bay was empty. It should have held hundreds of spawning salmon.

I was not surprised oil still stuck to this beach. It clings to Green, Knight, Montague, and many other islands as well. I was surprised, however, that we were still trying to extract it, that after billions spent on cleanup we still had this much faith in the power of technology.

On shore, we were immediately approached by three white men wearing hard hats and jeans. At first they acted guardedly, asking us who we were, what we wanted. But then, lured by the promise of a picture in the paper, they began showing us the latest oil cleanup technology, a new kind of drill pipe that was supposed to get the oil out from beneath the rocks, oil eight years old, oil that months of hand-scrubbing, summers of cold and hot water washing, years of biochemical treatment, had not budged.

While I listened to them talk of their invention, my attention was drawn beyond them to ten residents of Chenega Bay, Aleuts, dressed in protective gear, trying to clean this beach that, before the oil, they frequented to collect mussels and kelp, fish for salmon, hunt deer. They were silent. Only one spoke briefly, turning over a rock to show me oil glistening beneath, as fresh as if it had washed up yesterday.

On our way to Sleepy Bay we had passed Old Chenega, where the 1964 earthquake's tsunamis swept away twenty-three of the townspeople and so many buildings that the town was abandoned. Now residents of Chenega Bay, the new village, travel there once a year for three days to remember the dead. Now, too, they continue to clean up from the oil spill, which hit them twenty-five years to the day after the earthquake.

When we left, I looked back and saw the villagers sitting in a row on beach logs like cormorants on a rock ledge, eating lunch, staring out to sea. I wondered, did they see a better way to restore the Sound? Or were they as frustrated as I was?

I was grateful to leave that scene and head to Jackpot Bay, where I anticipated experiencing the newly protected place in solitude. Off Dangerous Passage, Jackpot spreads into a series of waterways, some connected like a string of pearls by narrow passages, another widening to embrace a massive waterfall, and one curving back to a small stream. When I'd been there four years earlier, the only evidence of humans I'd seen had been two small fishing boats.

What we found this time, though, made my heart heavy. Near the mouth of the stream, a small settlement had risen: three large wall tents, a couple of buoys on the water, a gas can on the beach, a bright blue tarp covering three fuel barrels, and trails crisscrossing the small headland. This was a research camp, Roger told me, peopled all summer.

We boated ashore and were met by three young graduate students, here for the summer helping with the pigeon guillemot project. Funded by the Trustee Council as restoration work, they studied a colony of these seabirds, whose population was devastated by the spill, on an islet in the middle of the bay. Every morning, these researchers climbed the island, found tunnels in which the birds nest, and reached their hands and arms inside, groping for eggs. They counted them. Later they would capture and band the chicks that hatch.

To my amazement, they weren't able to tell me what they hoped to learn from the project, or how their work might help the bird recover. They were uncomfortable with us, edgy. Another boat appeared, with the project director aboard. One of them took the skiff out and didn't return, though I asked her to see if I could talk with the director.

"He's probably giving her a hard time for talking with you," the other two told me. It was strange, as if they were hiding something.

Later I figured it out: They hid nothing. That's the problem. They could show no benefit, no restoration—just data and banded birds. Every day on that trip, we saw research boats and research camps. Before the spill, only a few researchers worked in the Sound. Now, though, with funds from the settlement, cadres of scientists study guillemots, river otters, sea otters, mussels, herring. All a result of the spill, of the $1 billion natural resource settlement. And few have helped the animals.

That evening I lay in my bunk, so upset I couldn't sleep. I recalled the last time I was in this place. It was four years after the oil spill, and I was aware that there were fewer seals, sea otters, birds. But I believed it was healing. Wounds take time, undisturbed time, to heal. I thought that, after the frenetic first two years' $2-billion cleanup and $15-million damage assessment, the Sound was now getting that undisturbed time to heal.

I was wrong. Eight years after the spill, more research went on in the Sound than did four years earlier. Now, instead of damage assessment, it is called restoration. Now there is a pot of money to fund it. Now dozens of projects employ hundreds of people during the season. The spill spawned a new industry whose center is here.

But it is not restoration. They are not working in the best interest of the wildlife, the wildlife that exists here and now. They are instead picking at the wound, keeping it open, creating new wounds. Yes, we know more about these animals being counted and darted, poked and prodded. But what good is that knowledge? They aren't more protected from oil spills; their lives aren't better, safer. Of dozens of affected species, only one, the bald eagle, has recovered.

Their lives are, instead, harder for all this research, much of it intensely intrusive. Harlequins, strikingly marked sea ducks, have suffered severe reproductive failure since the spill, and no one knows why. So the Trustee Council funded the "harlequin roundup": in the spring, when the birds are molting and flightless, researchers in kayaks circle a flock of swimming ducks and herd them into nets. Once caught, they have radio transmitters implanted in their bellies, and are released. So far, most have died.

Others have died in the name of restoration as well: sea otters, salmon, scoters, harbor seals. Hundreds of seabirds were shot and strapped with transmitters so researchers could chart where dead birds go. Harbor seals and Steller sea lions—now listed as endangered—were declining before the spill, likely from diminished food sources caused by overfishing. Oil-slicked haulouts exacerbated matters. Shortly after the spill, nearly two-dozen seals were "collected" so their stomach contents could be studied. Many others have since been captured and burdened with radios and antennas on their backs.

We define restoration as restitution for a loss, as returning to a previous and more desirable state, as renewing, giving back. These research projects, these vivisections, not only fail to do that—they make things worse. But, as with the high-technology beach cleanup, we continue to put our money—the Sound's money—into them. As one letter to the editor in the *Anchorage Daily News* said, "Research should not be the legacy of the spill; Prince William Sound should."

Unfortunately, intrusive research isn't the most blatant misuse of restoration money. There's the Seward Sealife Center, an aquarium touted as a research facility where tourists can see puffins and river otters and harbor seals. How is caging wild animals considered restoration? Of the $50 million it took to build the aquarium, $38 million came from the restoration fund. Each year, millions of dollars from the fund will go to support it. For one research project, healthy river otters have been captured and caged, and are being fed oiled food, after which their blood is tested—this to give researchers a benchmark for interpreting the blood samples they've already collected from otters in the Sound. In response to a letter in the *Daily News* denouncing this project, a researcher wrote that "we don't know whether oil affects river otters." Of course we do.

The money has been used to fund other buildings; in fact, nearly every community in the spill zone has a new facility from these funds. In Kodiak, it's a multimillion dollar industrial technology center; in Seward, a commercial shellfish hatchery. This isn't about restoration; it's about a pot of money, and everyone wants some.

In the latest round, the Trustee Council has set aside $140 million for a "Restoration Reserve," money that can be stretched to last for decades to, as one Trustee Council member said, "fund research by scientists who are still in grade school." They ought to be honest. They ought to call it the Research Reserve.

Many who clamor for a piece don't even link their request to restoration. An esteemed former legislator is pushing to use the reserve for science

education throughout the state. Letters from University of Alaska professors asking for an endowment ignore restoration as well; one professor says
only it "would serve the state well, now and in the future . . . the university
lags behind state development." It's about tenure and job security. It's about
self-interest, and short-term self-interest at that. It's not about the health of
the wild.

At a national Environmental History conference last August, sponsored by
the University of Alaska Anchorage, a panel discussed the *Exxon Valdez* oil
spill. Walt Parker, who has worked in oil transportation safety issues since
the inception of the Trans-Alaska Pipeline, said the risk of an oil spill in
Prince William Sound is greater now than in 1989. While much has been
spent on response, little has been spent on prevention. The pipeline is older
and less sturdy, and although the Oil Pollution Act of 1990 established new
tanker standards, including double hulls, none have been built.

"It was an old fleet in 1989," he said, "and now it's even older. The North
Pacific are the roughest waters in the world. These tankers have been operating in them now for another decade."

The best we can do for Prince William Sound is to do everything possible to prevent such a spill from recurring. We're not doing that. Instead
we're flushing beaches, sticking our hands in burrows, rounding up and
capturing, and implanting transmitters. All this science isn't restoration. It's
science.

At the same panel discussion, Stan Senner, science coordinator for the
Trustee Council, said, "Most of the recovery has and will come from natural
processes." This is clear admission that science can't fix it, that humans can't
fix it, from those responsible for restoration. So, what good are the buildings, science projects, beach cleanups paid for with restoration money?

Senner justifies the research by saying it "provides information that will
enable us to sustain the ecosystem over time." But we have no proof that
we can "sustain the ecosystem." Rather, we have the illusion that observing animals somehow helps them recover. The bald eagle recovered without
any help from science—all science did was record it. And few restorative
management decisions have come from ten years' worth of research.

What's worse, those decisions made are often baffling and contradictory.
This year, the river otter was moved to the "recovered" list and six were captured and caged in the aquarium for research, while at the same time river
otter trapping in the Sound was, for the first time ever, restricted.

If, as even Senner said, the Sound will recover of itself, the best restoration may be to simply let it be. We could limit the number of people in

the Sound, the number of boats and camps—a permit system, like Denali National Park's. I'd be willing, even if it meant I couldn't go there every summer. In the name of restoration, I'd be willing.

But things are heading in the opposite direction. The state is building a road connecting the highway system to Prince William Sound at Whittier, only forty miles south of Anchorage. It's estimated that the numbers of boats and people in the Sound will increase from 100,000 to more than 1.4 million a year. There will be more boats than river otters, more people than pigeon guillemots.

The Trustee Council did not make a move to stop this road, though only four lines in the road's Environmental Impact Statement were devoted to effects on the Sound, though even the researchers in Jackpot Bay said the road may do more damage than the oil. Despite their charge to restore the Sound, the Council did nothing to prevent what promises to be the next disaster.

It is hard to accept limits, limits to what we can do, to what we think we can do. It is hard to accept that the best thing may be to do nothing. This is why it's hard for us to see that so much of what goes on in the name of restoration does not help.

Of all that the Trustee Council has funded, habitat protection is the only thing that helps the place without inflicting more damage. Like double hulls and better-trained crews, it is prevention. But as my friend David says, if we consider the Sound a patient, then we ought to remember the healer's Hippocratic Oath: First, do no more harm.

With habitat protection, coastal forests slated for clear-cutting can be saved. Forests connected to oiled beaches and waterways; forests in whose streams spawning salmon lay eggs, the fry returning to the Sound; forests in whose trees nest birds who feed upon the fish in the Sound; forests along whose edges are fragile intertidal areas, nurseries where fresh and saltwater meet; forests entwined with the sea in mutually dependent relation: all can be saved.

Habitat protection allows for what we most need to restore: our relationship with the place. Not through management, and the arrogance to think we know what's best: that's what we use to justify science and technology. And not through a total absence of human interaction with the place. Restoring our right relationship with Prince William Sound requires learning, or remembering, a way to be in the natural world that doesn't desecrate or overrun, but that maintains and respects.

We find it through attentive love: through action based on the love that comes from awareness of what the place and its inhabitants need and desire. Attentive love requires an ethic of humility. It sees excessive control as a liability; it reveres the process of life; it knows that sometimes it's best to do nothing. Scientists like Barbara McClintock and Jane Goodall have shown us this ethic: McClintock says she listened to the corn, Goodall let herself be guided by the chimpanzees.

Attentive love requires a patient regard for an other who demands preservation and growth. It is how we raise our children. It requires faith in ourselves and in the beloved. And many people do it, in small and un-recognizable ways each day. Consider Roger who was constantly aware, constantly noticing every small thing about the place he has chosen to in-habit and be inhabited by. Having lived in the Sound eighteen years, Roger knew every inch. As he took me along Dangerous Passage, he stopped near a small island in Paddy Bay.

"There," he pointed to a tall Sitka spruce. "See the eagle's nest? This is the thirteenth summer they've nested here." At the mouth of Eshamy, he pointed out a spit of land. "A few falls ago," he told me, "I caught five bear hunters camped there. I chased them off, told them no hunting allowed on this land." He told me stories of catching kayakers littering and boaters dumping used oil. It had once been his job to patrol these waters, I knew, but I sensed that he would continue no matter who the owner was: in his eyes, the needs of the land don't change.

In attentive love, the natural world remains wild. As Jack Turner says in *The Abstract Wild,* "A place is wild when its order is created according to its own principles of organization—when it is self-willed land." Attentive love enhances this self-willed nature by only doing what is asked.

But we have to listen. Imagine the Trustee Council meeting to decide about research funding not in a conference room in Anchorage, but on the beach at Sleepy Bay, or by the stream at Jackpot Bay. Never before have they gone to the Sound as the Council. Imagine, though, that they each watched harlequin ducks in their habitat before deciding whether to fund another roundup. Imagine a gathering each year like the gathering of earth-quake survivors at Old Chenega: remembering and honoring. Imagine such a gathering for the tenth anniversary of the oil spill, instead of the two-day technology conference in Valdez or the three-day science conference in Anchorage.

If we listen, the Sound will tell us that we don't need to capture harle-quins, we don't need to band pigeon guillemots, we don't need to excavate beaches. The Sound will show us other paths of restoration.

On my last morning, Roger took me to a small beach on Chenega Island. I walked into the forest, following a small stream crossed with fallen logs and bending branches. Abandoning the stream, I followed an animal trail around boulders and up a steep bank. Sounds were muffled by thick moss: at my feet, on the branches, on the trunks around me. Every limb I touched felt mossy soft, wet and green. Walking was slow, for moss hid a tangle of fallen limbs and rocks.

I looked up at shafts of light pouring down upon small patches of the forest. So little light and sound in the middle of the day. One tree, larger than the rest, held several large moss platforms in its arms. I wondered if any were the nests of marbled murrelets.

Deep in the darkness of trees, marbled murrelets nest. They are small seabirds, indistinguishable as they bob on the ocean. But they are amazing. They spend days out at sea, then fly back into the old-growth spruce and hemlock forests, reaching speeds of one hundred miles an hour, little bolts of brown feather bodies among thick stands of rainforest trees. Zip. Into the forest. Zip. Out to sea, to feed on the fish. Like needle and thread, sewing together land and sea.

I paused at the base of the tree, and, not able to find steady footing, grabbed hold of the trunk. I leaned into it, tried to encircle it with my arms, but could not. It was more than six arm-lengths in circumference. Old growth, over five hundred years old—this tree was protected now. No one will cut it down and sell its thick old wood. An earthquake might fell it, a tsunami, but not a chainsaw. Even if a marbled murrelet did not now nest in it, one could. Even if a river otter didn't make the trail I followed back down to the stream, one could. It is the possibility of the wild that gives me hope. That this purchase, and others like it, leave open the possibility for the wild to live unhindered. That sounds like restoration.

(1999)

 Native

The Idea of a Local Economy

L ET US BEGIN BY ASSUMING WHAT APPEARS TO BE TRUE: THAT THE so-called "environmental crisis" is now pretty well established as a fact of our age. The problems of pollution, species extinction, loss of wilderness, loss of farmland, loss of topsoil may still be ignored or scoffed at, but they are not denied. Concern for these problems has acquired a certain standing, a measure of discussability, in the media and in some scientific, academic, and religious institutions.

This is good, of course; obviously, we can't hope to solve these problems without an increase of public awareness and concern. But in an age burdened with "publicity," we have to be aware also that as issues rise into popularity they rise also into the danger of oversimplification. To speak of this danger is especially necessary in confronting the destructiveness of our relationship to nature, which is the result, in the first place, of gross oversimplification.

The "environmental crisis" has happened because the human household or economy is in conflict at almost every point with the household of nature. We have built our household on the assumption that the natural household is simple and can be simply used. We have assumed increasingly over the last five hundred years that nature is merely a supply of "raw materials," and that we may safely possess those materials merely by taking them. This taking, as our technical means have increased, has involved always less reverence or respect, less gratitude, less local knowledge, and less skill. Our methodologies of land use have strayed from our old sympathetic attempts to imitate natural processes, and have come more and more to resemble the methodology of mining, even as mining itself has become more technologically powerful and more brutal.

And so we will be wrong if we attempt to correct what we perceive as "environmental" problems without correcting the economic oversimplification that caused them. This oversimplification is now either a matter of corporate behavior or of behavior under the influence of corporate behavior. This is sufficiently clear to many of us. What is not sufficiently clear, perhaps to any of us, is the extent of our complicity, as individuals and especially as individual consumers, in the behavior of the corporations.

What has happened is that most people in our country, and apparently most people in the "developed" world, have given proxies to the corporations to produce and provide *all* of their food, clothing, and shelter. Moreover, they are rapidly giving proxies to corporations or governments to provide entertainment, education, child care, care of the sick and the elderly, and many other kinds of "service" that once were carried on informally and inexpensively by individuals or households or communities. Our major economic practice, in short, is to delegate the practice to others.

The danger now is that those who are concerned will believe that the solution to the "environmental crisis" can be merely political—that the problems, being large, can be solved by large solutions generated by a few people to whom we will give our proxies to police the economic proxies that we have already given. The danger, in other words, is that people will think they have made a sufficient change if they have altered their "values," or had a "change of heart," or experienced a "spiritual awakening," and that such a change in passive consumers will cause appropriate changes in the public experts, politicians, and corporate executives to whom they have granted their political and economic proxies.

The trouble with this is that a proper concern for nature and our use of nature must be practiced not by our proxy-holders, but by ourselves. A change of heart or of values without a practice is only another pointless luxury of a passively consumptive way of life. The "environmental crisis," in fact, can be solved only if people, individually and in their communities, recover responsibility for their thoughtlessly given proxies. If people begin the effort to take back into their own power a significant portion of their economic responsibility, then their inevitable first discovery is that the "environmental crisis" is no such thing; it is not a crisis of our environs or surroundings; it is a crisis of our lives as individuals, as family members, as community members, and as citizens. We have an "environmental crisis" because we have consented to an economy in which by eating, drinking, working, resting, traveling, and enjoying ourselves we are destroying the natural, the god-given world.

We live, as we must sooner or later recognize, in an era of sentimental economics and, consequently, of sentimental politics. Sentimental communism holds in effect that everybody and everything should suffer for the good of "the many" who, though miserable in the present, will be happy in the future for exactly the same reasons that they are miserable in the present.

Sentimental capitalism is not so different from sentimental communism as the corporate and political powers claim. Sentimental capitalism holds in effect that everything small, local, private, personal, natural, good, and beautiful must be sacrificed in the interest of the "free market" and the great corporations, which will bring unprecedented security and happiness to "the many"—in, of course, the future.

These forms of political economy may be described as sentimental because they depend absolutely upon a political faith for which there is no justification, and because they issue a cold check on the virtue of political and/or economic rulers. They seek, that is, to preserve the gullibility of the people by appealing to a fund of political virtue that does not exist. Communism and "free-market" capitalism both are modern versions of oligarchy. In their propaganda, both justify violent means by good ends, which always are put beyond reach by the violence of the means. The trick is to define the end vaguely—"the greatest good of the greatest number" or "the benefit of the many"—and keep it at a distance.

The fraudulence of these oligarchic forms of economy is in their principle of displacing whatever good they recognize (as well as their debts) from the present to the future. Their success depends upon persuading people, first, that whatever they have now is no good, and second, that the promised good is certain to be achieved in the future. This obviously contradicts the principle—common, I believe, to all the religious traditions—that if ever we are going to do good to one another, then the time to do it is now; we are to receive no reward for promising to do it in the future. And both communism and capitalism have found such principles to be a great embarrassment. If you are presently occupied in destroying every good thing in sight in order to do good in the future, it is inconvenient to have people saying things like "Love thy neighbor as thyself" or "Sentient beings are numberless, I vow to save them." Communists and capitalists alike, "liberal" and "conservative" capitalists alike, have needed to replace religion with some form of determinism, so that they can say to their victims, "I am doing this because I can't do otherwise. It is not my fault. It is inevitable." The wonder is how often organized religion has gone along with this lie.

The idea of an economy based upon several kinds of ruin may seem a contradiction in terms, but in fact such an economy is possible, as we see. It is possible however, on one implacable condition: the only future good that it assuredly leads to is that it will destroy itself. And how does it disguise this outcome from its subjects, its short-term beneficiaries, and its victims? It does so by false accounting. It substitutes for the real economy, by which we build and maintain (or do not maintain) our household, a symbolic economy of money, which in the long run, because of the self-interested manipulations of the "controlling interests," cannot symbolize or account for anything but itself. And so we have before us the spectacle of unprecedented "prosperity" and "economic growth" in a land of degraded farms, forests, ecosystems, and watersheds, polluted air, failing families, and perishing communities.

This moral and economic absurdity exists for the sake of the allegedly "free" market, the single principle of which is this: commodities will be produced wherever they can be produced at the lowest cost, and consumed wherever they will bring the highest price. To make too cheap and sell too high has always been the program of industrial capitalism. The idea of the global "free market" is merely capitalism's so-far-successful attempt to enlarge the geographic scope of its greed, and moreover to give to its greed the status of a "right" within its presumptive territory. The global "free market" is free to the corporations precisely because it dissolves the boundaries of the old national colonialisms, and replaces them with a new colonialism without restraints or boundaries. It is pretty much as if all the rabbits have now been forbidden to have holes, thereby "freeing" the hounds.

The "right" of a corporation to exercise its economic power without restraint is construed, by the partisans of the "free market," as a form of freedom, a political liberty implied presumably by the right of individual citizens to own and use property.

But the "free market" idea introduces into government a sanction of an inequality that is not implicit in any idea of democratic liberty: namely that the "free market" is freest to those who have the most money, and is not free at all to those with little or no money. Wal-Mart, for example, as a large corporation "freely" competing against local, privately owned businesses has virtually all the freedom, and its small competitors virtually none.

To make too cheap and sell too high, there are two requirements. One is that you must have a lot of consumers with surplus money and unlimited wants. For the time being, there are plenty of these consumers in the "developed" countries. The problem, for the time being easily solved, is simply to keep them relatively affluent and dependent on purchased supplies.

The other requirement is that the market for labor and raw materials should remain depressed relative to the market for retail commodities. This means that the supply of workers should exceed demand, and that the land-using economy should be allowed or encouraged to overproduce.

To keep the cost of labor low, it is necessary first to entice or force country people everywhere in the world to move into the cities—in the manner prescribed by the United States' Committee for Economic Development after World War II—and second, to continue to introduce labor-replacing technology. In this way it is possible to maintain a "pool" of people who are in the threatening position of being mere consumers, landless and also poor, and who therefore are eager to go to work for low wages—precisely the condition of migrant farm workers in the United States.

To cause the land-using economies to overproduce is even simpler. The farmers and other workers in the world's land-using economies, by and large, are not organized. They are therefore unable to control production in order to secure just prices. Individual producers must go individually to the market and take for their produce simply whatever they are paid. They have no power to bargain or make demands. Increasingly, they must sell, not to neighbors or to neighboring towns and cities, but to large and remote corporations. There is no competition among the buyers (supposing there is more than one), who *are* organized, and are "free" to exploit the advantage of low prices. Low prices encourage overproduction as producers attempt to make up their losses "on volume," and overproduction inevitably makes for low prices. The land-using economies thus spiral downward as the money economy of the exploiters spirals upward. If economic attrition in the land-using population becomes so severe as to threaten production, then governments can subsidize production without production controls, which necessarily will encourage overproduction, which will lower prices— and so the subsidy to rural producers becomes, in effect, a subsidy to the purchasing corporations. In the land-using economies production is further cheapened by destroying, with low prices and low standards of quality, the cultural imperatives for good work and land stewardship.

This sort of exploitation, long familiar in the foreign and domestic economies and the colonialism of modern nations, has now become "the global economy," which is the property of a few supranational corporations. The economic theory used to justify the global economy in its "free market" version is again perfectly groundless and sentimental. The idea is that what is good for the corporations will sooner or later—though not of course immediately—be good for everybody.

That sentimentality is based in turn upon a fantasy: the proposition that the great corporations, in "freely" competing with one another for raw materials, labor, and market share, will drive each other indefinitely, not only toward greater "efficiencies" of manufacture, but also toward higher bids for raw materials and labor and lower prices to consumers. As a result, all the world's people will be economically secure—in the future. It would be hard to object to such a proposition if only it were true.

But one knows, in the first place, that "efficiency" in manufacture always means reducing labor costs by replacing workers with cheaper workers or with machines.

In the second place, the "law of competition" does *not* imply that many competitors will compete indefinitely. The law of competition is a simple paradox: Competition destroys competition. The law of competition implies that many competitors, competing on the "free market" will ultimately and inevitably reduce the number of competitors to one. The law of competition, in short, is the law of war.

In the third place, the global economy is based upon cheap long-distance transportation, without which it is not possible to move goods from the point of cheapest origin to the point of highest sale. And cheap long-distance transportation is the basis of the idea that regions and nations should abandon any measure of economic self-sufficiency in order to specialize in production for export of the few commodities or the single commodity that can be most cheaply produced. Whatever may be said for the "efficiency" of such a system, its result (and I assume, its purpose) is to destroy local production capacities, local diversity, and local economic independence.

This idea of a global "free market" economy, despite its obvious moral flaws and its dangerous practical weaknesses, is now the ruling orthodoxy of the age. Its propaganda is subscribed to and distributed by most political leaders, editorial writers, and other "opinion makers." The powers that be, while continuing to budget huge sums for "national defense," have apparently abandoned any idea of national or local self-sufficiency, even in food. They also have given up the idea that a national or local government might justly place restraints upon economic activity in order to protect its land and its people.

The global economy is now institutionalized in the World Trade Organization, which was set up, without election anywhere, to rule international trade on behalf of the "free market"—which is to say on behalf of the supranational corporations—and to *overrule,* in secret sessions, any national or regional law that conflicts with the "free market." The corporate program of global free trade and the presence of the World Trade Organization have legitimized extreme forms of expert thought. We are told confidently that if Kentucky loses its milk-producing capacity to Wisconsin, that will be a "success story." Experts such as Stephen C. Blank, of the University of California, Davis, have proposed that "developed" countries, such as the United States and the United Kingdom, where food can no longer be produced cheaply enough, should give up agriculture altogether.

The folly at the root of this foolish economy began with the idea that a corporation should be regarded, legally, as "a person." But the limitless destructiveness of this economy comes about precisely because a corporation is *not* a person. A corporation, essentially, is a pile of money to which a number of persons have sold their moral allegiance. As such, unlike a person, a corporation does not age. It does not arrive, as most persons finally do, at a realization of the shortness and smallness of human lives; it does not come to see the future as the lifetime of the children and grandchildren of anybody in particular. It can experience no personal hope or remorse, no change of heart. It cannot humble itself. It goes about its business as if it were immortal, with the single purpose of becoming a bigger pile of money. The stockholders essentially are usurers, people who "let their money work for them," expecting high pay in return for causing others to work for low pay. The World Trade Organization enlarges the old idea of the corporation-as-person by giving the global corporate economy the status of a super government with the power to overrule nations.

I don't mean to say, of course, that all corporate executives and stockholders are bad people. I am only saying that all of them are very seriously implicated in a bad economy.

Unsurprisingly, among people who wish to preserve things other than money—for instance, every region's native capacity to produce essential goods—there is a growing perception that the global "free market" economy is inherently an enemy to the natural world, to human health and freedom, to industrial workers, and to farmers and others in the land-use economies; and furthermore, that it is inherently an enemy to good work and good economic practice.

I believe that this perception is correct and that it can be shown to be correct merely by listing the assumptions implicit in the idea that corporations should be "free" to buy low and sell high in the world at large. These assumptions, so far as I can make them out, are as follows:

1. That stable and preserving relationships among people, places, and things do not matter and are of no worth.
2. That cultures and religions have no legitimate practical or economic concerns.
3. That there is no conflict between the "free market" and political freedom, and no connection between political democracy and economic democracy.
4. That there can be no conflict between economic advantage and economic justice.
5. That there is no conflict between greed and ecological or bodily health.

6. That there is no conflict between self-interest and public service.

7. That the loss or destruction of the capacity anywhere to produce necessary goods does not matter and involves no cost.

8. That it is all right for a nation's or a region's subsistence to be foreign based, dependent on long-distance transport, and entirely controlled by corporations.

9. That, therefore, wars over commodities—our recent Gulf War, for example—are legitimate and permanent economic functions.

10. That this sort of sanctioned violence is justified also by the predominance of centralized systems of production, supply, communications, and transportation, which are extremely vulnerable not only to acts of war between nations, but also to sabotage and terrorism.

11. That it is all right for poor people in poor countries to work at poor wages to produce goods for export to affluent people in rich countries.

12. That there is no danger and no cost in the proliferation of exotic pests, weeds, and diseases that accompany international trade and that increase with the volume of trade.

13. That an economy is a machine, of which people are merely the interchangeable parts. One has no choice but to do the work (if any) that the economy prescribes, and to accept the prescribed wage.

14. That, therefore, vocation is a dead issue. One does not do the work that one chooses to do because one is called to it by Heaven or by one's natural or god-given abilities, but does instead the work that is determined and imposed by the economy. Any work is all right as long as one gets paid for it.

These assumptions clearly prefigure a condition of total economy. A total economy is one in which everything—"life forms," for instance, or the "right to pollute"—is "private property" and has a price and is for sale. In a total economy significant and sometimes critical choices that once belonged to individuals or communities become the property of corporations. A total economy, operating internationally, necessarily shrinks the powers of state and national governments, not only because those governments have signed over significant powers to an international bureaucracy or because political leaders become the paid hacks of the corporations but also because political processes—and especially democratic processes—are too slow to react to unrestrained economic and technological development on a global scale.

And when state and national governments begin to act in effect as agents of the global economy, selling their people for low wages and their people's products for low prices, then the rights and liberties of citizenship must necessarily shrink. A total economy is an unrestrained taking of profits from the disintegration of nations, communities, households, landscapes, and ecosystems. It licenses symbolic or artificial wealth to "grow" by means of the destruction of the real wealth of all the world.

Among the many costs of the total economy, the loss of the principle of vocation is probably the most symptomatic and, from a cultural standpoint, the most critical. It is by the replacement of vocation with economic determinism that the exterior workings of a total economy destroy the character and culture also from the inside.

In an essay on the origin of civilization in traditional cultures, Ananda K. Coomaraswamy wrote that "the principle of justice is the same throughout . . . [it is] that each member of the community should perform the task for which he is fitted by nature. . . ." The two ideas, justice and vocation, are inseparable. That is why Coomaraswamy spoke of industrialism as "the mammon of injustice," incompatible with civilization. It is by way of the principle and practice of vocation that sanctity and reverence enter into the human economy. It was thus possible for traditional cultures to conceive that "to work is to pray."

Aware of industrialism's potential for destruction, as well as the considerable political danger of great concentrations of wealth and power in industrial corporations, American leaders developed, and for a while used, the means of limiting and restraining such concentrations, and of somewhat equitably distributing wealth and property. The means were: laws against trusts and monopolies, the principle of collective bargaining, the concept of one-hundred-percent parity between the land-using and the manufacturing economies, and the progressive income tax. And to protect domestic producers and production capacities it is possible for governments to impose tariffs on cheap imported goods. These means are justified by the government's obligation to protect the lives, livelihoods, and freedoms of its citizens. There is, then, no necessity or inevitability requiring our government to sacrifice the livelihoods of our small farmers, small business people, and workers, along with our domestic economic independence to the global "free market." But now all of these means are either weakened or in disuse. The global economy is intended as a means of subverting them.

In default of government protections against the total economy of the supranational corporations, people are where they have been many times before: in danger of losing their economic security and their freedom, both at once. But at the same time the means of defending themselves belongs to them in the form of a venerable principle: powers not exercised by government return to the people. If the government does not propose to protect the lives, livelihoods, and freedoms of its people, then the people must think about protecting themselves.

How are they to protect themselves? There seems, really, to be only one way, and that is to develop and put into practice the idea of a local economy—something that growing numbers of people are now doing. For several good reasons, they are beginning with the idea of a local food economy. People are trying to find ways to shorten the distance between producers and consumers, to make the connections between the two more direct, and to make this local economic activity a benefit to the local community. They are trying to learn to use the consumer economies of local towns and cities to preserve the livelihoods of local farm families and farm communities. They want to use the local economy to give consumers an influence over the kind and quality of their food, and to preserve and enhance the local landscapes. They want to give everybody in the local community a direct, long-term interest in the prosperity, health, and beauty of their homeland. This is the only way presently available to make the total economy less total. It was once, I believe, the only way to make a national or a colonial economy less total. But now the necessity is greater.

I am assuming that there is a valid line of thought leading from the idea of the total economy to the idea of a local economy. I assume that the first thought may be a recognition of one's ignorance and vulnerability as a consumer in the total economy. As such a consumer, one does not know the history of the products that one uses. Where, exactly, did they come from? Who produced them? What toxins were used in their production? What were the human and ecological costs of producing them and then of disposing of them? One sees that such questions cannot be answered easily, and perhaps not at all. Though one is shopping amid an astonishing variety of products, one is denied certain significant choices. In such a state of economic ignorance it is not possible to choose products that were produced locally or with reasonable kindness toward people and toward nature. Nor is it possible for such consumers to influence production for the better. Consumers who feel a prompting toward land stewardship find that in this economy they can have no stewardly practice. To be a consumer in the total economy, one must agree to be totally ignorant, totally passive, and totally dependent on distant supplies and self-interested suppliers.

And then, perhaps, one begins to *see* from a local point of view. One begins to ask, What is here, what is in me, that can lead to something better?

From a local point of view, one can see that a global "free market" economy is possible only if nations and localities accept or ignore the inherent instability of a production economy based on exports and a consumer economy based on imports. An export economy is beyond local influence, and so is an import economy. And cheap long-distance transport is possible only if granted cheap fuel, international peace, control of terrorism, prevention of sabotage, and the solvency of the international economy.

Perhaps one also begins to see the difference between a small local business that must share the fate of the local community and a large absentee corporation that is set up to escape the fate of the local community by ruining the local community.

So far as I can see, the idea of a local economy rests upon only two principles: neighborhood and subsistence.

In a viable neighborhood, neighbors ask themselves what they can do or provide for one another, and they find answers that they and their place can afford. This, and nothing else, is the *practice* of neighborhood. This practice must be, in part, charitable, but it must also be economic, and the economic part must be equitable; there is a significant charity in just prices.

Of course, everything needed locally cannot be produced locally. But a viable neighborhood is a community; and a viable community is made up of neighbors who cherish and protect what they have in common. This is the principle of subsistence. A viable community, like a viable farm, protects its own production capacities. It does not import products that it can produce for itself. And it does not export local products until local needs have been met. The economic products of a viable community are understood either as belonging to the community's subsistence or as surplus, and only the surplus is considered to be marketable abroad. A community, if it is to be viable, cannot think of producing solely for export, and it cannot permit importers to use cheaper labor and goods from other places to destroy the local capacity to produce goods that are needed locally. In charity, moreover, it must refuse to import goods that are produced at the cost of human or ecological degradation elsewhere. This principle applies not just to localities, but to regions and nations as well.

The principles of neighborhood and subsistence will be disparaged by the globalists as "protectionism"—and that is exactly what it is. It is a protectionism that is just and sound, because it protects local producers and is the best assurance of adequate supplies to local consumers. And the idea that local needs should be met first and only surpluses exported does not imply any prejudice against charity toward people in other places or trade with them. The principle of neighborhood at home always implies the principle of charity abroad. And the principle of subsistence is in fact the best guarantee of giveable or marketable surpluses. This kind of protection is not "isolationism."

Albert Schweitzer, who knew well the economic situation in the colonies of Africa, wrote nearly sixty years ago: "Whenever the timber trade is good, permanent famine reigns in the Ogowe region because the villagers abandon their farms to fell as many trees as possible." We should notice especially that the goal of production was "as many . . . as possible." And Schweitzer makes my point exactly: "These people could achieve true wealth if they could develop their agriculture and trade to meet their own needs." Instead they produced timber for export to "the world economy," which made them dependent upon imported goods that they bought with money earned from their exports. They gave up their local means of subsistence, and imposed the false standard of a foreign demand ("as many trees as possible") upon their forests. They thus became helplessly dependent on an economy over which they had no control.

Such was the fate of the native people under the African colonialism of Schweitzer's time. Such is, and can only be, the fate of everybody under the global colonialism of our time. Schweitzer's description of the colonial economy of the Ogowe region is in principle not different from the rural economy now in Kentucky or Iowa or Wyoming. A total economy for all practical purposes is a total government. The "free trade" which from the standpoint of the corporate economy brings "unprecedented economic growth," from the standpoint of the land and its local populations, and ultimately from the standpoint of the cities, is destruction and slavery. Without prosperous local economies, the people have no power and the land no voice.

(2001)

ERIC T. FREYFOGLE

The Culture of Owning

Americans have been altering the definition of property
rights to reflect changing times since Thomas Jefferson's day.
Given our evolving understanding of the health of the land,
the moment is ripe to do so again.

IT WAS A CALAMITOUS TIME, THE 1930S, OUT ON THE LAND AS WELL as in the cities. The crisis was most visibly an economic and social one: the soup lines, the Hoover camps, the migrant Okies. But it was more than that, or so it appeared to poet Archibald MacLeish and observers like him. American culture itself was in trouble, particularly on the Great Plains where plows, aridity, and human dreams had combined to create massive, billowing dust clouds that darkened skies a thousand miles eastward. Bad land use was one cause of the Dust Bowl, obvious to all who could see. But beneath that was a system of private property rights that allowed landowners to misuse nature, plowing land that should have been left in grass. And beneath that, getting to the heart of things MacLeish questioned, was America's concept of liberty, defined by too many as an individual's right to be left alone.

In "The Land of the Free," his much-acclaimed poem that appeared in 1938 with wrenching Depression-era images by Dorothea Lange, Margaret Bourke-White, and other WPA photographers, MacLeish would probe this concept of liberty, so tied to America's self image. Liberty as individual autonomy, as the right to do as one pleased, seemed to depend upon open land, available for the taking. The land, though, had largely run out, and now it was blowing away.

> *We wonder if the liberty was land*
> *We wonder if the liberty was grass*
> *Greening ahead of us: grazed beyond horizons*

So long as the grass remained alive and lay to the west, in an open landscape full of opportunity, liberty might prevail. But what happened when the last of the land was taken and the last of the grass turned under?

MacLeish's chief fear was that the loss of open land would threaten American democracy, precisely the fear that Thomas Jefferson had expressed generations earlier. If democracy was based on liberty and liberty was based on land, would democracy decline as the landless population rose? Jefferson's fear led him not just to expand the nation with the Louisiana Purchase but to push hard for the widespread distribution of land. "Legislators cannot invent too many devices for subdividing property," Jefferson advised. "It is not too soon to provide by every possible means that as few as possible shall be without a little portion of land."

Today's twenty-first-century fears about democracy take different forms and are probably better founded. But MacLeish was right about the troubling links between liberty, ownership, and land degradation. The established culture of owning, MacLeish recounted in his poem, had left a trail of its many failings. In the Midwest there were the vast Northwoods, now cut over and burning:

> *Millions of acres of stumps to remember the past by—*
> *To remember the Upper Peninsula hushed with pines:*
> *To remember the hemlocks singing in Wisconsin:*
> *To remember over the water the birches remembering*

In hilly lands everywhere, there were the gullies formed by the "rest-less rain" and the eroding soil, the land leaving "under our feet and our hands." When liberty was understood as the freedom to plow land, regardless of nature, the consequences would prove ill, for land and people. America needed a new understanding of liberty, MacLeish believed, based not on the right to be left alone but on something far different, leading in turn to new legal rules about the ownership of land.

The cultural problems MacLeish identified are by no means gone, and they have much to do with America's continuing land-use ills. Although less dramatically than during the Dust Bowl, bad land use still plagues our countryside, silting rivers, diminishing wildlife, creating hypoxic dead zones in waterways and oceans, and turning ecologically complex forests into monocultural plantations. Many people work hard attacking the ill effects of these environmental problems, but rarely do we cut to their cultural roots. These land uses are protected by a concept of liberty that largely retains the definition it had in the Dust Bowl: the right of individuals to use their land with little restraint. When we do see through this misguided myth, we come upon the outlines of a far better orientation toward land, private property, and liberty.

By the early 1990s the nation's push to protect ecologically sensitive lands had largely stalled. Soil erosion control measures had literally gained ground since the 1930s, as had efforts to expand wildlife refuges. In 1964, the Wilderness Act both culminated the effort to protect wild places and set the stage for expanded set-asides in the 1970s and 1980s. Indeed, progress had occurred on many fronts: floodplain protection ordinances, coastal-zone development restrictions, pollution-control and pesticide laws, wildlife protections on national forests, the Alaska Lands Act—all had promoted the land's healing and health. But a new sentiment was on the rise—or rather, a resurgence of an old sentiment—which came to political expression in a squabble fomented by then-Vice President Dan Quayle, having to do with the term "wetlands" as used in the federal Clean Water Act. Existing law defined wetlands in terms of the dominant plants that a parcel possessed. If land was covered chiefly by plants that required saturated soils to grow, then it qualified as a wetland and received the protection of federal wetlands law, even if the land surface was mostly dry.

Allying himself with developers who resisted this science-based definition, Quayle pushed for a radical cutback in the law's protective coverage. A wetland, he urged, should be underwater a good part of the time, science be damned. Before the law could apply to a particular land parcel, he proposed, government needed to show that the land had standing water two consecutive weeks every year. Had the test been adopted (it was not), millions of acres would have lost legal protection and the rate of wetlands destruction would have gone up.

For Quayle, liberty was the freedom of a landowner to develop land as she saw fit, just as it had been for Dust Bowl farmers. The land, of course, was private property, and as Quayle understood the institution of property, it existed chiefly to protect liberty of precisely this leave-me-alone type. The grasses he talked about were more likely *Carex* or *Spartina* than the buffalo grass of western Kansas, yet his respect for them was no greater than what the Dust Bowl farmers showed for the short-grass prairie.

Quayle's defense of individual liberty did more than just challenge specific rules on wetlands. Indirectly it also bolstered resistance to a principle that had guided environmental protection efforts for a quarter century: the idea that those who harm the environment should be held responsible for their actions. In the pollution context this principle is known as "polluter pays," and it requires polluters either to compensate for the damage they cause or buy the technology needed to control it. The same idea logically applies to land uses. Wetlands play key roles in filtering pollution and are ecologically connected in complex ways to surrounding lands and waters. When wetlands are filled, pollution levels rise, flooding increases, and wildlife suffers.

Beginning in the 1970s, the "polluter-pays" principle informed new laws governing many forms of pollution, yet it encountered tougher going in the land-use arena. Landowners strongly resisted taking responsibility for the polluted runoff their land uses caused. They also resisted accountability when they destroyed wildlife habitat, altered water flows, and let their topsoil slide into waterways and reservoirs. Rhetorically, landowners framed their resistance in terms of liberty and private property. Environmental laws limited their liberty to do as they pleased, interfering with their rights as landowners to make profitable uses of their lands. To bolster their defense, landowners also crafted a different policy argument, one that soon echoed loudly throughout the land: Sound land use that conserved resources, landowners asserted, brought benefits to the public. When a landowner practiced conservation, the entire community enjoyed the resulting gains, not the landowner alone. When trees were preserved along rivers they provided good shade to help cold-water fish species. When farms retained pastures and hayfields, they slowed drainage and aided grassland birds. Given these widespread benefits, the landowner groups argued, shouldn't the community in fairness shoulder the associated costs?

In the legal literature, this policy question has been around for years, and its resolution centers on what is termed the "harm-benefit test." The test goes like this: If a law tells a landowner to stop a harmful activity, the landowner has no cause to complain. The law is halting bad behavior (industrial air pollution, for instance), which the public has every right to deter. But when a law goes beyond that, telling a landowner that she has to use her land in a way that benefits the public, then the landowner ought to be paid for the costs of compliance. The public is being benefited; the public should pay.

This harm-benefit test is easy to apply in many specific settings. A landowner who spews toxic pollution in the river can be told to stop and cannot expect payment. When a landowner instead is asked to donate land for a public park, the case falls clearly on the other side; compensation is due. But where did wetlands protection fit in? Did a law compel the owner to devote lands to wetland uses such as open space, flood buffering, and wildlife habitat, therefore promoting an array of public goods? Or did it, by stopping the potential loss of those benefits, halt a harm?

Vice President Quayle stood among those who believed that land owner-ship included the inherent right to develop land, with little regard for its natural features. Land was land, and the rights of ownership took no ac-count of its variability. Conservation advocates for their part largely labored on the specific issues of the day: on floodplains, barrier islands, steep slopes, or whatever issue was drawing lawmakers' attention. As they pushed hard for limits on using sensitive lands they were nonetheless challenging as-sumptions about the meaning of owning land, yet rarely did conservation-ists frame their visions more fundamentally, in terms of the basic elements that private ownership should entail.

Today's observers, looking back upon the Dust Bowl, have little trouble seeing through some of the myths at work then, myths about individual power, the self-regulating market, and the human control of nature. But too many of the Dust Bowl myths are still clouding our vision, making it hard to perceive the path to healthier lands. Indeed, on issues relating to private land, some conservation efforts are heading us in the wrong cultural direction. Far from advancing us toward a sensible, ecologically informed understanding of private ownership, they are strengthening ideas of owner-ship that are distinctly miscast.

Many of the conservation problems on which America has made the least progress are those related to land—from the control of polluted runoff to urban sprawl to the protection of wildlife habitat. With 60 percent of the nation in private hands (more if Alaska is excluded), these lingering prob-lems are inextricably linked to unwise private behavior. To promote con-servation by private landowners, society must demand that they use their lands better. But the moment that idea rises up it collides with the cultural ideals of liberty and private property, as they are now understood. And from this collision it is but a short step to the now-popular claim that good land use benefits taxpayers and so should be funded by them.

This view of things is being bolstered by well-intentioned conservation strategies, used by governments and private groups. Encouraged by federal payment programs, farmers increasingly expect money whenever conserva-tion measures reduce their crop yields. When development would harm a particular landscape, the growing practice is to avert it by buying up "de-velopment rights" or purchasing a conservation easement. And rather than banning landowners from destroying critical wildlife habitat (a ban that's quite legal under the federal Endangered Species Act), the Fish and Wildlife

Service is now prone to pay them to leave the habitat alone, sometimes under long-term leases that include payments exceeding the land's total value. A message is embedded in these payment schemes, and it's coming through loud and clear: To own land is to have the right to degrade it ecologically. Payments are based on this assumption, and they help solidify and perpetuate it. Payments make far less sense, and can become distinctly problematic, when the assumption is set aside.

Hardly any institution is more in need of critical thought than private ownership. It is, in truth, a more flexible, value-laden, communal institution than people realize. Over the generations the rights of landowners have been redefined, again and again, in an evolutionary shift that still goes on.

In northern Idaho today, landowners grow bluegrass to harvest for seed. To produce lush grasses the growers burn their fields after the harvest. Predictably, the burning produces smoke and soot that annoys neighbors. In June 2002, some of them went to court to assert their own property rights and to protect the particular liberty that was most important to them, the liberty to be free of such disturbances. It was a classic case, and a timely one. Liberty lay on both sides of the dispute: the liberty to use land as you see fit and the liberty to protect yourself when your neighbor's actions cause harm. As the dispute would soon show, yet another type of liberty also was present: the liberty of citizens to come together to make laws for the governance of their interconnected landscapes.

To avoid liability under Idaho's trespass-and-nuisance law, the grass growers turned to the political realm for protection. Aided by Republican Governor Dirk Kempthorne, the growers convinced the state legislature to enact a statute that exempted them from liability for damages caused by their burning. In their nuisance suit, then still pending in court, the neighbors promptly challenged this new statute's constitutionality, claiming that it took away their own property rights by authorizing physical interferences with their lands. The trial court agreed, but in August 2004 the Idaho Supreme Court reversed the lower court, siding with the grass growers. Property rights, the high court proclaimed, are based upon state law, and it is entirely proper for the legislature to change that law. If the legislature wants to favor grass growers over their smoke-harmed neighbors it has every right to do so. Like all law, property law is subject to revision, even in its fundamentals.

The judicial ruling in *Moon v. North Idaho Farmers Association* is useful in revealing starkly how private property works and, implicitly, why it exists. Just as the Idaho Supreme Court explained, lawmakers wield ample power to control the mix of rights that ownership entails. The U.S. Constitution does protect property rights, but to a smaller extent than people typically assume. It is not a serious check on today's lawmakers as they reconsider and reconfigure the limited rights that landowners ought to possess. The way that property rights of neighbors are necessarily intertwined within a landscape is also clear here: The law can protect one owner's liberty (here, the grass grower's) only by curtailing the liberties of others (the neighboring landowners).

In the common view, property exists only to protect the liberty of the owner, who can use her rights as a shield to ward off complaints about her behavior. Property does work this way, but as an explanation of the institution it is seriously incomplete and begins at the wrong end. Whenever the law recognizes private property rights it enables an owner to draw upon the coercive engines of the state—its police, courts, and prisons—to restrict the liberties of other people. Private property, that is, arises out of the curtailment by landowners of the liberties of all other people. For one owner's liberty to go up, the liberties of others must go down. This clash of competing liberties is easy to see when a landowner exercises her right to exclude outsiders: When the no trespassing sign goes up, the liberty of hikers goes down. The same interconnection runs through other elements of land ownership, and in pretty much the same way. To favor Idaho's grass growers and their profits is to reduce the liberty of neighbors to enjoy clean air; to protect the neighbors is to reduce the liberty of the growers. In such disputes—indeed, in the vast majority of property disputes—there is no true "pro-liberty" or "pro-property" position that one can take.

To see this point is to realize why property cannot be defined sensibly by starting with the idea that it is first and foremost an individual right. The beginning point has historically been elsewhere, in an understanding of the common good. Is the public interest furthered by allowing grass burning or, instead, by protecting homeowners in their quiet enjoyment of the land? Only when political processes have decided upon the public interest and where it lies can we then revise the rights of landowners so that they promote that common good.

Americans have largely forgotten the links between property rights and the common good, a principle once regularly summed up with the Latin phrase *salus populi suprema lex est*—the good of the people is the supreme law. Private property, in truth, is a morally problematic institution in that it gives owners the legal power to harm or restrict the liberties of other people. Such uses of public power are legitimate, as philosophers have asserted for centuries, only when a valid moral justification exists to support them. Dominant myths notwithstanding, it's been clear for generations that the only sound way to justify private rights in land is to point to the contributions property makes to the common good. That's what the Idaho legislature had in mind, or so one hopes, when it decided to favor the grass growers—it made a political choice that defined the common good as being best served by the freedom to burn fallow fields. The legislature's decision can be challenged on policy grounds, to be sure. But what ought to be clear is the primacy of the common good in resolving the dispute. Lawmakers have the right and, indeed, the moral duty to revise property laws, keeping them in line with society's changing needs and its evolving visions of the common good.

The American "right to property" has had varied meanings over time; to the founders of the nation the phrase's multiple meanings were quite different from those of today. Even greater change has taken place in the mix of rights and responsibilities that ownership entails. But ownership has never included the right to conduct activities that are deemed harmful to others. The Latin phrase for this do-no-harm rule, *sic utere tuo ut alienum non laedas,* literally commanded that an owner cause no harm, either to other landowners or to the surrounding community. Over the generations lawmakers have given varied content to this rule. Inevitably, what one generation has found harmful another has sometimes viewed otherwise, and vice versa. Does private ownership include the legal right to fill wetlands, to burn bluegrass, or to plow the prairie in semiarid lands? The answer is as simple as it is incomplete. It does if lawmakers say it does; it does if, on balance, the recognition of this right would, in the estimation of elected officials, foster the commonweal.

In the recent past American law has allowed landowners to alter nature freely; it has defined property rights in abstract terms, independent of the land's features. Developing land, taming the frontier—these were at one time deemed to be unalloyed public goods. So we thought, and so our law said. Yet, if property law and the culture of owning could change to permit and encourage industrial land uses, despite the harm they caused, so too could they change to embrace today's far different values and circumstances. Property is a shifting, socially responsive institution. It is up to people today to decide the kind of property system that best serves their collective needs; it is up to them to decide what forms of liberty private property will promote.

As he ended his poem, Archibald MacLeish hinted at the answer to the question he raised: What could liberty mean when the land ran out? He suggested that the future required Americans to relinquish the idea of liberty as individual license to act as one pleased and to embrace the liberty that Thomas Jefferson and his colleagues had rated so highly a century and a half earlier, the liberty of free citizens to make rules for their shared life. In the Dust Bowl, MacLeish could see, Americans had failed to exercise sensibly this collective, positive form of liberty. Individual farmers had made mistakes, but the failure of the Dust Bowl was at root a collective one, for it was a failure of lawmakers who allowed private owners to use their lands in ways that harmed the good of the whole.

MacLeish's form of liberty, of course, is exercised often in many realms of lawmaking. But landowners could exercise it more effectively. An intriguing step in that direction is being taken in Montana, where state law now allows 60 percent of the landowners in a region to petition their county to set up a planning and zoning district to keep out unwanted development, even over the objections of a minority of landowners. In the Bozeman Pass area, a critical wildlife corridor, landowners in 2002 invited the Sonoran Institute to help them with this process. The announced aim of their effort: "To establish a permanent zoning district in the Bozeman Pass that protects the rural agricultural character and natural values of the area and builds citizen leadership in county growth management efforts." That is precisely the liberty that MacLeish had in mind, and it may lead to new American ideas about ownership.

As for the kinds of changes that might be made to the rights of landowners, most evident is the need for lawmakers to keep doing what they have long done: implementing new ideas that reflect our greater understanding of what constitutes land-use harm, new applications of the old *sic utere tuo,* do-no-harm rule of ownership. Filling a wetland can easily qualify as harm, and be banned as such. Stripping trees along a waterway, altering natural drainage in a significant way, plowing an erodible hillside, building on unstable slopes, ripping up rare wildlife habitat—these and similar forms of ecological degradation can also be viewed as harms. At times and places we already see them that way. But the cultural resistance is strong, and today's conservation payment programs, public and private, suggest that we are now backtracking. To buy lands for the public to use is entirely reasonable, but to pay to halt damaging behavior is to honor and entrench ideas about ownership that are outdated and pernicious.

As new laws reflecting our new understanding of the common good are put into place, they will produce new applications of the longstanding harm-benefit test. Once particular land uses are deemed harmful, then laws that command better behavior and activities will not be viewed as unfairly seizing public benefits from aggrieved private landowners; they'll be viewed as halting harmful activities, just as property law has done for centuries.

Well-crafted laws that consider the great variations in nature will also have the good effect of tailoring landowner rights to the land itself. It is ecological foolishness to define landowner rights as if all tracts of land were alike. Rights in wetlands should not be the same as those in high and dry fields; rights in sloping lands or in biologically rich habitats need not be defined as if these natural conditions did not exist.

It is not just in clear cases of land degradation, though, where changes in property law might take place. The landowner's right to develop is by no means beyond scrutiny. So long as legislatures are evenhanded in their work they may significantly reduce development rights, just as lawmakers in other countries have done over decades. It is also not clear why landowners should enjoy the strong right to exclude outsiders that they now do. This right has not always been recognized, even in the United States. In some countries, such as Sweden and Great Britain, the public enjoys a right to roam and landowners can only exclude people to halt actual interferences with their land uses.

In the push for new laws, however, we would do well as a people to remember the Dust Bowl and the failure of the generation then in charge to foster new ideas of ownership. Property law is not a separate component in the land-use equation. It is intertwined with and dependent upon the larger culture and America's ideals. New land-use laws simply cannot outpace American culture, not by much and not for long. And so there is the need to work on the meanings of liberty and equality and on America's ingrained, costly practice of viewing nature in fragmented terms rather than as the complex, interconnected systems we know them to be. Let us recover modes of liberty that have to do with collective governance, as MacLeish suggested, and with the right to live in healthy places. Let us evolve a sense of equality that respects the equal moral worth of people while also respecting the great variety in our lands.

(2005)

Listening to the Other

Can a sense of place help the peace-making process?

A CHUNK OF PALE, LIMEY DOLOMITE SITS ON MY DESK, A FRAGMENT of my ancestors' homeland. Sometimes I fit it inside my fist, as a way to remind me of the very ground from which my grandmother was torn around the time of World War I. Once a chink between larger, more durable cobbles in the dry masonry walls of the stone hut where she resided during her girlhood, this rock speaks to me like no other. The day I plucked it from the wall of my sitti's dwelling, I noticed how similar its texture and color were to the ridges flanking the Bekaa Valley. Those ridges rise into the Anti-Lebanon Mountains, along the present-day border of Lebanon with Syria—a place less than one hundred fifty miles from bullet-riddled Jerusalem, and less than two hundred miles from bombed-out Iraq.

Like the stone that now rests on my desk, my grandmother was displaced from her region of origin. During the time when my grandparents were forced to flee from Lebanon, warring was almost constant. The Turks conscripted over 240,000 Arabs into their forces, and roughly 40,000 of them were killed, while another 150,000 deserted their posts. At least 40,000 of the Lebanese deserters—Arabs who refused to fight for the Ottoman Empire against their own people—soon fled with their families to the Americas.

They left the Bekaa Valley as depopulated and broken as Ireland was after the Great Potato Famine. Those who stayed faced a gnawing famine of their own, accompanied by a plague of locusts of biblical proportions. After World War I erupted, at least 100,000 Lebanese died of starvation, leaving the pastures, orchards, and vineyards of the Bekaa with less than half the shepherds and grape-pickers they had sheltered prior to the war.

I think of these upheavals whenever I read passages of Diane Abu-Jaber's novel *Crescent,* Joseph Geha's short stories in *Through and Through,* or even Andre Dubus III's *House of Sand and Fog.* These stories are not necessarily analogous to those of my own immigrant family; in fact, I love them all the more for the surprises and anomalies they offer. Like the poems of Israeli dissident Yehuda Amichai, French-Lebanese novelist Venus Khoury-Gata, Lebanese-American poet David Williams, and Palestinian-American troubadour Naomi Shihab Nye, they offer me fresh perspectives when I might otherwise wallow in despair.

These dissidents and refugees are speaking to something that Americans are not reading in the pages of the *New York Times,* seeing in the live coverage on CNN, or hearing in the ever more subdued commentaries from National Public Radio. Their stories reveal how racism and social injustice not only hurt individuals and their families but impair the capacity of those people to adequately care for the land, and one another.

These days, I hold that chunk of dolomite in the palm of my hand as I pray for peace, and contemplate what a lasting peace might mean for all the displaced people roaming this planet.

By some counts, political and economic refugees recently uprooted from their ancestral homelands now number two billion. Let me take that statistical abstraction and strip it down for you. Wherever you travel in this world, it is likely that one out of every three people whose paths you cross are fleeing or have fled from their mother country. They are cultural and ecological orphans, uprooted from the natal grounds in which their stories and songs, their environmental sensibilities and ethics, were first and most vividly nursed and nurtured.

We live during an era in which there are as many descendants of refugees around us as people who have stayed put, living in the same places where their ancestors lived. Many of us whose forebears were displaced have endeavored long and hard to regain some sense of nativity in our adopted homelands. But it is difficult to rekindle such sensibilities in a new place, surrounded by cultures and environments foreign to us.

In many ways, this is the deepest struggle of my own life. After growing up among a cohesive clan of Lebanese Americans hidden within the Indiana Dunes along Lake Michigan, I moved westward to work with O'odham, Seri, Navajo, and Hopi families who have lived in the same stretches of Southwest deserts for centuries if not millennia. Blessed by the chance to learn from tribal elders as we work together to document ancient shrines, gather wild plants, or sow native crop seeds, I have been regularly humbled by how little I can ever learn about the desert within which their lives and stories are rooted. The detail with which their oral histories instruct them how to live in their peculiar homelands is so rich that I would have difficulty picking it all up even if I were to become a fluent speaker of their indigenous languages. While working with these elders to document their land rights and genealogies, I sometimes feel I am listening to multiple generations of in-place peoples speaking to me in an unbroken chain. Juxtaposed with them, my own brokenness—my own sense of having been displaced—seems painfully obvious.

At the same time, I sometimes see the similarities between their limestone mesas and those where my relatives still live in Syria and Lebanon; I hear in my head echoes of songs from 'a biladna, the beloved ground that my grandfather simply referred to in English as "The Old Country." It was a place where, on a hot day, Baba could always find the shade of some centuries-old fig tree to rest beneath, where he could slowly savor the fruitiness of a dried al-barquq apricot, where the fragrance of the wild thyme he called zaatar filled the air, and where, off in the distance, he could hear lost lambs bleating longingly for their mothers.

In many ways, I am one of those lambs. You may be one yourself, cut off from the places that nurtured your forebears: the motherlands.

I grew up only vaguely understanding what labels like Arab or Middle-Easterner meant. Some of my aunts and uncles claimed to be Syrian while others declared themselves Lebanese, depending on who politically controlled the Bekaa Valley when they emigrated. But there was something altogether richer, darker, and more unpredictable about them compared to my mother's Irish family, which had learned and mastered the norms of midwestern American behavior over several generations. I felt their distinctiveness largely through the savory foods we shared—food unlike anything in midwestern cafeterias at the time—and through the words of Arabic still sprinkled into all of our conversations, words that my aunts instructed us over and over again to pronounce with verve.

But when the Six Days War between Egypt and Israel splashed blood across the headlines of our hometown paper in 1967, my image of myself began to change. Some Jewish kids who lived nearby stopped playing with me; when I asked them why, I was told that Arabs were trying to kill Jews in their holy lands. My father scolded my mother for responding to a local journalist's request for her to discuss the Jewish-Arab conflict from the perspective of an American who had married into an Arab family—as if my father, a city councilman and veteran, was somehow less American. But her answer, published in the newspaper the next day, delighted even him: "I'm not so much worried about what's happening over there because I'm spending all my time trying to help Jewish and Arab kids get along right here where we live."

There were other times when I felt blackballed by Jewish-American social groups and by Israeli exchange students at my school, but they were rare exceptions. In fact, it was easy for me to have as many Jewish friends as Christian (or Muslim) ones while growing up. Perhaps that is why it has been so difficult to fathom the increase in hate crimes against Arabs and Muslims in the U.S.—crimes that include a Zionist-extremist plot to assassinate a Lebanese-American congressman from California. This unprecedented hatred of Arab speakers has really emerged within just the last few years, as international events stimulated new strains of intolerance across America and the world at large.

Wherever we now live—and most certainly in the United States, Afghanistan, Iraq, Indonesia, Cuba, Yemen, the Philippines, Germany, North Korea, or the British Isles—we can hardly escape from the news of warfare. We spend most of our lives within earshot of the latest reports of battles, suicide bombs, ambushes, and air raids. Despite how the media attempts to portray them, these conflicts cannot be so easily passed off as a series of isolated, low-intensity skirmishes.

Let's be clear: A half-century of relative peace has been eclipsed by a period marked by bloodbaths. Beyond the many casualties and refugees currently being tallied by hospitals and relief agencies, many more people stand to be killed, wounded, or displaced unless we collectively yearn with all of our hearts for a different kind of news. It must be news of certain peace, one in which people of many faiths and many colors are once again assured the right to celebrate their own distinctive senses of place, not in exile, but at home, even alongside one another. We have to relearn ways to connect a sense of place with a sense of peace.

Peace and place. I have always sensed that these two words have a bit of the same ring to them in modern English, but had not thought much about their semantic overlap until recently. I wonder if Middle English speakers who pronounced peace more like pais noticed its resonance with terms for place in Spanish (país) and in French (pays). Oddly, I hadn't appreciated the simplest of facts: that anyone who feels secure, grateful, and satisfied in a particular place is likely to feel at peace. Or that those who have fled war or other forms of violence are left not in peace but in struggle. They not only grieve for what they have lost; they are often unable to see the beauty of their newfound land because the salt of their own tears continues to blind them. They feel humiliated by those who have taken over their homeland, and feel any wounds that the land has suffered as their own.

If we listen, much of what we may hear around us is the keening of displaced peoples, struggling to regain some modicum of dignity, which they pray will come through reconnecting with their ancestral lands. As the late

Edward Said so eloquently observed, that is why we hear such desperation from Palestinian families evicted from their homes in the West Bank by Jewish "settlers"; they are frustrated because they do not currently have any legal recourse in Israeli courts to negotiate for a return to their land. That may also be what underlies the vindictiveness seen in certain Kurds who have been forced back and forth between Turkey and Iraq, unable to retain control of land that has been the legacy of their families for centuries.

The unfulfilled need to live in peace, in place, is what fueled the struggle against Apartheid in South Africa, and what continues to drive the Mayan farmers who feel that their only hope for staying on the land is to join ranks with Zapatista rebels in Chiapas. It is also why the forced relocation of Navajo families from the Big Mountain region of northern Arizona has been largely unsuccessful after years of bitter struggle against federal and tribal bureaucrats. Overcome by the fear that they will be permanently ripped away from the land that has given them much of their identity and sense of connectedness, these people feel a desperation that cannot be quenched by token gestures. They are hurt, and like the wounded of any species, they respond with fury to anyone who tries to dislodge them. It is not just their sense of home that is threatened, but the opportunity to have a reciprocal and mutually sustaining relationship with the land itself.

For too long we have assumed that confronting racism and social in-justice were altogether different challenges from safeguarding land rights, practicing multigenerational land stewardship, or protecting cultural and biological diversity. But from my own fieldwork as a conservation activist and ethnobiologist, I see these seemingly disparate threads woven tightly together nearly every place I go. I see it among my O'odham friends, who used to drive past a sign in a national park that warned tourists to "Watch Out for Cattle, Deer and Indians." They had been displaced from living near one of their sacred sites by preservationists who wanted the park and did not understand that the wildlife attracted to that desert oasis was lured there by habitats that the O'odham themselves had stewarded for centuries.

I also see it among my Hopi neighbors, whose springs have dried up since the Peabody Coal Company began mining the aquifer underlying their land some thirty years ago. They feel that both their culture and their environment have suffered because of water-pricing deals made without their consultation. As I have assisted indigenous communities in their at-tempts to rectify such damage, I have realized that these situations were triggered by a mindset that treats landed peoples as ignorant and inferior, and that they result in the loss of both culturally important habitats and as-sociated biodiversity.

To describe such tragedies, we tend to use the term "environmental injustice." But why not use that concept to understand what is happening in Palestine, Iraq, Israel, Lebanon, and Bali? What if we begin to view the crisis in the Middle East not merely as an economic and political struggle, but one in which two formerly displaced peoples are attempting to reaffirm their love and attachment to the place on Earth that they consider to be most sacred? What if we admit that, from the Gulf War to the present, both sides have damaged the capacity of the land to sustain anyone who lives on it, and have contaminated one water reserve after another, rendering them undrinkable? What would we lose if all parties were sanctioned to renew their efforts to restore traditional ways of caring for the land? While some diplomats might question the worth of such values in negotiating a peace settlement, I doubt that this approach could fare any worse than the Road Map for Peace and the Oslo Accord.

The connections between peace, place, and environmental justice are deeply rooted, if one is willing to listen to the stories these cultures have to tell. Unfortunately, much of our society has retreated into a comfort zone where they only listen to voices like their own. It is this chronic inattention to root values that makes the destabilizing events of the past three years all the more heartbreaking and bewildering.

In the week prior to September 11, 2001, I had a jarring experience. A sense of foreboding welled up within me that haunts me to this day. I was driving through the piñon-studded mesas and sandy valleys of Navajo and Hopi country. Soothed by the stunning serenity of the Colorado Plateau, I hardly noticed that the car radio was on until an NPR commentary shook me from my reverie.

In a matter-of-fact tone, a National Public Radio correspondent reported that diplomats from the United States and Israel had declined to attend the World Conference against Racism, Racial Discrimination, Xenophobia and Related Intolerance because they were unwilling to be publicly confronted by diplomats and activists from countries that were calling their policies in the Middle East "racist." The commentator mentioned the contention, widely shared by conference attendees, that Palestinians were being denied their basic civil, spiritual, and land rights by a brutal Israeli regime propped up by billions of dollars of U.S. military aid.

Merely hearing this made me pull off the road and stop, so strong was the thudding of my heart against the shell of my chest. Within a week's time, those now-infamous mushrooms billowed over buildings that had once stood as the most invincible symbols of American strength.

Let me clarify: I am not asserting that Al-Qaeda chose to attack U.S. landmarks and people simply because our diplomats refused to attend the conference on racism the week before. I do believe, however, that if Americans had been listening to Arab concerns all along—at that world conference and in other international debates on human rights—there would have been far fewer people sympathetic with the goals of Al-Qaeda, and many more would have condemned Al-Qaeda's horrifying means.

Of course the mushrooms over the World Trade Center and the Pentagon were not the only seeds of violence to germinate and grow in our midst. In the aftermath of September 11, a 1,700 percent rise in hate crimes against Arab Americans, against visitors from Arab and other Muslim-dominated countries, and against others from Asia and Africa occurred on American soil. More than seven hundred violent incidents targeted Arabs and Muslims, Arab Americans, or those perceived to be Arab Americans in thirteen states during the nine weeks after the September 11 attacks. These hate crimes included several murders, arsons, and bombings, aggravated assaults with handguns, pepper spray, and stones, as well as lootings and death threats.

In the town where I grew up, a car was intentionally driven into the wall of a gas station managed by a Yemeni-American citizen; in another city where I once lived, a Sikh wearing "an Arab-like" turban was shot and killed. On the Northern Arizona University campus where I currently work, several misguided students burned the Qur'an, on the erroneous premise that those holy teachings had fostered the attacks on New York and Washington, D.C. Our campus was also intruded upon by federal agents who attempted to interrogate foreign students from Middle Eastern countries at all hours of day and night, without initially presenting legal papers that in any way justified such interviews.

And ever since I pointed out to security officials at the Flagstaff Airport that they were only subjecting "people of color" to extensive searches and filed a formal complaint, I have been pulled over for interrogation every time I have flown out of my hometown. When friends ask me how I feel about this insult, I can only reply that it is minor compared to what most Arabs attempting to enter this country are subjected to. Two Lebanese cousins of mine—both girls under fifteen years of age—were denied visas to revisit my family in the U.S. on the grounds that they were either seeking to marry Americans to gain U.S. citizenship or that they were potentially dangerous.

If such outrageous examples of racial profiling and harassment were merely random acts by individual citizens or overly strident officers—unsupported by governmental institutions or by the public at large—perhaps the Arab community could feel that recourse was available to them. But such recourse is hardly possible when the federal government has gained sweeping powers to detain immigrants or foreign nationals indefinitely with little or no due process, and without having to prove that the detainees are in fact terrorists. And even though the U.S. Patriot Act gives sweeping new powers to military and police investigating suspected terrorists, the FBI, the departments of justice and state, as well as local police officials in at least ten states have still been found culpable of both misconduct and overstepping their powers in recent actions against Arabs and Muslims living within our borders.

Rather than being outraged by this state of affairs, 43 percent of all Americans surveyed by the *Washington Post* thought that the terrorist attacks should make them "personally more suspicious of people who appear to be of Arab descent." I am saddened by the fact that nearly half of our country's population has lost its empathy with 3.5 million of their fellow citizens of Arab ancestry, and with 7 million other Americans who embrace the Islamic faith; that they have come to mistrust the fifth of the human family who either practice Islam (1.2 billion individuals) or speak Arabic (200 million individuals), the predominant language in some twenty nations.

Meanwhile, I am one of many Arab Americans who feel the anguish of trying to express our grief for both American lives that have been lost or touched deeply by this tragedy, and for those of our innocent Arab brethren who have been killed, jailed, or humiliated by our own government. As my late mentor Bill Stafford used to say, "every war has two losers."

Xenophobia, the fear of the Other, is a malady that not only mutes and distorts Americans' responses to some 200 million Arabic speakers. It also confers a deafness to the wisdom, warmth, and warnings spoken in some thirty-five hundred languages other than English that have persisted on this planet. While the privileged and educated of nearly every other nation in the world routinely strive to speak, read, and understand several languages, America appears to be among the few that does not generally regard being multilingual as the ultimate indicator of civility and worldliness.

That is a sad oversight, especially as it leads us to ignore the incredible insights into land stewardship and community building that can be found in so many native and minority languages. The rich lexicons associated with Native American farming cultures regarding the care of plants, animals, and soils are but one widely recognized example. For instance, ancient terms embedded in the O'odham language can tangibly guide farmers toward means for renewing the fertility of their field's soils with flood-carried organic debris; without this culture-specific technical vocabulary at their disposal, desert farmers would likely fall back on conventional practices that allow the soils to wash away. Should such terms disappear along with some three thousand languages now endangered by the economically driven homogenization of linguistics worldwide, will knowledge of sustainable technologies and practices die with them?

Our lack of linguistic proficiency limits our competency in cross-cultural contexts of all sorts, including the resolution of conflict and negotiation of peace. Our inability to understand the meanings and morals embedded in specific languages is matched only by our illiteracy regarding linguistics as a whole. To be sure, most Americans do not fathom the relatively minor differences among Semitic languages such as Arabic, Hebrew, and Aramaic, let alone grasp how large the differences are between Arabic and Persian (or Farsi).

We can do better. Why not use our love of oral storytelling and written literature as a means of entering and more fully understanding worlds where few Americans have traveled? Once we engage ourselves with the rich legacy of Arab storytelling and poetry that continues to thrive in the Middle East, as well as in the multiethnic neighborhoods of America, we will find our ears opened to incredible imagery and word music that celebrates the deep connection between being at peace and in place.

Over the last two years I have been spending much of my early morning hours in a ritual of reawakening, one that helps me feel kinship with people in faraway places. Whenever I hear more world news that pushes me into deeper sorrow, I stop my business-as-usual and reach for books that remind me how refugees themselves have rekindled hope in their lives. I have been surprised at how often one theme surfaces in their poems: the link between finding peace and reconnecting with their ancestral lands. There are so many ways that this theme can be freshly expressed—as is evident in the poems of Mahmoud Darwish, recipient of the 2001 Prize for Cultural Freedom from the Lannan Foundation.

Darwish, who was born in the village of Birwe in Upper Galilee, was only six years old when the Israeli Army destroyed his village along with 416 other Palestinian villages. Israelis later pushed a new road through the ruins of his village, and in doing so bulldozed its last remaining cemetery, tearing from the earth the remains of the poet's ancestors and former neighbors. Darwish will not let that village and those who have inhabited it be forgotten. Although he has been forced to live and write in exile from

Palestine for nearly half of his life, he was allowed to return in 1996, when he was greeted at the airport by thousands of fellow Palestinians chanting his most popular poems. One of those poems, "On This Earth," suggests that his unshakable relationship to his natal ground has given him much of his courage and strength over the years:

> We have on this earth what makes life worth living: April's
>   hesitation, the aroma of bread
> at dawn, a woman's point of view about men, the works of
>   Aeschylus, the beginning
> of love, grass on a stone, mothers living on a flute's sigh and
>   the invaders' fear of memories.
>
> We have on this earth what makes life worth living: the
>   final days of September, a woman
> keeping her apricots ripe after forty, the hour of sunlight in
>   prison, a cloud reflecting a swarm
> of creatures, the peoples' applause for those who face death
>   with a smile,
> a tyrant's fear of songs.
>
> We have on this earth what makes life worth living: on this
>   earth, the Lady of Earth,
> mother of all beginnings and ends. She was called
>   Palestine. Her name later became
> Palestine. My Lady, because you are my Lady, I deserve life.

Laila 'Allush describes herself as an Arab Israeli, a label that often confuses the unacquainted. But when they learn that her poems are collected in a book called *Spices on the Open Wound*, their confusion is transformed into pure curiosity and compassion. Despite all the horrors she has witnessed in the Middle East, she has chosen to follow "The Path of Affection":

> Along the amazing road drawn from the throat of recent dates . . .
> Along the amazing road drawn from my old Jerusalem,
> And despite the hybrid signs, shops, and cemeteries,
> My fragmented self drew together to meet the kin of New Haifa . . .
> The earth remained unchanged as of old,
> With all its mortgaged trees dotting the hills,
> And all the green clouds and the plants

Fertilized with fresh fertilizers,
And efficient sprinklers . . .
In the earth there was an apology for my father's wounds,
And all along the bridges was my Arab countenance,
In the tall poplars,
In the trains and windows,
In the smoke rings.
Everything is Arab despite the change of tongue,
Despite the trucks, the cars, and the car lights . . .
All the poplars and my ancestor's solemn orchards
Were, I swear, smiling at me with Arab affection.
Despite all that had been eliminated and coordinated and the
*   "modern" sounds . . .*
Despite the seas of light and technology . . .
O my grandparents, the rich soil was bright with Arab reserve,
And it sang out, believe me, with affection.

What I love about this poem is that no one can take away 'Allush's af-fection for the land—or its affection for those who have cared for it. The land may become occupied, its fields and orchards may be built upon or its irrigation systems may be modernized, but it is still the land her people love in their dreams and in their hearts. Should anyone attempt to rekindle their deep bond with the land, there can be a healing of the most horrific wounds, and the possibility of returning the "brightness" that can be found in any land-based culture.

'Allush speaks of the possibilities of reconciliation and repatriation un-folding in geologic time, not rushing to occur at the expense of people or the land itself. She cares for the land not as property but as family. Despite all the changes that the present occupants of the land have made, she does not condemn them as much as accept that they too will pass in their time. It is as though the land itself may one day forgive the transgressions that have taken place. Neither the land nor her people can ultimately be re-moved from their primordial relationship with one another.

Such poems by refugees speak of a love of place that cannot be van-quished. I wish there were a way of allowing that love to guide the peace-making process—rather than assuming that it inevitably pits Palestinian Christians and Muslims against Israeli Jews, Kurds against Sunni and Shiite Iraqis, Navajos against Hopis in an irreconcilable struggle.

If there has ever been a graphic reminder of how the resulting placeless-ness wounds the Earth, it is the juxtaposition of two maps from the *Atlantic*

Monthly that my friend David Hancocks and I pondered over not long ago. One was a map showing where endangered species are most densely clustered due to loss of habitat; the other depicted where people with the shortest residencies on the land happen to dwell. Although not completely identical, their patterns were strikingly similar, suggesting that the same forces that generate refugees also generate endangered species. Or, to put it another way, wherever cultural communities stay rooted on the land, plants and animals also stay, escaping extinction.

Meanwhile, I am more troubled than I have ever been by the current Israeli efforts to fence Palestinians into a small portion of the West Bank or to expel them altogether; and by similar struggles in Iraq, Afghanistan, Rwanda, and Zaire. In Africa alone, there are more than three million refugees recently displaced from their homelands. The scatter of internecine strife across the face of the Earth today is alarmingly reminiscent of what historians recount of the years just prior to World War I, when many such racist-oriented skirmishes coalesced into something dreadfully global. Even if these widespread events do not metastasize into a universal conflict, the current unrest should convince us all to dedicate a portion of our efforts toward tangible actions to make peace a reality once again.

The ravages of war last far longer than the duration of any "official" combat; our cultures and our habitats remain wounded for years, even decades. Every war we avoid allows millions to remain in place, and keeps the vibrant places of the Earth from being dismembered. It is the healing power of the land and our shared history with it that offers hope of a brighter future.

(2004)

SCOTT RUSSELL SANDERS

Staying Put

T WO FRIENDS ARRIVED AT OUR HOUSE FOR SUPPER ONE MAY EVENING along with the first rumblings of thunder. As my wife and I sat talking with them on our front porch, we had to keep raising our voices a notch to make ourselves heard above the gathering storm. The birds, more discreet, had already hushed. The huge elm beside our door began to sway, limbs creaking, leaves hissing. Black sponges of clouds blotted up the light, fooling the street lamps into coming on early. Above the trees and rooftops, the murky southern sky crackled with lightning. Now and again we heard the pop of a transformer as a bolt struck the power lines in our neighborhood. The pulses of thunder came faster and faster, until they merged into a continuous roar.

We gave up on talking. The four of us, all Midwesterners teethed on thunderstorms, sat down there on the porch to our meal of lentil soup, cheddar cheese, bread warm from the oven, sliced apples, and strawberries. We were lifting the first spoonfuls to our mouths when a stroke of lightning burst so nearby that it seemed to suck away the air, and the lights flickered out, plunging the whole street into darkness.

After we had caught our breath, we laughed—respectfully, as one might laugh at the joke of a giant. The sharp smell of ozone and the musty smell of damp earth mingled with the aroma of bread. A hill of pleasure ran up my spine. I lit a pair of candles on the table, and the flames rocked in the gusts of wind.

In the time it took for butter to melt on a slice of bread, the wind fell away, the elm stopped thrashing, the lightning let up, and the thunder ceased. The sudden stillness was more exciting than the earlier racket. A smoldering yellow light came into the sky, as though the humid air had caught fire. We gazed at one another over the steady candle flames and knew without exchanging a word what this eerie lull could mean.

"Maybe we should go into the basement," my wife, Ruth, suggested.

"And leave this good meal?" one of our friends replied.

The wail of a siren broke the stillness, not the lesser cry of ambulance or fire engine or squad car, but the banshee howl of the civil defense siren at the park a few blocks away.

"They must have sighted one," I said.

"We could take the food down with us on a tray," Ruth told our guests.

"It's up to you," I told them. "We can go to the basement like sensible people, or we can sit here like fools and risk our necks."

"What do you want to do?" one of them asked me.

"You're the guests."

"You're the hosts."

"I'd like to stay here and see what comes," I told them.

Ruth frowned at me, but there we stayed, savoring our food and the sulphurous light. Eventually the siren quit. When my ears stopped ringing, I could hear the rushing of a great wind, like the growl of a waterfall. An utter calm stole over me. The hair on my neck bristled. My nostrils flared. Heat rose in my face as though the tip of a wing had raked over it.

Although I found myself, minutes later, still in the chair, the faces of my wife and friends gleaming in the candlelight, for a spell I rode the wind, dissolved into it, and there was only the great wind, rushing.

The tornado missed us by half a mile. It did not kill anyone in our vicinity, but it ripped off chimneys, toyed with cars, and plucked up a fat old maple by the roots.

Prudent folks would have gone to the basement. I do not recommend our decision; I merely report it. Why the others tarried on the porch I cannot say, but what kept me there was a mixture of curiosity and awe. I had never seen the whirling black funnel except in cautionary films, where it left a wake of havoc and tears. And now here was that tremendous power, paying us a visit. When a god comes calling, no matter how bad its reputation, would you go hide? If the siren had announced the sighting of a dragon, I would have sat there just the same, hoping to catch a glimpse of the spiked tail or fiery breath.

As a boy in Ohio I knew a farm family, the Millers, who not only saw but suffered from three tornadoes. The father, mother, and two sons were pulling into their driveway after church when the first tornado hoisted up their mobile home, spun it around, and carried it off. With the insurance money, they built a small frame house on the same spot. Several years later, a second tornado peeled off the roof, splintered the garage, and rustled two cows. The younger of the sons, who was in my class at school, told me that he had watched from the barn as the twister passed through, "And it never even mussed up my hair." The Millers rebuilt again, raising a new garage on the old foundation and adding another story to the house. That upper floor was reduced to kindling by a third tornado, which also pulled out half the apple trees and slurped water from the stock pond. Soon after that I left Ohio, snatched away by college as forcefully as by any cyclone. Last thing I heard, the family was preparing to rebuild yet again.

Why did the Millers refuse to budge? I knew them well enough to say they were neither stupid nor crazy. After the garage disappeared, the father hung a sign from the mailbox that read: *Tornado Alley.* He figured the local terrain would coax future whirlwinds in their direction. Then why not move? Plain stubbornness was a factor. These were people who, once settled, might have remained at the foot of a volcano or on the bank of a flood-prone river or beside an earthquake fault. They had relatives nearby, helpful neighbors, jobs and stores and school within a short drive, and those were all good reasons to stay. But the main reason, I believe, was because the Millers had invested so much of their lives in the land, planting orchards and gardens, spreading manure on the fields, digging ponds, building sheds, seeding pastures. Out back of the house were groves of walnuts, hickories, and oaks, all started by hand from acorns and nuts. Honeybees zipped out from a row of white hives to nuzzle clover in the pasture, April through October, perennial flowers in the yard pumped out a fountain of blossoms. This farm was not just so many acres of dirt, easily exchanged for an equal amount elsewhere; it was a particular place, intimately known, worked on, dreamed over, cherished.

Psychologists tell us that we answer trouble with one of two impulses, either fight or flight. I believe that the Millers' response to tornados and my own keen expectancy on the porch arose from a third instinct, that of staying put. When the pain of leaving behind what we know outweighs the pain of embracing it, or when the power we face is overwhelming and neither fight nor flight will save us, there may be salvation in sitting still. And if salvation is impossible, then at least before perishing we may gain a clearer vision of where we are. By sitting still I do not mean the paralysis of dread, like that of a rabbit frozen beneath the dive of a hawk. I mean something like reverence, a respectful waiting, a deep attentiveness to forces much greater than our own. If indulged only for a moment, as in my case on the porch, this reverent impulse may amount to little; but if sustained for months and years, as by the Millers on their farm, it may yield marvels. The Millers knew better than to fight a tornado, and they chose not to flee. Instead they devoted themselves, season after season, to patient labor. Instead of withdrawing, they gave themselves more fully. Their commitment to the place may have been foolhardy, but it was also grand. I suspect that most human achievements worth admiring are the result of such devotion.

The tornado memories dramatize a choice we are faced with constantly: whether to go or stay, whether to move to a situation that is safer, richer, easier, more attractive, or to stick where we are and make what we can of it. If the shine goes off our marriage, our house, our car, do we trade it for a new one? If the fertility leaches out of our soil, the creativity out of our job, the money out of our pocket, do we start over somewhere else? There are voices enough, both inner and outer, urging us to deal with difficulties by pulling up stakes and heading for new territory. I know them well, for they have been calling to me all my days. I wish to raise here a contrary voice, to say a few words on behalf of staying put, confronting the powers, learning the ground, going deeper.

In a poem written not long before he leapt from a bridge over the Mississippi River, John Berryman ridiculed those who asked about his "roots" ("as if I were a *plant*"), and he articulated something like a credo for the dogma of rootlessness:

> *Exile is in our time like blood. Depend on*
> *interior journeys taken anywhere.*
>
> *I'd rather live in Venice or Kyoto,*
> *except for the languages, but*
> *O really I don't care where I live or have lived.*
> *Wherever I am, young Sir, my wits about me,*
> *memory blazing, I'll cope & make do.*

("Roots")

It is a bold claim, but also a hazardous one. For all his wits, Berryman in the end failed to cope well enough to stave off suicide. The truth is, none of us can live by wits alone. For even the barest existence, we depend on the labors of other people, the fruits of the earth, the inherited goods of our given place. If our interior journeys are cut loose entirely from that place, then both we and the neighborhood will suffer.

Exile usually suggests banishment, a forced departure from one's homeland. Famines and tyrants and wars do indeed force entire populations to flee; but most people who move, especially within the industrialized world, do so by choice. Salman Rushdie chose to leave his native India for England, where he has written a series of brilliant books from the perspective of a cultural immigrant. Like many writers, he has taken his own condition to represent not merely a possibility but a norm. In the essays of *Imaginary Homelands* he celebrates "the migrant sensibility," whose development he regards as "one of the central themes of this century of displaced persons." Rushdie has also taken this condition to represent something novel in history:

> The effect of mass migrations has been the creation of radically new types of human beings: people who root themselves in ideas rather than places, in memories as much as in material things; people who have been obliged to define themselves—because they are as defined by others—by their otherness; people in whose deepest selves strange fusions occur, unprecedented unions between what they were and where they find themselves.

In the history of my own country, that description applies just as well to the Pilgrims in Plymouth, say, or to Swiss homesteading in Indiana, or to Chinese trading in California, or to former slaves crowding into cities on the Great Lakes, or to Seminoles driven onto reservations a thousand miles from their traditional land. Displaced persons are abundant in our century, but hardly a novelty.

Claims for the virtues of shifting ground are familiar and seductive to Americans, this nation founded by immigrants and shaped by restless movers. From the beginning, our heroes have been sailors, explorers, cowboys, prospectors, speculators, backwoods ramblers, rainbow-chasers, vagabonds of every stripe. Our Promised Land has always been over the next ridge or at the end of the rail, never under our feet. One hundred years after the official closing of the frontier, we have still not shaken off the romance of unlimited space. If we fish out a stream or wear out a field, or if the smoke from a neighbor's chimney begins to crowd the sky, why, off we go to a new stream, a fresh field, a clean sky. In our national mythology, the worst fate is to be trapped on a farm, in a village, in the sticks, in some dead-end job or unglamorous marriage or played-out game. Stand still, we are warned, and you die. Americans have dug the most canals, laid the most rails, built the most roads and airports of any nation. In today's newspaper I read that, even though our sprawling system of interstate highways is crumbling, the President has decided that we should triple it in size, and all without raising our taxes a nickel. Only a populace drunk on driving, a populace infatuated with the myth of the open road, could hear such a proposal without hooting.

So we Americans are likely to share Rushdie's enthusiasm for migration, for the "hybridity, impurity, intermingling, the transformation that comes of new and unexpected combinations of human beings, cultures, ideas, politics, movies, songs." Everything about us is mongrel, from race to language, and we are stronger for it. Yet we might respond more skeptically when Rushdie says that "to be a migrant is, perhaps, to be the only species of human being free of the shackles of nationalism (to say nothing of its ugly sister, patriotism)." Lord knows we could do with less nationalism (to say nothing of its ugly siblings, racism, religious sectarianism, or class snobbery). But who would pretend that a history of migration has immunized the United States against bigotry? And even if, by uprooting ourselves, we shed our chauvinism, is that all we lose?

In this hemisphere, many of the worst abuses—of land, forests, animals, and communities—have been carried out by "people who root themselves in ideas rather than places." Rushdie claims that "migrants must, of necessity, make a new imaginative relationship with the world, because of the loss of familiar habitats." But migrants often pack up their visions and values with the rest of their baggage and carry them along. The Spaniards devastated Central and South America by imposing on this New World the religion, economics, and politics of the Old. Colonists brought slavery with them to North America, along with smallpox and Norway rats. The Dust Bowl of the 1930s was caused not by drought but by the transfer onto the Great Plains of farming methods that were suitable to wetter regions. The habit of our industry and commerce has been to force identical schemes onto differing locales, as though the mind were a cookie-cutter and the land were dough.

I quarrel with Rushdie because he articulates as eloquently as anyone the orthodoxy that I wish to counter: the belief that movement is inherently good, staying put is bad; that uprooting brings tolerance, while rootedness breeds intolerance; that imaginary homelands are preferable to geographical ones; that to be modern, enlightened, fully of our time is to be displaced. Wholesale displacement may be inevitable; but we should not suppose that it occurs without disastrous consequences for the earth and for ourselves. People who root themselves in places are likelier to know and care for those places than are people who root themselves in ideas. When we cease to be migrants and become inhabitants, we might begin to pay enough heed to respect where we are. By settling in, we have chance of making a durable home for ourselves, our fellow creatures, and our descendants.

What are we up against, those of us who aspire to become inhabitants, who wish to commit ourselves to a place? How strong, how old, is the impulse we are resisting?

Although our machines enable us to move faster and farther, humans have been on the move for a long time. Within a few clicks on the evolutionary clock our ancestors roamed out of their native valleys in Africa and spread over the Eurasian continent. They invaded the deserts, the swamps, the mountains and valleys, the jungle and tundra. Drifting on boats and rafts, they pushed on to island after island around the globe. When glaciers locked up enough seawater to expose a land bridge from Asia to North America, migrants crossed into this unknown region, and within a few thousand years their descendants had scattered from the Bering Straits to Tierra del Fuego.

The mythology of those first Americans often claimed that a tribe had been attached to a given spot since the beginning of time, and we in our craving for rootedness may be inclined to believe in this eternal bond between people and place; but archaeology suggests that ideas, goods, and populations were in motion for millennia before the first Europeans reached these shores, hunters and traders and whole tribes roving about, boundaries shifting, homelands changing hands. Even agricultural settlements, such as those associated with the mound-building cultures in the Mississippi and Ohio valleys, reveal a history of arrivals and departures, sites used for decades or centuries and then abandoned. By comparison to our own hectic movements, an association between people and place lasting decades or centuries may seem durable and enviable; but it is not eternal.

What I am saying is that we are a wandering species, and have been since we reared up on our hind legs and stared at the horizon. Our impulse to wander, to pick up and move when things no longer suit us in our present place, is not an ailment brought on suddenly by industrialization, by science, or by the European hegemony over dark-skinned peoples. It would be naive to think that Spanish horses corrupted the Plains Indians, tempting a sedentary people to rush about, or that snowmobiles corrupted the Inuit, or that Jeeps corrupted the Aborigines. It would be just as naive to say that the automobile gave rise to our own restlessness; on the contrary, our restlessness gave rise to the automobile, as it led to the bicycle, steamboat, and clipper ship, as it led to the taming of horses, lacing of snowshoes, and carving of dugout canoes. With each invention, a means of moving farther, faster, has answered to a desire that coils in our genes. Mobility is the rule in human history, rootedness the exception.

Our itch to wander was the great theme of the English writer Bruce Chatwin, who died in 1989 from a rare disease contracted in the course of his own incessant travels. For Chatwin, "the nature of human restlessness" was "the question of questions." One hundred pages of *The Songlines,* his best-known work, are filled with notebook entries supporting the view that "man is a migratory species." In a posthumous collection of essays entitled *What Am I Doing Here,* he summed up his observations:

> [W]e should perhaps allow human nature an appetitive drive for movement in the widest sense. The act of journeying contributes towards a sense of physical and mental wellbeing, while the monotony of prolonged settlement or regular work weaves patterns in the brain that engender fatigue and a sense of personal inadequacy. Much of what the ethnologists have designated "aggression" is simply an angered response to the frustrations of confinement.

I am dubious about the psychology here, for I noticed Chatwin's own frustrations in the passage, especially in the irritable phrase about "the monotony of prolonged settlement or regular work"; but I agree with his speculation that deep in us there is "an appetitive drive for movement."

The movement chronicled in *The Songlines*—the purposeful wandering of the Australian Aborigines—may suggest a way for us to harness our restlessness, a way to reconcile our need to rove with our need to stay put. As hunter-gatherers in a harsh continent, the Aborigines must know their land thoroughly and travel it widely in order to survive. According to their belief, the land and all living things were created in a mythic time called the Dreaming, and the creative spirits are still at work, sustaining the world. Humans keep the world in touch with the power of the Dreaming by telling stories and singing songs. The whole of Australia is crisscrossed by pathways known to the Aborigines, who must walk them at intervals, performing the songs that belong to each path. Every tribe is responsible for the tracks within its own territory, and for passing down the appropriate songs from generation to generation. "There was hardly a rock or creek in the country," Chatwin remarks," "that couldn't or had not been sung." The movement of the Aborigines is not random, therefore, but deliberate, guided by hunger and thirst, but also by the need to participate in the renewal of the world. The land supplies the necessities of life, and in return humans offer knowledge, memory, and voice.

The Aboriginal walkabout illustrates "the once universal concept," in Chatwin's words, "that wandering re-establishes the original harmony . . . between man and the universe." Unlike vagabonds, who use up place after place without returning on their tracks, the Aborigines wed themselves to one place, and range over it with gratitude and care. So that they might continue as residents, they become stewards. Like the rest of nature, they move in circles, walking again and again over sacred ground.

The Australian Aborigines are among the "inhabitory peoples" whom Gary Snyder has studied in his search for wisdom about living in place, a wisdom he described in *The Old Ways:*

> People developed specific ways to be in each of those niches: plant knowledge, boats, dogs, traps, nets, fishing—the smaller animals, and smaller tools. From steep jungle slopes of Southwest China to coral atolls to barren artic deserts—a spirit of what it was to be there evolved, that spoke of a direct sense of relation to the "land"—which really means, the totality of the local bio-region system from cirrus clouds to leaf-mold.

Such knowledge does not come all at once; it accumulates bit by bit over generations, each person adding to the common lore.

Even nomads, whose name implies motion, must be scholars of their bioregion. As they follow herds from pasture to pasture through the cycle of the year, they trace a loop that is dictated by what the land provides. For inhabitory peoples, listening to the land is a spiritual discipline as well as a practical one. The alertness that feeds the body also feeds the soul. In Native American culture, "medicine" is understood not as a human invention, but as a channeling of the power by which all things live. Whether you are a hunter-gatherer, a nomad, a farmer, or a suburbanite, to be at home in the land is to be sane and whole. Your own health and that of your community derive from the health of the soil, the waters, the air, the plants, and the beasts.

The Aborigines worked out an accommodation with their land over forty thousand years, no doubt through trial and error. They would not have survived if their mythology had not soon come to terms with their ecology. Even so, their population was never more than about one-hundredth as large as that of modern Australia. We who live in North America are engaged in our own trails and errors, which are greatly magnified by the size of our population and the power of our technology. A man with a bulldozer can make a graver mistake in one day than a whole tribe with digging sticks can make in a year. In my home region, mistakes are being made seven days a week—with machinery, chemicals, guns, plows, fountain pens, bare hands. I suspect the same is true in every region. But who is keeping track? Who speaks for the wordless creatures? Who supplies memory and conscience for the land?

Half a century ago, in *A Sand County Almanac,* Aldo Leopold gave us an ecological standard for judging our actions: "A thing is right when it tends to preserve the integrity, stability, and beauty of the biotic community. It is wrong when it tends otherwise." We can only apply that standard if, in every biotic community, there are residents who keep watch over what is preserved and what is lost, who see the beauty that escapes the frame of the tourist's windshield or the investor's spreadsheet. "The problem," Leopold observed, "is how to bring about a striving for harmony with land among a people many of whom have forgotten there is any such thing as land, among whom education and culture have become almost synonymous with landlessness." To be landless is not to lack property but to lack responsibility.

In the preface to his *Natural History of Selborne,* the eighteenth-century English vicar, Gilbert White, notes that a comprehensive survey of England might be compiled if only "stationary men would pay some attention to the districts on which they reside." Every township, every field and creek, every mountain and forest on Earth would benefit from the attention of stationary men and women. No one has understood this need better than Gary Snyder (speaking here in an interview from *The Real Work*):

> One of the key problems in American society now, it seems to me, is people's lack of commitment to any given place—which, again, is totally unnatural and outside of history. Neighborhoods are allowed to deteriorate, landscapes are allowed to be strip-mined, because there is nobody who will live there and take responsibility; they'll just move on. The reconstruction of people and of a life in the United States depends in part on people, neighborhood by neighborhood, county by county, deciding to stick it out and make it work where they are rather than flee.

We may not have forty years, let alone forty thousand, to reconcile our mythology with our ecology. If we are to reshape our way of things, as the songs of the Aborigines follow their terrain, many more of us need to *know* our local ground, walk over it, care for it, fight for it, bear it steadily in mind.

But if you stick in one place, won't you become a stick-in-the-mud? If you stay put, won't you be narrow, backward, dull? You might. I have met ignorant people who never moved; and I have also met ignorant people who never stood still. Committing yourself to a place does not guarantee that you will become wise, but neither does it guarantee that you will become parochial. Who knows better the limitations of a province or a culture than the person who has bumped into them time and again? The history of settlement in my own district and the continuing abuse of land hereabouts provoke me to rage and grief. I know the human legacy here too well to glamorize it.

To become intimate with your home region, to know the territory as well as you can, to understand your life as woven into the local life does not prevent you from recognizing and honoring the diversity of other places, cultures, ways. On the contrary, how can you value other places if you do not have one of your own? If you are not yourself *placed,* then you wander the world like a sightseer, a collector of sensations, with no gauge for measuring what you see. Local knowledge is the grounding for global knowledge. Those who care about nothing beyond the confines of their parish are in truth parochial, and are at the least mildly dangerous to their parish; on the other hand, those who *have* no parish, those who navigate among postal zones and area codes, those for whom the world is only a smear of highways and bank accounts and stores, are a danger not just to their parish but to the plant.

Since birth, my children have been surrounded by images of the earth as viewed from space, images that I first encountered when I was in my twenties. Those photographs show vividly what in our sanest moments we have always known—that the Earth is a closed circle, lovely and rare. On the wall beside me as I write there is a poster of the big blue marble encased in its white swirl of clouds. That is one pole of my awareness; but the other pole is what I see through my window. I try to keep both in sight at once.

For all my convictions, I still have to wrestle with the fear—in myself, in my children, and even in some of my neighbors—that our place is too remote from the action. This fear drives many people to pack their bags and move to some resort or burg they have seen on television, leaving behind what they learn to think of as the boondocks. I deal with my own unease by asking just what action I am remote *from*—a stock market? a debating chamber? a drive-in mortuary? The action that matters, the work of nature and community goes on everywhere.

Since Copernicus we have known better than to see the earth as the center of the universe. Since Einstein we have learned that there is no center; or alternatively that any point is as good as any other for observing the world. I take this to be roughly what medieval theologians meant when they defined God as a circle whose circumference is nowhere and whose center is everywhere. I find a kindred lesson in the words of Zen master,

Thich Nhat Hanh: "This spot where you sit is your own spot. It is on this very spot and in this very moment that you can become enlightened. You don't have to sit beneath a special tree in a distant land." If you stay put, your place may become a holy center, not because it gives you special access to the divine, but because in your stillness you hear what might be heard anywhere. The Sioux medicine man, Black Elk, explained that in a vision he saw "the whole hoop of the world" encircling his own sacred mountain peak in the Black Hills of South Dakota. Although he gazed into the heart of Creation, this did not mean that he was standing in a privileged location, Black Elk went on to say, "because anywhere is the center of the world." There are no privileged locations. No place has a corner on the truth. All there is to see can be seen from anywhere in the universe, if you know how to look; and the influence of the entire universe converges on every spot.

Except for the rare patches of wilderness, every place on Earth has been transformed by human presence. "Ecology becomes a more complex but far more interesting science," René Dubos observes in *The Wooing of Earth*, "when human aspirations are regarded as an integral part of the landscape." Through "long periods of intimate association between human beings and nature," Dubos argues, landscape may take on a "quality of blessedness." The understanding of how to dwell in a place arises out of the sustained conversation between people and land.

If our fidelity to place is to help renew and preserve our neighborhoods, it will have to be informed by what Wendell Berry in *Standing by Words* calls "an ecological intelligence: a sense of the impossibility of acting or living alone or solely in one's own behalf, and this rests in turn upon a sense of the order upon which any life depends and of the proprieties of place within that order." Proprieties of place: actions, words, and values that are *proper* to your home ground. I think of my home ground as a series of nested rings, with house and family and marriage at the center, surrounded by the wider and wider hoops of neighborhood and community, the bioregion within walking distance of my door, the wooded hills and karst landscape of southern Indiana, the watershed of the Ohio Valley, and so on outward—and inward—to the ultimate source.

The longing to become an inhabitant rather than a drifter sets me against the current of my culture, which nudges everyone into motion. Newton taught us that a body at rest tends to stay at rest, unless acted on by an outside force. We are acted on ceaselessly by outside forces—advertising, movies, magazines, speeches—and also by the inner force of biology. I am not immune to their pressure. Before settling in my present home, I lived in seven states and two countries, tugged from place to place in childhood by my father's work and in early adulthood by my own. This itinerant life is so common among the people I know that I have been slow to conceive of an alternative. Only by knocking against the golden calf of mobility, which looms so large and shines so brightly, have I come to realize that it is hollow. Like all idols, it distracts us from the true divinity.

The ecological argument for staying put may be easier for us to see than the spiritual one, worried as we are about saving our skins. Few of us worry about saving our souls, and fewer still imagine that the condition of our souls has anything to do with the condition of our neighborhoods. Talk about enlightenment makes us nervous, because it implies that we pass our ordinary days in darkness. You recall the scene in *King Lear* when blind and wretched old Gloucester, wishing to commit suicide, begs a young man to lead him to the edge of the cliff. The young man is Gloucester's son, Edgar, who fools the old man into thinking they have come to a high bluff at the edge of the sea. Gloucester kneels, then tumbles forward onto the level ground; on landing, he is amazed to find himself alive. He is transformed by the fall. Blind, at least he is able to see his life clearly; despairing, he discovers hope. To be enlightened, he did not have to leap to someplace else; he only had to come hard against the ground where he already stood.

I am encouraged by the words of a Crow elder, quoted by Gary Snyder in *The Practice of the Wild:* "You know, think if people stay somewhere long enough—even with people—the spirits will begin to speak to them. It's the power of the spirits coming up from the land. The spirits and the old powers aren't lost, they just need people to be around long enough and the spirits will begin to influence them." No need to put out your eyes like Gloucester in order to see. No need to be grim. I embrace the Buddhist advice: learn what you can, live as mindfully as you can, treat with loving kindness all the creatures that share the sunlight with you, and be joyful.

My friend Richard, who wears a white collar to his job, recently bought forty acres of land that had been worn out by the standard local regimen of chemicals and corn. Evenings and weekends, he has set about restoring the soil by spreading manure, planting clover and rye, and filling the eroded gullies with brush. His pond has gathered geese, his young orchard has tempted deer, and his nesting boxes have attracted swallows and bluebirds. Now he is preparing a field for the wildflowers and prairie grasses that once flourished here. Having contemplated this work since he was a boy, Richard will not be chased away by fashion or dollars or tornadoes. On a recent airplane trip he was distracted from the book he was reading by thoughts of renewing the land. So he sketched on the flyleaf a plan of labor for the next ten years. Most of us do not have forty acres to care for, but they should not keep us from sowing and tending local crops.

I think about Richard's ten-year vision when I read a report that shows computer users grow impatient if they have to wait more than a second to see the results of their decisions. If a machine or a program takes longer than a second to respond, customers will shun it. I use a computer, but I am wary of the haste it encourages. Few answers that matter will come to us in a second; some of the most vital answers will not come in ten years, or a hundred.

When the chiefs of the Iroquois nation sit in council, they are sworn to consider how their decisions will affect their descendants seven generations into the future. Seven generations! Imagine our politicians thinking beyond the new opinion poll, beyond the next election, beyond their own lifetimes, two centuries ahead. Imagine our bankers, our corporate executives, our advertising moguls weighing their judgments on that scale. Looking seven generations into the future, could a developer pave another farm? Could a farmer spray another pound of poison? Could the captain of an oil tanker flush his tanks at sea? Could you or I write checks and throw switches without a much greater concern for what is bought and sold, what is burned?

As I write this, I hear the snarl of earthmovers and chain saws a mile away destroying a farm to make way for another shopping strip. I would rather hear a tornado whose damage can be undone. The elderly woman who owned the farm had it listed in the National Register, then willed it to her daughters on condition they preserve it. After her death, the daughters, who live out of state, had the will broken, so the land could be turned over to the chain saws and earthmovers. The machines work around the clock. Their noise wakes me at midnight, at three in the morning, at dawn. The roaring abrades my dreams. The sound is a reminder that we are living in the midst of a holocaust. I do not use the word lightly. The earth is being pillaged, and every one of us, willingly or grudgingly, is taking part. We ask how sensible, educated, supposedly moral people could have tolerated slavery or the slaughter of Jews. Similar questions will be asked about us by our descendants, to whom we bequeath an impoverished planet. They will demand to know how we could have been party to such waste and ruin. They will have good reason to curse our memory.

What does it mean to be alive in an era when the earth is being devoured, and in a country which has set the pattern for that devouring? What are we called to do? I think we are called to the work of healing, both inner and outer: healing of the mind through a change in consciousness, healing of the earth through a change in our lives. We can begin that work by learning how to abide in a place. I am talking about an active commitment, not a passive lingering. If you stay with a husband or wife out of laziness rather than love, that is inertia, not marriage. If you stay put through cowardice rather than conviction, you will have no strength to act. Strength comes, healing comes, from aligning yourself with the grain of your place and answering to its needs.

"The man who is often thinking that it is better to be somewhere else than where he is excommunicates himself," we are cautioned by Thoreau, that notorious stay-at-home (*Journal*, November 20, 1857). The metaphor is religious: to withhold yourself from where you are is to be cut off from communion with the source. It has taken me half a lifetime of searching to realize that the likeliest path to the ultimate ground leads through my local ground. I mean the land itself, with its creeks and rivers, its weather, seasons, stone outcroppings, and all the plants and animals that share it. I cannot have a spiritual center without having a geographical one; I cannot live a grounded life without being grounded in a *place*.

In belonging to a landscape, one feels a rightness, at-homeness, a knitting of self and world. This condition of clarity and focus, this being fully present, is akin to what the Buddhists call mindfulness, what Christian contemplatives refer to as recollection, what Quakers call centering down. I am suspicious of any philosophy that would separate this-worldly from other-worldly commitment. There is only one world, and we participate in it here and now, in our flesh and our place.

(1992)

What Came Next

Following Up on the Stories in The Future of Nature

The initiatives, movements, ideas, people, and organizations that have been described in *Orion* in the last fifteen years have not stood still. All of them have changed and evolved; some for the better, some not. We asked contributors to *The Future of Nature* to apprise readers of how affairs related to their original articles have changed since their first publication.

Action

Reinhabiting Environmentalism (1999)

Writing in 1999 I was celebrating what I hoped would be the reemergence of conversations that sought to connect the environment and human rights. I also was anticipating—yearning for—a more tranquil, comfortable new century and worried that in a less urgent atmosphere the impulse for these discussions might be lost again.

The new century has turned out to be anything but tranquil. Social, economic, and political forces have combined with chemical, physical, and biological processes to produce a bewildering storm of urgency. It demands elucidation, yet defies conventional reductionist explanations. It's an ideal climate for these conversations to continue—to understand that polar bears starving on melting Arctic ice, New Orleans and Bangladesh drowning, the poverty and malnourishment that afflict 80 percent of the people on the planet, and our adventure in Iraq, are symptoms of the same persistent resistance to comprehend the human and biotic communities as one.

The conversations—the "continuing seminar" that Aldo Leopold proposed in 1948—has reconvened in a global forum. I worry only that they might not proceed fast enough.

—Peter Sauer

Consent of the Governed (2003)

Several more Pennsylvania townships have enacted ordinances denying constitutional rights to corporations. The townships have also begun expanding the reach of the ordinances by, for example, asserting, "Natural communities and ecosystems possess inalienable and fundamental rights to exist and prosper." The town of Barnstead, New Hampshire, has also passed a Water Rights and Local Self-Government Ordinance banning corporations from withdrawal of water for resale as well as stripping them of other constitutional rights. The board of supervisors of Campbell County in Virginia will soon vote on a similar measure that would restrict corporate use of toxic sludge.

In June of 2006 the voters of Northern California's Humboldt County passed an initiative that outlawed non-local corporations from contributing to local elections or ballot questions. The initiative, referred to as Measure T, defines a local corporation as one whose owners, stockholders, and employees all live within the county. It also explicitly denies corporations the ability to invoke "constitutional rights or protections" in order to challenge the law. Democracy Unlimited of Humboldt County (DUHC) of Eureka, California, led the initiative campaign.

Jeff Milchen, founder of ReclaimDemocracy.org, observes that local battles against chain stores provide ripe opportunities for reasserting citizen authority over corporations and prods some of these communities to strip corporations of presumed political rights through laws like Measure T. Kaitlin Sopoci-Belknap, director of Democracy Unlimited and campaign co-manager for Measure T, agrees. "The key is to create concrete campaigns around issues that folks already care about in order to broaden and deepen the growing movement to challenge the illegitimate notion that a corporation possesses 'rights' at all," she says. "Ultimately we need communities across the country to stand up for themselves in order to build a true democracy movement in the United States."

—Jeffrey Kaplan

The Union Makes Them Strong (2005)

Since forgoing a re-election run for the position as District 11 director of the United Steelworkers of America—a position he held for sixteen years—David Foster has dedicated himself full-time to working on "blue-green alliances." In June 2006 he became executive director of the new Strategic Alliance, which solidifies an alliance between the labor and environmental movements.

The issues the alliance focuses on most today, he says, include global warming, clean energy, trade, and the creation of a "green" chemical industry. He reiterates today just why labor and environmentalists are natural allies, and why it was necessary to do this work full-time: "The United States and other Western countries are fundamentally undermining the basic reforms the labor movement had been striving for in the twentieth century. And the same is happening with the environmental movement, too," he says. "I saw us losing all that." There are challenges ahead, he knows, not the least of which has to do with banging up against a free market economy that doesn't treat humans—or the environment—very well. But the reality is, he says, "the jobs that last will be jobs based on environmental sustainability. In a global economy, we can't talk anymore about one without the other."

Since researching this story, by the way, I've kept at my desk a quote from former Rep. Ken Hechler (D-WV), who led the charge to pass legislation in 1970 compensating miners who had contracted Black Lung disease: "You are in politics whether you like it or not. If you sit it out on the sidelines, you are throwing your influence on the side of corruption, mismanagement, and the forces of evil." Amen.

—*Laura Paskus*

Got Tape? (2003)

About a year after I finished "Got Tape?" the landowners pulled out of the deal allowing Open Space to buy the property over a five-year period. They wanted retail price, or nothing. In a hearing highly influenced by our community activist group, however, the land was no longer zoned retail.

This is what the landowners told me: Way back when they were trying to farm and make a living in the manner they loved, city water rights changed. Though farmers once had priority, suburban lawns now had first water rights and whatever was left trickled down to farmers. Colorado is a semi-arid climate. No water, no crops, no income. Local farmers were forced out of business. The landowners would forever hold a grudge. This old anger came to the fore when negotiations for selling to Open Space began. The deal fell through.

For four years the land remained undeveloped. I rode my bike by daily thinking that, had the owners sold to Open Space, they would now have four years' worth of interest in hand.

In 2006 a residential developer paid retail price for the property. They'll make up the difference in density of units. However, the City will not back down on rezoning issues, which require a decent portion of the acreage be devoted to open space. They have insisted on integrating trails into the plan. These will connect to forty-eight miles of existing trails, all of which may help turn this commercially driven suburb into a walking community. As I write this update, I can hear the backhoes and bulldozers just beginning to rev their engines.

About one month before the developer broke ground, Oliver was committed to a V.A. mental hospital. He was the one family member who had stayed behind, living on the property he grew up on. He was waving a loaded gun, desperately pointing it at anyone who neared the place. He did not want to leave.

—BK Loren

Refugees

Conservation Refugees (2005)

Transnational conservation organizations and the worldwide movement of indigenous peoples share a goal that is vital to all of us—a healthy and diverse biota. Both are communities of integrity led by some of the most admirable, dedicated people in modern civilization, both care deeply for the planet. Together they are capable of preserving more biological diversity than any other two institutions on it. Yet sadly they have been terribly at odds with one another—violently at times—due mostly to conflicting views of nature, radically different definitions of "wilderness," and profound misunderstandings of each other's science and culture. The result of this century-old conflict is thousands of unmanageable protected areas and an intractable debate over who holds the key to successful conservation in the most biologically rich areas of the world.

I wrote this article for *Orion* with the hope that, one day, conservationists and native people could come to agreement that they need each other badly. My hope was that together they could create a new conservation paradigm that honors and respects the lifeways of people who have been living sustainably for generations on what can only be fairly regarded as their native land, who in exchange will blend with their ancient traditional knowledge systems the comparatively new sciences of ecology and conservation biology, in search of new and better ways to preserve the diversity of species that is vital to all life on Earth. At this point, as the entire planet seems poised to tip into ecological chaos, there may be no other way.

—Mark Dowie

Jeremiad for Belarus (2004)

Six years after my introduction to life in Chernobyl-contaminated Belarus, there is good news and there is bad news. Three years of annual inflation well above 200 percent has slowed, Belarus's economy is growing, and the impact is visible in Cherikov where many more roads and sidewalks have been paved, theoretically preventing foot traffic from stirring radioactive dust particles. Salaries have doubled (to an average $35 a month, about one-third of pre-Chernobyl levels) making life for many more comfortable, if not more certain. Government and NGO aid has once again made it possible for Cherikov's school children to spend a month each year in a clean territory receiving health checks, and clean food and air in which to play.

In the absence of human competition or predation, wildlife is thriving in the nearby Exclusion Zone, as it is in the zone around the Chernobyl nuclear power station in Pripyat, Ukraine. But the extent to which people, wildlife, and the environment were harmed by the accident is still debated. Texas Tech researchers Ronald Chesser and Robert Baker wrote in a December 2006 issue of *American Scientist,* "Conflicting reports on the genetic and biological impacts of environmental radiation make it difficult for even the most seasoned scientist to make sense of all the data."

Their recommendation that the "proper null hypothesis should be that the effects of the Chernobyl environment on an organism do not differ from effects outside the environment" is sound science. Is it, however, sound social policy? The Price-Anderson Act, reauthorized in 2005, precludes injured victims from directly suing nuclear vendors or manufacturers responsible for an accident, and restricts plaintiffs' abilities to access any state laws that might go above and beyond federal protections. Unlike evacuated Katrina victims who can at least hope their lawsuits with insurance companies will eventually provide the monetary means to rebuild lives and homes, those of us living in the path of radioactive plumes will have no recourse. Like Irene Kulbakina, whose most recent letter announces that she and Sasha have given up hope of ever being able to leave their contaminated town and so are taking a forty-year mortgage on a three-room flat, our government's refusal to take Chernobyl seriously enough to consider the long-term consequences of constant exposure to radioactivity will ensure that in the event of a catastrophe at one of our aging nuclear power facilities, we too will simply live through the null hypothesis while the nascent field of radio-ecology tries to catch up with regulatory hubris.

—Hope Burwell

Moving Mountains (2006)

Since I wrote "Moving Mountains," three important things have happened: two good and one bad. First the bad news. On March 13, 2006, the West Virginia Surface Mine Board overturned the Department of Environmental Protection ruling that banned Massey Energy from building a second coal silo behind the Marsh Fork Elementary School. A few days later, protesters gathered at the state capitol to demand that a new school be built for the children. A sit-in ensued, and the protesters were arrested in not the gentlest of fashion. As of now, neither Governor Manchin nor Senator Byrd has offered to help find these children a decent, healthy, non-life-threatening place to learn.

Now the good news. On March 23, former coal lobbyist Steven Griles was sentenced to six months in prison for lying about his ties to Jack Abramoff. As deputy secretary of the interior under George W. Bush, Griles worked callously to weaken environmental regulations on strip mining. He changed one word of the Clean Water Act—replacing "waste" with "fill"—so that toxic mining debris could then be dumped into rivers as benign fill material. Griles, more than anyone, is responsible for the out-of-control mountaintop removal mining that is destroying central Appalachia. His admission of guilt, along with his incarceration, is a welcome development and perhaps a sign that the foxes can no longer have their way in the hen house.

And lastly, on March 27, a federal judge demanded the immediate stoppage of four mountaintop removal operations in West Virginia. He agreed with Earthjustice and the Appalachian Center for the Economy and the Environment that the Army Corps of Engineers had not properly studied the risk to the surrounding watersheds. Since 2000, the Corps has felt intense pressure by the Bush administration to "fast-track" the permitting process without performing environmental impact assessments. As the *New York Times* editorialized: "Local residents who have watched the destruction of their landscape hope the ruling will lead to tighter regulation of other mountaintop mining proposals. The greater hope is that the government can be persuaded to stop the practice altogether."

—*Erik Reece*

The Black Mesa Syndrome (1998)

In the nine years since "The Black Mesa Syndrome" was published, Black Mesa has seen good news and bad news. First, the good news: In 2005, after thirty-five years of operation, the Mohave Power Plant in Laughlin, Nevada, along with its slurry pipeline supply system (which used over a billion gallons of water a year to transport pulverized coal to Laughlin), as well as the Black Mesa mine which supplied the five million tons of coal, shut down.

The shutdown was the result of a series of successful lawsuits by environmental and Native American groups over irresponsible water use and the amount of pollution spewed out by the plant, built in 1970 by the Bechtel Corporation without scrubbers or antipollution equipment. Rather than spend an estimated $1 billion to upgrade, the operating utilities of Las Vegas, Phoenix, and Los Angeles decided to shut the plant down. Its last day of operation was December 31, 2005. Black Mesa strip-mining continued at the Kayenta mine site with approximately seven million tons of coal going to the Navajo Power Station at Page. (The Navajo tribe has no operating control or interest in the Navajo power plant.)

Then, in 2006, the law of unintended consequences took over. Irl Engelhardt, chairman of Peabody Coal, set in motion a new life-of-the-mine permit for the Black Mesa mine. In the intervening years Peabody Coal Company has morphed into Peabody Energy Inc., a public company (stock exchange symbol, BTU) with friends in the White House, and the largest coal supplier in the world. The new Black Mesa Project involves re-opening the Mohave Plant, rebuilding the slurry pipeline, drawing water from a new aquifer source, and obtaining a mining permit for as long as the coal is retrievable from the Black Mesa site. It is worth repeating that coal slurryline technology is highly controversial; in every white community where coal slurry pipelines have been proposed, they have been defeated on the grounds of destruction of groundwater.

In January 2007 the Office of Surface Mining held public hearings in chapter houses around the Navajo and Hopi reservations about the new Black Mesa Project. The Hopi didn't attend because they were engaged in their ceremonial year; the Navajo did attend and were described in one account as "fractious." They objected to being shown a movie about the 753-page Environmental Impact Statement and then told to give any comments they might have to a court reporter sitting off to the side of the room. How, they asked the OSM official, if the hearing didn't allow for public discussion, did the meeting fulfill the legal requirements for public input?

Words like climate change, mercury, sulfates, asthma, arsenic, acid rain, and smog have yet to enter this debate. Black Mesa continues to be the most intense area of coal-fired energy and coal strip-mining in the nation. Arizona gets 300 out of 365 days with sunshine. Unlike California, which announced an aggressive solar energy policy in 2006, Arizona is not pursuing an energy policy of new solar initiatives, nor does it seem to be a priority in the governor's office. Peabody Coal is sponsoring a national advertising campaign touting "clean coal" and coal as the energy technology of the future. The Black Mesa Syndrome is still in effect.

—*Judith Nies*

Boundaries

On Waste Lonely Places (1994)

After I wrote "Waste Lonely Places"—nearly fifteen years ago—I felt I'd mined out a personal theme and so turned toward other areas of interest. I did so with Jim Harrison's admonition in mind, that to grow artistically one must do more than cover old ground. I spent several years reading and thinking, and when I began writing again, the work I produced was poetry, a lot of it having to do with waste places. Landfills, fields, empty skies— these sorts of places seem to be an intractable part of my personal mythology. I see now that to write well about airport fences or the dead-end by a cornfield is not to cover old ground but to move with integrity toward a fuller understanding both of "waste" places and of myself.

—*John Landretti*

Reverence

The Rise and Fall of Natural History (2001)

I wish I could say that the conclusions and trends I expressed in this essay have all since been reversed and corrected. Unfortunately, such is not the case. If anything, the mass phenomenon of nature illiteracy has only grown in the succeeding years. The devices that people use to separate themselves from what they see as a boring, hostile, or insufficiently stimulating world have grown in number, allure, power, and sophistication. Everyone, it seems, is plugged in, even as they are tuned out from natural history. I've heard of whole classes of third-graders given Palm pilots, and students, who could not even tell you what an arthropod is, all have, or want, iPods. Even when people leave their homes or cars to walk or run, often as not they do so attached to an audio engine that is guaranteed to isolate them from the sounds around them. Perhaps most insidious of all in this regard is an epidemic addiction to the blandishments of the mediating screen: especially e-mailing, blogging, Internet surfing, and video gaming. Not that any of these are evil in themselves, but their collective effect has been to create a species of modern human exactly the opposite of what poet Robinson Jeffers called for when he wrote "not man apart." Meanwhile, No Child Left Behind has culled much of what remained of nature study in the classroom and an increasingly litigious and fearful culture has cut back still further on field trips, leaving no time for pure exploration.

Yet, even as I relate this depressing litany, I must also recognize some equally encouraging developments. One is the irrepressible urge toward natural history that continues to burst out in some children, parents, and elders reacquainting with something they once loved and then misplaced. A child I got to know on Vashon Island called herself "the Girl Naturalist." Now that she is almost off to college, pretty, socially adept, and gifted in many areas, I wondered if her passion had survived. While staying with her parents recently, I asked Moria, "Are you still 'the Girl Naturalist'?" She opened her door to show me her room: there was no longer any question. She will always be a naturalist. The same can be said for a young butterfly-smitten friend who has returned safely to college from two tours in Iraq, and many others I meet who don't throw over their young enthusiasm for mere electronic temptation. Even global warming, for all its perils, is stimulating the fields of faunistics and floristics (finding out just where plants and animals occur, and why) with a whole new energy and urgency.

But the most exciting development against the final burial of natural history in the schools and neighborhoods came with the publication of Richard Louv's book *The Last Child in the Woods: Saving Our Children from Nature Deficit Disorder.* Louv's insights, abundantly documented in *Orion,* have given voice to what many have feared, suspected, and articulated, but never as well or as richly: that youthful contact with nature is being lost. Not only does *Last Child* elegantly make this case, but it also offers hope—ways to bring the children back into the woods, and bring the woods to them. Louv's Children and Nature Network is making rapid progress toward reform in this area, including the introduction of "No Child Left Inside" bills in several legislatures. If natural history is to rise again, it will depend not only on educators, not only on conservationists, but most of all upon the children: for children, once fascinated with the world, may stay that way for a lifetime.

—*Robert Michael Pyle*

These Green Things (1994)

Today, Garden Project Apprentices continue their work growing and delivering vegetables. However, growing vegetables to sell at local restaurants proved to be time and labor intensive, and the profits were never enough to support the program without growing more—ostensibly limiting the capacity of the program to also grow for donation. We felt that community service was a key part of the program and that former prisoners benefited from being able to serve the community. By 2000, the program was dedicated to growing for donation. Soon, Garden Project vegetables were donated to hundreds of poor families and seniors per week via a community distribution network that included more than forty organizations.

Garden Project participants have worked on a variety of greening and cleanup programs around the city. In addition, we created a program with the neighborhood police precinct whereby officers helped deliver produce in the neighborhood, helping the Project to get its food to more people and officers to connect with the neighborhoods. Community centers began their own programming with Garden Project vegetables, and one began offering cooking classes. A local elementary school started basic nutrition classes. In these ways and more, the work of the Project has reverberated throughout the city.

Unfortunately, the Tree Corps program was funded by the city, and as San Francisco's commitment to the urban forest dwindled, so did support for the Tree Corps, causing the program to end in 2002. Nonetheless, by that time, the program had planted more than ten thousand street trees in San Francisco.

The Garden Project continues to respond to the changing needs of the population we serve. Today, in addition to working with former prisoners, The Garden Project also has a program specifically for at-risk young adults, called The Earth Stewards Program, which began in 2004. It is an intensive thirty-eight-week training program in which participants learn to earn a wage, continue their education, build life skills, and contribute to the community through environmental projects. After completing the program, participants enter the Trade Apprenticeship Program sponsored by the San Francisco Public Utilities Commission. Stewards learn basic horticulture and landscaping through farm and site-specific projects. Through each project, participants learn about the environment and leave a tangible mark in the community.

—*Cathrine Sneed*

Assailed (2002)

Although the "cosmological riffing" in this essay is grounded in firsthand experience of the Rockies in early spring, the writing didn't begin to achieve power until I began to contemplate the relationships between certain key words. *Cosmology* and *scripture*, for instance. *Science* and *reverence*. *Reason* and *intuition. Wonder* and *knowledge. Skepticism* and *faith.* As I watched the world-drama out my window and meditated upon these terms, I grew aware that some words are so alive, and so much bigger than me, that it's a mistake, in defining them, to believe that I have defined them once and for all. Some words are like weather systems: despite our best attempts to define and carefully deploy them, new energies keep flowing into them, forcing us to rethink and redefine. Some words are so potent that they deploy us to achieve *their* ends, rather than the other way around.

What follows are some of the key words probed in "Assailed," reimagined and redefined in light of the experiences I underwent as I worked on the essay. A couple of terms did not make it into the finished piece. That doesn't mean they weren't crucial to the finished product. No scaffolding, no cathedral.

cosmology: the living, breathing, never-to-be-literalized stories of science and spiritual tradition, dealing with the universe as an ordered whole, and with the general laws which govern that whole.

science: the observation, identification, description, experimental investigation, and theoretical explanation of phenomena, now "scientifically proven" to be devastating beyond belief when practiced as a substitute religion claiming to be sufficient unto itself.

tradition: the action of transmitting or handing down, from one person to another or from generation to generation, beliefs, teachings, insights, customs, and the like, especially by word of mouth, via stories, poetry, scriptures and other art forms, and via demonstrable example and practice (as opposed to knowledge handed down solely through books, computer data, didactic writings, lectures, videos of lectures, and the like).

maya (Sanskrit): the physical universe, i.e., cosmic illusion, including all forms and beings except Divine Being; everything that is not God; in some scriptures, "God's shadow."

imagination: that faculty of mind by which are formed images or concepts of external objects not present to the senses, and of their relations to each other or to the subject; the human ability to form concepts or perceive images beyond those derived from external objects; the creative faculty in its highest aspect (William Blake: "Imagination is Christ").

story: an imaginative account or narrative, be it fiction or nonfiction, spiritual or scientific, frivolous or profound.

poetry: Gary Snyder's definition is in my experience nonpareil: "the skilled and inspired use of the voice and language to embody rare and powerful states of mind that are in immediate origin personal to the singer, but at deep levels common to all who listen."

reason: to think in a connected, sensible, or logical manner; to employ the faculty of reason in forming conclusions; in relation to the numinous, however, it is reasonable of our reason to admit its complete inability to grasp that which transcends it, and fall silent.

mysticism: reliance on intuition or exalted feeling as a means of acquiring genuine knowledge of realities inaccessible to reason; especially an experience (fleeting, or lasting) of the Divine via ecstatic contemplation, "satori experience," indescribable feelings of love, inexplicable awareness of Presence, and the like; (Keats: "fellowship with essence").

wonder: a state of serene astonishment brought on by a marvelous object, or better, by an ordinary object suddenly seen as a marvel; "the aura of truth, or halo of it; the invisible caress of truth touching our very skin."

barzakh (Arabic): something that separates—yet in a sense also *joins*—two things, yet is part of neither thing, as, for example, the line that separates shadow from sunlight, oil from water, land from sea, the physical from the spiritual, the mind of man from the mind of God. (Ibn al-Arabi: "A *barzakh* separates a known from an unknown, an existent from a nonexistent, a negated from an affirmed, an intelligible from a nonintelligible.")

supernatural: not the "more than natural" or the inexplicably weird or occult or ghostly or unnatural; on the contrary, the subtlest, finest forms of the natural; the *extra*-natural; the *really really natural.*

language: the whole body of words and of methods of combining words used by a nation, people, or race; a "tongue."

beyond-language: the *barzakh* between a "tongue" and the numinous, between words and all that is beyond them, between the natural and extra-natural—especially love and the Divine.

reagent (Chemistry): a reactive substance employed as a test to determine the presence of some other substance by means of the reaction produced.

love: the reagent that determines the presence of the *really really natural* here in the living cosmos.

—David James Duncan

Monsters

The Pirates of Illiopolis (2005)

In March 2007—nearly three years after the explosion—the U.S. Chemical Safety Board in Washington, D.C. issued its formal and final report on Formosa Plastics. It concluded that the accident occurred when a worker who was cleaning out empty reactors took a wrong turn on a stairwell, approached a cluster of full reactors, and overrode a safety valve on a pressurized vessel that was not empty. Vinyl chloride sprayed into the room and ignited, resulting in a massive detonation. No gauges, indicators, or warning lights informed workers on the lower level of a reactor's operating status, and workers had no radios to communicate with operators on the upper level. The Chemical Safety Board found that both Formosa and its previous owner, Borden Chemical, were aware of the catastrophic potential of such mistakes but failed to implement measures sufficient "to prevent human error or minimize its consequences."

The facility—which never blew up during its incarnation as a World War II munitions plant but turned into a fireball while making plastic for kitchen floors—has been permanently closed. Its charred hull sits at the exact geographic center of Illinois and is visible for miles in all directions.

—*Sandra Steingraber*

Radioactive Roadtrip (2003)

Since the election of President Bush in 2000, the focus of activities at the NTS has swung away from civilian projects and again toward nuclear ones, in particular the development of tactical "bunker busters" and the "reliable replacement warhead." Although funding for the former was dropped from recent Department of Energy budgets, some analysts speculate that research is being funded through the more opaque Department of Defense.

A related test explosion of a 700-ton ammonium nitrate and fuel oil bomb was planned for 2007 by the Defense Threat Reduction Agency, a branch of the Department of Defense responsible, ironically, for reducing the threat of weapons of mass destruction. The test, which was to study the effect of ground shocks propagating against underground tunnels, was diverted by lawsuits noting that such a large explosion would run the risk of throwing into the atmosphere soil made radioactive in previous nuclear tests. The use of smaller explosions has not been ruled out.

The reliable replacement warhead project seeks to put redesigned hydrogen bombs on the U.S. Navy's Trident missiles by 2012, although there is considerable debate about whether or not it is necessary to replace the existing warheads. The Bush administration claims it has no intent to test the new weapon, but it seems unlikely that the U.S. Strategic Command would accept it for deployment without testing its reliability. The American government has still not signed the Comprehensive Test Ban Treaty, and the executive order forestalling the testing of nuclear weapons, a moratorium first signed by President George G.W. Bush in 1992, can be reversed with a single signature.

—*William L. Fox*

In the Name of Restoration (1999)

Eighteen years after oil flooded Prince William Sound, the ecosystem has not recovered, yet we continue to rely on science and technology rather than show any restraint. Less than a third of the species and habitats harmed by oil are listed as recovered. Some continue to decline, most notably Pacific herring, upon which over forty species—from salmon to orcas to murrelets—depend.

Science has simply observed this lack of recovery; it hasn't led to any significant restrictions on human activity in the Sound. To the contrary, there are new roads, new boat facilities, more boats and people, and increased fishing and hunting—all compromising recovery.

In 2006, under a reopener clause in the settlement, the government requested $92 million from Exxon for unanticipated injury. Astonishingly, instead of using these funds for restoration, such as buying back commercial herring fishing permits, they plan to spend another decade doing more beach cleanup. What's surprising isn't the lingering oil, but the lack of ecosystem recovery. This calls into question the very idea of ecosystem resilience: Prince William Sound may never recover.

What's more, Exxon continues to appeal the 1994 punitive verdict, denying compensation to commercial fishermen and subsistence communities. Meanwhile, many of these plaintiffs have died, without closure from Exxon.

There's some good news: only one single-hull tanker, sister ship of the *Exxon Valdez*, remains in the fleet, and safety measures on new tankers go beyond federal mandates. These measures have not, however, been applied elsewhere.

As Prince William Sound struggles to recover, and as more oil spills occur worldwide, we continue to confuse science with restoration, and knowledge with healing.

—*Marybeth Holleman*

Native

Staying Put (1992)

Like many of my essays, "Staying Put" began in private bewilderment, and like a few of my essays it wound up tapping into a widely-shared concern. What bewildered me was the puzzle about where to live—whether to stay in southern Indiana, where my wife and I had settled following graduate school, or to move someplace else where we might find greater sympathy for the causes we embraced and for the making and reading of books. I knew the attraction of moving on and starting afresh; I also knew the fears of getting stuck. Stay in one place, the voices told me, and you'll become backward and dull. Move on, and you'll be able to shed responsibilities, reinvigorate your life, maybe find a larger audience. I was wooed to leave my job at Indiana University, and I considered doing so. But for a host of reasons, some of them laid out in this essay, I decided, in common with my wife, to stay put and see what I could learn and contribute right here.

As I came to recognize the roots of my own restlessness, in personal history and American culture, I also came to recognize the damage caused to individuals, families, communities, and the land by our nation's cult of mobility. I realized that fidelity to place is inseparable from other sorts of commitment—to marriage and lifelong partnerships, to neighbors and friends, to a cause, to the habit of art, to learning, to spiritual practice. The searching begun in this essay gradually expended into a book, also called *Staying Put*, with the subtitle, "Making a Home in a Restless World."

Over the past twenty years, *Orion* has published work of mine that became pivotal chapters or lead essays in half a dozen books—not only *Staying Put*, but also *Secrets of the Universe, Writing from the Center, Hunting for Hope, The Force of Spirit*, and *A Private History of Awe*. The magazine has nurtured me as a writer as well as a reader, inviting me to think more deeply about our place in nature, about right living, about the links between social justice and conservation, and about the source of things. For these gifts, and for all the people who have sustained *Orion* over the years, I am profoundly grateful.

—*Scott Russell Sanders*

Barry Lopez is the author of several works of fiction and nonfiction, including *Arctic Dreams,* for which he received the National Book Award, and *Of Wolves and Men,* a finalist for the National Book Award and winner of the John Burroughs Medal. His fiction, including *Field Notes, Light Action in the Caribbean,* and most recently *Resistance,* as well as his nonfiction, are regularly translated into other languages, and he contributes to a wide range of magazines, among them *Granta, Harper's, Outside, National Geographic, Manoa,* and *Orion.* As Visiting Distinguished Scholar at Texas Tech University he has helped develop changes in curriculum in the Honors College, has established a lecture series in social and environmental justice, and has initiated a reconciliation with the Comanche Nation. He is the recipient of awards from the Guggenheim, Lannan, and National Science foundations and, in 2002, was awarded the John Hay Medal by the Orion Society. Mr. Lopez's work has taken him to nearly seventy countries. He is a Fellow of The Explorers Club, an advisor to Theater Grottesco in Santa Fe, and is on the steering committee for Quest for Global Healing. Since 1970 he has lived on the Upper McKenzie River in western Oregon. See www.BarryLopez.com.

Contributors

Wendell Berry's poems, essays, and works of fiction have won him numerous honors and a wide following. His most recent books include *Given: New Poems, The Way of Ignorance and Other Essays,* and *Andy Catlett: Early Travels.* He lives and farms in his native Kentucky.

Hope Burwell's Chernobyl-related articles have appeared in several magazines and newspapers. She earned an award from the Society for Environmental Journalists, as well as an honorable mention in *2004 Best Science and Nature Writing.* Burwell gives lectures on life in post-Chernobyl Belarus, and continues to act as director of Strong Like a Willow: A Belarus Relief Project.

Mark Dowie teaches science and environmental reporting at the University of California Graduate School of Journalism. He is currently coordinating a series of courses there on the environment in China. He has won over twenty major journalism prizes, including four National Magazine Awards, a George Polk Award, and he was awarded the bronze medallion for Outstanding Investigative Journalism by Investigative Reporters and Editors.

William J. Cronon is the Frederick Jackson Turner and Vilas Research Professor of History, Geography, and Environmental Studies at the University of Wisconsin-Madison. He is the author of several books, including *Changes in the Land: Indians, Colonists, and the Ecology of New England, Uncommon Ground: Rethinking the Human Place in Nature,* and *Nature's Metropolis: Chicago and the Great West,* which was nominated for the Pulitzer Prize in History.

John Daniel, the author of seven books of essays, memoir, and poetry, lives and writes in the Coast Range foothills west of Eugene, Oregon. His most recent book, *Rogue River Journal,* won a 2006 Book Award from the Pacific Northwest Booksellers Association. He has also received a Wallace Stegner Fellowship in Poetry at Stanford University, two Oregon Book Awards for literary nonfiction, and a fellowship from the National Endowment for the Arts.

Alison Hawthorne Deming is the author of several poetry collections, including *Science and Other Poems, The Monarchs,* and *Genius Loci,* and a collection of essays, *Temporary Homelands.* Among other awards, she has received a Wallace Stegner Fellowship at Stanford University, two NEA Fellowships, and a Pushcart Prize. She is a professor of creative writing at the University of Arizona as well as the former director of the University of Arizona Poetry Center.

David James Duncan is the author of the novels *The River Why* and *The Brothers K* and several works of nonfiction. His work has won a Lannan Fellowship, the 2001 Western States Book Award for Nonfiction, a National Book Award nomination, three PNBA Awards, two Pushcarts, the American Library Association's 2003 Award (with Wendell Berry) for the Preservation of Intellectual Freedom, and other honors. He lives near Missoula, Montana.

William L. Fox has published numerous books about cognition and landscape, and fourteen collections of poetry. He has received awards from the Guggenheim Foundation, National Science Foundation, National Endowment for the Humanities, and been a visiting scholar at the Getty Research Institute and Australia National University. He is a Fellow of the Royal Geographical Society and the Explorer's Club. He lives in Burbank, California.

Eric T. Freyfogle writes widely on issues of people and nature, especially private rights and the governance mechanisms society develops to guide our living on the land. His books include *On Private Property: Finding Common Ground on the Ownership of Land, The Land We Share: Private Property and the Common Good,* and *Why Conservation Is Failing and How It Can Regain Ground.* He is a professor of law at the University of Illinois at Urbana-Champaign.

Marybeth Holleman's most recent book is *The Heart of the Sound: An Alaskan Paradise Found and Nearly Lost.* Her work has appeared in dozens of journals and anthologies, including *North American Review, Alaska Quarterly Review, Christian Science Monitor, Ice-Floe, Sierra, American Nature Writing,* and *Solo.* She also teaches creative writing at the University of Alaska Anchorage. Raised in the Appalachians of North Carolina, she transplanted to Alaska's Chugach Mountains over twenty years ago.

Derrick Jensen is the author of *Endgame, A Language Older Than Words,* and *The Culture of Make Believe.* Author, teacher, activist, small farmer, and a leading voice of uncompromising dissent, he speaks and lectures widely. Jensen holds a degree in creative writing from Eastern Washington University, a degree in mineral engineering physics from the Colorado School of Mines, and has taught at Eastern Washington University and Pelican Bay State Prison. He lives in Crescent City, California.

Van Jones is the founder and president of the Ella Baker Center for Human Rights. Based in Oakland, the Center champions police reform, juvenile justice reform, violence prevention, and ecologically sound job creation. A Yale-educated attorney, Van has also served on numerous national boards, including: the National Apollo Alliance, the Beatitudes Society, WITNESS, and Bioneers.

Jeffrey Kaplan's essays and articles have appeared in many regional and national newspapers and periodicals. He lives and works in the San Francisco Bay Area.

John Landretti is a writer and poet whose interests include the natural sciences, myth, and all things spiritual. His work has appeared in *The Best Spiritual Writing 2001* and *The Anatomy of Memory.* He teaches at an anti-poverty program in the Twin Cities.

BK Loren's work has been published in *Parabola* and *The Best American Spiritual Writing of 2004.* She lives and writes in the middle of the Denver-Boulder suburbs on land she remembers as farms and orchards. She's been involved in many fights to retain the integrity of the place.

Oren Lyons is a Faithkeeper of the Turtle Clan of the Onondaga Nation, and a professor of American studies at the State University of New York (SUNY) at Buffalo. He is also the publisher of *Daybreak,* a national Native American magazine.

Bill McKibben is an *Orion* columnist and the author of ten books on the environment and other topics. A former staff writer for the *New Yorker,* his work appears in *Harpers, Atlantic,* the *New York Review of Books,* and a variety of other national publications. A scholar-in-residence at Middlebury College, he is the recipient of Guggenheim and Lyndhurst fellowships and the Lannan Prize in Nonfiction Writing. His most recent book is *Deep Economy: The Wealth of Communities and the Durable Future.*

Lowell Monke is associate professor of education at Wittenberg University in Springfield, Ohio. He spends much of his time helping adults understand why computers aren't good for kids.

Gary Paul Nabhan is a Lebanese-American food writer and ethnobiologist. On the home front, he coordinates the Canyon Country Fresh "local foods" network in Northern Arizona and is founder of the Renewing America's Food Traditions consortium. "Listening to the Other," in an updated form, will appear in his forthcoming book, *Arab/American: Landscape, Agriculture, and Cuisine in Arabian and American Deserta.*

Judith Nies is the author of three books: *Native American History,* a chronology of American history in two parallel timelines; *Nine Women: Portraits from the American Radical Tradition;* and the forthcoming *The Girl I Left Behind: A Narrative History of the 1960s.* She first encountered the Black Mesa project as a congressional speechwriter in the 1970s and has followed it for thirty-five years. She currently teaches nonfiction writing at Massachusetts College of Art in Boston.

Laura Paskus is a writer living in Albuquerque, New Mexico, who has written about environmental issues for *High Country News, Audubon Magazine,* and the *Santa Fe Reporter.* The daughter of union members herself, she believes the time is right for new alliances, in which progressive activists can pool their resources and work together for the rights everyone deserves, including fair wages and health care, as well as safe workplaces and healthy environments.

Robert Michael Pyle, a life-long naturalist, has written *Wintergreen, The Thunder Tree, Where Bigfoot Walks, Chasing Monarchs, Walking the High Ridge, Sky Time in Gray's River,* and several standard butterfly books. A John Burroughs Medalist and Guggenheim Fellow, Pyle has contributed his column "The Tangled Bank" to *Orion* for nearly fifty issues. He lives with artist and botanist Thea Linnaea Pyle along a tributary of the Lower Columbia River, where he is completing a novel and a collection of poems.

Erik Reece teaches writing at the University of Kentucky in Lexington. His work appears in *Harper's,* the *Oxford American,* and other publications. He was the recipient of the Sierra Club's David R. Brower Award, and his *Harper's* story on which *Lost Mountain* is based won the Columbia University School of Journalism's 2005 John B. Oakes Award for Distinguished Environmental Journalism.

Scott Russell Sanders, a contributing editor of *Orion,* is a distinguished professor of English at Indiana University. Among his more than twenty books are novels, collections of stories, and works of personal nonfiction, including *Staying Put, Hunting for Hope,* and *A Private History of Awe.* His writing has won the AWP Creative Nonfiction Award, the John Burroughs Essay Award, and the Lannan Literary Award.

Peter Sauer's writings on consanguinities between culture and nature have appeared in *Orion* since 1992 and he has written two regular columns for the magazine, as well as feature length essays and articles. He lives in Salem, New York.

David Sobel is the director of teacher certification programs in the Education Department and co-director of the Center for Place-based Education at Antioch New England Graduate School. His books include *Children's Special Places, Beyond Ecophobia: Reclaiming the Heart in Nature Education, Mapmaking with Children: Sense of Place Education for the Elementary Years* and *Place-based Education: Connecting Classrooms and Communities.*

A regular columnist for *Orion,* activist and essayist **Rebecca Solnit** is the author of twelve books including *Storming the Gates of Paradise, Hope in the Dark, Wanderlust,* and *River of Shadows.* In 2003 she won the Lannan Literary Award and the National Book Critic's Award in criticism. She lives in the West.

Cathrine Sneed is the founder of The San Francisco Garden Project. Over four thousand former prisoners have gone through the program. Her work with The Garden Project has been featured widely in venues including the *New York Times,* the *Economist,* the *Chicago Tribune,* the *Los Angeles Times,* and A&E Channel's *Uncommon Americans.* She has been honored with such awards as the National Caring Award, the Hero for the Earth Award, and the National Foundation for the Improvement of Justice Award.

Sandra Steingraber grew up an hour north of Illiopolis in Tazewell County, Illinois, just downwind from an ethanol distillery, an aluminum foundry, a coal-burning power plant, two chemical plants, and a company that turns scrap metal into barbed wire. She currently lives in upstate New York and is the author of *Living Downstream: An Ecologist Looks at Cancer and the Environment* and *Having Faith: An Ecologist's Journey to Motherhood.* She holds a Ph.D. in biology and a master's degree in creative writing.

Ginger Strand is the author of the novel *Flight,* and a forthcoming nonfiction book about Niagara Falls, *Inventing Niagara.* She has published essays and stories in *Harper's, Swink,* the *Iowa Review, Raritan,* and is a frequent contributor to the *Believer.* She lives in New York City, where she writes and teaches environmental criticism at Fordham University.

Charles Wohlforth is a life-long Alaskan who spends his time outdoors, skiing and boating, and caring for his four children with his wife. He began his writing career at the weekly *Homer News* and became a full-time freelancer in 1993. He is the author of many books and articles, most notably 2004's *The Whale and the Supercomputer: On the Northern Front of Climate,* which won the *Los Angeles Times* Book Award for Science and Technology.

milkweed
editions

Founded as a nonprofit organization in 1980,
Milkweed Editions is an independent
publisher. Our mission is to identify, nurture
and publish transformative literature, and
build an engaged community around it.

milkweed.org

Interior design by Wendy Holdman
Typeset in Adobe Garamond Pro
by Prism Publishing Center